From Counterculture to Cyberculture

from Counterculture to Cyberculture

Stewart Brand, the Whole Earth Network, and the Rise of Digital Utopianism

Fred Turner

The University of Chicago Press / Chicago and London

Fred Turner is assistant professor of communication at Stanford University. He is the author of *Echoes of Combat: The Vietnam War in American Memory*.

The University of Chicago Press, Chicago 60637
The University of Chicago Press, Ltd., London
© 2006 by Fred Turner
All rights reserved. Published 2006
Printed in the United States of America

15 14 13 12 11 10 09 08 07 06   1 2 3 4 5

ISBN-13: 978-0-226-81741-5 (cloth)
ISBN-10: 0-226-81741-5 (cloth)

Library of Congress Cataloging-in-Publication Data

Turner, Fred.
    From counterculture to cyberculture : Stewart Brand, the Whole Earth
network, and the rise of digital utopianism / Fred Turner.
        p. cm.
    Includes bibliographical references and index.
    ISBN 0-226-81741-5 (cloth : alk. paper)
    1. Computers and civilization.   2. Brand, Stewart.   3. Information
technology—History—20th century.   4. Counterculture—United States—
History—20th century.   5. Computer networks—Social aspects.
6. Subculture—California—San Francisco—History—20th century.
7. Technology—Social aspects—California, Northern.   8. Whole earth
catalog.   I. Title: Stewart Brand, the Whole Earth network, and the rise
of digital utopianism.   II. Title.

QA76.9.C66T875 2006
303.48'33—dc22

                                                        2005034149

∞ The paper used in this publication meets the minimum requirements of the
American National Standard for Information Sciences—Permanence of Paper
for Printed Library Materials, ANSI Z39.48-1992.

Contents

Illustrations follow page 140.

Acknowledgments

If I've learned anything in the last seven years, it's that ideas live less in the minds of individuals than in the interactions of communities. The ideas in this book are no exception: they owe their origin to a far-flung network of extraordinarily generous teachers, colleagues, friends, and interviewees, to all of whom I'm very grateful.

I first began thinking about the Whole Earth network and the politics of information technology while I was a PhD student in the Department of Communication at the University of California, San Diego. My professors there offered me an ideal mix of direction and freedom. They consistently demanded that I reach across disciplinary boundaries, pursue difficult questions, and find my own voice on the page. As my early interests gelled into a dissertation, Professors Michael Schudson, Robert Horwitz, Chandra Mukerji, Geoffrey Bowker, Lev Manovich, Philip Agre, and Steven Epstein each introduced me to new literatures, read multiple drafts of chapters, and patiently helped me frame my fascination with the *Whole Earth Catalog* in analytical terms. Together, they offered me a model of what a life devoted to engaged, public-minded scholarship and committed teaching could be. I would also like to thank my fellow graduate students—Lonny Brooks, Cynthia Chris, Carol Christopher, Tarleton Gillespie, Mary Gray, Steve Jackson, Sujeong Kim, Barbara Osborn, Mauro Porto, Matt Ratto, and Jennifer Rayman—for their encouragement and friendship.

Three years into my work at UCSD, I moved to Boston and began teaching at the Massachusetts Institute of Technology's Sloan School of Management. MIT is the kind of place where you can be hired to play in one intellectual sandbox and suddenly find yourself jumping into others; fortunately, that's what happened to me. There I had the incredible luck to find three new teachers: Professors JoAnne Yates, Pablo Boczkowski, and Joe Dumit. They introduced me to much of the literature in the fields of organizational sociology and science and technology studies that informs this book. Sloan also allowed me to teach with a highly experienced and delightful group of colleagues, including Lori Breslow, Neal Hartman, Leigh Hafrey, and Melissa Raffoni, all of whom made coming to work a treat. At the same time, I found my way to MIT's Comparative Media Studies Program, where Professors Henry Jenkins, William Uricchio, and David Thorburn taught me a great deal about the dynamics of digital media and contemporary culture. So did three graduate students with whom I worked: David Spitz, Anita Chan, and Zhan Li. I also want to thank Catherine Friedman, then head of MIT's Dewey Library, and her staff for going to exceptional lengths to keep my office bookshelves well stocked.

Since 2003 I have been happily housed in the Department of Communication at Stanford University. Writing this book at Stanford has been a delight for a number of reasons. For one, many of the events I have written about took place within shouting distance of my office. Thus I have been allowed to enjoy one of the peculiar pleasures of those who study the past: the chance to walk through a landscape and in the same moment to see it as it is and imagine it as it used to be. But more than that, I am grateful to my colleagues in the department. Jeremy Bailenson, Jim Bettinger, Henry Breitrose, Jim Fishkin, Dawn Garcia, Ted Glasser, Shanto Iyengar, Jan Krawitz, Jon Krosnick, Marion Lewenstein, Marcyliena Morgan, Cliff Nass, Byron Reeves, Don Roberts, Kris Samuelson, and Bill Woo have all shared the kind of insights and offered the kind of support that make writing a book possible. The department's administrative and technical staff have been unfailingly helpful as well. I would like to thank Susie Ementon, Joan Ferguson, Michael Forte, Joyce Ichinose, Barbara Kataoka, Kathleen Magner, Mark Urbanek, and Mark DeZutti for all their hard work on this project's behalf. And I would like to thank two undergraduate research assistants, Adam Maenhout and Joel Lewenstein, for their unstinting hustle.

Outside the department, I have enjoyed the support of faculty and staff from around the university. Steve Barley, co-director of the Center for Work, Technology, and Organization, and Woody Powell, professor of education and director of the Scandinavian Consortium for Organizational Research, have both pushed me to rethink the relationship between media technologies and organizations. Both have also given me rich opportunities to test my ideas within their respective research groups. Professors Scott Bukatman of the Art Department, Michael Shanks of Classics, and Tim Lenoir of History (now at Duke), together with the graduate students and visitors of the Critical Studies in New Media Seminar, have kept me focused on thinking about the ways that emerging media may shape the future.

Without the staff of the Stanford University libraries, this book could not have been written. Under the leadership of University Librarian Michael Keller, the library has collected not only the archives of the *Whole Earth Catalog* and the personal papers of Stewart Brand, but also a whole host of records covering the past fifty years of technological and cultural change in the region. Henry Lowood, curator of science and technology at the library, has generously guided me through these materials, as have Alex Pang, Steven Mandeville-Gamble, and Sean Quimby. Chris Bourg and Glen Worthey have continued to point me to new digital resources, while Roberto Trujillo, Polly Armstrong, Margaret Kimball, Christy Smith, Peter Whidden, and the whole staff of the Special Collections Department have bent over backward to help me work with previously unexamined archival materials.

Over the past two years, as the book began to take shape, I have had the opportunity to think it through out loud with several engaged and congenial groups. I would particularly like to thank Jennifer Light and the faculty and students of Northwestern University's Department of Communication Studies, and AnnaLee Saxenian, Nancy Van House, and the University of California, Berkeley, School of Information Management and Systems for allowing me to present my work in progress and for making it better with their comments. For the same reasons, I am also grateful to David Silver, Adrienne Massanari, and the Ford Foundation for organizing the miniconference "Critical Cyberculture Studies" at the University of Washington, and to Geoffrey Bowker, the Social Science Research Council, and Santa Clara University's Center for Science, Technology, and Society for convening the two-day session "Digital Cultural Institutions and the Future of Access." I also thank fellow panelists and audiences at the annual meetings of the Association of Internet Researchers, the International Communication Association, the Society for the History of Technology, and the Society for Social Studies of Science, all of whom offered valuable feedback on my work.

Once the manuscript had solidified, a small group of colleagues and friends bore down on it, challenged my arguments, and made it a much stronger book than it otherwise would have been. I'm especially grateful to Hsiao-Yun Chu, Sharon Ghamari-Tabrizi, Roy Rosenzweig, Jonathan Sterne, and the anonymous readers for the University of Chicago Press for their rigor and care, and to my agent, Geri Thoma, and my editor, Doug Mitchell, for their steady encouragement and warmth.

Perhaps the people to whom this book owes the most are those whose lives and work it explores. They have been extraordinarily open and forthcoming, devoting hours and sometimes days to helping me understand their histories. For all of their help, I'd like to thank Bob Albrecht, Dennis Allison, John Perry Barlow, Reva Basch, Keith Britton, Lois Britton, John Brockman, Michael Callahan, John Coate, Doug Engelbart, Bill English, Lee Felsenstein, Cliff Figallo, David Frohman, Asha Greer (formerly Barbara Durkee), Katie Hafner, Paul Hawken, Alan Kay, Kevin Kelly, Art Kleiner, Butler Lampson, Liza Loop, John Markoff, Jane Metcalfe, David Millen, Nancy Murphy, Richard Raymond, Danica Remy, Howard Rheingold, Louis Rossetto, Peter Schwartz, Mark Stahlman, Gerd Stern, Shirley Streshinsky, Larry Tesler, Paul Tough, Jim Warren, and Gail Williams. Most of all, I thank Stewart Brand, whose openness to this project has been a lesson in itself.

I am also grateful to a number of people and institutions for permission to quote conversations and to reprint previously published material. I conducted all interviews myself. All quotations from Stewart Brand's personal papers appear with his permission and courtesy of the Department of Special Collections, Stanford University Libraries. All quotations from materials in the *Whole Earth Catalog* Records appear courtesy of the Department of Special Collections, Stanford University Libraries. "All Watched Over by Machines of Loving Grace," from *The Pill versus The Springhill Mine Disaster,* © 1968 by Richard Brautigan, has been reprinted with the permission of Sarah Lazin Books. Portions of chapter 2 have been adapted from "Buckminster Fuller: A Technocrat for the Counterculture," in *New Views on R. Buckminster Fuller,* edited by Hsiao-Yun Chu and Roberto Trujillo, © 2006 Board of Trustees of the Leland Stanford Jr. University, forthcoming from Stanford University Press, used by permission. Parts of chapters 4 and 8 have been drawn from "How Digital Technology Found Utopian Ideology: Lessons from the First Hackers' Conference," in *Critical Cyberculture Studies: Current Terrains, Future Directions,* edited by David Silver and Adrienne Massanari (New York University Press, forthcoming), and are used by permission. Portions of chapter 5 first appeared as "Where the Counterculture Met the New Economy: Revisiting the WELL and the Origins of Virtual Community," *Technology and Culture* 46, no. 3 (July 2005): 485–512 (© 2005 by The Johns Hopkins University Press, used by permission).

Above all, I would like to thank my wife, Annie Fischer, and my daughter, Althea Turner. They've crisscrossed the country as I've chased my curiosities and they've done it with grace and patience. I adore them both.

Introduction

In the mid-1990s, as first the Internet and then the World Wide Web swung into public view, talk of revolution filled the air. Politics, economics, the nature of the self—all seemed to teeter on the edge of transformation. The Internet was about to "flatten organizations, globalize society, decentralize control, and help harmonize people," as MIT's Nicholas Negroponte put it.[1] The stodgy men in gray flannel suits who had so confidently roamed the corridors of industry would shortly disappear, and so too would the chains of command on which their authority depended. In their place, wrote Negroponte and dozens of others, the Internet would bring about the rise of a new "digital generation"—playful, self-sufficient, psychologically whole— and it would see that generation gather, like the Net itself, into collaborative networks of independent peers.[2] States too would melt away, their citizens lured back from archaic party-based politics to the "natural" agora of the digitized marketplace. Even the individual self, so long trapped in the human body, would finally be free to step outside its fleshy confines, explore its authentic interests, and find others with whom it might achieve communion. Ubiquitous networked computing had arrived, and in its shiny array of interlinked devices, pundits, scholars, and investors alike saw the image of an ideal society: decentralized, egalitarian, harmonious, and free.

But how did this happen? Only thirty years earlier, computers had been the tools and emblems of the same unfeeling industrial-era social machine whose collapse they now seemed ready to bring about. In the winter of 1964, for instance, students marching for free speech at the University of California at Berkeley feared that America's political leaders were treating them as if they were bits of abstract data.

One after another, they took up blank computer cards, punched them through with new patterns of holes—"FSM" and "STRIKE"—and hung them around their necks.[3] One student even pinned a sign to his chest that parroted the cards' user instructions: "I am a UC student. Please do not fold, bend, spindle or mutilate me."[4] For the marchers of the Free Speech Movement, as for many other Americans throughout the 1960s, computers loomed as technologies of dehumanization, of centralized bureaucracy and the rationalization of social life, and, ultimately, of the Vietnam War. Yet, in the 1990s, the same machines that had served as the defining devices of cold war technocracy emerged as the symbols of its transformation. Two decades after the end of the Vietnam War and the fading of the American counterculture, computers somehow seemed poised to bring to life the countercultural dream of empowered individualism, collaborative community, and spiritual communion. How did the cultural meaning of information technology shift so drastically?

As a number of journalists and historians have suggested, part of the answer is technological. By the 1990s, the room-sized, stand-alone calculating machines of the cold war era had largely disappeared.[5] So too had the armored rooms in which they were housed and the army of technicians that supported them. Now Americans had taken up microcomputers, some the size of notebooks, all of them available to the individual user, regardless of his or her institutional standing. These new machines could perform a range of tasks that far exceeded even the complex calculations for which digital computers had first been built. They became communication devices and were used to prepare novels and spreadsheets, pictures and graphs. Linked over telephone wires and fiber-optic cables, they allowed their users to send messages to one another, to download reams of information from libraries around the world, and to publish their own thoughts on the World Wide Web. In all of these ways, changes in computer technology expanded the range of uses to which computers could be put and the types of social relations they were able to facilitate.

As dramatic as they were, however, these changes alone do not account for the particular utopian visions to which computers became attached. The fact that a computer can be put on a desktop, for instance, and that it can be used by an individual, does not make it a "personal" technology. Nor does the fact that individuals can come together by means of computer networks necessarily require that their gatherings become "virtual communities." On the contrary, as Shoshanna Zuboff has pointed out, in the office, desktop computers and computer networks can become powerful tools for integrating the individual ever more closely into the corporation.[6] At home, those same machines not only allow schoolchildren to download citations from the public library; they also turn the living room into a digital shopping mall. For retailers, the computer in the home becomes an opportunity to harvest all sorts of information about potential customers. For all the utopian claims surrounding the emergence of the Internet, there is nothing about a computer or a computer network that *necessarily* requires that it level organizational structures, render the individual more psychologically whole, or drive the establishment of intimate, though geographically distributed, communities.

How was it, then, that computers and computer networks became linked to visions of peer-to-peer ad-hocracy, a leveled marketplace, and a more authentic self? Where did these visions come from? And who enlisted computing machines to represent them?

To answer these questions, this book traces the previously untold history of an extraordinarily influential group of San Francisco Bay area journalists and entrepreneurs: Stewart Brand and the Whole Earth network. Between the late 1960s and the late 1990s, Brand assembled a network of people and publications that together brokered a series of encounters between bohemian San Francisco and the emerging technology hub of Silicon Valley to the south. In 1968 Brand brought members of the two worlds together in the pages of one of the defining documents of the era, the *Whole Earth Catalog*. In 1985 he gathered them again on what would become perhaps the most influential computer conferencing system of the decade, the Whole Earth 'Lectronic Link, or the WELL. Throughout the late 1980s and early 1990s, Brand and other members of the network, including Kevin Kelly, Howard Rheingold, Esther Dyson, and John Perry Barlow, became some of the most-quoted spokespeople for a countercultural vision of the Internet. In 1993 all would help create the magazine that, more than any other, depicted the emerging digital world in revolutionary terms: *Wired*.

By recounting their history, this book reveals and helps to explain a complex intertwining of two legacies: that of the military-industrial research culture, which first appeared during World War II and flourished across the cold war era, and that of the American counterculture. Since the 1960s scholarly and popular accounts alike have described the counterculture in terms first expressed by its members—that is, as a culture antithetical to the technologies and social structures powering the cold war state and its defense industries. In this view the 1940s and 1950s are often seen as a gray time shaped by rigid social norms, hierarchical institutions, and the constant demands of America's nuclear face-off with the Soviet Union. The 1960s seem to explode onto the scene in a Technicolor swirl of personal exploration and political protest, much of it aimed at bringing down the cold war military-industrial bureaucracy. Those who accept this version of events tend to account for the persistence of the military-industrial complex today, and for the continuing growth of corporate capitalism and consumer culture as well, by arguing that the authentically revolutionary ideals of the generation of 1968 were somehow co-opted by the forces they opposed.

There is some truth to this story. Yet, as it has hardened into legend, this version of the past has obscured the fact the same military-industrial research world that brought forth nuclear weapons—and computers—also gave rise to a free-wheeling, interdisciplinary, and highly entrepreneurial style of work. In the research laboratories of World War II and later, in the massive military engineering projects of the cold war, scientists, soldiers, technicians, and administrators broke down the invisible walls of bureaucracy and collaborated as never before. As they did, they embraced both computers and a new cybernetic rhetoric of systems and information. They began to imagine institutions as living organisms, social networks as webs of information, and the gathering and interpretation of information as keys to understanding not only the technical but also the natural and social worlds.

By the late 1960s, so too did substantial elements of the counterculture. Between 1967 and 1970, for instance, tens of thousands of young people set out to establish communes, many in the mountains and the woods. It was for them that Brand first published the *Whole Earth Catalog*. For these back-to-the-landers, and for many others who never actually established new communities, traditional political mechanisms for creating social change had come up bankrupt. Even as their peers organized political parties and marched against the Vietnam War, this group, whom I will call the New Communalists, turned away from political action and toward technology and the transformation of consciousness as the primary sources of social change. If mainstream America had become a culture of conflict, with riots at home and war abroad, the commune world would be one of harmony. If the American state deployed massive weapons systems in order to destroy faraway peoples, the New Communalists would deploy small-scale technologies—ranging from axes and hoes to amplifiers, strobe lights, slide projectors, and LSD—to bring people together and allow them to experience their common humanity. Finally, if the bureaucracies of industry and government demanded that men and women become psychologically fragmented specialists, the technology-induced experience of togetherness would allow them to become both self-sufficient and whole once again.

For this wing of the counterculture, the technological and intellectual output of American research culture held enormous appeal. Although they rejected the military-industrial complex as a whole, as well as the political process that brought it into being, hippies from Manhattan to Haight-Ashbury read Norbert Wiener, Buckminster Fuller, and Marshall McLuhan.

Through their writings, young Americans encountered a cybernetic vision of the world, one in which material reality could be imagined as an information system. To a generation that had grown up in a world beset by massive armies and by the threat of nuclear holocaust, the cybernetic notion of the globe as a single, interlinked pattern of information was deeply comforting: in the invisible play of information, many thought they could see the possibility of global harmony.

To Stewart Brand and later to other members of the Whole Earth group, cybernetics also presented a set of social and rhetorical resources for entrepreneurship. In the early 1960s, not long after graduating from Stanford University, Brand found his way into the bohemian art worlds of San Francisco and New York. Like many of the artists around him at the time, and like Norbert Wiener, in whose writings on cybernetics they were immersed, Brand quickly became what sociologist Ronald Burt has called a "network entrepreneur."[7] That is, he began to migrate from one intellectual community to another and, in the process, to knit together formerly separate intellectual and social networks. In the *Whole Earth Catalog* era, these networks spanned the worlds of scientific research, hippie homesteading, ecology, and mainstream consumer culture. By the 1990s they would include representatives of the Defense Department, the U.S. Congress, global corporations such as Shell Oil, and makers of all sorts of digital software and equipment.

Brand brought these communities together in a series of what I will call *network forums*. Drawing on the systems rhetoric of cybernetics and on models of entrepreneurship borrowed from both the research and the countercultural worlds, Brand established a series of meetings, publications, and digital networks within which members of multiple communities could meet and collaborate and imagine themselves as members of a single community. These forums in turn generated new social networks, new cultural categories, and new turns of phrase. In 1968 Brand founded the *Whole Earth Catalog* in order to help those heading back to the land find the tools they would need to build their new communities. These items included the fringed deerskin jackets and geodesic domes favored by the communards, but they also included the cybernetic musings of Norbert Wiener and the latest calculators from Hewlett-Packard. In later editions, alongside discussions of such supplies, Brand published letters from high-technology researchers next to firsthand reports from rural hippies. In the process, he offered commune-based subscribers a chance to see their own ambitions as commensurate with the technological achievements of mainstream America, and he gave technologists the opportunity to imagine their diodes and relays as tools, like those the commune dwellers favored, for the transformation of individual and collective consciousness. Together, the creators and readers of the *Whole Earth Catalog* helped to synthesize a vision of technology as a countercultural force that would shape public under-standings of computing and other machines long after the social move-ments of the 1960s had faded from view.

In the 1980s and 1990s, as computers became ever smaller and more interconnected, and as corporations began to employ increasingly flexible modes of production, Brand and his colleagues repeated this process at the WELL, in the Global Business Network, through *Wired,* and in a series of meetings and organizations associated with all three. In each case, a net-work entrepreneur (often Brand himself) gathered members of multiple communities within a single material or textual space. The members of those networks collaborated on the various projects at hand and developed a shared language for their work. Out of that language emerged shared un-derstandings—of the potential social impact of computing, of information and information technologies as metaphors for social processes, and of the nature of work in a networked economic order. Often enough, the systems on which network members appeared became models in their own right of these new understandings. Even when they did not, members often took the insights they had gleaned back into their social and professional worlds. In this way ideas born within *Whole Earth*–derived network forums became key frames through which both public and professional technologists sought to comprehend the potential social impact of information and infor-mation technologies. Over time, the network's members and forums helped redefine the microcomputer as a "personal" machine, computer communi-cation networks as "virtual communities," and cyberspace itself as the digi-tal equivalent of the western landscape into which so many communards set forth in the late 1960s, the "electronic frontier."

At the same time, and by means of the same social processes, members of the Whole Earth network made themselves visible and credible spokesmen for the socio-technical visions that they had helped create. Traditionally, so-ciologists have depicted journalists in terms set by the professional norms of newspapers and magazines: as reporters of a consensus achieved among communities from which they were analytically, if not actually, separated. In this view, a reporter's prestige depends on her or his ability to dig up new in-formation, report it in a compelling way, and make it visible to a broad public (which itself is seen as analytically distinct from either the community of sources or the community of journalists). Brand and other writers and editors associated with the Whole Earth publications developed extraordinary repu-tations as journalists, winning, among other prizes, the National Book Award (for the *Whole Earth Catalog*) and the National Magazine Award (for *Wired*).

They did so, however, by building the communities on whose activities they were reporting. Within Whole Earth–sponsored network forums, and within the books and articles they spawned, representatives of the technological world met leaders from politics and business, as well as former counterculturalists. Together, their conversations turned digital media into emblems of network members' own, shared ways of living, and evidence of their individual credibility. Again and again, Brand, and later Kevin Kelly, Howard Rheingold, John Perry Barlow, and others, gave voice to the techno-social visions that emerged in these discussions.

As they did, they were welcomed into the halls of Congress, the boardrooms of major corporations, and the hotels of Davos, Switzerland, home of the World Economic Forum. By the mid-1990s, throughout much of the mainstream press and in business and government as well, the networked entrepreneurship of the Whole Earth group and its self-evident financial and social success had become evidence for the transformative power of what many had begun to call the "New Economy." According to a raft of politicians and pundits, the rapid integration of computing and telecommunications technologies into international economic life, coupled with dramatic rounds of corporate layoffs and restructuring, had given rise to a new economic era. Individuals could now no longer count on the support of their employers; they would instead have to become entrepreneurs, moving flexibly from place to place, sliding in and out of collaborative teams, building their knowledge bases and skill sets in a process of constant self-education. The proper role of government in this new environment, many argued, was to pull back, to deregulate the technology industries that were ostensibly leading the transformation, and, while they were at it, business in general.

Proponents of this view included telecommunications executives, high-tech stock analysts, and right-wing politicians. Kevin Kelly, a former editor of the quarterly *Whole Earth Review,* which had grown out of the original *Catalog,* helped to bring them all to the pages of *Wired.* As the magazine's executive editor, he argued that the world was a series of interlocking information systems, all of which were working to corrode the bureaucracies of the industrial era. To Kelly and the other creators of *Wired,* the suddenly public Internet appeared to be both the infrastructure and the symbol of the new economic era. And if it was, they suggested, then those who built their lives around the Net and those who sought to deregulate the newly networked marketplace might in fact be harbingers of a cultural revolution. In the pages of *Wired,* at least, this new elite featured the citizens of the WELL, the members of the Global Business Network, and the founders of the Electronic Frontier Foundation—all groups well woven into the fabric of the Whole Earth community—as well as Microsoft's Bill Gates, libertarian pundits such as George Gilder, and, on the cover of one issue, conservative Republican Congressman Newt Gingrich.

To those who think of the 1960s primarily as a break with the decades that went before, the coming together of former counterculturalists, corporate executives, and right-wing politicians and pundits may appear impossibly contradictory. But as the history of the Whole Earth network suggests, it isn't. As they turned away from agonistic politics and toward technology, consciousness, and entrepreneurship as the principles of a new society, the communards of the 1960s developed a utopian vision that was in many ways quite congenial to the insurgent Republicans of the 1990s. Although Newt Gingrich and those around him decried the hedonism of the 1960s counterculture, they shared its widespread affection for empowering technologically enabled elites, for building new businesses, and for rejecting traditional forms of governance. And as they rose to power, more than a few right-wing politicians and executives longed to share the hip credibility of people like Stewart Brand.

This book, then, does not tell the story of a countercultural movement whose ideals and practices were appropriated by the forces of capital, technology, or the state. Rather, it demonstrates that the New Communalist wing of the counterculture embraced those forces early on and that in subsequent years, Stewart Brand and the Whole Earth network continued to provide the intellectual and practical contexts within which members of the two worlds could come together and legitimate one another's projects. At the same time, however, this book is not a biography of Stewart Brand. Brand certainly deserves a biography, and one will no doubt be written in the years to come, but this book makes relatively little effort to understand Brand's personal history except insofar as it illuminates his role in reshaping the politics of information. Brand has had a substantial influence in other areas, especially ecology and architectural design, as well as a fascinating personal life, but these will have to wait for other chroniclers. My aim here is to make visible Brand's impact, and that of the networks he helped build, on our understandings of computing and its possible relations to social life. Within this story, Brand is both an influential actor in his own right and an exemplary promoter of a new, networked mode of techno-social life; so too are the journalists, consultants, and entrepreneurs of the Whole Earth network, which is by now far-flung. My challenge in writing this book has been to keep in view simultaneously Brand's unique individual talents, the networking tactics he employed, and the increasing influence of the networks he helped build.

For that reason, I begin with an overview of the broad transformation in popular perceptions of computing that has occurred over the past forty years, and a reminder of the forgotten affinities between cold war research culture and the counterculture of the New Communalists. I then turn to following Stewart Brand, first into the early 1960s art scene, then to the communes of the Southwest, into the back rooms of Bay area computer science in the 1970s, and on into the corporate world in the 1980s and 1990s. Along the way, I pause to examine in some detail the networks and network forums that Brand has built. As these explorations suggest, Brand's influence on popular understandings of technology has depended not only on his considerable talent for spotting the forward edges of social and technological change, but also on the richness and complexity of the networks he has assembled. I conclude by arguing that Brand's entrepreneurial tactics, and the now-widespread association of computers and computer-mediated communication with the egalitarian social ideals of the counterculture, have become important features of an increasingly networked mode of living, working, and deploying social and cultural power.

Although it is tempting to think of that mode as a product of a revolution in computing technology, I argue that the revolution it represents began long before the public appearance of the Internet or even the widespread distribution of computers. It began in the wake of World War II, as the cybernetic discourse and collaborative work styles of cold war military research came together with the communitarian social vision of the counterculture.

CHAPTER 1

The Shifting Politics of the Computational Metaphor

On December 2, 1964, just before noon, more than five thousand students streamed into an open-air plaza in front of the University of California at Berkeley's Sproul Hall. As they sat down on the pavement, one of their leaders, Mario Savio, stepped up to a microphone. With the towering gray columns of Sproul behind him, he tried to articulate what he and his audience had mobilized to fight. The university, he shouted, was an "autocracy." Its Board of Regents was a "Board of Directors," and its president, Clark Kerr, was a "manager." Extending the corporate analogy, he argued that the faculty were little more than "employees" and the students, "raw material." But, shouted Savio, "we're a bunch of raw material that don't mean . . . to be made into any product, don't mean to end up being bought by some clients of the university. . . . We're human beings." With that, he uttered three sentences that would come to define not only the Free Speech Movement at Berkeley, but the countercultural militancy of the 1960s across America and much of Europe as well: "There's a time when the operation of the machine becomes so odious, makes you so sick at heart, that you can't take part, you can't even tacitly take part. And you've got to put your bodies upon the gears and upon the wheels, upon the levers, upon all the apparatus, and you've got to make it stop. And you've got to indicate to the people who run it, to the people who own it, that unless you're free, the machine will be prevented from working at all."[1]

Savio's speech conjured up images of predigital industry, of factory floors and wheels and levers and of the bodies that work them. Yet, for Savio and the community of students to whom he spoke, the word *machine* also referred to a social world that had become increasingly

✓ organized around information and information technologies.[2] Just a year
before the unrest of the Free Speech Movement, Clark Kerr had published a
series of lectures in which he suggested that the university was "a mechanism—a series of processes producing a series of results—a mechanism
held together by administrative rules and powered by money."[3] He argued
that this mechanism served two purposes: first, citing economist Fritz
Machlup's recent studies on the increasing importance of information to the
economy, he argued that the university generated new knowledge and new
workers for an emerging "information society." In that sense, both he and
his students agreed that the university was an information machine. Second,
he suggested that this machine had a particular role to play in the ongoing
cold war. "Intellect has . . . become an instrument of national purpose," he
wrote, "a component part of the 'military-industrial complex.' . . . In the war
of ideological worlds, a great deal depends on the use of this instrument."[4]

For the students of the Free Speech Movement, the university's role as
knowledge producer could not be separated from its engagement with cold
war politics. Moreover, the entanglement threatened many at a deeply personal level. To the protestors, the university was both a knowledge factory
in its own right and a microcosm of the rigid, highly rationalized military-
industrial complex it served. In that sense it modeled the hierarchical world
of cold war corporate adulthood for which many feared they were being
trained. And at the time, no machine more commonly represented this
stratified, depersonalized social order than the computer. Hal Draper, a
librarian at Berkeley in 1964, explained that for a student, "the mass university of today is an overpowering, over-towering, impersonal, alien machine
in which he is nothing but a cog going through pre-programmed motions—
the IBM syndrome." As Mario Savio later told an interviewer, he and many
others felt that "At Cal you're little more than an IBM card."[5]

For Savio and the students of the Free Speech Movement, the corporate
world, the university, the military, and the punch-card universe of information seemed to be mirrors of one another. Each presented the otherwise
whole and authentic individual with a world in which he or she must pare
away some part of his or her self in order to participate. In the military or
the corporate world, or, for that matter, in the university, people would have
to learn to play assigned organizational roles. These roles, many argued at
the time, might reduce their otherwise complex and creative natures to the
two-dimensional dullness of an IBM card. In a sense, each of these systems
threatened to alienate the individual from her or his own lived experience.
It became particularly important, therefore, for the students to put their
bodies in Sproul Hall, as they did in the sit-in that followed Savio's speech. If
the university was a giant machine for the abstracting of individuals into

informational raw material for the knowledge industry, then how could they assert their humanity more powerfully than by laying their bodies across the stairways and office floors of the institution?

Thirty years later, the same aspects of computing that threatened to dehumanize the students of the Free Speech Movement promised to liberate the users of the Internet. On February 8, 1996, John Perry Barlow, an information technology journalist and pundit, and a former lyricist for the house band of the San Francisco LSD scene, the Grateful Dead, found himself at his laptop computer in Davos, Switzerland. While attending the World Economic Forum, an international summit of politicians and corporate executives, he had watched the American Congress pass the *Telecommunications Act,* and with it a rider called the *Communications Decency Act,* which aimed to restrict pornography on the Internet. Incensed by what he perceived to be the rider's threat to free speech, Barlow drafted the "Declaration of the Independence of Cyberspace" and posted it to the Internet. According to Barlow, the "Governments of the Industrial World" had become "weary giants of flesh and steel." Organized into hyperrationalized bureaucracies devoted to enforcing their laws by military means, these governments, he wrote, belonged to the past. Thanks to the advent of digital technologies,

> We are creating a world that all may enter without privilege or prejudice accorded by race, economic power, military force, or station of birth.
>
> We are creating a world where anyone, anywhere may express his or her beliefs, no matter how singular, without fear of being coerced into silence or conformity.

That world existed principally in the exchange of digital signals between interlinked computers—that is, in cyberspace. Speaking directly to the governments of the material world, Barlow argued:

> Your legal concepts of property, expression, identity, movement, and context do not apply to us. They are all based on matter, and there is no matter here.
>
> Our identities have no bodies, so, unlike you, we cannot obtain order by physical coercion. We believe that from ethics, enlightened self-interest, and the commonweal, our governance will emerge.[6]

For Barlow, digital technologies had ceased to be emblems of bureaucratic alienation and had become instead the tools by which bureaucracy and alienation could be overthrown. Echoing the high-flown rhetoric of the Free Speech Movement, Barlow suggested that Americans had once again found themselves at a moment of social revolution. But this time, the forces of information were on the side of the people. In Mario Savio's view, the power of computers to render the embodied lives of individual students as bits of computer-processed information symbolized the power of the factory to turn people into corporate drones and the power of the militarized state to turn young people into soldiers. For Barlow, though, that same power offered men and women the chance to enter a world of authentic identity and communal collaboration. Freed from the institutions that structured privilege in the material world, the individual in Barlow's cyberspace could join a society much like the one imagined by the Free Speech Movement—a world in which hierarchy and bureaucracy had been replaced by the collective pursuit of enlightened self-interest.

Nor was Barlow alone. For instance, Silicon Valley journalist and venture capitalist Esther Dyson, in her much-read 1997 guide to the social impact of computer networks, *Release 2.0: A Design for Living in the Digital Age,* argued that the Internet would soon dissolve the bureaucracies of the marketplace by stripping away the material bodies of individuals and corporations. Within the electronic confines of the digital marketplace, she claimed, both person and firm would be reduced to packages of information. At the same time, digital technologies would render information about products and markets ubiquitous. Together these features would allow individuals and corporations to negotiate with one another from positions of equality. Dyson was persuaded that digital media would free individuals from the ostensibly tyrannical rule of corporate hierarchies much as they would liberate Barlow's citizens from the impositions of government.

Dyson and Barlow, as well as many other commentators at the time, saw the Internet serving as a rhetorical prototype for new, flexible, and mobile ways of working and living.[7] "Like the Net, my life is decentralized," wrote Dyson, reminding her readers of how much and where she traveled. "I live on the Net," she explained. "It's the medium I use to communicate with many of my friends and colleagues. I also depend on it professionally: It's the primary subject about which I write, talk, and consult, and the basis of most of the companies I invest in, both in the United States and in Eastern Europe." Likewise, Barlow reminded his readers, "I live at barlow@eff.org. That is where I live. That is my home. If you want to find me, that's the only place you're liable to be able to do it, unless you happen to be looking at me at that moment—physically. . . . There really is no way to track me. I have not been in one place for more than 6 days since April."[8] Metaphorically, Barlow and Dyson had become packets of information, shuttling from boardroom to conference to media outlet. Their sense of place had become dislocated and their sense of home, like their notion of a home on the Net, distributed.

For Kevin Kelly, executive editor of *Wired,* this new way of living and the ways in which digital technologies served and modeled it marked a revolutionary transformation in human understanding. In one of the most widely read business manuals of the 1990s, *New Rules for the New Economy,* Kelly explained that "the principles governing the world of the soft—the world of intangibles, of media, of software, and of services—will soon command the world of the hard—the world of reality, of atoms, of objects, of steel and oil, and the hard work done by the sweat of brows." The savvy worker would have to become a networker. "Those who obey the logic of the net, and who understand that we are entering into a realm with new rules," he intoned, "will have a keen advantage in the new economy."⁹ Along with this understanding of work, he argued, a singular, almost mystical understanding of the power of information and information systems had begun to arise: "the computational metaphor." In 1998 Kelly explained that human beings were slowly but surely moving toward believing that "the universe is a computer." Already, computer experts had begun to model life in computer science terms on their machines. For some time now, many had believed that "thinking is a type of computation, DNA is software, evolution is an algorithmic process." Soon enough, he argued, human beings would begin to imagine all of biology as an instantiation of computer logic. "Is this embrace just a trick of language?" he asked. "Yes, but *that* is the unseen revolution. We are compiling a vocabulary and a syntax that is able to describe in a single language all kinds of phenomenon [*sic*] that have escaped a common language until now. It is a new universal metaphor. It has more juice in it than previous metaphors: Freud's dream state, Darwin's variety, Marx's progress, or the Age of Aquarius. And it has more power than anything else in science at the moment. In fact the computational metaphor may eclipse mathematics as a form of universal notation."¹⁰

At one level, Kelly's notion that the material world can be imagined as an information system belongs very much to the 1990s. It underpins his claims that the entrepreneurial networks of the business world resemble the systems of nature. And it runs throughout Dyson's and Barlow's arguments that the Internet models a world free from bureaucracy and psychological fragmentation. Yet it also presents a historical puzzle. The idea that the material world could be thought of as an information system and modeled on computers emerged not with the Internet, but much earlier, in and around the government-sponsored research laboratories of World War II, and particularly around the Radiation Laboratory at MIT. These laboratories helped drive the development of computing in America. They also formed the foundations of the same military-industrial-academic complex against which Berkeley students marched in 1964. Somehow, by the 1990s, a metaphor born at the heart of the military research establishment had become an emblem of the sort of personal integrity, individualism, and collaborative sociability that so many had claimed the very same establishment was working to destroy.

The computational metaphor of the 1990s embraced other contradictions too. For the marchers of the Free Speech movement, disembodiment—that is, the transformation of the self into data on an IBM card—marked the height of dehumanization. For Kelly, Dyson, and Barlow, however, it marked the route to new forms of equality and communion. Somehow, somewhere, disembodiment had come to be seen as a route to a more holistic life. Likewise, for the students who turned toward Mario Savio, the link between computers and commerce represented a threat. As Savio's speech suggested, the students of the Free Speech Movement were afraid not only of becoming victims of a social machine, but also of becoming fuel for the engines of economic production. In the 1990s, the computer once again served as a metaphor for the organization of production and labor, but this time that link promised to liberate both individuals and society. How was it that the informational economy came to be seen not as an oppressive force, but as a site of political and cultural change?

In order to answer this question, we need to revisit the research world out of which the computational metaphor arose in the 1940s and 1950s and the countercultural world of the 1960s. Contrary to the perceptions of many in the counterculture in the 1960s and of many scholars since, the two worlds had a great deal in common. They shared a celebration of intellectual work, of technology, and of collaborative work styles. Both reveled in the economic and technological abundance of post–World War II America. The research laboratories of World War II, and the military-industrial-academic bureaucracies that grew out of them, were far more flexible, entrepreneurial, and individualistic places than many remember today. By the same token, certain elements of the counterculture embraced the ideas, the social practices, and the machines that emerged inside the world of military research even as they vocally attacked cold war bureaucracies. Even as they sought to find new ways to live psychologically and socially integrated lives, some members of the counterculture turned toward the heart of the technocracy itself in search of tools and models for their work.

The Forgotten Openness of the Closed World

In the wake of Hiroshima and Nagasaki and the decades of nuclear tension that followed, it has become difficult to think of the weapon laboratories of World War II in any but the apocalyptic terms set by the Manhattan Project.

As a generation of cultural historians has shown, the end of World War II and the arrival of the atomic era unleashed a wave of quietism and fear across American society.[11] Gender boundaries stiffened, racial tensions slipped from public discussion, and leaders and citizens alike came to dread a vague but seemingly pervasive Communist menace. As Paul Edwards has demonstrated, computers played a central role as both tools and symbols in this period. In Washington, government planners used computers to model the possible effects of nuclear holocaust; in North Dakota, Alaska, and elsewhere, air force generals used computers to track potential attacks on the United States.[12] In both cases, the planet was transformed into a closed informational system for purposes of military command and control. Cognitive psychologists in turn began to imagine that the brain was a form of digital hardware and its actions a form of software, that thinking was a type of computing and memory simply a matter of data retrieval. Together, such analogies supported what Edwards has called a "closed world discourse."[13] Within this discourse, the mind of the individual man and the command centers of America's nuclear defense establishment both seemed to be mechanized tools of management and control. Both seemed devoted to maintaining firm boundaries—national in the case of the military, masculine in the case of individual military leaders. The world in which they lived and worked seemed to be dominated by large, bureaucratic organizations. Like their leaders and like the information machines on which they depended, these organizations seemed to many to be closed, unfeeling systems.

It was such closed-world visions that the students of the Free Speech Movement rose up against. Yet, even though the computational metaphor provided rhetorical support for the discourse of the closed world, the metaphor had in fact emerged from and would ultimately also help perpetuate an extraordinarily flexible, entrepreneurial, and, for its participants, often deeply satisfying style of research. As numerous historians of technology have pointed out, World War II triggered a transformation in American science.[14] Before the war, science and scientists seemed to stand outside politics. University-based researchers generally drew their funding from their universities or from industry. By and large, they maintained clear distinctions between science and engineering and between military and civilian research.[15] When Germany invaded Poland, however, these relatively independent specialists found themselves thrown into new interdisciplinary and interinstitutional collaborations. In 1940 former MIT professor and administrator Vannevar Bush persuaded Franklin Roosevelt to create the National Defense Research Committee, through which government dollars for military research would be funneled to civilian contractors, and to put him in charge of it. A year later the committee became the Office of Scientific Research and Development (OSRD). Over the next five years, the OSRD pumped some $450 million into researching and developing war-related technologies.[16]

In the process, the OSRD knit together a fabric of military-industrial-academic collaborations that has persisted to this day. Much of its wartime funding went to large research universities, such as MIT ($117 million), Caltech ($83 million), and Harvard ($30 million), but a great deal also went to industrial manufacturers such as General Electric ($8 million), RCA, Du Pont, and Westinghouse (who each received amounts less than $6 million).[17] The need to control the flow of this funding and the need to manage the movement of men and material led to a massive expansion of government bureaucracy. Government agencies, the universities housing military research, and the corporations building new military machines all saw extraordinary and, at the macro level, largely hierarchical growth.[18] The technologies produced in this manner—including radar, the atomic bomb, submarines, aircraft, and even digital computers—tended to be large, complex, and under centralized command as well. In contrast, the laboratories within which the research and development took place witnessed a flourishing of nonhierarchical, interdisciplinary collaboration. At sites such as Los Alamos and the Oak Ridge National Laboratory, theoretical physicists, experimentalists, and electrical and mechanical engineers began to work together on a daily basis and toward a common end for the first time.[19]

One of the most effective and most visible laboratories of the war was MIT's Radiation Laboratory. Founded in late 1940 with a half-million-dollar grant from the National Defense Research Committee, the Rad Lab, as it was commonly known, aimed to develop more effective ways to track and shoot down the bombers then plaguing Britain.[20] Driven first by the urgency of keeping Britain in the war, and then, after Pearl Harbor, by America's own military needs, the Rad Lab grew rapidly. Six months after its founding, it employed some two hundred researchers and technicians; by the end of the war, it employed thirty-nine hundred. Between 1940 and 1945, it developed $25 million worth of equipment for the military.[21] Before it closed at the end of the war, the laboratory enjoyed the support of government funders, military clients, industrial subcontractors, and an academic host—all of whom represented, from a structural point of view at least, the sort of bureaucracies that would become emblematic of the closed world. Over the next twenty years, engineers and administrators associated with the Rad Lab and with MIT during the war went on to play key roles in a wide variety of Defense Department–sponsored research initiatives. The Rad Lab itself became a model for the sorts of large-scale military engineering projects that defined the cold war, including the Semi-Automated Ground Environment (SAGE) air defense system and the Atlas and Polaris missile systems.[22]

Even though it operated with the support of large bureaucracies, however, the Rad Lab was a site of flexible, collaborative work and a distinctly nonhierarchical management style. Its name may conjure up images of a single laboratory room, but the Rad Lab was in fact a collection of inter-linked research projects housed together at MIT. Along with work on radar, the Lab developed technologies for long-range navigation, the aiming of anti-aircraft guns, and fire control. It brought together scientists and mathematicians from MIT and elsewhere, engineers and designers from industry, and many different military and government planners. Among these various professionals, and particularly among the engineers and designers, entrepreneurship and collaboration were the norm, and independence of mind was strongly encouraged. Formerly specialized scientists were urged to become generalists in their research, able not only to theorize but also to design and build new technologies.[23] At the same time, scientists and engineers had to become entrepreneurs, assembling networks of technologists, funders, and administrators to see their projects through. Neither scientists nor administrators could stay walled off from one another in their offices and laboratories; throughout the Rad Lab, and even after hours, in the restaurants and living rooms of Cambridge, the pressures to produce new technologies to fight the war drove formerly specialized scientists and engineers to cross professional boundaries, to routinely mix work with pleasure, and to form new, interdisciplinary networks within which to work and live.[24]

The new networks helped generate new ways of thinking and speaking. Drawing on the literature of anthropology, historian of science Peter Galison has described the Rad Lab as a "trading zone."[25] Like members of linguistically distinct tribes who come together to trade goods and services, he argues, the scientists, technologists, and administrators of the Rad Lab developed "contact languages" with which to exchange ideas and techniques toward the common end of producing weapons systems. These languages ranged from "the most function-specific jargons through semispecific pidgins, to full-fledged creoles"; they also included nonverbal elements, such as shared tools, which could be used to demonstrate concepts across disciplinary boundaries or serve as sites for collaborative work.[26] According to Galison, scientists, engineers, and administrators in the wartime laboratories worked not so much as members of a single culture, but rather as members of different professional subcultures bound together by common purpose and a set of linguistic tools they had invented to achieve it.[27]

It was precisely this process and this institutional context that gave rise to the computational metaphor and the new philosophy of technology in which it made its first public appearance: Norbert Wiener's cybernetics.[28] A former mathematics prodigy, Wiener had joined the faculty of MIT in 1919 and soon began collaborating with Vannevar Bush, a professor of electrical engineering at the time. By the 1930s Wiener had achieved substantial renown for his work in mathematics, but he had also continued to venture into other disciplines, including electrical engineering, biology, and the study of computers. He worked especially closely with Bush, for instance, on the development of analog computers in the 1930s. He also began attending a monthly seminar on scientific method conducted by Mexican physiologist Arturo Rosenblueth at the Harvard Medical School. As Wiener recalled in 1948, he and Rosenblueth shared the idea that the most interesting areas for scientific work were the "boundary regions" between disciplines.[29] They had also begun to imagine an institutional structure that would facilitate such work. Wrote Wiener,

> We had dreamed for years of an institution of independent scientists, working together in one of these backwoods of science, not as subordinates of some great executive officer, but joined by the desire, indeed by the spiritual necessity, to understand the region as a whole, and to lend one another the strength of that understanding.
>
> We had agreed on these matters long before we had chosen the field of our joint investigations and our respective parts in them. The deciding factor in this new step was the war.[30]

Norbert Wiener began doing war-related research even before the United States entered the fighting, and soon after the Rad Lab was formed, he turned his attention to the problems of tracking and shooting down enemy aircraft.[31] As a mathematician, Wiener worked to devise statistical methods for determining the future course of an airplane based on its location and motion. Together with a young engineer named Julian Bigelow, he also designed a machine that they called a "predictor" that would embody these methods. Early in the process, Wiener and Bigelow recognized that the enemy bomber and the anti-aircraft fire-control system each depended on both mechanical and human components. From a theoretical point of view, this combination of the organic and the mechanical presented a problem. In his 1956 memoir, *I Am a Mathematician,* Norbert Wiener explained that "in order to obtain as complete a mathematical treatment as possible of the over-all control problem, it is necessary to assimilate the different parts of the system to a single basis, either human or mechanical. Since our understanding of the mechanical elements of gun pointing appeared to us to be far ahead of our psychological understanding, we chose to find a mechanical analogue of the gun pointer and the airplane pilot."[32] In other words, Wiener and Bigelow began to imagine the soldiers who controlled the airplanes and the anti-aircraft apparatus as mechanical devices so as to be able to model their behavior using mathematical formulas. The analogue they chose was the servomechanism.[33] Wiener and Bigelow noticed that both the pilot and the anti-aircraft gunner observed patterns of error in their attempts to attack and escape and regulated their behavior accordingly. In this respect, like the nineteenth-century governor that once regulated steam engines, each responded to what Wiener and Bigelow called "negative feedback."[34]

By conceptualizing pilots and gunners as servomechanisms, Wiener and Bigelow also found a way to imagine the material world in terms of the computational metaphor. That metaphor in turn encoded two sometimes overlapping, and sometimes competing, socio-technical visions: the automaton and the self-regulating system. By imaginatively transfiguring soldiers into mechanisms, Wiener and Bigelow suggested that human beings were at some level machines.[35] Underlying all their messy, fleshy, emotional complexity, human beings could be modeled as mechanical information processors. Moreover, if this was the case, they could be replaced by faster and more reliable mechanical devices. With their anti-aircraft predictor, Wiener and Bigelow helped lay the foundation for a vision of the automated human being and the automated organization that would haunt American public life well into the 1960s.

At the same time, however, by means of the same imaginative transformation of men into information processing devices, Wiener and Bigelow offered up a picture of humans and machines as dynamic, collaborating elements in a single, highly fluid, socio-technical system.[36] Within that system, control emerged not from the mind of a commanding officer, but from the complex, probabilistic interactions of humans, machines, and events around them. Moreover, the mechanical elements of the system in question—in this case, the predictor—enabled the human elements to achieve what all Americans would agree was a worthwhile goal: the shooting down of enemy aircraft. In the predictor, Wiener and Bigelow presented an example of a system in which men and machines collaborated, amplifying their respective capabilities, sharing control, and ultimately serving the human good of stopping the Nazi onslaught. Over the coming decades, this second vision of benevolent man-machine systems, of circular flows of information, would emerge as a driving force in the establishment of the military-industrial-academic complex *and* as a model of an alternative to that complex.

Wiener and Bigelow began almost immediately to generalize their vision of a self-directing system governed by feedback to other fields. In early 1942, Wiener and Bigelow had begun to think about the biological realm and approached Arturo Rosenblueth. Their discussions led to the 1943 publication of a paper, "Behavior, Purpose, and Teleology," in which they suggested that behavior and purpose in biological systems proceeded according to the same feedback dynamics that governed the sorts of mechanical and biomechanical systems Wiener and Bigelow had been developing in the Rad Lab. But this was only the beginning. Within a year, Wiener began to imagine duplicating the human brain with electrical circuits. By 1948 he had transformed the computational metaphor into the basis of a new discipline. In his book *Cybernetics; or, Control and Communication in the Animal and the Machine,* he defined cybernetics as a field focused on "the study of messages as a means of controlling machinery and society," with machinery seeming to include, by analogy at least, biological organisms. For Wiener, the world, like the anti-aircraft predictor, was composed of systems linked by, and to some extent made out of, messages. Drawing on Claude Shannon's information theory (published in 1948, but likely familiar to Wiener much earlier), Wiener defined messages as "forms of pattern and organization."[37] Like Shannon's information, Wiener's messages were surrounded by "noise," yet they somehow maintained their integrity. So too did organisms and machines: incorporating and responding to feedback through structural mechanisms, Wiener explained, both kept themselves in a state of homeostasis. In that sense, Wiener believed that biological, mechanical, and information systems, including then-emerging digital computers, could be seen as analogues of one another. All controlled themselves by sending and receiving messages, and, metaphorically at least, all were simply patterns of ordered information in a world otherwise tending to entropy and noise.

Wiener also believed that these systems could serve as models for social institutions and for society at large. Two years after publishing *Cybernetics,* Wiener published the far more accessible and intellectually more expansive volume *The Human Use of Human Beings: Cybernetics and Society.* There he argued that society as a whole, as well as its constituent organizational parts, functioned much like organisms and machines. That is, society could be seen as a system seeking self-regulation through the processing of messages. In Wiener's analogy, for instance, public information systems such as the media served as servomechanisms. The TV screen became to the society as a whole what the radar screen was to the World War II gunner—a system through which to measure and adjust the system's performance. Wiener believed that the media ideally served to "correct" the actions of public leaders by offering them accurate information about the performance of society as a whole. Likewise, within the smaller unit of the government agency or the corporation, Wiener argued that leaders should actively solicit feedback from their colleagues and employees. In particular, they should avoid adhering to a strictly top-down style of communication: "Otherwise," wrote Wiener, "the top officials may find that they have based their policy on a complete misconception of the facts that their underlings possess."[38]

Both *Cybernetics* and *The Human Use of Human Beings* were best sellers, and together with Claude Shannon and Warren Weaver's 1949 *Mathematical Theory of Communication,* they sparked a decade's worth of debate about the proper role of computers in society. Given the many pages they devoted to analyzing complex mathematical formulas, *Cybernetics* and *The Mathematical Theory of Communication* would not seem to be likely candidates for popular acclaim. Yet, in an America that had recently defeated Nazi Germany and Hirohito's Japan and invented a weapon that could eradicate life on earth, the computational metaphor that underlay these books gave voice to two issues then much in the public eye: the sudden importance of science and its ambiguous social potential. On the one hand, as Wiener himself pointed out, cybernetics suggested that digital processes might lead to a malevolent automation of human and biological processes. At the end of *Cybernetics,* for example, he described a computer of the future that could play chess.[39] Though such computers have become commonplace today, to readers of the early cold war era, Wiener's image suggested that a human being could be substantially translated into a system of wires and electrodes — at least for the purposes of playing a board game. His image conjured up the swarm of recent propaganda images of hyperrational, unfeeling Nazis. Like a Hollywood Nazi, the computer played chess efficiently, but without feeling. It sought only to dominate and control. This vision sparked several fears, as Wiener saw it. Computers, he suggested, might step beyond the reaches of human control and begin to act on their own.[40] On the other hand, they might become the tools of unfeeling politicians and capitalists and those individuals' desire to automate the social institutions they dominated. Over the next fifteen years, Wiener remained particularly afraid of industrial automation and even sought out union leader Walter Reuther to suggest how workers might combat the threats it posed.[41]

Wiener's fear of automation would echo down through the 1950s and would reappear both in technical discussions of the potential social impact of computing and in radical critiques of postwar society. Yet, in his vision of organisms, machines, and society itself as overlapping systems of information exchange, Wiener also offered a much more benevolent view of the political implications of information technology. Following Shannon, Wiener viewed information as pattern within noise and therefore as a model of material and social order. In Wiener's own words, disorganization and randomness, whether in the realm of information or in the realm of politics, was something "which without too violent a figure of speech we may consider evil."[42] Information systems, in part simply by virtue of being *systems,* exemplified organization. What is more, because of their feedback mechanisms, Wiener believed they sought to maintain order within themselves. In both senses, Wiener viewed information systems as sources of moral good. Moreover, to an America that had just spent five years combating a dictatorial German regime and that would soon confront a new dictator in the person of Joseph Stalin, a systems view of information offered an appealingly nonhierarchical model of governance and power. Cybernetic systems as Wiener saw them were self-regulating and complete in and of themselves, at least in theory. They had only to process information by means of their constituent parts and respond to the feedback offered, and order would emerge. Embedded in Wiener's theory of society as an information system was a deep longing for and even a model of an egalitarian, democratic social order. To the readers of *Cybernetics,* computers may have threatened automation from above, but they also offered metaphors for the democratic creation of order from below.

At the same time, for scientists and technologists, cybernetics and the systems theories that followed it remained the preeminent language of collaboration in the multidisciplinary world of cold war research.[43] Vannevar Bush had feared the long-term consequences of government influence on civilian research and development and had hoped that the military-industrial-academic collaborations he helped establish would not outlive World War II. Nevertheless, as soon as the war ended, they became the basis for a series of massive military research projects, including the Intercontinental Ballistic Missile, the SAGE air defense system, and the Polaris Intermediate Range Missile. All of these projects depended heavily on computers, on interdisciplinary and interinstitutional collaborations, and on a systems approach to engineering.[44] Over the next twenty years, cybernetics and systems theory more generally provided a rhetoric and a conceptual framework with which to link the activities of each of these actors to the others and to coordinate their work as a whole.

The power of cybernetics and systems theory to facilitate interdisciplinary collaboration emerged in large part thanks to the entrepreneurship of Norbert Wiener and the research climate of World War II. Wiener did not create the discipline of cybernetics out of thin air; rather, he pulled its analytical terms together by bridging multiple, if formerly segregated, scientific communities. Wiener borrowed the word *homeostasis* from the field of physiology and applied it to social systems; he picked up the word *feedback* from control engineering; and from the study of human behavior, he drew the concepts of *learning, memory, flexibility,* and *purpose.*[45] Wiener could assemble pieces from such diverse sources because he was in steady collaborative contact with representatives from each of these domains at the Rad Lab, in his famous hallway wanderings at MIT, and in his sojourns to the Harvard Medical School. In the course of these peregrinations, he discussed physiology with Arturo Rosenblueth, feedback with the engineers of the Rad Lab, and, very likely, human behavior with both. Like the anti-aircraft predictor itself, the rhetoric of cybernetics was the product of interdisciplinary entrepreneurial work. Thus, the key terms of early cybernetics can be seen to have emerged as elements of a local contact language in and around the multiple trading zones of World War II Cambridge.

The rhetoric of cybernetics not only embodied, but also actively facilitated, networking and entrepreneurship. At the local level of the Rad Lab, cybernetics offered a contact language through which work on weapons devices could be organized; devices such as the anti-aircraft predictor offered sites for collaboration. Yet, as Geoffrey Bowker has argued, the locally developed tactics of cybernetic rhetoric also allowed it to spread across multiple fields of research and to become a "universal discipline."[46] Because of the changes in scientific practice brought about by World War II, specialists in one discipline began to do things that had previously been considered the proper domain of specialists in other areas. They could justify such leaps across disciplinary boundaries by drawing on the rhetoric of cybernetics. If biological principles were at work in machines, then why shouldn't a physiologist contribute to work on computers? If "information" was the lifeblood of automatons, human beings, and societies alike, why shouldn't a mechanical engineer become a social critic? With such justifications, Wiener and a string of later cyberneticians and systems theorists reached across disciplinary boundaries and claimed a universal relevance for their new "science."

In this process, two rhetorical tactics played especially important roles: the use of prototypes and what Bowker has called "legitimacy exchange," a term that refers to the process by which experts in one area draw on the authority of experts in another area to justify their activities. As Bowker explains, "An isolated scientific worker making an outlandish claim could gain rhetorical legitimacy by pointing to support from another field—which in turn referenced the first worker's field to support its claim. The language of cybernetics provided a site where this exchange could occur."[47] Legitimacy exchange helped transform cybernetics from a relatively local contact language suited to the particular needs of scientists in wartime Cambridge into a discourse commonly used for coordinating work across multiple research projects and multiple professional communities. As Bowker suggests, cybernetics facilitated not only the interlinking of research, development, and production activities, but also the development of new interpersonal and interinstitutional networks and, with them, the exchange and generation of a networked form of power. To the extent that members of two or several disciplines could succeed in creating a relatively closed system of interlegitimation, they could make it extraordinarily difficult for nonexperts (e.g., noncyberneticians) to challenge their individual agendas. They could and did stake claims for research funding, material resources, and popular attention. Working together, in pairs and networks, each acquired a legitimacy that none could have had alone without the exchange of legitimacy afforded by cybernetic rhetoric.

Legitimacy exchange drew not only on rhetoric, but on material artifacts as well. Andrew Pickering has pointed out that cyberneticians created a variety of "monsters"—artifacts that seemed to straddle the line between mechanical devices and living systems. These artifacts included Wiener and Bigelow's anti-aircraft predictor, a homeostat developed by British psychiatrist and cybernetic theorist Ross Ashby, and a number of others.[48] In each case, the artifact served as a prototype of other sorts of systems and of cybernetic principles more generally. In Wiener's case, the anti-aircraft predictor modeled not only the behavior of aircraft, but also the probabilistic nature of biological, mechanical, and social systems of all sorts. Ashby's homeostat modeled processes of self-regulation that could be observed in biological and social domains as well. As Katherine Hayles has observed, such devices "functioned as exchangers," bringing "man and machine into equivalence."[49] In the process, they served to exemplify in real, concrete terms—and thus to legitimate—the claims of cyberneticians and systems theorists that just as information itself spanned multiple domains, their theory could be deployed in multiple disciplines.

Over the two decades following World War II, such claims found a home in massive military research projects; in a variety of academic disciplines, including management theory, clinical psychology, political science, biology, and ecology; and ultimately in the urban renewal projects of Lyndon Johnson's Great Society.[50] As Katherine Hayles and Steve Heims have shown, cybernetics's migration into the social and, to some extent, the physical and biological sciences was driven in large part by the Macy Conferences.[51] Sponsored by the Macy Foundation in the late 1940s and early 1950s, these meetings brought together biologists, physicists, and mathematicians, including cyberneticians such as Arturo Rosenblueth and Warren McCulloch, psychiatrists such as Ross Ashby, and sociologists and anthropologists such as Gregory Bateson and Margaret Mead. Over time, the Macy Conferences helped refine a number of cybernetic concepts, including the relationship between a system and its observers and the nature of feedback. They also sent individual participants back to their home disciplines with a deep systems orientation toward their work and a habit of deploying the informational and systems metaphors. In this way the Macy meetings helped transform cybernetics into one of the dominant intellectual paradigms of the postwar era.[52]

As important as they were, though, these conferences were only one force driving the spread of systems thinking. At the same time that the Macy meetings were introducing cybernetics into new intellectual circles, the military research projects of the cold war were turning its systems orientation into everyday practice. Like the Macy Conferences, these projects brought together specialists from a variety of disciplines, and for the specialists involved, systems theory became a way of life. The SAGE air defense project, for example, began as an attempt to establish an early warning system against Soviet bombers armed with nuclear weapons. Like the Rad Lab before it, SAGE was based at MIT; involved a complex range of military, industrial, and academic players; and organized its work in a highly collaborative fashion. Far from implementing a rigid command hierarchy, the managers of SAGE coordinated the project's many elements through a set of distributed, interdisciplinary meetings. The air defense system they developed depended on a series of geographically distributed radar sets, linked to computers that could monitor and coordinate the information they sent back. For this work, the SAGE planners turned to the Whirlwind computer already under development in a project led by MIT professor Jay Forrester. The Whirlwind was about to become the first interactive digital computer to be used (by SAGE personnel) primarily for information management and control rather than computation.[53] At the same time, they helped turn the computational metaphor into a tool with which to imagine, manage, and facilitate such highly interdisciplinary, networked forms of cooperation. The power of this metaphor can be seen in an influential 1950 report written by the Truman administration's Defense Systems Engineering Committee— the same committee that would ultimately press to integrate the Whirlwind computer into the nation's air defense system. In their report, the committee outlined the means by which air defense ought to be organized: not only in terms of armaments and airplanes, but in terms of the computational metaphor of cybernetics. "The Air Defense system," they wrote,

> is an organism. . . . What then are organisms? They are of three kinds: animate organisms, which comprise animals and groups of animals, including men; partly animate organisms which involve animals together with inanimate devices such as in the Air Defense System; and inanimate organisms such as

vending machines. All these organisms possess in common: sensory components, communication facilities, data analyzing devices, centers of judgment,
directors of action, and effectors, or executing agencies. . . .

It is the function of an organism . . . to achieve some defined purpose.[54]

Before the system was deployed in 1958, the SAGE project would train
an entire generation of computer engineers, scientists, and technicians.
These men (and they were almost exclusively men) would go on to found
numerous university computer science departments, to set up MIT's Project MAC (which introduced computer time-sharing), to help establish key
computer companies (such as the Digital Equipment Corporation), and
even to help initiate the ARPANET, which would become the basis of the
Internet.[55] As they created the military-industrial-academic infrastructure
out of which individualized and networked computing would emerge, these
engineers, along with their colleagues on the ICBM and Polaris projects and
on dozens of other military command-and-control system development
projects, brought with them not only a habit of entrepreneurship and interdisciplinary collaboration, but also the discourse of cybernetics and systems
theory and the computational metaphor on which it depended. Even as they
built the large military research projects and the massive weapons that
would come to symbolize cold war technocracy, the researchers of SAGE
and later projects carried forward a collaborative style and a rhetoric of collaboration born in the weapons laboratories of World War II.

The Countercultural Embrace of Technology and Consciousness

Even though it grew out of and facilitated interdisciplinary forms of cooperation, the computational metaphor did not yet carry with it the visions of
a disembodied, egalitarian polis and the postinstitutional, peer-to-peer marketplace with which it would be associated in the mid-1990s. On the contrary, those social ideals emerged as key features of a nationwide youth
movement that rose up in the 1960s in large part *against* the institutions
within which cybernetics served as a lingua franca.

By the late 1950s, many Americans had begun to fear that the military, industrial, and academic institutions that had brought the atomic bomb into
being were beginning to transform all of American life. Under the shadow
of nuclear war, the often freewheeling, collaborative practices of cold war
research and development almost disappeared from public view.[56] What remained was a vision of expertise and hierarchy and, for critics on the left, of
a society dominated by pyramidal organizations run by buttoned-down,
psychologically fragmented men. "As the means of information and of

power are centralized," wrote sociologist C. Wright Mills in 1956, "some men come to occupy positions in American society from which they can look down upon . . . and by their decisions mightily affect, the everyday worlds of ordinary men and women."[57] Under the controlling eye of this "power elite," Mills argued, ordinary Americans found themselves trapped in corridors and offices, unable to envision, let alone take charge of, the entirety of their work or their lives. Ordinary people lacked the ability to "reason about the great structures—rational and irrational—of which their milieux are subordinate parts," he explained.[58] So too, in a way, did the men at the top. For critics like Mills, both the masters of bureaucracy and their minions suffered from a paring away of emotional life and a careful separation of psychological functions. After World War II, rationalization had begun to give rise to "the man who is 'with' rationality but without reason, who is increasingly self-rationalized and also increasingly uneasy." This man, continued Mills, was a "Cheerful Robot."[59]

Mills's critique could be heard echoing throughout the 1960s in works as varied as Jacques Ellul's *The Technological Society* (1964), John Kenneth Galbraith's *The New Industrial State* (1967), Herbert Marcuse's *One-Dimensional Man* (1964), Lewis Mumford's *The Myth of the Machine* (1967), Theodore Roszak's *The Making of a Counterculture* (1969), and Charles Reich's *The Greening of America* (1970). Like Mills, these authors suggested that society was undergoing a rapid process of centralization and rationalization, a process both supported by new technologies and designed to help build them. The resulting social order went by a variety of names—the "technostructure" (Galbraith), the "technological society" (Ellul), and "technocracy" (Roszak). In each case, critics pointed to computers and automation as forces driving the rise of this new way of life. Though little read today, for instance, Lewis Mumford was among the most eloquent and popular of the anti-automationists. In *The Myth of the Machine,* he turned a cold eye on post–World War II technological research. While noting that the era had given rise to a new "experimental mode" and to such varied technologies as nuclear energy and supersonic transportation, Mumford argued that it had also brought into being a new generation of technocrats and a new generation of technologies through which they might rule: "With this new 'megatechnics' the dominant minority will create a uniform, all-enveloping, superplanetary structure, designed for automatic operation. Instead of functioning actively as an autonomous personality, man will become a passive, purposeless, machine-conditioned animal whose proper functions, as technicians now interpret man's role, will either be fed into the machine or strictly limited and controlled for the benefit of de-personalized, collective organizations."[60]

Such visions of the social world as an automated machine found a large and passionate audience on the college campuses of the 1960s. The generation that came of age early in the decade had been born into a world of extraordinary contradictions. On the one hand, the children of the cold war years witnessed an astonishing growth in American affluence. Teenagers found themselves surrounded by appliances and automobiles and opportunities for education and employment that their parents, growing up in the Depression, could hardly have imagined. As many commentators remarked at the time, this affluence transformed adolescence into a true interregnum between the freedom of childhood and the employment and family demands of adulthood.[61] For the ever-increasing numbers of middle- and upper-class youths in particular, adolescence became a time for personal exploration.

On the other hand, universities became sites where adolescents could do that work together. In the postwar years, thanks in no small part to government funding for scientific and technological research, the American university system expanded at an exponential rate. The years immediately before the war saw only 14 percent of college-age youth attending universities. By 1961 the percentage had risen to 38, and by 1970 it had topped 50.[62] In 1959 a little over 3 million Americans were enrolled in college; by 1973 the number had climbed to 8.5 million.[63] These shifts represented not only the extension of formal education to whole new segments of the population, but also a broader movement toward meritocracy in education, especially at elite institutions. Until the mid-1950s, universities such as Harvard and Yale often admitted students on the basis of family connections. By the mid-1960s, largely due to the rise of educational testing, more merit-based standards had taken hold, and students from a wider range of social backgrounds found themselves on campuses that had been off-limits to their parents.[64]

Even as their horizons widened, though, the youth of the late 1950s and early 1960s found themselves beset by fears of the atomic bomb and of growing up to take their place in the sort of closed social world that they imagined had brought it into being. Elaine Tyler May has pointed out that the dominant social style of the middle and upper classes during the postwar years could be described as "containment." As the interpersonal corollary to the closed-world visions of military and government planners, containment referred to a way of being in which men and women sought to constrain their emotions, maintain their marriages, and build safe, secure, and independent homes. Like the air force soldiers who scanned America's borders for incoming Soviet bombers, many Americans took to monitoring the boundaries of their own lives. These efforts, however, did not keep nuclear nightmares at bay. On the contrary, for Americans in the 1950s, and

especially American children, nuclear warfare remained a terrifying and imminent prospect. In 1967 social psychologist Kenneth Keniston interviewed
a group of young men and women who had taken part in a series of anti–
Vietnam War efforts. Hoping to uncover the roots of their activism, he
asked them to recall their earliest memories. One young woman described
the day an encyclopedia salesman sold her mother volume A of the *Encyclopedia Britannica*: "I remember reading it and seeing a picture of an atomic
bomb and a tank going over some rubble. And I think I became hysterical.
I screamed and screamed and screamed."[65]

This woman was hardly unique. As schoolchildren, she and her class-
mates had been taught to "duck and cover" under their desks if they should
happen to see a nuclear flash. They had been shown government-sponsored
films in which children their own age sprinted through neighborhoods that
been reduced to atomic rubble, hunting for the local fallout shelter.[66] Ever
since the Soviet Union first tested an atomic bomb in 1949, Americans, and
particularly young Americans, had suffered under a thick cloud of nuclear
anxiety. For the college students of the early 1960s, that anxiety fused with
fears for their own professional futures. Thanks to the power of postwar industry, they would have no trouble finding jobs. Yet many feared that to take
those jobs would be to enter the bleak ranks of the bureaucracy that had
brought forth nuclear weapons and, later, the Vietnam War. "There are
models of marriage and adult life, but . . . they don't work," recalled the
same young woman who had discovered the atomic bomb in the encyclopedia. "There is that whole conflict about being professional, leading a
middle-class life which none of us have been able really to resolve. How do
you be an adult in this world?"[67]

In response to this question, and to the threat of technological bureaucracy
more broadly, the youth of the 1960s developed two somewhat overlapping
but ultimately distinct social movements.[68] The first grew out of the struggles
for civil rights in the Deep South and the Free Speech Movement and became
known as the New Left. Its members registered formerly disenfranchised
voters, formed new political parties, and led years of protests against the Vietnam War. The second bubbled up out of a wide variety of cold war–era cultural springs, including Beat poetry and fiction, Zen Buddhism, action painting, and, by the mid-1960s, encounters with psychedelic drugs. If the New
Left turned outward, toward political action, this wing turned inward, toward questions of consciousness and interpersonal intimacy, and toward
small-scale tools such as LSD or rock music as ways to enhance both. By the
end of the decade, as youth everywhere adopted its drug habits and its sartorial styles, this branch of the youth movement, and ultimately youthful
protestors as a whole, came to commonly be called "the counterculture."

Today, it is the counterculture's hedonism that many Americans remember best. Since the publication of the book that first put the term into mass circulation, Theodore Roszak's 1969 *The Making of a Counterculture,* commentators have taken that hedonism as evidence that the youth movements of the era represented a clean break with cold war society. For those on the right, the drug use and open sexuality of long-haired youths marked a deep challenge to mainstream America. In 1976, for instance, sociologist Daniel Bell pronounced that the counterculture had brought with it the end of the Protestant ethic. For many on the left, the counterculture seemed to threaten the end of traditional political struggle. To former members of the New Left such as Todd Gitlin, hippies were a seductive force, tempting the leaders of the antiwar movement to abandon their organizing for the theatrical politics of the Yippies. Historians who have followed his lead have pointed to the ways in which the counterculture opened the doors of the youth movement to the complex delights of consumer culture. To others, such as Herbert Marcuse and a subsequent generation of cultural theorists, the hippies' hedonism marked the birth of a new, performative sensibility with which to challenge the social and emotional rigidities of mainstream culture.[69]

Even as these critiques have acknowledged the power of the cultural dimensions of activism in the 1960s, however, they have obscured the intellectual underpinnings of the hippie style of protest and the ways in which that style echoed ideas, social practices, and attitudes toward technology that had emerged in the center of the cold war research world. For many in the counterculture, though by no means all, the work of expanding consciousness and increasing interpersonal intimacy was not an end in itself; it was a means by which to build alternative, egalitarian communities. Although historians and pundits alike remain fascinated with the sex, drugs, and rock and roll of the era, few today recall that in 1967 many of the hippies who made San Francisco's Haight-Ashbury neighborhood the epicenter of the famed "Summer of Love" left the city early that fall and, together with thousands of others, helped launch the largest wave of communalization in American history. In the two centuries before 1965, historians and sociologists have estimated that Americans established between five hundred and seven hundred communes.[70] Between 1965 and 1972, they have estimated that somewhere between several thousand and several tens of thousands of communes were created, with most appearing between 1967 and 1970.[71] Judson Jerome, perhaps the most rigorous surveyor of the movement, has estimated that in the early 1970s, some 750,000 people lived in a total of more than ten thousand communes nationwide.[72]

Many of these new communities sprang up on hillsides and wooded lots far from America's urban capitals. Former hippies from the Haight, for instance, helped establish farms and rural homesteads in northern California, Colorado, New Mexico, and Tennessee. Other communes came to life in the apartments and row houses of Berkeley, Cambridge, and many other cities, often in direct confrontation with long-standing ordinances prohibiting cohabitation by groups of unmarried adults. As Timothy Miller has explained, many communes were organized along religious lines, some came together around a shared political orientation, and still others formed around a shared sexual orientation.[73] By far the most visible of the communes at the time, however, were those founded by the hippies of San Francisco and their confreres on the East Coast.[74] For them, the mind-expanding turn toward sexuality and toward the small-scale technologies of psychedelia and music was not only a turn away from the constrained cultural style of middle-class cold war America; it was a turn toward what they imagined could become a new nation, a land of small, egalitarian communities linked to one another by a network of shared beliefs.

For this reason, I will call both those who actually established such communes and those who saw the transformation of consciousness as the basis for the reformation of American social structure *New Communalists*. In doing so, I hope to tease apart an important strand of countercultural thought and practice that has become so thoroughly entangled with the terms *counterculture* and *New Left* over the years as to have been rendered nearly invisible. By identifying the intellectual roots, the social ambitions, and the extensive historical influence of those who turned toward technology and mind as foundations of a new society, I also hope to clear up two historical misconceptions. Many historians today still read the youth movements of the 1960s as a generational rejection of the cold war world into which they were born. Among New Communalists, though, this was simply not the case: even as they set out for the rural frontier, the communards of the back-to-the-land movement often embraced the collaborative social practices, the celebration of technology, and the cybernetic rhetoric of mainstream military-industrial-academic research. More recently, analysts of digital utopianism have dated the communitarian rhetoric surrounding the introduction of the Internet to what they have imagined to be a single, authentically revolutionary social movement that was somehow crushed or co-opted by the forces of capitalism.[75] By confusing the New Left with the counterculture, and the New Communalists with both, contemporary theorists of digital media have often gone so far as to echo the utopians of the 1990s and to reimagine its peer-to-peer technologies as the rebirth in hardware and software of a single, "free" culture that once stood outside the main-stream and can do so again.[76]

A closer look at the New Left and the New Communalists, however, reveals critical differences between the two movements and suggests that neither achieved a complete break with the society it aimed to change. From its earliest days, the New Left was a primarily political movement, albeit one with communitarian strains. In June 1962, fifty-nine student radicals gathered in Port Huron, Michigan, and penned what would become the founding document of the Students for a Democratic Society (SDS). SDS did not constitute the whole of the New Left by any means, but its Port Huron Statement still stands as one of the clearest expressions of the movement's appeal to college-educated youth of the time. The authors of the document identified two forces driving their desire to organize. One was the rise of the civil rights movement, which revealed a level of bigotry in the American South that by 1962 had compelled many of the white college students gath-ered in Port Huron to become engaged in nonviolent forms of resistance. The other was the cold war and the threat of nuclear annihilation. "Our work," they explained, "is guided by the sense that we may be the last gen-eration in the experiment with living." As the founders of SDS saw it, the denigration of African Americans and the possibility of destroying the hu-man species had emanated from the same source: a highly bureaucratized society whose structures virtually required individuals to become psycho-logically fragmented and thus capable of atrocious behavior.[77] If bigotry was to end and the world was to survive, a new kind of social structure would have to be built.

In this new world, they explained, "the goal of man and society should be finding a meaning in life that is personally authentic."[78] For many in the New Left, as for many New Communalists, the bureaucracies of cold war America and the nuclear cloud that hung over it seemed to threaten to de-stroy the individual's sense of his or her own reality. As historian Douglas Rossinow has shown, the founders of the New Left carried with them a deep anxiety, a ferocious sense of their own "weightlessness" in the face of world events, and a "deadening alienation" from the culture within which they were about to become adults.[79] They responded to this experience by developing two forms of political activism. The first, and by far the domi-nant mode, was straightforward organizing for political change. Across the 1960s, New Left activists demonstrated on behalf of Free Speech rights and Black Power. They protested the industrial activities and bureaucratic orga-nization of the universities, and, most visibly of all, they led demonstrations against the Vietnam War. In each area, the New Left did what insurgent political movements have often done: they wrote statements, formed parties, chose leaders, and marched.

Many members of the New Left took activism to be the fundamental mission of the movement. To eliminate individual alienation and bring about a less violent and more psychologically satisfying society, they believed, the movement would need to engage in political struggle. At the same time, within SDS and the New Left more broadly, many hoped that they might begin to live out some of the new political structures they were working to create. If, as the Port Huron Statement suggested, an effective democracy facilitated individual participation and individual independence, then SDS should do the same. SDS became a party that elected its leaders and staged annual conventions, but its members often tried to make decisions by consensus and, at least in some quarters, retained a distrust of hierarchical organization. And as they came together, first in the Civil Rights and Free Speech Movements and later in protests against the Vietnam War, members of the SDS experienced a feeling of solidarity and community that many had not known before. In its early years, wrote Todd Gitlin, who was elected president of SDS in 1963, "the SDS circle had founded a surrogate family, where for long stretches of time horizontal relations of trust replaced vertical relations of authority." These relations intensified for others as the decade wore on. In 1966 Greg Calvert, who was elected national secretary of SDS that year, argued that SDS should not only "destroy the power which had created the loveless anti-community" of mainstream America, but actively seek to create a new community within its own ranks. "We would ourselves create the community as love," he said.[80]

Within SDS, then, and within the New Left as a whole, the young, predominantly white, middle- and upper-class rank and file did go some way toward building an alternative community structure. At the same time, though, especially in its early years, the New Left retained an allegiance to mainstream political tactics and an antipathy to the psychedelic mysticism common to the counterculture. The New Left may have sought to build a new world, but it did so using the traditional techniques of agonistic politics. If elements within the New Left began to experience forms of solidarity like those they helped to build into the world outside the movement, they did so as an after-effect of their own organizing. Within the New Left, true community and the end of alienation were usually thought to be the result of political activity, rather than a form of politics in their own right.

The reverse was true among the New Communalists. For the proto-hippies, artists, and mystics who began coming together in Manhattan and San Francisco after World War II, political activism was at best beside the point and at worst part of the problem. Like the founders of the New Left, these early counterculturalists wanted to challenge the social order of the cold war and, by doing so, bring about a new, less violent, and more psychologically authentic world. Unlike many in the New Left, however, most retained a deep distrust not only of traditional politicians, but of any and all formal chains of command. In late 1967 the San Francisco–based underground newspaper the *Seed* published a poem that gives a feel for the attitude toward politics that would soon inform the New Communalist movement:

> Beware of leaders, heroes, organizers.
> Watch that stuff. Beware of structure freaks.
> They do not understand.
> We know the system doesn't work because we're living in its ruins. We
>   know that leaders don't work out because they have all led us only to
>   the present, the good leaders equally with the bad. . . . What the system
>   calls organization—linear organization—is a systematic cage, arbitrarily
>   limiting the possible. It's never worked before. It always produced the
>   present.[81]

For the New Communalists, the key to social change was not politics, but mind. In 1969 Theodore Roszak spoke for many when he argued that the central problem underlying the rationalized bureaucracy of the cold war was not political structure, but the "myth of objective consciousness." This state of mind, wrote Roszak, emerged among the experts who dominated rationalized organizations, and it was conducive to alienation, hierarchy, and a mechanistic view of social life. Its emblems were the clock and the computer, its apogee "the scientific world view, with its entrenched commitment to an egocentric and cerebral mode of consciousness." Against this mode, Roszak and others proposed a return to transcendence and a simultaneous transformation of the individual self and its relations with others: "This . . . is the primary project of our counter culture: to proclaim a new heaven and a new earth so vast, so marvelous that the inordinate claims of technical expertise must of necessity withdraw in the presence of such splendor to subordinate and marginal status in the lives of men. To create and broadcast such a consciousness of life entails nothing less than the willingness to open ourselves to the visionary imagination on its own terms."[82]

Roszak's call echoes the Romantic nineteenth-century voices of Emerson and Whitman and, before them, the millennial ambitions of the early American Puritans. Perhaps no dream in American culture has recurred as often as the one in which a group of spiritual adepts remake the world they have inherited in the image of their own ideals. For Roszak and the New Communalists, this dream entailed a rejection of industrial-era technocratic bureaucracy. As they drove their funky school buses off into the hills of Marin County and the deserts of New Mexico, the back-to-the-landers intended to build self-sufficient retreats in which they might rediscover what they imagined to be pre-industrial forms of intimacy and egalitarian rule. At the same time, though, the countercultural dream of transcendence signaled a move toward the embrace of knowledge and collaborative styles of knowledge work that had emerged at the heart of mainstream American research and industrial culture during World War II.

This can be seen especially clearly in a book that, along with Roszak's *The Making of a Counterculture,* helped to define the intellectual framework of the New Communalist movement: Charles Reich's *The Greening of America.* Reich argued that socioeconomic history could be divided into three phases, each with its own associated consciousness. Consciousness I, he explained, emerged during the agricultural era of the nineteenth century and represented the values of farmers and small businessmen. By the middle of the twentieth century, Consciousness I had been replaced by Consciousness II, in which industrial bureaucracies sought to manage people and nature through complex organizations and new technologies of control and communication. Like Roszak and other critics of technological bureaucracy, Reich held this second era responsible for the global threat of nuclear disaster and the highly localized experience of psychological distress. Under the industrial regime, Reich wrote, "it is impossible to know, talk to, or confront the whole man, for that wholeness is precisely what does not 'exist.'"[83]

Consciousness III would create the missing wholeness. Unlike its predecessors, Consciousness III rejected "relationships of authority and subservience" in favor of bureaucratically leveled communities, harmonious collaborations in which each citizen was "honest" and "together" with every other.[84] Within such communities, citizens would serve as examples to one another; the communities in turn would serve as examples to the world. That the citizens in question would largely be white, affluent, and young was beside the point: "Today there is only one class," wrote Reich. "The economic class struggle has been transcended by the interest of everyone in recapturing their humanity."[85] In Reich's view, men and women of all classes were locked in a struggle to reclaim their consciousnesses; the affluent young represented the vanguard of this struggle; when they succeeded first in changing their minds and then in building new communities around those new minds, the technocratic machine would finally be brought to a halt.

By turning to consciousness as a source of social change, Reich and the New Communalists who put his ideas into practice turned away from the political struggles that preoccupied both the New Left and the Democratic and Republican parties. But even as they did, they opened new doors to mainstream culture, and particularly to high-technology research culture. If the mind was the first site of social change, then information would have to become a key part of a countercultural politics. And if those politics rejected hierarchy, then the circles-within-circles of information and systems theory might somehow make sense not only as ideas about information, but also as evidence from the natural world for the rightness of collective polity. Finally, if the self was the ultimate driver of social change, and if class was no more, then individual lifestyle choices became political acts, and both consumption and lifestyle technologies—including information technologies—would have to take on a newly political valence.

For both the New Left and the New Communalists, technological bureaucracy threatened a drab, psychologically distressing adulthood at a minimum and, beyond that, perhaps even the extinction of the human race. For the New Left, movement politics offered a way to tear down that bureaucracy and simultaneously to experience the intimacy of shared commitment and the possibility of an emotionally committed adulthood. For the New Communalists, in contrast, and for much of the broader counterculture, cybernetics and systems theory offered an ideological alternative. Like Norbert Wiener two decades earlier, many in the counterculture saw in cybernetics a vision of a world built not around vertical hierarchies and top-down flows of power, but around looping circuits of energy and information. These circuits presented the possibility of a stable social order based not on the psychologically distressing chains of command that characterized military and corporate life, but on the ebb and flow of communication.

In the summer of 1967, a long-haired poet named Richard Brautigan transformed this vision into blank verse. Walking through the streets of Haight-Ashbury, he handed his fellow pedestrians a broadsheet on which he had printed the following poem:

All Watched Over by Machines of Loving Grace

I like to think (and
the sooner the better!)
of a cybernetic meadow
where mammals and computers
live together in mutually
programming harmony

like pure water
touching clear sky.

I like to think
(right now, please!)
of a cybernetic forest
filled with pines and electronics
where deer stroll peacefully
past computers
as if they were flowers
with spinning blossoms.

I like to think
(it has to be!)
of a cybernetic ecology
where we are free of our labors
and joined back to nature,
returned to our mammal
brothers and sisters,
and all watched over
by machines of loving grace.

As Brautigan's poem suggests, by the end of the 1960s, some elements of
the counterculture, and particularly that segment of it that headed back to
the land, had begun to explicitly embrace the systems visions circulating
in the research world of the cold war. But how did those two worlds come
together? How did a social movement devoted to critiquing the technological bureaucracy of the cold war come to celebrate the socio-technical visions
that animated that bureaucracy? And how is it that the communitarian ideals
of the counterculture should have become melded to computers and computer networks in such a way that thirty years later, the Internet could appear to so many as an emblem of a youthful revolution reborn?

For answers to these questions, we need to turn to the biography of
Stewart Brand and the history of the Whole Earth network.

CHAPTER 2

Stewart Brand Meets the Cybernetic Counterculture

In the spring of 1957, at the height of the cold war, Stewart Brand was a nineteen-year-old freshman at Stanford University, and he was deeply worried. Even though Europe lay more than six thousand miles to the east, Brand had begun to write at length in his diary about his fear that the Soviet Union would soon attack the United States. If the Soviets invaded, he wrote, he could expect

> That my life would necessarily become small, a gear with its place on a certain axle of the Communist machine. Perhaps only a tooth on the gear. . . .
> That my mind would no longer be my own, but a tool carefully shaped by the descendants of Pavlov.
> That I would lose my identity.
> That I would lose my will.
> These last are the worst.[1]

Some fifty years later, and more than a decade after the collapse of the Soviet Union, Brand's fears might appear overwrought. But for Brand and other members of his generation in the late 1950s, the possibility of a Soviet attack felt very real. Brand was born in 1938 in Rockford, Illinois, a town not far south of Milwaukee, which specialized in making machine tools. His father was an advertising copywriter and a ham radio operator; his mother, a Vassar-educated homemaker and "space fanatic."[2] In the Brand household, technologies of communication and travel presented vistas of individual and national progress. Both radio sets and rocket ships connected the Brand family to a universe beyond midsized, middle-class, midwestern Rockford.

Thanks primarily to his mother, Brand became a space buff himself. He still keeps a well-worn copy of his childhood favorite, Chesley Bonestell's New Frontier primer *The Conquest of Space*, in his Sausalito, California, office. Even so, Brand suffered from a deep fear of technological Armageddon. "In [the] early '50s somebody compiled a list of prime targets for Soviet nuclear attack," he later remembered, "and we [Rockford] were [number] 7, because of the machine tools." For the young Stewart Brand, as for many other American children in the era, the possibility that the world might come to an end at any moment hung steadily in the air. As a child, he recalled, "I had a nightmare—one of those horrible, vivid, never forget nightmares—there was chaos and then I looked around and I was the only person left alive in Rockford . . . a knee-high creature. So I had an early allergy to nukes."[3]

By the time Brand reached college, alongside the dread of nuclear holocaust, another fear lurked as well: the fear of growing up to become the kind of adult who lived and worked in a hyperrationalized world. While he wrote extensively about the Soviets in his journals, Brand dwelled very little on the risks an invasion might pose to America as a nation. Instead, he focused on the ways that such an invasion might prevent his achieving personal independence and on how it would force him to become a member of a gray, uninspired, Orwellian mass. The Soviets of Brand's imagination were mechanical creatures who would stomp out every trace of individuality if given half a chance. In one sense, as symbols, they pointed backward, calling up the lockstep Nazis of American propaganda some fifteen years before. Yet they also looked forward, to an adulthood in which Brand himself might be compelled to give up his individuality. Both of these senses of *invasion* came to the fore in Brand's diary of 1957, when he wrote: "If there's a fight, then, I will fight. And fight with a purpose. I will not fight for America, nor for home, nor for President Eisenhower, nor for capitalism, nor even for democracy. I will fight for individualism and personal liberty. If I must be a fool, I want to be my own particular brand of fool—utterly unlike other fools. I will fight to avoid becoming a number—to others and to myself."[4]

For Stewart Brand, the national struggle to save America and the world from Soviet assault and nuclear holocaust was intimately entwined with his individual adolescent struggle to become his own person. And Brand was not unique in this respect. For college students of his time, the imagined gray mass of the Soviet Army was a mirror image of the army of gray flannel men who marched off to work every morning in the concrete towers of American industry. The soldier in his uniform was simply another form of what sociologist William Whyte called the "Organization Man."[5] Cut off from his emotions, trained to follow a chain of command, the Soviet soldier and the American middle manager alike seemed to many to be little more than worker bees inside ever-growing hives of military-industrial bureaucracy. In the 1940s and 1950s, that bureaucracy had brought forth nuclear weapons; in the 1960s it would lead Americans into the Vietnam War. As they came of age, Stewart Brand and others of his generation faced two questions: How could they keep the world from being destroyed by nuclear weapons or by the large-scale, hierarchical governmental and industrial bureaucracies that had built and used them? And how could they assert and preserve their own holistic individuality in the face of such a world?

As he sought to answer those questions, Brand turned first to the study of ecology and a systems-oriented view of the natural world. Later, after graduating from Stanford and serving several years as a draftee in the army, he found his way into a series of art worlds centered in Manhattan and San Francisco. For the artists of those communities, as for Brand's professors at Stanford, cybernetics offered a new way to model the world. Even at the height of the cold war, many of the most important artists of this period, figures such as John Cage and Robert Rauschenberg, embraced the systems orientation and even the engineers of the military-industrial research establishment. Together they read Norbert Wiener and, later, Marshall McLuhan and Buckminster Fuller; across the late 1950s and well into the 1960s, they made those writings models for their work. At the same time, both the artists he met and the authors they read presented the young Stewart Brand with a series of role models. If the army and the cold war corporate world of Brand's imagination moved according to clear lines of authority and rigid organizational structures, the art worlds of the early 1960s, like the research worlds of the 1940s, lived by networking, entrepreneurship, and collaboration. As he moved among them, Brand came to appreciate cybernetics as an intellectual framework and as a social practice; he associated both with alternative forms of communal organization.

Ecology as Alternative Politics

Brand first encountered systems-oriented ways of thinking at Stanford in a biology class taught by Paul Ehrlich. By the end of the decade, Ehrlich was famous for predicting in his book *The Population Bomb* (1968) that population growth would soon lead to ecological disaster. In the late 1950s, however, he was concentrating on the fundamentals of butterfly ecology and systems-oriented approaches to evolutionary biology. These preoccupations reflected the extraordinary influence of cybernetics and information theory on American biology following World War II. At the level of microbiology, information theory provided a new language with which to understand heredity. Under its influence, genes and sequences of DNA became information systems, bits of text to be read and decoded. In the 1950s, as Lily Kay has pointed out, microbiology became "a communication science, allied to cybernetics, information theory, and computers." Information theory also exerted a tremendous pull on biological studies of organisms and their interaction. Before World War II, biologists often focused on the study of individual organisms, hierarchical taxonomies of species, and the sexual division of labor. Afterward, many shifted toward the study of populations and the principles of natural selection in terms modeled on cybernetic theories of command and control.[6]

Ehrlich's research and teaching in this period strongly reflected this shift. A preoccupation with systems-oriented models of the natural world informed both his lectures and the 1963 textbook *The Process of Evolution* in which he and coauthor Richard Holm summarized much of Ehrlich's thinking in the period. Ehrlich and Holm deliberately "de-emphasized taxonomic ideas such as species and subspecies." Instead of a world arrayed in Linnaean hierarchies, they offered a vision of life as "a complex energy-matter nexus."[7] Individuals, populations, and the landscapes they inhabited were entwined in constant exchanges—exchanges so pervasive that, as in the case of algae and fungi, individuals were sometimes hard to distinguish from whole populations. For Ehrlich and Holm, the classic dualities of mind and matter, actor and action, masked a series of more essential truths: individuals were elements within systems and were systems in their own right. As such, they both responded to and helped shape the flows of energy that governed all matter. This was also true for humans at the cultural level: according to Ehrlich and Holm, culture had grown out of man's biological evolution and had become a force through which humans could recursively influence their biological development. For Ehrlich and Holm, and the young Stewart Brand, cultural activities such as politics, art, conversation, and play took on a deep significance for the survival of the species. At a moment when humans threatened to destroy themselves with nuclear weapons, concrete expressions of culture offered a way to help them move forward and escape annihilation.[8]

For Brand, Ehrlich's systems orientation offered an intellectual alternative to the cold war dualisms with which he had been struggling. If hierarchical leaders such as those in the Kremlin ruled by applying force from above, and so squeezed the individuality out of their subjects, biological systems as Ehrlich described them maintained order by means of evolutionary forces at work in the life of every individual. With an analytical framework drawn from ecology and evolutionary biology, Brand could simultaneously explain the threat of the Soviet Union to the United States and the threat of hierarchies to the individual. That is, he could imagine both the Soviet

Union and bureaucratic hierarchies more generally as monocultures, systems devoted to reducing the individual variations that helped ecosystems evolve. Brand could also begin to view the political confrontation between the Soviet Union and the United States and its potential for nuclear holocaust in evolutionary terms. On the one hand, thanks to nuclear weapons, humanity found itself at a new evolutionary moment. Like other species, it had arrived at the brink of its own destruction. But on the other hand, unlike other species, it could recognize its predicament and choose to make changes. In this context, the choices that individuals made in the cultural realm became freighted with truly cosmic, evolutionary significance. In September 1958 Brand explained in his diaries that "the responsibility of evolution is on each *individual* man, as for no other species. Since the business of evolution for man has gone over to the mental and psychological phase, each person may contribute and influence the heritage of the species." For this reason, he wrote a month later, "the matter [of] freedom—social, psychological, and potential—is of the highest importance."[9] For Brand, even as a student at Stanford, the ability to think outside the dominant paradigm of cold war conflict both marked and made possible an advancement in human evolution. The liberation of the individual was simultaneously an American ideal, an evolutionary imperative, and, for Brand and millions of other adolescents, a pressing personal goal.

Cybernetic Art Worlds

The question was, How could that liberation be achieved in daily life? Brand's search for individual freedom led to a decade-long migration among a wide variety of bohemian, scientific, and academic communities. In the course of these travels, Brand encountered both communal ways of living and a series of technocentric, systems-oriented theories that served as ideological supports for communalism. Often enough, the theories themselves were not explicitly theories of social organization so much as theories of local social practices, such as how to make art or how to take LSD or how to run a business meeting. As he moved among these communities, however, and later, when his *Whole Earth Catalog* became a forum in which such communities met, Brand began to see how the systems orientation of Paul Ehrlich's population biology, combined with new, countercultural modes of living, might offer an appealingly individualistic lifestyle—not only for him, but also for anyone else who could abandon the halls of bureaucratic America.

Soon after graduating from Stanford, Brand was drafted into the army, where he spent the next two years, first as an infantryman and later as a photographer. At the beginning, Brand took to military life and decided to become a Ranger. Midway through Ranger school, though, he decided to quit. "I wrote out every argument on both sides, knowing the conclusion was foregone, but comforted by the list," he told his diary at the time. "My vision widened, the Rangers looked admirable but wrongly zealous. And they wanting to be soldiers and I not." Although he liked the Rangers' parachute training and their camaraderie, Brand gradually come to loathe military regimentation. After leaving the Rangers, he became an army photographer at Fort Benning, Georgia; at Fort Dix, New Jersey; and briefly at the Pentagon. While stationed in Washington, he began to feel restless in his off-duty hours. "I was looking for the wrong thing," he wrote in his diary. "I was looking for San Francisco beauty, San Francisco people, San Francisco happiness—the bohemian style. . . . Therefore, Resolved—to go posh. To frequent the theaters, music halls, galleries, and homes not as an interloper taking all he can learn, but as a learning participant."[10]

Brand remained somewhat isolated in Washington, but when he returned to Fort Dix, he found his way into a swirling New York art scene. In the summer of 1960, Brand had met a young San Francisco painter named Steve Durkee; by 1961 Durkee had moved into a lower-Manhattan loft, where Brand began to visit him on weekends from Fort Dix. As he did, he began to explore a social landscape at once deeply in synch with the systems perspectives he had encountered at Stanford and entirely out of synch with the relatively ordered, hierarchical world of cold war college and military life.

Lower Manhattan in the late 1950s and early 1960s played host to a community of artists preoccupied with finding new relationships to their materials and audiences. When Brand arrived, the most influential members of the scene included musician John Cage, painter Robert Rauschenberg, and performance artist Allan Kaprow. These artists had inherited an essentially Romantic tradition, especially in painting, within which the artist struck a heroic pose. Art historian David Joselit has pointed out that the abstract expressionism that dominated American painting in the 1940s and 1950s celebrated painters as nearly mythic figures engaged in powerful acts of symbolic creation. Journalists for magazines such as *Life, Fortune,* and *Harper's Bazaar* amplified this mythology, depicting painters like Jackson Pollock as living emblems of the freedom of cold war American culture.[11]

Cage, Rauschenberg, and Kaprow worked to undermine this tradition. Since the mid-1940s, Cage had been exploring Zen Buddhism. Within Zen, he later wrote, nature was "an interrelated field or continuum, no part of which can be separated from or valued above the rest." In keeping with Zen tradition, Cage argued that the artist should not speak *to* his or her audience *about* the natural world, but should instead use art to heighten the audience member's sensitivity to experiences of all kinds. Neither the artist nor the audience should be cut away from or valued above the rest of nature; on the contrary, the process of art should work to integrate them both more closely into the natural systems of which they were already part. Whereas the high modernists of midcentury New York had become famous by making images of their own intentions, which were captured in brush strokes, Cage insisted that "the highest purpose [of an artist] is to have no purpose at all. This puts one in accord with nature in her manner of operation." For Cage, the rational, ordering mind that Theodore Roszak would later call "objective consciousness" had no place in art. Robert Rauschenberg agreed. "I don't want painting to be just an expression of my personality," he explained. "And I'm opposed to the whole idea of conception-execution—of getting an idea for a picture and then carrying it out. I've always felt as though, whatever I've used and whatever I've done, the method was always closer to a *collaboration* with materials than to any kind of conscious manipulation and control."[12]

At one level, the work of Cage and Rauschenberg represented an attack on the hierarchies of cold war art and cold war artistic process. While emblematic artists of cold war American culture such as such as the abstract expressionists worked to demonstrate a mastery of the canvas and to create a product that could then be sold as evidence of that mastery, Cage and Rauschenberg offered up a view of artistic practice as a leveled collaboration among artist, audience, and materials. At another level, though, their work echoed and ultimately celebrated a migration toward the decentralized, systems-oriented forms of thought then occurring at the center of the scientific establishment. Writing in the *Hudson Review* at about the time that Stewart Brand was making his weekend forays into Manhattan, for example, art critic and professor Leonard B. Meyer described this movement and its effects on American art in this period. His view was that American artists had begun to work from the premise that "man is no longer . . . the center of the universe" and that the universe itself, as revealed by quantum physics, was an indeterminate system. In the work of Cage and Rauschenberg, he was right: for them, the making of art had become the building of systems of pattern and randomness, and thus, in Claude Shannon's sense, of information.[13]

For Stewart Brand, such insights echoed Paul Ehrlich's systems view of the natural world. They also offered new models for living. Starting in the early 1950s, Cage and his friends began to build artistic systems that would play out in real time. In 1952, for instance, at Black Mountain College in North Carolina, Cage created an event called Theatre Piece No. 1 in which audience members found themselves surrounded by Robert Rauschenberg's "White Paintings" and, among them, Merce Cunningham performing improvised dances, M. C. Richards reading poetry on a ladder, David Tudor playing piano, and Cage himself delivering a lecture. In 1958 Allan Kaprow christened these sorts of events "happenings."[14] Kaprow had studied with Cage at the New School for Social Research. At the turn of the decade, he and artists such as Jim Dine, Claes Oldenburg, and Red Grooms blended Cage's systems orientation to artistic production with the abstract expressionist painters' focus on action. They developed a form of art in which artists, audience, and materials worked together to blur the boundary between art and life. Using materials gathered out of everyday life, they built theatrical environments inhabited by performers, objects, and bits of text, and invited audience members to wander through. On any given evening, art fans in jackets and ties might find themselves walking through a room hung with sheets of paper, a man on a swing swaying back and forth over their heads. They might watch artists roll around in chicken guts on the floor. Or they might visit a "shrine" made out of junkyard metal and paper trash. Like Cage's music or Rauschenberg's paintings, Kaprow and company's happenings brought to life a world of chance experience built out of everyday materials. Within that world traditional artistic hierarchies were leveled. The artist, the audience, the experience of theater, the experience of daily life—all were equivalent elements in a single complex system of exchange.

To Brand, happenings offered a picture of a world where hierarchies had dissolved, where each moment might be as wonderful as the last, and where every person could turn her or his life into art. After his discharge from the army in 1962, Brand began to look for such worlds in earnest. Over the next six years, he traveled back and forth between the artistic bohemias of New York City and the emerging hippie scene in Haight-Ashbury. He visited Indian reservations in the Southwest, government-sponsored psychological researchers in Palo Alto, California, and, ultimately, a series of communes. Each of these settings provided a glimpse of a new way of living. Together, they began to supply the people and ideas whose interconnections would underlie the formation of the Whole Earth network in the years to come.

Among the first communities into which Brand found his way was the influential art tribe USCO. Around 1962 Steve Durkee met up with a San Francisco–based poet named Gerd Stern. Within a year, Stern began collaborating on a series of multimedia performances with a young technician from the San Francisco Tape Music Center named Michael Callahan. By 1964 Durkee, Stern, and Callahan, together with a floating circus of friends and family, had taken up residence in an old Methodist church in

Garnerville, New York, about an hour north of Manhattan. They christened their art troupe USCO—short for "The US Company." Over the next four years, they transformed the "happening" into a psychedelic celebration of technology and mystical community that found its way into the burgeoning LSD scene in San Francisco and the pages of *Life* magazine.

Brand worked off and on with USCO as a photographer and a technician between 1963 and 1966, living at the Garnerville church for short periods between his travels. Within USCO, he encountered the first stirrings of the New Communalist movement. Like Cage and Rauschenberg, the members of USCO created art intended to transform the audience's consciousness. They also drew on many diverse electronic technologies to achieve their effects. Strobe lights, light projectors, tape decks, stereo speakers, slide sorters—for USCO, the products of technocratic industry served as handy tools for transforming their viewers' collective mind-set. So did psychedelic drugs. Marijuana and peyote and, later, LSD, offered members of USCO, including Brand, a chance to engage in a mystical experience of togetherness. And USCO's work did not stop at the end of each performance. Gathering at their church in Garnerville and then again at performance sites around the country, the members of USCO lived and worked together steadily for a period of years. Like a cross between a touring rock entourage and a commune, USCO was more than a performance team. It was a social system unto itself. Through it, Brand encountered the works of Norbert Wiener, Marshall McLuhan, and Buckminster Fuller—all of whom would become key influences on the Whole Earth community—and began to imagine a new synthesis of cybernetic theory and countercultural politics.

USCO was founded on a fusion of Eastern mysticism and ecological, systems thinking. Its members chose the name USCO in accordance with the teachings of Ananda K. Coomeraswamy, an early-twentieth-century scholar of Indian art then popular among Manhattan bohemians. Coomeraswamy had asserted that artists in traditional societies were as anonymous as tradesmen. The members of USCO saw themselves returning to a more traditional mode of tribal living and collective craftsmanship. The tribe would be bound together through various rituals involving drugs, mystical forces, and electrical technologies. As art critic Naomi Feigelson put it in 1968, "Collectively and individually USCO is hung up on light and its symbolic meanings, on the Kaballah and mysticism, on the divine geometry of living things and electrical phenomena."[15] But USCO's founders were also steeped in the literature of cybernetics. Gerd Stern, a European Jew and a World War II–era refugee, saw Norbert Wiener as a child of European transplants like himself and was thoroughly versed in his writings. In large part for this reason, light, electricity, and mystical "energy" generally played a role in USCO's work very much like the one "information" plays in Wienerian cybernetics: they became universal forces that, functioning as the sources and content of all "systems" (biological, social, and mechanical), made it possible for individual people, groups, and artifacts to be seen as mirrors of one another. A promotional brochure for a 1968 USCO presentation at New York's Whitney Museum of Art described the group this way: USCO "unites the cults of mysticism and technology as a basis for introspection and communication."[16]

Like Wiener's cybernetics, USCO's techno-mystical ideology emerged out of and supported multidisciplinary collaboration in a workshop setting. The group's productions ranged from three-dimensional poems, with flashing lights and bold-faced words, to multimedia slide, light, and sound shows and psychedelic posters. Each production required input by artists with a variety of technical skills, and the collaboration in turn required both a contact language in which the artists could speak to one another and a rationale to drive their production. Techno-mysticism filled both bills. "They have an artistic point of view," wrote Naomi Feigelson in 1968, "a critical, philosophical approach to life, and a goal beyond today. They are a group of individual artists, each disciplined in his own craft, and all together they are on a work trip." For the artists of USCO, technical work on multimedia projects offered a way to plug in to mystical currents that flowed among the group's members and within each of them. Like the anti-aircraft gunner operating Wiener's theoretical predictor, they could see themselves as parts of a techno-social system, serving new machines and being served by them. Such a vision did not mean that the members of USCO entirely escaped the questions of leadership and issues of gender politics that they ascribed to mainstream society. On the contrary: former members recall that Durkee and Stern served as alpha males to the group and frequently, if indirectly, struggled to control its direction.[17] Although women (notably Durkee's wife, Barbara), played important roles in the group, leadership fell to men. Nevertheless, with their mystical conviction of collective unity, the members of USCO could confront the hard-bodied, bifurcated universe of cold war politics and its potentially world-ending nuclear weapons with a vision of transpersonal and potentially transnational harmony.

To bring that vision to life in performance, USCO operated on organizational principles that would have been quite familiar to Brand from his studies with Paul Ehrlich. Rather than work with a transmission model of communication, in which performers or others attempt to send a message to their audience, USCO events tried to take advantage of what Gerd Stern called "the environmental circumstance." That is, USCO constructed all-encompassing technological environments, theatrical ecologies in which the audience was simply one species of being among many, and waited to observe their effects. As Steve Durkee put it, they built artistic worlds just like "God created the universe."[18] Early projects were relatively simple. In 1963, for instance, Stern developed a project called "Verbal American Landscape," in which three slide projectors showed, in random sequence, photographs—many taken by Stewart Brand—of individual words found on road signs and billboards. Viewers were left to piece the words together into meanings of their own. Gradually "Verbal American Landscape" was absorbed into more complex shows. In a 1963 performance entitled "Who R U?" at the San Francisco Museum of Art, Stern and Callahan added highway sounds to the mix, moving them from speaker to speaker in the showroom. They also had individuals placed in booths around a central auditorium, miked their conversations, and replayed them simultaneously in an eighteen-channel remix. By 1965 this show had morphed into a program called "We R All One," in which USCO deployed slide and film projections, oscilloscopes, music, strobes, and live dancers to create a sensory cacophony. At the end of the performance, the lights would go down, and for ten minutes the audience would hear multiple "Om's" from the speakers. According to Stern, the show was designed to lead viewers from "overload to spiritual meditation."[19] In the final moments, the audience was to experience the mystical unity that ostensibly bound together USCO's members.

Comprehensive Designers: Marshall McLuhan and Buckminster Fuller

By the mid-1960s, USCO's performances marked the cutting edge of countercultural art. USCO had built multimedia backdrops for talks by Timothy Leary (whose Millbrook, New York, mansion received regular visits from USCO members) and Marshall McLuhan. In 1966 they supplied multimedia designs for Murray the K's World—a huge discotheque created within an abandoned airplane hangar—that appeared on the cover of *Life* magazine. In May of that year, they built an installation they called "Shrine" at New York's Riverside Museum. Audience members sat on the floor around a large aluminum column. Around them, a nine-foot-high hexagon featured Steve Durkee's paintings of Shiva and the Buddha, as well as flashing lights and other psychedelic imagery. They inhaled burning incense and listened to a sound collage and stayed as long as they liked. USCO called the installation a "be-in" because of the ways audience members were supposed to inhabit and not simply observe the work. On September 9, 1966, *Life* featured USCO's "Shrine" in a cover story on psychedelic art and introduced the notion of a "be-in" to a national readership for what was almost certainly the first time.[20]

USCO's performances brought with them two important transformations of the earliest artistic happenings. First, they aimed not only to help their audiences become more aware of their surroundings but also to help them imagine themselves as members of a mystical community. Second, to bring about that understanding, USCO turned to the materials of everyday life and to new electronic communication technologies. These turns grew in large part out of USCO's engagement with the technocentric visions of Marshall McLuhan and Buckminster Fuller. Each of these theorists depicted technology as a tool for social transformation. At the same time, both turned their backs on the bureaucratic world of mainstream technocratic production. In their writings and their speeches, each cultivated a style of orphic collage. To readers raised on the declarative sentences of Ernest Hemingway, McLuhan and Fuller offered a kaleidoscopic alternative. Words and ideas collided with one another across their texts, sparking insights, creating flashpoints, energizing their readers. What is more, McLuhan and Fuller seemed to live lives in synch with their prose. Even though McLuhan held a teaching post in Canada, both he and Fuller traveled constantly in the mid-1960s. For the young people who flocked to their lectures, their peregrinations offered a model of an entrepreneurial, individualistic mode of being that was far from the world of the organization man—and yet a mode in which they still didn't need to give up the stereos and automobiles and radios that industrial society had created. Ultimately, McLuhan, and especially Fuller, would offer Stewart Brand both ways of imagining technology as a source of social transformation and living models of how to become a cultural entrepreneur.

By the time Marshall McLuhan came to the attention of the artists in USCO, he had been a professor of English literature, primarily at the University of Toronto, for nearly twenty years. He had edited a volume of Tennyson's poetry, converted to Catholicism, and spent most of his working life in Canada. Little in this work suggested that he would become the most popular media theorist of the 1960s. Yet, alongside his teaching and his work on poetry, McLuhan developed a fascination with technology and its role in psychological and cultural change. Most critics trace this interest to his reading of the Canadian economic historian Harold Innis.[21] But McLuhan also drew extensively on the work of Norbert Wiener. As McLuhan's first PhD student, Donald Theall, has pointed out, McLuhan encountered Norbert Wiener's *Cybernetics* in the summer of 1950. According to Theall, who was studying with McLuhan at the time, McLuhan rejected the mathematical theory of communication that Wiener laid out in *Cybernetics* but was deeply influenced by the vision of the social role of communication outlined in Wiener's 1950 volume *The Human Use of Human Beings*.[22] McLuhan began reading the work of other cyberneticians, and in 1951 he took up Jürgen Ruesch and Gregory Bateson's *Communication: The Social Matrix of Psychiatry*. According to Ruesch and Bateson, the self that was the subject of psychiatry was enmeshed in and largely shaped by a complex web of information exchange. In keeping with Wiener's cybernetics, they viewed social life as a system of communication and the individual as both a key element within that system and a system in his or her own right. When McLuhan was engaging with cybernetics, he was also exploring tribalism and art with his colleague Edmund Carpenter, an authority on the Inuit. In 1953 Carpenter and McLuhan established a series of weekly seminars on communication and media and a journal entitled *Explorations*. Together, journal and seminar served as a forum for McLuhan to brew up many of the insights for which he became famous.

The twin interests in cybernetic approaches to communication media and tribal forms of social organization that McLuhan developed in the early 1950s became key elements of his media theories in the early 1960s and important influences on the art worlds of that period. In 1962 and 1964 McLuhan published *The Gutenberg Galaxy* and *Understanding Media,* which, together, argued that transformations in communication technology were bringing about the retribalization of society. *The Gutenberg Galaxy* asserted that mankind was leaving a typographic age and entering an electronic one. With its sequential orientation, its segmented letters and words, McLuhan claimed, the technology of type had tended to create a world of "lineal specialism and separation of functions." That is, he held type responsible in large part for the development of rationalization, bureaucracy, and industrial life. By contrast, he said, electronic technologies had begun to break down the barriers of bureaucracy, as well as those of time and space, and so had brought human beings to the brink of a new age. In *The Gutenberg Galaxy* McLuhan described the new age in tribal terms: electronic media had linked all of humanity into a single "global village." In *Understanding Media,* McLuhan linked both the new tribalism and its promise of a return to a prebureaucratic humanism to a more cybernetic rhetoric of human-machine entanglement as well. "Today," he wrote, "we have extended our central nervous system itself in a global embrace, abolishing both space and time as far as our planet is concerned."[23] In McLuhan's view, the individual human body and the species as a whole were linked by a single nervous system, an array of electronic signals fired across neurons in the human body and circulating from television set to television set, radio to radio, computer to computer, across the globe.[24]

This worldwide web of electronic signals carried a mystical charge for many. In McLuhan's work, the charge tended to invoke a vision of mystical Christian unity, but for the young bohemians of the 1960s, it did not need to refer to anything more dogmatic than the felt sense of generational togetherness. At one level, USCO's motto—"We Are All One"—echoed McLuhan's Catholic striving toward a universal humanism. When the members of USCO built their multimedia environments, they hoped their audiences would feel their own, individual senses meld into the global nerve system of electronic media. At a more local level, though, the "we" of USCO's motto referred primarily to the members of USCO itself, the vanguard techno-tribesmen who recognized the power of McLuhan's vision. Even as they labored to introduce their audiences to the notion that all humans were one, the members of USCO created a workaday world in which the members of USCO were themselves brought into a state of collaborative unity through their work with electronic media. In that sense, the "we" of USCO's motto reflected a *turning away* from the global humanism of McLuhan's vision and back toward a more traditional notion of a visionary avant-garde. Early on, the members of USCO painted two words over the doors to the Garnerville church that captured this mix of anti-authoritarian humanism and tribal elitism well: "Just Us."

The same tension between global humanist ideals and local elite practice would haunt much of the New Communalist movement over the next decade, and the Whole Earth network for years after that. But in the early 1960s, the linking of the global and the local helped account for much of Marshall McLuhan's appeal within the emerging counterculture. McLuhan's simultaneous celebration of new media and tribal social forms allowed people like Stewart Brand to imagine technology itself as a tool with which to resolve the twin cold war dilemmas of humanity's fate and their own trajectory into adulthood. That is, McLuhan offered a vision in which young people who had been raised on rock and roll, television, and the associated pleasures of consumption need not give those pleasures up even if they rejected the adult society that had created them. Even if the social order of technocracy threatened the species with nuclear annihilation and the individual young person with psychic fragmentation, the media technologies produced by that order offered the possibility of individual and collective transformation. McLuhan's dual emphases also allowed young people to imagine the local communities they built around these media not simply as communities built around consumption of industrial products, but as model communities for a new society. In McLuhan's writing, and in the artistic practice of groups like USCO and, later, the psychedelic practices of groups like San Francisco's Merry Pranksters, technologies produced by mass, industrial society offered the keys to transforming and thus to saving the adult world.

No one promoted this doctrine more fervently than the technocratic polymath Buckminster Fuller. Architect, designer, and traveling speechmaker, Fuller became an inspiration to Stewart Brand, the Whole Earth network, and the New Communalist movement as a whole across the 1960s. The geodesic domes Fuller patented soon after World War II came to be favored housing on communes throughout the Southwest. Fragments of his idiosyncratic conceptual vocabulary, such as "tensegrity," "synergy" and "Spaceship Earth," bubbled up steadily in discussions of how and why alternative communities should be built. And Fuller himself—seventy years old in 1965, short, plump, bespectacled, and, when he spoke in public, often clad in a three-piece suit with an honorary Phi Beta Kappa key dangling at the waist— seemed to model a kind of childlike innocence that many New Communalists sought to bring into their own adulthoods.[25] If the politicians and CEOs of mainstream America were distant and emotionally reserved, Fuller was playful and engaged. And like his young audiences, he displayed a highly individualistic turn of mind and a deep concern with the fate of the species.

Fuller made his name designing futuristic technologies such as the three-wheeled Dymaxion car and, most famously, the geodesic dome, but the roots of his interests reached deep into America's pre-industrial past. Born in 1895, Fuller was the latest in a long line of Unitarian ministers, lawyers, and writers. His great-aunt, Margaret Fuller, had joined Ralph Waldo Emerson to cofound the *Dial,* the preeminent literary journal of American Transcendentalism and the first magazine to publish Henry David Thoreau. Margaret served as an intellectual model for the young Buckminster. "When I heard that Aunt Margaret said, 'I must start with the universe and work down to the parts, I must have an understanding of it,' that became a great drive for me," he recalled.[26] For the Transcendentalists, as later for Fuller himself, the material world could be imagined as a series of corresponding forms, each linked to every other according to invisible but omnipresent principles. Emerson explained the point this way:

> The law of harmonic sound reappears in the harmonic colors. The granite
> is differenced in its laws only by the more or less of heat from the river that
> wears it away. The river, as it flows, resembles the air that flows over it; the air
> resembles the light which traversed it with more subtle currents; the light
> resembles the heat which rides with it through Space. Each creature is only a
> modification of the other; the likeness in them is more than the difference,
> and their radical law is one and the same. A rule of one art, or a law of one
> organization holds true throughout nature.[27]

Fuller, like Emerson, saw the material world as the reflection of an otherwise intangible system of rules. But unlike Emerson and the Transcendentalists, Fuller linked that system of rules not only to the natural world, but also to the world of industry. During World War I, Fuller had watched his four-year-old daughter Alexandra die of infantile paralysis, contracted in part, he believed, because the family's home was badly built. At the time, he was working as a contractor with the navy. Earlier, as a junior officer, he had seen how, with proper coordination, extraordinary industrial resources could be mustered to solve military problems. In his view, his daughter had died directly from a disease but indirectly from a failure to distribute the world's resources appropriately.[28] This conviction grew during World War II and the early years of the cold war, when once again Fuller saw the full scope of industrial production at work, as well as the inequality with which the world's resources were distributed. What humankind required, he came to believe, was an individual who could recognize the universal patterns inherent in nature, design new technologies in accord with both these patterns and the industrial resources already created by corporations and the military, and see that those new technologies were deployed in everyday life.

In a 1963 volume called *Ideas and Integrities,* a book that would have a strong impact on USCO and Stewart Brand, Fuller named this individual the "Comprehensive Designer."[29] According to Fuller, the Comprehensive Designer would not be another specialist, but would instead stand outside the halls of industry and science, processing the information they produced, observing the technologies they developed, and translating both into tools for human happiness. Unlike specialists, the Comprehensive Designer would be aware of the system's need for balance and the current deployment of its resources. He would then act as a "harvester of the potentials of the realm," gathering up the products and techniques of industry and redistributing them in accord with the systemic patterns that only he and other comprehensivists could perceive. To do this work, the Designer would need to have access to all of the information generated within America's burgeoning technocracy while at the same time remaining outside it. He would need to become "an emerging synthesis of artist, inventor, mechanic, objective economist and evolutionary strategist."[30] Constantly poring over the population surveys, resource analyses, and technical reports produced by states and industries, but never letting himself become a full-time employee of any of these, the Comprehensive Designer would finally see what the bureaucrat could not: the whole picture.

Being able to see the whole picture would allow the Comprehensive Designer to realign both his individual psyche and the deployment of political power with the laws of nature. In contrast to the bureaucrat, who, so many critics of technocracy had suggested, had been psychologically broken down by the demands of his work, the Comprehensive Designer would be intellectually and emotionally whole. Neither engineer nor artist, but always both simultaneously, he would achieve psychological integration even while working with the products of technocracy. Likewise, whereas bureaucrats exerted their power by means of political parties and armies and, in Fuller's view, thus failed to properly distribute the world's resources, the Comprehensive Designer would wield his power systematically. That is, he would analyze the data he had gathered, attempt to visualize the world's needs now and in the future, and then design technologies that would meet those needs. Agonistic politics, Fuller implied, would become irrelevant. What would change the world was "comprehensive anticipatory design science."[31]

Both Stewart Brand and the members of USCO were steeped in Fuller's writings by the mid-1960s. Brand would go on to write to Fuller, to attend his lectures, and, in the first edition of the *Whole Earth Catalog,* to claim that "the insights of Buckminster Fuller are what initiated this catalog." In retrospect, it is easy to understand Fuller's appeal to cold war American youth. Like McLuhan, he simultaneously embraced the pleasures and power associated with the products of technocracy and offered his audiences a way to avoid becoming technocratic drones. Moreover, according to Fuller the proper deployment of information and technology could literally save the human species from annihilation. As he put it in *Ideas and Integrities,* "If man is to continue as a successful pattern-complex function in universal evolution, it will be because the next decades will have witnessed the artist-scientist's spontaneous seizure of the prime design responsibility and his successful conversion of the total capability of tool-augmented man from killingry to advanced livingry—adequate for all humanity."[32] In Fuller's view, the Comprehensive Designer not only did not need to don a gray flannel suit when he went to work; he actually needed to become an artist and an intellectual migrant. To a generation preoccupied with the fear of becoming lockstep corporate adults on the military model of Brand's imagined Soviet Army, Buckminster Fuller offered a marvelously playful alternative.

Fuller's vision of the Comprehensive Designer carried with it, nonetheless, intellectual frameworks and social ideals formulated at the core of military research culture. Foremost among these was Fuller's notion of the world as an information system. In his numerous autobiographical writings, Fuller traces the origins of his ideas about the world as a system to his Transcendental lineage and especially to his time on board ships—which he considered closed systems—when he was a naval officer. Yet his writings also bear the imprint of cold war–era military-industrial information theory. For Fuller, as for Wiener and the systems analysts of later decades, the material world consisted of information patterns made manifest. The patterns could be modeled and manipulated by information technologies, notably the computer. The computer in turn could suffice as a model for the human being. After all, although Fuller's Comprehensive Designer promises to be psychologically integrated as specialists are not, that integration depends on the Designer's ability to process vast quantities of information so as to perceive social and technological patterns. Fuller's Comprehensive Designer is, from a functional point of view at least, an information processor, and as such he is a descendent of cold war psychology and systems theory as much as a child of Fuller's own imagination.

Even Fuller's work style echoes the collaborative ethos of World War II research. According to Fuller and, later, his countercultural admirers, the Comprehensive Designer came by his comprehensive viewpoint only by stepping away from the industrial and military institutions in which specialists had long been trapped. Only the freestanding individual "could find the time to think in a cosmically adequate manner," he explained. Fuller himself lived accordingly: for most of his career, he migrated among a series of universities and colleges, designing projects, collaborating with students and faculty—and always claiming the rights to whatever the collaborations produced.[33] In his writings, Fuller offered his travels as a model of the proper behavior for a Comprehensive Designer and suggested that such a life was genuinely new. Yet a quick glance back at MIT's Rad Lab in World War II would have reminded Fuller's audiences that interdisciplinary migration and multi-institutional collaboration were key features of the military research world.

Fuller's debts to the military-industrial complex went unremarked within USCO. In the New York art world of the mid-1960s, Fuller seemed to speak for the avant-garde. His belief that new technological environments could transform societies into leveled, harmonious systems echoed the ways Allan Kaprow and others claimed that artistic environments might transform their audiences. And his call for a corps of Comprehensive Designers held enormous appeal. In keeping with Fuller's views, the members of USCO went on to design comprehensive media environments that could inspire a new, more harmonious social world. In USCO's Garnerville church, as in the writings of Wiener, McLuhan, and Fuller, traditional party-based politics fell away. In its place, a creative, independent elite sought to put the world back in balance by manipulating information and technology.

Indians, Beats, and Hippies

Even as Brand was participating in the technocentric rituals of USCO, he was continuing to search for new, flexible modes of living in other realms as well. Soon after Brand left the army, an old family friend, Dick Raymond, commissioned him to take photographs of the Warm Springs Indian Reservation in central Oregon for a brochure. Over the next three years, when he was not working with USCO, Brand visited the Warm Springs Reservation and Blackfoot, Navajo, Hopi, and Papago reservations as well. When he began this project, he saw Native Americans in terms long set by Anglo-American myth. They were the custodians of the American landscape and, as such, guides to the preservation of the American wilderness. Over time, however, Brand began to reimagine Native Americans in light of his readings of McLuhan and Fuller. In his journals of 1964, he wrote that a new era was dawning. The old era had been dominated by a "Protestant consciousness"; under it, "mystery subsided into number, uniform and linear. Specialization gradually pervaded Western society, became malignant, and then suddenly, with the acceleration of electricity and computer automation, it passed its own breakpoint into an era of tribal endeavor and cosmic consciousness still un-named. Americans dwelling in the wilderness of changing eras are re-learning to be natives from the most native Americans, The Indians, studying with the new clarity the ancient harmony of a shared land-heritage." For Brand, as for many counterculturalists in the decade to follow, Native Americans became symbolic figures of authenticity and alternative community.[34] If the white-collar man of the 1950s had become detached from the land and from his own emotions, the Native American could show him how to be at home again, physically and psychologically. If the large corporations and governments of the twentieth century were organized in psychologically and socially divisive hierarchies, the world of the Native American was organized into tribes. Polis, family, community: within Brand's heavily idealized vision of Native Americans, all three exist harmoniously as elements of a single unity, the tribe. And if technology had finally begun to draw Americans toward a "cosmic consciousness," well, the Indians had been there all along.

Not long after he started working with the Warm Springs Indians, Brand read a book that seemed to confirm his inkling that Indians might hold the key to a nonhierarchical world, Ken Kesey's 1962 novel *One Flew Over the Cuckoo's Nest*. There Kesey told the story of McMurphy, an individualistic con man imprisoned in a mental hospital, and his struggle against his rigid, unfeeling floor manager, Nurse Ratched (also known as "Big Nurse"). His narrator was another patient, the Native American Chief Bromden.

McMurphy's struggle with Ratched and Chief Bromden's ultimate escape from the ward served, in Brand's view, as emblems of his own struggle to establish an independent identity. The novel, he wrote in his journal, gave him "the answer to my dilemma between revolution against the Combine and preservation of things like old Indian ways. No dilemma. They're identical. As Kesey writes it, the battle of McMurphy versus Big Nurse is identical with [Warm Springs] Indians versus Dalles Dam [on Oregon's Columbia River] or me versus the Army."[35] For Brand, the hierarchical institutions of the hospital in Kesey's book and the government on the reservation mirrored each other. McMurphy's struggle for independence was Brand's own, and Chief Bromden's escape from the hospital at novel's end neatly described Brand's own desire for de-institutionalized freedom. As he read *One Flew Over the Cuckoo's Nest* and as he traveled from reservation to reservation, Brand, like Kesey, began to link his own struggle against hierarchy and his generation's struggle against technocracy to a mythic American past.

As he did so, however, he found a way to bring a countercultural version of that past to life. In 1963 Brand wrote a low-key letter introducing himself to Ken Kesey and soon after met him face-to-face. By that time, Kesey was not only an increasingly famous author, but the host of a burgeoning psychedelic scene on the San Francisco peninsula as well. In 1958 Kesey had come to Palo Alto as a graduate student in Stanford's creative writing program. Over the next few years, the program admitted a stellar roster, including future novelists Larry McMurtry, Ed McClanahan, Robert Stone, and Gurney Norman. While there, Kesey wrote much of *One Flew Over the Cuckoo's Nest*. He also began to develop an affection for psychedelic drugs. In 1959 Kesey became a subject in a series of experimental protocols at the Veterans Hospital in Menlo Park, sponsored by the CIA's MK-ULTRA program. Doctors in these experiments gave volunteer subjects various psychedelic drugs and observed their behavior. In return they offered the subjects small amounts of cash. Between 1959 and 1960, Kesey tried LSD, psilocybin mushrooms, mescaline, and the amphetamine IT-290.[36] The CIA believed that these drugs had the potential to become weapons in the cold war, breaking down the psyches of spies, for instance, and making them more amenable to questioning.[37] Kesey saw quite a different effect:

> The first drug trips were, for most of us, shell-shattering ordeals that left
> us blinking kneedeep in the cracked crusts of our pie-in-sky personalities.
> Suddenly people were stripped before one another and behold! As we looked,
> and were looked on, we all made a great discovery: we were beautiful. Naked
> and helpless and sensitive as a snake after skinning, but far more human than
> that shining knightmare that had stood creaking in previous parade rest.

We were alive and life was us. We joined hands and danced barefoot amongst the rubble. We had been cleansed, liberated! We would never don the old armors again.[38]

For Kesey, LSD served as a weapon in the same generational struggle that occupied Stewart Brand. Symbolically, Kesey's "knightmare" echoes Brand's undergraduate fear of growing up to don psychic armor on behalf of a militarized corporate state. In this context, LSD was a benevolent wake-up call, one that allowed Kesey to step out of the regimented ranks of adulthood and become childlike, flexible, barefoot and dancing. Stewart Brand's first experience taught him a somewhat different lesson. Brand was first given LSD in December of 1962 at the International Federation for Advanced Study (IFAS), an organization founded a year earlier by Myron Stolaroff, an engineer from the Ampex Corporation, and Willis Harman, a professor of engineering at Stanford and later a futurist at the Stanford Research Institute. Stolaroff and Harman had built the institute in order to explore the psychological effects of LSD; by 1962 they were charging subjects like Brand five hundred dollars for a daylong trip guided by one of several local psychologists. The man in charge of Brand's procedure was Jim Fadiman, who later served for several months at Stanford Research Institute's Augmentation Research Center—the division that in 1963 sponsored Douglas Engelbart's research on networked computing. According to Brand's journals, he received two doses of LSD, one in a "goblet" and the other, an hour later, by injection. Fadiman and others then had Brand look at a mural, a yin-yang mandala, and a series of other images, including pictures of his family. They played classical music. They asked Brand how he felt ("very *thing*" he replied).[39] Eventually, the session ended and Brand wandered off to dinner at Fadiman's house, still high.

Brand was put off by the highly structured, pseudoscientific trappings of the IFAS procedure, but the notion that psychedelic drugs could alter one's perceptions took. Brand soon began to hang out with a group devoted to "tripping" in every sense: the Merry Pranksters. The Pranksters had first come together around Kesey's house on Perry Lane on the edge of the Stanford campus. Not long after he began visiting the Veterans Hospital in Menlo Park, Kesey began bringing drugs home. A scene began to emerge: some of the writers from Stanford, the artist Roy Seburn, psychologist Richard Alpert (later known as Baba Ram Dass), guitarist Jerry Garcia, Page Browning—all had begun to appear for various parties. Within a year, Kesey had put together a new scene, with Page Browning and Gurney Norman remaining from the original Perry Lane crew, and in the fall of 1964 he and the Pranksters painted up an old school bus and drove east on the first leg of the legendary tour chronicled in Tom Wolfe's *The Electric Kool-Aid Acid Test*. Brand did not go with them. As Wolfe put it, Brand represented "the restrained, reflective wing of the Merry Pranksters."[40]

Even so, to Brand the Pranksters were a West Coast version of USCO's techno-tribalism. If USCO had emerged out of an East Coast engagement with cold war avant-garde art, the Pranksters drew on the bohemian energy of San Francisco's Beatnik scene. Since the mid-1940s, the Beats had built a small, highly influential social world, and with it a literature and a way of being that had an extraordinary impact on the counterculture, especially on its West Coast contingent. The origins of the Beat movement can probably best be dated to 1944, when novelists William Burroughs and Jack Kerouac met poet Allen Ginsberg in Manhattan.[41] Over the next fifteen years, these three writers traveled to Europe, North Africa, New York, and San Francisco; together with writers and artists in each of those locations, they built a vision within which, as Ginsberg put it, "existence itself was God." For the Beats, cold war society was plagued by mechanical ways of living and thinking. In the years after World War II, Ginsberg later recalled, "there was a definitive shrinkage of sensation, of sensory experience, and a definite mechanical disorder of mentality that led to the cold war. . . . The desensitization had begun, the compartmentalization of the mind and heart, the cutting off of the head from the rest of the body, the robotization of mentality."[42] In response to this mechanistic world, Ginsberg and company launched a celebration of individual, embodied experience.[43] Drawing on influences ranging from German historian and mystic Oswald Spengler and nineteenth-century American Romantics such as Walt Whitman to psychologist Wilhelm Reich and semanticist Alfred Korzybski, they imagined that both the material world and the social world were imbued with meaning. That meaning could be experienced as an ecstatic state of enlightenment that was itself in tune with the deeper, mystical laws of experience: satori.

The Merry Pranksters thought the Beats offered a model of how to step outside mainstream American culture, build an alternative community, and pursue psychic wholeness even within the bowels of a militarized state. Yet the Pranksters extended the Beat vision as well. Like the Beats, they sought to experience a condition of harmonious flow, and they turned to drugs to do it. Also like the Beats, they saw the whole world as their stage and their own lives as roles that could be played for pleasure. Like USCO, however, the Pranksters appropriated technologies developed in industrial and sometimes military contexts (including LSD) and put them to work as tools for the transformation of self and community. Although Brand later recalled that Kesey and the Pranksters were unfamiliar with Buckminster Fuller's writings and with cybernetic theory when he first met them, their techno-logical performances suggest a deep sympathy with both.[44] For Kesey and company, body and landscape, community and state, and sometimes even biological and electronic systems were mirrors of one another. Metaphori-cally, when they drove their school bus into the heart of the United States, its sheet-metal skin coated with Day-Glo paint, its insides and often outsides wired with speakers and microphones, its inhabitants hairy, costumed, nick-named, and alert, Kesey and the Pranksters dropped a tab of LSD into the belly of America. They wanted to turn the country on, to do for the nation what LSD had done for them as individuals and as a community. They wanted to show cold war America an alternative and apparently a much more adventurous, harmonious, and fun way to live. The bus was both the vehicle by which to make this new lifestyle visible and a prototype of that lifestyle itself. Are you "on the bus"? asked the Pranksters. Or not?

Both on and off the bus, the Pranksters played with the boundaries between self, community, and technology. As they drove across America, they kept a movie camera rolling. If all the world was a stage, they were liv-ing here and now, in the real, material space of everyday life, and at the same time inside a movie, in media space. They were both themselves and char-acters in a scene—a pattern of self-understanding that they saw as congru-ent with the experience of self on LSD. In part, they were self-consciously seeking to make history, and of course they did. Yet they were also working out a new relationship to technologies of communication and transporta-tion. At one party, for instance, Tom Wolfe recalls seeing Kesey and a half dozen Pranksters sprawled out across the floor, high on LSD, ululating. They were pretending to be a "Humanoid Radio." This was partly a party joke, a prank. "The idea was to try to hit that beam and that mode that would enable you to communicate with beings on other planets, other galaxies. . . . They were all high as hell," wrote Wolfe.[45] But it also marked a weird attempt to appropriate the radio's ability to transcend distance and reach faraway minds with a single, disembodied signal. In the Pranksters' world, LSD and radio were harbingers of New Communalist possibilities. They were communication technologies through which humans could not only exchange information, but, at least imaginatively, merge with one another in a spiritually harmonious state.

Whereas USCO took up technology to make art, the Merry Pranksters deployed technology expressly to create a new consciousness and a new form of social organization. In this sense, the Pranksters represent a key ori-gin point not only for the psychedelic side of the counterculture, but for the New Communalist movement. By 1965 the San Francisco Bay area had seen the Free Speech Movement emerge at Berkeley and had witnessed its first antiwar protests as well. In this increasingly politicized atmosphere, Kesey and the Pranksters turned away from the politics of struggle and embraced the politics of consciousness. On October 15, 1965, Kesey was invited to speak at a rally against the Vietnam War in Berkeley. Organizers expected a fiery speech and a joining of the New Left and the growing counterculture. But rather than orate, Kesey simply stood up and announced to the audience, "You know, you're not gonna stop this war with this rally, by marching. . . . That's what *they* do."[46] He then pulled out his harmonica and played "Home on the Range." In keeping with psychedelic visions of transpersonal harmony (and with cybernetic and Romantic visions of a world linked by invisible currents of energy and information), Kesey rejected as fundamentally false the dynamics of confrontation called for by the moment and by the logic of the cold war more generally. He simply stood up and demanded that the audience not confront their enemies, but instead turn away from them and come together elsewhere.

After some confusion, the audience ignored him and continued their march. But in retrospect, Kesey's action marked a key moment in the public emergence of a New Communalist style of social action. For the Free Speech and antiwar movements, to attempt to change society meant to pursue claims on the existing political structure. In both cases, demonstrators asked for changes in policies—the policies of a university in the first case and of a nation in the second. Kesey sought nothing from established politicians, other than to be left alone. Having rejected agonistic politics, he asked demonstrators to turn away from the centers of established political power and look inward, toward each other. In place of politics, he offered the experience of togetherness; in place of a rigid, violent society, he presented the possibility of a leveled, playful community.

At the same time, he exhibited a style of leadership that would soon characterize Stewart Brand's work at the *Whole Earth Catalog* and that, over the next three decades, would migrate into debates around the social impact of digital technologies. At the Vietnam Day rally, Kesey simultaneously denied his role as a leader and assumed it, albeit in a new way, by playing his harmonica. Like the members of USCO, the Pranksters worked to step outside traditional political arrangements and celebrated a tribal togetherness. But unlike USCO, they also had a single, de facto leader: Kesey, called "the Chief" by the Pranksters. It was Kesey's earnings from *One Flew Over the Cuckoo's Nest* that had paid for the bus trip in 1964, and it was Kesey who was paying most if not all of the group's expenses (which Wolfe estimated at a hefty twenty thousand dollars per year). But neither Kesey nor anyone else would acknowledge this power explicitly. Wolfe put it this way: "Kesey took great pains not to make his role explicit. He wasn't the authority, someone else was: 'Babbs says . . .' 'Page says . . .' He wasn't the leader, he was the 'non-navigator.' He was also the non-teacher. . . . Kesey's explicit teachings were all cryptic, metaphorical; parables, aphorisms." Within the Pranksters, Wolfe argued, Kesey's leadership and the group's direction were "The Unspoken Thing."[47]

Rather than identify the power to lead with Kesey himself, Kesey and the Pranksters turned to various devices to distribute and, ostensibly, level that power. One of the devices was a simple spinner. The Pranksters regularly played a game in which a number of them would sit in a circle. Someone would spin the spinner, and whoever it pointed to would then have full power over the group for the next thirty minutes. Another tool they used was the *I Ching*. When important decisions loomed, Kesey and others—like hippies everywhere in the coming years—would throw a set of coins, find a correlated bit of text in the book, and use it as the basis for taking action.

The spinner and the *I Ching* did serve to take power out of the hands of designated leaders. If the former turned group members into followers, it did so only temporarily, and only with the members' consent. If the latter threw up an obscure ancient fortune, it also demanded that one work out its meaning on one's own. In both cases, the individual remained empowered. But within the context of the Pranksters, these devices also served an ideological function. That is, they not only distributed some power among group members and decision-making devices, but they also diverted attention from the very real and centralized leadership Kesey was exerting. Having walked away from what they believed were the excesses of the traditional party politics practiced by the American government and its cold war allies and enemies, Kesey and the Pranksters did everything they could to deny the fact of concentrated power in their midst. In a pattern that would become familiar around the digital technologies of the 1990s, they reassigned it, at least temporarily and at least symbolically, to devices.

For Stewart Brand, Kesey became a role model and a collaborator. In January of 1966, Brand and Kesey mingled the Pranksters' vision of power with USCO's high-tech tool kit to create the single event that, more than any other, would take the San Francisco psychedelic scene public: the Trips Festival. Over the preceding year, Kesey and the Pranksters had staged about a dozen "Acid Tests."[48] According to Tom Wolfe, Kesey had originally dreamed up the notion of an acid test as a multimedia LSD fest to be staged within one of Fuller's geodesic domes with psychedelic lighting by Gerd Stern of USCO. In the end, the tests tended to be more modest—they included long-hair gatherings featuring LSD in various venues in Palo Alto, Portland, San Francisco, Los Angeles, and even Mexico. The Grateful Dead supplied much of the music. Toward the end of 1965, Brand and Ramón

Sender Barayón, a composer of electronic music and a friend of USCO's Michael Callahan, thought up the Trips Festival as a way to bring the burgeoning scene together. Together, they found promoter Bill Graham (then a member of the San Francisco Mime Troupe) and hired the Longshoreman's Hall in San Francisco for three nights: Friday, January 21, through Sunday, January 23. By this time, the federal government had outlawed LSD, so posters promised an Acid Test—a full-blown psychedelic experience—without LSD.

As it turned out, the Trips Festival featured plenty of LSD. But more importantly, it represented a coming together of the Beatnik-derived San Francisco psychedelic scene and the multimedia technophilia of art troupes such as USCO. On the first night, Brand and some friends performed his multimedia piece *America Needs Indians*. When he developed it during his time with USCO, *America Needs Indians* consisted of sound tracks, three slide projection systems, and four Native American dancers. Brand thought of it as an immersive experience, a "peyote meeting without peyote." In the open, industrial space of the Longshoremen's Hall however, the piece looked tiny, like "a teepee and some slide projectors," according to one visitor.[49] That evening, visitors wandered throughout the hall, sometimes dancing, talking and playing with bits of electronic gear scattered around the floor.

The second night brought the scene into focus. Kesey had called for the audience "to wear ecstatic dress and to bring their own gadgets (A.C. outlets will be provided)," and they did. Audience members painted in Day-Glo colors danced and watched their dancing rebroadcast live on a series of closed-circuit televisions. The hosts had arranged for live microphones and sound gear for anyone to play with. Five slide projectors splashed images on the wall; light machines scanned the room. Two bands played: the Grateful Dead and Big Brother & the Holding Company. Above it all hovered Kesey. Stationed on a balcony and wearing a space suit, he wrote messages on acetate slides and projected them onto a wall below. Jerry Garcia, lead guitarist with the Dead, recalled the feeling that characterized the early Acid Tests and the Trips Festival: "Thousands of people, man, all helplessly stoned, all finding themselves in a room of thousands of people, none of whom any of them were afraid of. It was magic, far-out beautiful magic."[50]

According to Tom Wolfe, it was also the start of the Haight-Ashbury era. The festival grossed $12,500 within three days and had spent very little in the way of overhead. Two weeks later, Bill Graham could be found staging a trips festival every weekend at the Fillmore. Within a year, teenagers from across America would be streaming into Haight-Ashbury, looking for the sort of bohemian utopia Graham was marketing. Reporters for *Time* and *Life* were not far behind. Almost immediately, San Francisco became Oz to a generation that had feared it would grow up into a black-and-white Kansas of a world—if it lived long enough in the face of nuclear weapons and the draft to grow up at all. In myth, if not always in fact, Kesey and the Merry Pranksters became San Francisco's wizards, and as they did, they made visible to mainstream Americans the possibility of living a mobile, tribal life, a world in which the role-playing and psychological fragmentation common to the institutions of technocracy dissolved in a whirlwind of drugs, music, and travel and left standing only a more authentic, and seemingly childlike, self. For the teenagers then beginning to think of heading west, and for the reporters packing their bags to follow suit, the Trips Festival and the San Francisco scene heralded the birth of a new and open world.

The Trips Festival marked Stewart Brand's emergence as a countercultural entrepreneur—but in a deeply technocratic mold. Ten years earlier, Brand had feared that he would grow up into a world where he would have to partition his psyche and wield what power he had from within a hierarchical organization. He would have to become a soldier, cut off from both the world around him and the world within him by his uniform and his place in the ranks. At the Trips Festival, in contrast, Brand acted as a Comprehensive Designer. He built a world in which he and the dancers on the floor were part of a single, leveled social system. At one level, that system responded to the norms of the countercultural critique of technocracy. It shunned hierarchy in favor of anarchic togetherness; it turned away from emotionally removed, objective consciousness and toward a delicious, embodied, experiential magic. Like the happenings of Allan Kaprow and the music of John Cage, the Trips Festival transformed every moment into an all-encompassing now—itself a version of Beatnik satori.

At another level, though, the swirling scene at the Trips Festival, and Brand's role in it, represented a coming together of the New Communalist social ideals then emerging and the ideological and technological products of cold war technocracy. The festival itself was a techno-social hybrid. The Longshoreman's Hall surrounded dancers with the lights, images, and music of electronic media. The bodies of many dancers were infused with LSD. To the extent that they felt a sense of communion with one another, the sensation was brought about by their integration into a single techno-biological system within which, as Buckminster Fuller put it, echoing Norbert Wiener, the individual human being was simply another "pattern-complex." Brand himself had organized the event in keeping with the systems principles he had encountered at Stanford and afterward. Far from asserting direct control over events, he had built an environment, a happening, a laboratory. He had set forth the conditions under which a system might evolve and flower, and he had stocked the biological and social worlds of those who entered that system with technologies that allowed them to feel as though the boundaries between the social and the biological, between their minds and their bodies, and between themselves and their friends, were highly permeable. He had helped found a new tribe of technology-loving Indians, artistic engineers of the self. Very soon these new Comprehensive Designers would set out from San Francisco to found their own communities in the wilderness.

When they got there, thought Brand, what they would need most would be tools and information.

CHAPTER 3

The *Whole Earth Catalog* as Information Technology

After the Trips Festival, Brand continued to show *America Needs Indians* and to develop other slide shows and multimedia events. Part performance artist, part social reformer, part genial party host, he moved from project to project, trying to create holistic media environments of the kind favored by USCO and the Merry Pranksters. He also turned to making buttons:

> One afternoon, probably in March in 1966, dropping a little bit of LSD, I went up onto the roof and sat shivering in a blanket sort of looking and thinking. . . . And so I'm watching the buildings, looking out at San Francisco, thinking of Buckminster Fuller's notion that people think of the earth's resources as unlimited because they think of the earth as flat. I'm looking at San Francisco from 300 feet and 200 micrograms up and thinking that I can see from here that the earth is curved. I had the idea that the higher you go the more you can see earth as round.
>
> There were no public photographs of the whole earth at that time, despite the fact that we were in the space program for about ten years. I started scheming within the trip. How can I make this photograph happen? Because I have now persuaded myself that it will change everything if we have this photograph looking at the earth from space.[1]

The next week, Brand printed up a batch of buttons that read "Why Haven't We Seen a Photograph of the Whole Earth yet?" and started selling them at Berkeley's Sather Gate. When a dean threw him out, his removal was covered by the *San Francisco Chronicle*.

At about the same time, Brand got married. In 1965, at a meeting of the National Congress of American Indians, he had met Lois Jennings, a former mathematician for the U.S. Navy and a member of the Grand Traverse band of the Ottowa. They married in the spring of 1966, and in late 1967 they moved to Menlo Park, where Brand began working at his friend Dick Raymond's nonprofit educational foundation, the Portola Institute. Founded a year earlier, the Portola Institute housed and helped develop a variety of influential Bay area organizations, including the Briarpatch Society, the Ortega Park Teachers Laboratory, the Farallones Institute, the Urban House, the Simple Living Project, and Big Rock Candy Mountain publishers, as well as its most visible production, the *Whole Earth Catalog*. As Theodore Roszak has suggested, Portola's efforts were all designed "to scale-down, democratize, and humanize our hypertrophic technological society."[2] When Stewart Brand joined, much of Portola's energy was directed toward providing computer education in the schools and developing simulation games for the classroom. The person leading that effort was Bob Albrecht, who later entered personal computer lore as a cofounder of the *People's Computer Company* and a key member of the Homebrew Computer Club.

The Portola Institute served as a meeting ground for counterculturalists, academics, and technologists in large part because of its location. Within four blocks of its offices, one could find the offices of the Free University— a polyglot self-education project that offered all sorts of courses, ranging from mathematics to encounter groups, usually taught in neighboring homes—and two off-center bookstores (Kepler's and East-West). A little farther away was the Stanford Research Institute, where Dick Raymond had worked for a number of years, and not far beyond that, Stanford University. In addition, many of Portola's members represented multiple communities. Albrecht had worked at Control Data Corporation and brought with him advanced programming skills and links to the corporate world of computing, along with a commitment to empowering schoolchildren. Brand and Raymond both had extensive experience in the Bay area psychedelic scene. And Portola's various projects kept its members in circulation: teachers, communards, computer programmers—all came through the offices at one time or another.[3]

In his first few months at Portola, Brand moved from project to project, unsure of what to focus on. In March of 1968, however, his father died, leaving him an inheritance of about one hundred thousand dollars in stock. On the flight home from Illinois, Brand began thinking about how many of the people he knew from the Bay area countercultural scene had lately begun to move out into rural areas to live communally. As he described it at the end of the *Last Whole Earth Catalog* three years later, imagining his friends "starting their own civilization hither and yon in the sticks" got him thinking about the L.L.Bean catalog. This led him to fantasize about something he called the "Access Mobile." It would consist of a catalog and a "road show" and would offer "all manner of access materials and advice for sale cheap," including books, camping gear, blueprints for houses and machines, and subscriptions to magazines.[4] That spring, Brand spent much of his time scouring local bookstores, writing to publishers, and identifying items for a potential catalog. In July he printed up a six-page, mimeographed list of approximately 120 items for sale, put samples of many of them in a Dodge pickup, and with his wife, Lois, drove out to New Mexico and Colorado to visit the communes then appearing in the plains and hills. In one month, he and Lois sold some two hundred dollars' worth of goods.

Over the next four years, Stewart and Lois Brand turned that first mimeographed sheet into one of the defining documents of the American counterculture. Sized somewhere between a tabloid newspaper and a glossy magazine, divided into seven categories, and, in its National Book Award–winning 1971 incarnation, spread out over 448 pages, the *Whole Earth Catalog* featured a smorgasbord of books, mechanical devices, and outdoor recreational gear. A novel or a piece of literary journalism might have offered its readers a narrative thread to follow through the text from beginning to end, or a coherent authorial voice to cling to when the plot got murky, but the *Catalog* offered a cacophony of artifacts, voices, and visual design. Home weaving kits and potters' wheels banged up against reports on the science of plastics. Bamboo flutes shared space with books on computer-generated music. Readers couldn't actually buy any of these goods through the *Catalog*—to make purchases they would have to visit the Whole Earth Truck Store in Menlo Park, California, or turn to other retailers. But they could write in to recommend new products, to respond to other contributors' reviews, or to simply describe experiences that might be of interest to other *Whole Earth* readers. Neither book, nor magazine, nor traditional mail-order outlet, the *Whole Earth Catalog* represented something new in American publishing, and no one at the time could say quite what.

To journalists like Ed McClanahan, writing in *Esquire* magazine, it appeared that "the whole diffuse business . . . was held together by some mysterious principle of internal dynamics, some inscrutable law of metaphysics which I simply didn't understand, which no one who hadn't actually been close to the very center of the entire *Whole Earth* operation could even begin to define."[5] Nearly forty years later, that law looks less like an abstract principle of metaphysics than the product of Stewart Brand's network entrepreneurship and the convergence of systems theory and New Communalist politics that it facilitated. At one level, Brand's migrations throughout the 1960s represented a personal quest to find an alternative to the gray adult world he so feared in 1957. At another, though, they marked his emergence as an intellectual and cultural broker and, more broadly, the increasing importance of mobility and networking as an American cultural style. As he migrated from Stanford to the art worlds of Manhattan and the psychedelic bohemias of San Francisco, Brand became a key link between very different countercultural, academic, and technological communities. When he founded the *Whole Earth Catalog* in 1968, he gathered those communities into a single textual space.

That space in turn became a *network forum*—a place where members of these communities came together, exchanged ideas and legitimacy, and in the process synthesized new intellectual frameworks and new social networks. By coining the term *network forum* I aim to bridge two important ideas in science and technology studies: Peter Galison's notion of the "trading zone" and Susan Leigh Star and James Griesemer's "boundary object." Network forums function like a trading zone in that they are sites where representatives of multiple disciplines come together to work and, as they do, establish contact languages for purposes of collaboration. Yet, for Galison, as for the anthropologists on whom he draws, trading zones are physical sites such as laboratories. In a 1989 study of Berkeley's Museum of Vertebrate Zoology, Star and Griesemer suggested that a media artifact could serve some of the same collaborative ends. Like Galison, they showed that scientific work required collaboration by members of a wide variety of subdisciplines. Those individuals, they argued, found ways to collaborate and yet retain their individual allegiances to their fields of origin in part through the creation and circulation of "boundary objects"—that is, "objects which both inhabit several intersecting social worlds *and* satisfy the informational requirements of each." For Star and Griesemer, these objects included indexed repositories of collected objects, maps, diagrams, standardized forms, and objects with commonly agreed-upon boundaries but with content that could be viewed differently by different members.[6]

A network forum displays properties of both the trading zone and the boundary object. Like the boundary object, it can be a media formation such as a catalog or an online discussion system around or within which individuals can gather and collaborate without relinquishing their attachment to their home networks. But like the trading zone, it is also a place within which new networks can be built, not only for social purposes, but for the purpose of accomplishing work. Within the network forum, as within the trading zone, contributors create new rhetorical tools with which to express and facilitate their new collaborations. Network forums need not be confined to media. Think tanks, conferences, even open-air markets—all can serve as forums in which one or more entrepreneurs gather members of multiple networks, allow them to communicate and collaborate, and so facilitate the formation of both new networks and new contact languages. Media-based network forums such as the *Whole Earth Catalog*, however, are in part built out of these new languages and are in part sites for their display. Ultimately, the forums themselves often become prototypes of the shared understandings around which they are built.[7]

The *Whole Earth Catalog* played all of these roles, first for its contributors and its original, commune-based readership and, within three years, for readers far and wide. A comprehensive survey of the *Whole Earth Catalog*'s contents and contributors from its founding in 1968 through 1971 reveals that it featured contributions from four somewhat overlapping social groups: the world of university-, government-, and industry-based science and technology; the New York and San Francisco art scenes; the Bay area psychedelic community; and the communes that sprang up across America in the late 1960s. When these groups met in its pages, the *Catalog* became the single most visible publication in which the technological and intellectual output of industry and high science met the Eastern religion, acid mysticism, and communal social theory of the back-to-the-land movement. It also became the home and emblem of a new, geographically distributed community. As they flipped through and wrote in to its several editions, contributors and readers peered across the social and intellectual fences of their home communities. Like the collaborative researchers of World War II, they became interdisciplinarians, cobbling together new understandings of the ways in which information and technology might reshape social life. Together, they came to argue that technologies should be small-scale, should support the development of individual consciousness, and therefore should be both informational and personal. Readers who wrote in also celebrated entrepreneurial work and heterarchical forms of social organization, promoted disembodied community as an achievable ideal, and suggested that techno-social systems could serve as sites of ecstatic communion.

Over time, both these beliefs and the networks of readers and contributors who developed them, along with the *Catalog* itself, helped create the cultural conditions under which microcomputers and computer networks could be imagined as tools of liberation.

Communities of Consciousness

Brand later argued that to the extent that the *Whole Earth Catalog* reflected a particular "theory of civilization," it was a theory developed on the communes. By the summer of 1967, nearly a half million American soldiers were

[74] Chapter 3

stationed in Vietnam and more were being drafted every day. Antiwar protests had taken on a new intensity, with marchers burning draft cards in Boston's Arlington Street Church and confronting armed troops at the Pentagon. American cities had turned into battlefields as well; in 1967 alone, 167 experienced riots, most with racial overtones. In July, days of rioting in Detroit left 43 residents dead, almost 2,000 injured, and 5,000 homeless. The federal government had to call in some fifteen thousand state police and National Guardsmen to restore order.[8] In the fall of that year, the twin ills of a growing war abroad and intensifying violence at home helped drive thousands of young, college-educated, and predominantly white Americans to seek out rural havens. Not all communes were rural, of course—there was an increase in different city-based cooperative living arrangements as well—but for the hundreds that were in the countryside, the hinterlands of America seemed to promise the possibility of building a new, collaborative society. If the rest of America was preoccupied with violence and political struggle, the communes would take up the politics of consciousness. If Americans were at war with one another and with foreign enemies, the citizens of the communes would build self-sufficient, nonhierarchical communities based on interpersonal harmony. And the land itself—imagined as fertile, open, welcoming—would become a new frontier on which the commune dwellers could explore the limits of their own minds, their own bodies, and their own collective possibilities.

Yet even as they set out to escape mainstream technocratic society, founders of the intentional communities of the Southwest embraced the technophilic, consciousness-oriented value systems that Brand had encountered earlier in USCO and among the Merry Pranksters and, beyond them, though less explicitly, the collaborative research culture of cold war America. In the late 1960s and early 1970s, intentional communities tended to be organized along one of two lines: either free-flowing anarchy or rigid, usually religious, social order.[9] Both types of communities, however, embraced the notion that small-scale technologies could transform the individual consciousness and, with it, the nature of community. They also celebrated the imagery of the American frontier. Many communards saw themselves as latter-day cowboys and Indians, moving out onto the open plains in order to find a better life.[10]

Early in their travels, for instance, Stewart and Lois Brand visited one of the first and most influential of the nonreligious communities, Drop City. Founded in 1965, Drop City blossomed in a cluster of geodesic domes on the plains of Colorado, near the town of Trinidad. Like USCO and, to some extent, the Merry Pranksters, Drop City was devoted to pursuing collective harmony and creating traveling pieces of multimedia theater, in this case called Droppings. Cofounder Peter Rabbit explained at the time, "There is no political structure in Drop City. Things work out; the cosmic forces mesh with people in a strange complex intuitive interaction. . . . When things are done the slow intuitive way the tribe makes sense."[11] At Drop City, individuals were free to come and go whenever they liked and to pursue what interested them moment to moment. This freedom they believed would lead to a greater state of collective harmony, with one another and with unseen forces in the universe. "We dance the joydance, we listen to the eternal rhythm, our feet move to unity . . . live-love-joy-energy are one," wrote Rabbit, echoing the tenets of USCO. "We are all one."[12]

As in the performances of USCO and the Pranksters, the citizens of Drop City and other communes depended on small-scale technologies to link them together. LSD, peyote, rock and roll—each revealed the fundamental links between all living things and the otherwise invisible energies governing the material world. So too did the tools required to do the work of daily life. This was especially true in communes organized along religious lines. In early 1968, Stewart Brand's old friends Steve and Barbara Durkee of USCO, now disciples of the Indian guru Meher Baba, established the Lama Foundation near Taos, New Mexico. One of a cluster of communes in the region, the Lama Foundation was designed to facilitate personal spiritual transformation. The goal of the foundation was "to awaken consciousness," explained Steve Durkee at the time.[13] In order to facilitate this process, the foundation, like Drop City, claimed to do away with hierarchical forms of government. "We're anti-priesthood," said Durkee. "The world that makes sense is a world where each man and each woman lives out time and the cycles of the seasons, where no man is a priest and every man is a priest, and where the duty to maintain the cosmos is dependent on everybody instead of just a select few. . . . There are no priests here because everybody is a priest. There are none other than the elect."[14] In point of fact, Durkee and a committee called the Caretakers maintained a firm grip on the community. Yet, in theory at least, relations between individual members, and between members and cosmic forces, were to be governed in part by small-scale technologies and their deployment in collaborative labor. "Everything we do here is a kind of karma yoga," explained Barbara Durkee. "Chopping wood or carrying water, done in the right spirit, are meditation. . . . We praise God by building domes." For the members of the Lama Foundation, as for the Transcendentalists of New England, "The essence of spirituality [was] practicality."[15] And in that context, small-scale tools offered both a way to get a job done and a route toward the transformation of one's self, one's community, and, ultimately, the world.

Yet, even though it aimed to draw commune dwellers closer to themselves and their fellow citizens, the antinomian celebration of consciousness and its pursuit through the deployment of small-scale technologies and hands-on work did not prevent either social friction or the reassertion of traditional gender roles and racial politics. The do-your-own-thing ethos of the anarchic communes tended to drive away those with more structured ambitions. At Drop City, for instance, the day-to-day chaos created by the group's anarchistic politics, along with an overwhelming number of visitors in the summer of 1967, caused many of the founders to leave within three years. The stresses of building a community from scratch affected religious groups as well. Only five years after they came to New Mexico, the Durkees had left the Lama Foundation. What order obtained on many communes depended less on systems of explicit social control than on social resources and cultural habits imported from the New Communalists' former lives. More than a few communes were built with inherited money and sustained with welfare checks and food stamps. And many commune residents felt at home in large part because they were surrounded by others like themselves. As a resident of the New Buffalo commune outside Taos put it, "Here the one thing you're sure of is that you're pretty much on each other's side."[16]

Even as they imagined themselves to be colonizing new social frontiers, many New Communalists recreated the conservative gender, class, and race relations of cold war America. By 1967, within the New Left at least, women had begun to claim power in large part by asserting their rights in the political sphere.[17] On the communes of the New Communalist movement, by contrast, women often pursued authority by asserting a neotraditional femininity in the domestic sphere. As sociologist Rosabeth Moss Kanter has shown, communes outside the New Communalist tradition frequently divided up the childrearing, cooking, and cleaning commonly associated with the nuclear family, and as a result, a woman's status often had relatively little to do with her partnerships with men. In the rural communes of the back-to-the-land movement, however, men and women often pursued a neoprimitive, tribal ideal in which men made "important" decisions while women tended the kitchen and the children. Brand's wife Lois had grown up in suburban Maryland. She later recalled that on the communes she and Stewart visited, work was commonly divided along gender lines. "It wasn't that far removed from what I'd grown up with at home," she explained. "My brother cut the lawn and I did the dishes." On the communes, she reported, men worked on construction projects while "women put the Clorox in the water to keep everyone from getting sick."[18]

In many rural groups, men and women framed their gender roles in terms of an imaginary American frontier. They were not simply tribesmen, but settlers, and the process of rediscovering themselves and a down-home landscape they had imagined but never known became part of the thrill of being together—particularly for men. In 1970 journalist William Hedgepeth described gender relations at New Buffalo thus: "Without becoming bogged-down in sexual identity crises and the 'feminine mystique' type traumas that idle females flagellate themselves with back in Suburbia, the New Buffalo girls fulfill themselves naturally not only in sewing, cooking, cleaning or child-tending, but also in freely voicing their views and mystical visions, and then acting upon them. . . . 'We're trying to live a way that's never been lived before,' says Siva [a female New Buffalo resident]. 'There's no double standard here. We'll find out *together* how this works.'"[19] Yet, despite Hedgepeth's picture of mystically inflected domesticity, many communes, including New Buffalo, did not so much leave suburban gender relations behind as recreate them within a frontier fantasy. One man who lived at New Buffalo could have been speaking for many at other communes when he told Hedgepeth, "A girl just becomes so . . . so *womanly* when she's doing something like baking her own bread in a wood stove. I can't explain it. It just turns me on."[20]

Race relations echoed patterns found elsewhere in the counterculture. Virtually all of the back-to-the-landers were white, and most were under thirty years of age, well-educated, socially privileged, and financially stable. Explicit prejudice against African Americans or other people of color would have been unwelcome on almost all communes. In fact, by the late 1960s, more than a few New Communalists, like some on the New Left, saw themselves as social revolutionaries. "We are very much like the Vietcong," explained Bill Wheeler, who founded Wheeler's Ranch in California's Sonoma County. "We are a form of guerilla warfare and we're going to take our losses." At the same time, however, very few nonwhites took part in the New Communalist migrations of the time, and those who did were often as well-educated and well-off as their white counterparts.[21]

Throughout the New Communalist movement, it was far more common for young, white, highly mobile hippies to find their interests in conflict with those of the comparatively impoverished and immobile populations of Hispanics and African Americans among whom they often settled.[22] As communes sprang up around Taos, New Mexico, for example, realtors celebrated the hippie-driven rise in land values while other local residents seethed. William Hedgepeth recalled watching a long-time Hispanic resident tell some new, white arrivals, "You see the scenery. We see a battleground." By the summer of 1969, teachers in the Taos public schools had banded together to write an antihippie resolution decrying the commune-dwellers' "excesses in drug addiction, sexual immorality, obscene behavior . . . and public exhibitions of perversion and licentiousness."[23] As this resolution suggests, part of the problem was simply that hippies brought with them an alien code of behavior. In addition, though, their arrival tapped into memories of very old patterns of colonization and migration. A Chicano member of New Mexico's Reality Construction Company commune told a visiting reporter, "Every time a white hippie comes in and buys a Chicano's land to escape the fuckin' city, he sends that Chicano *to* the city to go through what he's trying to escape *from*, can you dig it? What can you do with that bread out here, man? Nothing. Then when that money's gone, see, the Chicano has to *stay* in the city, cause now he ain't got no land to come back to. He's stuck, and the hippie's free. That's why they don't dig the fuckin' hippies, man."[24]

And yet, in their own minds at least, the New Communalists were not simply colonizers. They may have bought up lands that formerly belonged to farmers and laborers, and they may have appropriated what they imagined to be working-class styles of manual labor and associated values of craft; but above all, they saw themselves as well-equipped refugees from technocracy. Drawing on the education, money, and technological savvy provided by the American mainstream and, less self-consciously, on its frontier mythology, they aimed to build communities that not only would serve as alternatives to a buttoned-down society, but would ultimately save that society from itself. If nuclear weapons and the Vietnam War, and perhaps even the urban riots that had plagued the last decade, were the products of a technocratic bureaucracy, then small-scale tools, the pursuit of higher consciousness, and the development of rural collaboratives might undermine the bureaucracy itself and, in the process, forecast a new, more harmonious future.

The *Whole Earth Catalog* as a Network Forum

In Brand's view, as in that of the USCO artists, the underlying principles of such a future had already been mapped by scientists and technologists in terms of energy and information—that is, in terms of systems theory. Brand drew on that theory to design a catalog that would supply the communes with goods but that would also link their political project to the ideals and practices of the American research establishment. In 1971 Brand recalled that at the *Catalog*'s founding, "the problem was How to Generate a Low-Maintenance High-Yield Self-Sustaining Critical Information Service"—a system for alerting communards to the latest social and technological developments and for linking them to one another. At the same time, though, Brand aimed to imitate the goals and tactics of American research culture.

Brand recalled, also in 1971, that he had "imagined us becoming primarily a research organization, with nifty projects everywhere, earnest folk climbing around on new dome designs, solar generators."[25] Some years later, he explained the link between service to the counterculture and the *Catalog*'s research orientation thus: "If [the commune dwellers] were going to go back to basics, they needed to know where the basics were. And I didn't either. But I set in motion a thing by which by purveying the stuff, and being a node of a network of people purveying it to each other. . . . I would get to learn whatever that network was learning. So it's being paid to get an education kind of thing. And it was designed as a system. I knew about systems. I had studied cybernetics."[26]

At one level, then, the *Catalog* served to make items of use available to an emerging, geographically distributed network of communes. At another, it served as a textual forum within which back-to-the-landers could meet one another, as well as technologists, academics, and artists, and share information. At both of these levels, systems theory became a contact language and a structuring principle. It organized the *Catalog*'s contents and shaped the reader's role in regard to those contents. Coupled to the New Communalist critique of hierarchical politics, it also provided Stewart Brand with a theory of editorial process and management practice that was particularly well suited to the coordination of multiple communities. Married to the frontier rhetoric of "cowboys and Indians," systems theory offered *Whole Earth* readers a way to link their countercultural attempts to transform themselves and their communities to the trajectory of American myth. Like its New Communalist audience, the *Catalog* celebrated small-scale technologies—and, again, itself—as ways for individuals to improve their lives. But it also offered up those tools—and itself—as prototypes of a new relationship between the individual, information, and technology. Like the scientific entrepreneurs of MIT's Rad Lab, the New Communalist adventurers of the *Whole Earth Catalog* were to become independent, collaborative, and mobile, and they were to build the norms of their communities into technologies and information systems that would both support those communities and model their ideals to the outside world.

At the start, the *Catalog* was a fairly modest proposition. After their first foray to the communes, Stewart and Lois returned to Menlo Park, hired two assistants, and, with a small portion of Brand's inheritance, as well as several thousand dollars Lois had inherited from her grandmother, printed one thousand copies of the first *Whole Earth Catalog*.[27] On its cover the first *Catalog* featured a photograph of the earth taken from space by a 1967 NASA expedition under the words, "WHOLE EARTH CATALOG / access to tools." On the back was a photograph of a solar eclipse under the words, "We can't put it together. It is together." Inside approximately 133 items were listed, more or less evenly distributed across seven thematic categories:

Understanding Whole Systems
Shelter and Land Use
Industry and Craft
Communications
Community
Nomadics
Learning

For the first, 61-page, edition of the *Catalog*, which retailed for five dollars, Brand selected virtually all the items; by 1971, a year in which the *Catalog* sprawled over 448 pages, sold more than a million copies, and won the National Book Award, many items had been recommended and reviewed by readers. Ninety-eight of the items listed in the first edition, and a similar portion in later editions, were books. At the front of the *Catalog*, in "Understanding Whole Systems," works by Buckminster Fuller met books on geology and biology; a little later, in "Community," the *Merck Manual* could be found alongside a chronicle of kibbutz life and a catalog of art prints. The *Catalog* listed periodicals as well, some emanating from the counterculture, such as the *Modern Utopian* and the *Realist*, others more mainstream, like *National Geographic* and *Scientific American*. The *Catalog* also offered mechanical and electrical devices, such as a forty-nine-hundred-dollar Hewlett-Packard desktop calculator (depicted directly above an entry for Norbert Weiner's book *Cybernetics* in the "Communication" section) and a one-man sawmill, as well as catalogs for companies ranging from L.L.Bean to Allied Electronics. The *Catalog* presented these items within a design framework that echoed the frontier preoccupations of the back-to-the-land movement and the psychedelic design inclinations of the contemporary alternative press. Each page featured multiple typefaces, many seemingly created in the nineteenth century. They appeared on plain, rough paper—the tactile antithesis of the glossy magazine. At the same time, the *Catalog* offered a riot of photographs, bits of text, and reader commentary that would have been familiar to readers of underground papers such as the *San Francisco Oracle* or the *Berkeley Barb*. Like its choice of products, the *Catalog*'s design mingled the psychedelic, the nostalgic, and the practical.[28]

The first *Catalog* did not sell quickly, but it did sell—enough for Stewart, Lois, and their staff to imagine producing a series of catalogs.[29] In January of 1969, as part of this process, Brand published the first quarterly update to the *Catalog*, which he called the *Supplement*. In addition to product news, the *Supplement* offered articles and letters from and about the communities Brand had visited. The first issue of the *Supplement*, for instance, included letters from Pranksters Ken Kesey and Ron Bevirt; Peter Rabbit of Drop City and, more recently, the Libre Commune; and Steve Durkee from the Lama Foundation, and an exchange between Steve Baer, who had designed the dome housing at Drop City, and Dave Evans, a staffer at Doug Engelbart's Augmented Human Intellect project at the Stanford Research Institute. It also featured a detailed description of how to build a solar water heater, four pages of free events and services in New York City, and announcements for several experiments in living and building, including an advertisement for Paolo Soleri's desert utopia, Arcosanti, and a proposal for "A Libertarian Nomadic Association in Southern California." As the *Catalog* gave access to tools, the *Supplement* gave readers a view of the communal world in which the tools were being used and a way to contact its members.

Over the next three years, the *Whole Earth Catalog* and the *Supplement* grew exponentially and so did their audience.[30] Before they announced that they would cease publication with the *Last Whole Earth Catalog* of 1971, Stewart, Lois, and a growing staff produced six different semiannual editions of the *Catalog*, of which some 2.5 million copies were ultimately sold, and nine quarterly *Supplements*.[31] By 1971 the number of items listed in the *Catalog* had increased nearly tenfold to 1,072. In 1968 Brand had designed the *Catalog* specifically for a commune-bound readership; within three years, the *Catalog* could be found in bookstores and living rooms in cities and suburbs across America. For many, the *Catalog* provided a first, and sometimes overwhelming, glimpse of the New Communalists' intellectual world. Gareth Branwyn, for instance, a journalist who later wrote for *Wired* magazine, recalled the day in 1971 when he saw his first copy of the *Catalog*: "I was instantly enthralled. I'd never seen anything like it. We lived in a small redneck town in Virginia—people didn't think about such things as 'whole systems' and 'nomadics' and 'Zen Buddhism.' . . . The *Whole Earth Catalog* changed my life. It was my doorway to Bucky Fuller, Gregory Bateson, whole systems, communes, and lots of other things that formed a foundation to a world model I've been building ever since."[32]

As the *Catalog* grew, the categories around which it was organized, and the structuring principles and editorial practices underlying those categories, remained consistent. So did the *Catalog*'s products. Although later editions tended to list an increasing number of items connected to the growing outdoor recreation industry, such as camping gear and down jackets, as well as other consumer-oriented goods, the *Catalog*'s products tended to accumulate over time rather than to be replaced. Virtually all of the items listed in the 1968 *Whole Earth Catalog* could be found again in the final edition three years later.

Looking over the range of items and the categories in which they were arranged, today, we can trace all of them back to one or another of the communities Brand visited across the 1960s. The biology and geology books of "Understanding Whole Systems" emanated from the interest Brand developed in natural systems at Stanford; the Fuller works, from his time at USCO and his visits to Fuller's lectures. The domes depicted in "Shelter and Land Use" could be found throughout the communes of the Southwest, while the buckskin jackets depicted in "Industry and Craft" echoed the sorts of clothing once worn by the Native Americans Brand had long admired and the hippies of Haight-Ashbury as well. Desktop calculator maker Hewlett-Packard was headquartered just down the road in Palo Alto, and the *I Ching* offered in the "Learning" section had by then become ubiquitous in psychedelic circles. In the early issues of the *Catalog*, though not in the much larger editions of 1970 and 1971, it is virtually impossible to find an item offered that is not intimately linked to a community to which Brand belonged, if only somewhat marginally, between 1960 and 1968.

In linking and arranging the *Catalog*'s artifacts, Brand displayed not only the range of his interpersonal networking, but his allegiance to the organizational and rhetorical principles of systems theory as well. For Brand, the *Whole Earth Catalog* was simultaneously a whole system in its own right and a tool for its readers to use in improving the whole systems that were their lives and the world in which they lived. Readers were offered the chance to adopt two positions simultaneously in regard to the *Catalog*, and to their lives. Consider the *Catalog*'s opening statement. On the inside cover of every edition, Brand defined the *Catalog*'s purpose:

> We *are* as gods and might as well get good at it. So far, remotely done power and glory—as via government, big business, formal education, church—has [sic] succeeded to the point where gross defects obscure actual gains. In response to this dilemma and to these gains a realm of intimate, personal power is developing—power of the individual to conduct his own education, find his own inspiration, shape his own environment, and share his adventure with whoever is interested. Tools that aid this process are sought and promoted by the WHOLE EARTH CATALOG.

Brand's definition clearly states the countercultural critique of hierarchical, establishment institutions as emotionally and geographically remote from the lives of citizens and, on the whole, destructive. At the same time, he intimates that he and the reader are like gods in at least two senses, one local and one global, and both familiar from Buckminster Fuller's *Ideas and Integrities* and, before that, Norbert Wiener's *Cybernetics*. On the local level, the individual reader is like a god in having the power to conduct his life as he wishes, as long as he can find the appropriate tools. For Brand, as for Fuller and Wiener, the system of the universe is complete—it is not something we can put together, but something already "together" in its own right. At the local level, our job is to turn its energies and resources to our own purposes. In keeping with the countercultural critique of hierarchy, we must pursue our own, individual transformation and the transformation of the world. These transformations depend on our understanding the world as a system of invisible forces; if effectively carried out, they will result in our living lives more in synch with those forces—lives that will be more meaningful, more satisfying or, in Norbert Wiener's terms, more homeostatically stable.

At the global level, like Fuller's Comprehensive Designer or perhaps a cold war military planner, Brand's reader enjoys the power of a god to survey the whole earth below him. The front cover of many editions of the *Whole Earth Catalog* featured an image of the earth seen from space. Simply by picking up the *Catalog*, the reader became a visionary of a sort. This vision, though, had been made possible by the cameras of NASA and, more generally, by the fact that he was a member of the most technologically advanced generation on earth. In the *Whole Earth Catalog*, cold war technocracy itself had granted its opponents the power to see the world in which they lived as a single whole.

These two perspectives are built into the reading experience of the *Catalog* as well. At one level, the *Catalog* was a "Whole Earth" in its own right. That is, it was a seemingly comprehensive informational system, an encyclopedia, a map. Simply by picking it up and flipping through its seven sections, the reader could become an astronaut looking down from space on a textual representation of a new earth. At another level, the *Catalog* offered its readers ways to enter its world and become "as gods" in a local sense too. The reader could order the "tools" on display and so help to create a realm of "intimate, personal power" in her or his own life (albeit by entering the commercial sphere first). One reader explained the distinction thus: "Walking to the bathhouse today, holding my new twenty-ounce hammer, I suddenly understood the *Whole Earth Catalogue* meaning of 'tool.' I always thought tools were objects, things: screw drivers, wrenches, axes, hoes. Now I realize that tools are a process: using the right-sized and shaped object in the most effective way to get a job done."[33]

For this reader, as for others, the *Catalog* sparked an understanding of tools as means not only to get a job done, but also to enter into a process.

The process would accomplish tasks but also would transform the individual into a capable, creative person. Within this process, artifacts such as calculators and books could clearly be of assistance, but so could other people. In addition to providing information on how to order material goods, the *Catalog* and, to an even greater extent, the *Supplement*, each told readers how to reach out to one another. For Brand, the *Catalog* was both a "whole system" and a "tool" for readers, and so were readers themselves. They could write in and use the pages of the *Catalog* to tell one another about their experiences with particular products. Via the *Supplement*, they could learn of ongoing countercultural projects and contact one another to join in. The *Catalog* and the *Supplement* became looking glasses through which to peer down and see a reflection of an emerging world and, at the same time, spot doorways through which they could enter that world.

The principles of systems theory helped to structure not only the readers' position in regard to the *Catalog*, but the world depicted within it. Throughout the 1960s, Brand had visited communities ranging from rural Native American reservations to downtown Manhattan art lofts to the Stanford Research Institute. In bringing together the array of tools and ideas he had encountered among these groups, he relied on the principle of juxtaposition to provide a sense of excitement and, paradoxically, coherence, for the reader. "How you get energy is, you take polarities and slap them next to one another," he explained in 1970. "If you get into cybernetics and your head is just a minute ago full of organic gardening and ecology, then cybernetics starts to come alive for you in a different way." But this juxtaposition was never ideologically neutral. As Geoffrey Bowker has pointed out, juxtaposition is a core element of the cybernetic practice of universal rhetoric and of its ideological component, legitimacy exchange.[34] These principles are at work on virtually every page of the *Whole Earth Catalog*, and in its overarching structure as well. Together they offer a way for the members of the New Communalist movement to claim some of the legitimacy of the American research community. They also work to legitimate mainstream forces of consumption, technological production, and research as hip.

Consider the *Catalog's* categories. On the face of it, the category "Nomadics" has no necessary relationship with, say, "Communications." As the collection of high-technology devices and books on high-technological theory gathered under this heading suggest, "Communications" conjures up the world of cutting-edge electronics research. "Nomadics," in apparent contrast, calls us back to a pre-electronic era and suggests visions of wandering tribes. Some of its contents, such as *National Geographic* magazine or a book called *Survival Arts of the Primitive Paiutes*, deal explicitly in images of these tribes. Others, such as books on wilderness survival and catalogs of backpacks and tents, offer tools that modern readers can use to imitate their wanderings. Nevertheless, juxtaposed on the contents page of the first *Whole Earth Catalog*, these categories do not appear unrelated; rather, the *Catalog's* statement of purpose and arrangement of categories suggest that understanding their relationship is part of the larger process of "Understanding Whole Systems." And to the extent that the reader does in fact perceive using high-tech electronic devices and modern backpacks as somehow equivalent to participating in the wandering of pretechnological tribes, he is able to see both the technological world (of SRI, of Hewlett-Packard) and the tribal world (of ancient Native Americans and contemporary counterculturalists) as equally legitimate elements of a single system. Within the pages of the *Whole Earth Catalog*, each of these communities offers a set of tools, practices, and symbolic resources that can be taken up by members of the other—as ideas, if one simply reads the *Catalog*; as artifacts, if one buys the products on display; as practices, if one puts them to use. Moreover, the categories "Communications" and "Nomadics" do not merely rub shoulders; they make possible the exchange of legitimacy across conceptual and community boundaries. Equipped with a backpack and a book on cybernetics, the neotribal New Communalist can roam from commune to commune, imagining himself as simultaneously ancient and contemporary. He is an Indian; he is also an engineer.

This sort of legitimacy exchange takes place at the micro-level as well. On a single page in the "Understanding Whole Systems" section, for instance, the first *Whole Earth Catalog* depicts two books of photographs: Hanns Reich's *The World from Above* and Joseph Royce's *Surface Anatomy*.[35] At the top of the page, Brand has printed four images from Reich's book that illustrate abstract patterns on the surface of the earth seen from an airplane: rivers flowing, houses boxed up into blocks, clouds billowing from a volcano. Beneath these are five images from *Surface Anatomy*. Each depicts a portion of a naked human body: the torsos of an old man and a young girl; the clenched fists of a baby and an adult. Juxtaposed with the images of the earth, these pictures suggest an analogy: the human skin and the skin of the earth both cover whole worlds, whole systems, as it were. Those systems are composed of abstract patterns, patterns that not only live within each of them, but that also flow through and across both of them. The reader can survey these images, can see them from above, thanks to the hidden presence of modern technologies (the camera, the airplane), even as he finds himself conceptually implicated in the analogy. After all, the reader's flesh has a surface anatomy of its own; the skin of his hands is not so different from the skin in the photographs. Perhaps he is a "whole system" as well. Perhaps he is both a citizen of the earth and, as a packet of informational patterns, its emblem too, just as he is both a reader of the *Whole Earth Catalog* (a system of tools) and, potentially, a tool for others in his own right.

In this dizzying string of analogies, we can hear echoes of Ralph Waldo Emerson, Norbert Wiener, and, of course, Buckminster Fuller. But for many of the readers of the *Whole Earth Catalog*, the analogies were more than the stuff of Romantic or cybernetic theory. They could be lived. In keeping with Brand's statement of its purpose, and with the collective ambitions of the New Communalists, the *Catalog's* structure and rhetorical strategies worked to shape an imagined reader who was a visionary, with a view of the planet's condition, and a local actor, with the ability to shape the larger world by shaping his local surroundings. Scrambling across the industrial landscape, plucking its technological fruits and replanting them in his own garden, this reader would be nomad and technocrat, local citizen and Comprehensive Designer. In the pages of the *Whole Earth Catalog* and its *Supplement*, readers could glimpse individuals who seemed to be leading this life, even as, by interacting with the *Catalog* itself, they could mimic some of the practices on which such a life would be based.

They could also read extensive descriptions of this new way of being, written by other readers. In the July 1969 *Supplement*, for instance, a reader wrote in from the Ant Farm art and design collective in Space City, Texas.[36] Beside a picture of a naked man and a naked woman posed in front of a wall of electronic devices, their shoulders draped in cable, he described a figure called the "Cowboy Nomad" and tried to place him in history:

THE FRONTIER DAYS WERE LAND OWNIN, PUTTING DOWN ROOTS, SELF SUFFICIENT FARMER STABILITY. THE COWBOY WAS LIVING IN ANOTHER LIFE STYLE, SACRIFICING COMFORT FOR FREEDOM AND MOBILITY.

THE COWBOY NOMAD CARRIED ALL HIS LIFE SUPPORT SYSTEMS WITH HIM BEING RESTRICTED BY WHAT HIS VECHICLE (HORSE) COULD CARRY.

COWBOY NOMAD EQUIPMENT: SAFETY MATCHES / KWIK START ENERGY BANDANA / CLIMATE PROTECTION TOOL BED ROLL / THROW DOWN SLEEP ANYWHERE SADDLE BAGS / HAD CARRY STORAGE PAK SIDE IRON / TAKE YOUR OWN JUDICIAL.

SOCIETY TODAY IS AMBIGUOUS, LAWS ENFORCE STATIC LIVING PATTERNS WITH VOTER RESIDENCY LAW, DRIVERS LICENSE STATE JURISDICTION, STATES RIGHTS KEEP YOU IN YOUR PLACE, IN A CIVILIZATION DESIGNED FOR MOBILITY. UNLIKE THE COWBOY, WE CAN GET QUICK FOOD, NEWS, SUPPLIES, ANYWHERE ON THE ROAD IN THE UNIVERSAL COMMERCIAL SERVICES MATRIX (YOU CAN GET COCA

COLA ANYWHERE IN THE WORLD) THE HOWARD JOHNSONS ARE ALL THE SAME AS
THE SEVEN ELEVEN, O-TOT-UM, PAK-A-SAK, LITTLE GENERAL, BABY GIANT,
PIK-A-PAK, TOM THUMB MARKET. IF WE PUT YOU IN AN AMERICAN SUPERMARKET
DISORIENTED TIME CLIP, HOW LONG WOULD IT TAKE YOU TO GUESS THE CITY
YOU ARE IN?

YET THERE ARE COWBOY NOMADS TODAY, LIVING IN ANOTHER LIFE STYLE, AND
WAITING FOR ELECTRONIC MEDIA, THAT EVERYONE KNOWS IS DOING IT, TO BLOW
THE MINDS OF THE MIDDLE CLASS AMERICAN SUBURBANITE. WHILE THEY WAIT
THE COWBOY NOMADS (OUTLAWS) SMOKE LOCO WEED AROUND ELECTRIC
CAMPFIRES.

"WILL YOU BE STAYING HERE IN DODGE CITY, MR MAVERICK?"

"WELL MAM, I RECKON I'D GET AWFUL ITCHY BOOTS SITTING AROUND IN ONE
PLACE VERY LONG."[37]

Grafted onto the historical figure of the American cowboy, this new "Cowboy Nomad" is part Marshall McLuhan and part Ken Kesey. He roams, but he takes his electronic (and psychedelic) technology with him. He can't bear the commercial American landscape or the middle class, and yet he lives off the bounty they have produced. And he is a "he"—there are no women in sight.

The Cowboy Nomad figure reappears throughout the *Catalog*, in a variety of guises. In 1970 Gurney Norman summoned up images of Daniel Boone and eighteenth-century Native American warriors, melded them into the figure of what he called the "Long Hunter," and suggested that they offered fit models for contemporary life:

The metaphor is inescapable: today's middle-class consumer culture as a
Mother Country to cut loose from; then a period of long-learning, in which
modern frontiersmen gain the individual competence that allows them to do
the necessary, practical things. Indians were the original teachers. They are
with us still, their ways and attitudes remain as models, to emulate and learn
from. But today, they are joined by others who qualify as "Indians" of a sort,
by virtue of their skills which allow them to function as teachers, as shamen
[*sic*], as knowers of The Way. Certain thinkers, certain mystics, certain far-out
entrepreneurs, qualify, but so do certain small farmers and artisans, aborigines
of a kind, native to their places, there on the land to be learned from by
modern Long Hunters willing to range beyond the settled places in search of
education and adventure.[38]

Norman's "Long Hunter," like the Cowboy Nomad, acts out in myth what the reader of the *Whole Earth Catalog* is asked to act out in the process of reading. Like the reader, the Long Hunter is simultaneously to survey the landscape as a whole and acquire the specialized knowledge of nomads and entrepreneurs. He is to reject *middle-class* consumer culture (the feminized "Mother country"), though not the process of consumption. Mobile, flexible, masculine, he is to consume knowledge and information and carry it with him on his migrations.

In short, despite the talk of cowboys and Indians, he is to become a member of an information-oriented, entrepreneurial elite. Like a Prankster playing the "Humanoid Radio" game, he is to be able to channel both the electrical currents running through his calculators and radios and the mystical currents of "The Way." He is also to inhabit what Buckminster Fuller called an "outlaw area," a place to experiment outside the strictures of everyday law.[39] For the New Communalists, in keeping with the rhetoric of the American frontier, these areas were represented by rural America. But even for these groups, the "outlaw area" was as much an idea as an actual landscape. And that idea had come to life in other areas of American society as well— particularly the space program. In the January 1970 edition of the *Supplement*, Brand printed portions of an article by physicist Freeman Dyson, father of 1990s dot-com guru Esther Dyson, that made this connection clear. Space, wrote Dyson, would always be big enough to provide a home for "rebels and outlaws." There they could "experiment undisturbed with the creation of radically new types of human beings, surpassing us in mental capacities as we surpass the apes."[40]

In Buckminster Fuller's "outlaw area," and in Dyson's social-Darwinist vision of space, we can glimpse the first intimations of the libertarian "cyberspace" of the early 1990s. Likewise, even as they summon up Daniel Boone and Buffalo Bill Cody, the figures of the Cowboy Nomad and the Long Hunter point toward the entrepreneurial high-tech engineers of the dot-com craze and their missionary zeal. In each of these instances, the symbolic consequences of legitimacy exchange reach across countercultural, scientific, and technological communities. As it links communes such as Drop City and the Lama Foundation to centers of high technology such as SRI and groups devoted to techno-social exploration, such as USCO and the Pranksters, the *Catalog* also facilitates the blending of their symbolic repertoires. Out of this blending, there emerged the image of a new kind of person, one who moved from task to task pursuing information and using technical tools in an experimental manner for the advancement of himself or herself and society. The text of the *Whole Earth Catalog*, organized according to the principles of systems theory, served the reader as a tool in this process and also, through both the reader reports it printed and the reading practices its structure suggested, offered him or her an opportunity to try on this new sort of self.[41]

This self was not alone. If the *Whole Earth Catalog* served as a guide to a new way of being an individual, it also modeled and offered access to new ways of being in community. "I think the whole scene is tantamount to a sort of community in print, with the crafty taciturn old bastards hawking and spitting into the fire, and occasionally laying one on us out of the experience store," wrote reader Rolan Jacopetti in the March 1969 *Supplement*. "Sheeeeeeeit, son, you talkin' geodesic domes . . . hell, I recollect me and Bucky once . . ." [42] In part that community was a function of network representation. In the *Supplement* and to a lesser extent in the *Catalog*, living members of actual communities wrote in to the *Whole Earth*, chatting, recommending products, and so on. The products themselves represented and invoked the networks in which Brand first encountered them. Together, the *Catalog* and the *Supplement* became textual forums within which a geographically dispersed collection of individuals and groups could come together, in text and sometimes pictures, and recognize each other as members of a single community. In a sense, *Catalog* and *Supplement* became town squares.

In their design and in their management and editorial practices, the *Catalog* and the *Supplement* were governed in keeping with principles derived both from the New Communalist critique of hierarchical organization and agonistic politics and from the systems orientation of population biology and cybernetics. A more traditional text, including a catalog, might have featured hierarchical elements of organization at several levels. It might have privileged a single author's voice, recounting events or framing products from that author's singular perspective. Or it might have arranged items or information in such a way as to emphasize that some things or ideas were more important than others. In the *Catalog*, Brand and his staff undercut these potential hierarchies. Instead of a single author's voice, Brand featured the voices of various reviewers and letter-writers and bits of text from the products themselves. A few items, such as Buckminster Fuller's writings, received extra space, but virtually all of the rest received between one-quarter and one-half of a page. Although the section "Understanding Whole Systems" stands at the front of the publication like a front door, helping to frame the reader's experience, should he enter that way, the *Catalog*'s seven categories are not otherwise ranked. They are of more or less equal size and can be entered and exited by the reader at will, with no loss of comprehension for the *Catalog* as a whole.[43]

As a manager, Brand used a series of strategies to distribute power and work to readers and to downplay his own authority. First, he called for readers to suggest and review items for the *Catalog,* offering them ten dollars for an accepted evaluation. Those who first suggested or reviewed an item would have their name listed in the *Catalog.* In this way Brand accomplished several entrepreneurial purposes: he enlarged the range of the *Catalog's* contents by appealing to "experts" outside his organization; he increased his readers' sense of commitment to and involvement with his organization; and he increased the *Catalog's* own value to the community it served. In the process, he invited the reader to become a producer of economic value, a contributor to a textual community, and still a buyer of the *Catalog.*

Brand exercised the ultimate power to include or exclude material, however. It was his money at stake, and in the end the *Whole Earth Catalog* was his organization.[44] In a sense, Brand sought to manage "as a god." That is, in keeping with Fuller's call for Comprehensive Designers, as well as his own experiences of environmental biology, he sought to set what he called the "initial conditions" of what he hoped would become a self-sustaining system.[45] "What you're trying to do is nourish and design an organism which can learn and stay alive while it's learning," Brand later wrote. "Once that process has its stride, don't tinker with it, let it work for you."[46] As he had seen Ken Kesey do with the Merry Pranksters, Brand downplayed his own power within the system. Apart from the "Purpose" section at the start of each *Catalog,* his editorial comments and reviews tended to be brief, modest, and casual. They projected a take-it-or-leave-it tone and a sense that their author saw his readers as equals. Brand took the process farther by publishing the full financial accounts of the *Whole Earth Catalog* in every issue after the first. While mainstream publications kept their numbers to themselves and made their workings a mystery, the *Whole Earth Catalog* invited its readers in. The *Catalog* may have been a system like other publications, but by publishing its accounts, Brand suggested that it was an open system, one over which its readers as much as its producers retained control.

As a theory of management, Brand's cybernetic notion of organization-as-organism allowed him to turn away from the agonistic jockeying for power that he imagined characterized life in the hierarchical organizations of the 1950s and toward a process that he called "Transcendental planning." This method of management, he explained, involved a recognition of one's individual interests and one's interests in the collective good. "You are you, and you are working in your self-interest because that's life, and you are also the event, or the thing you're working on, that's kind of big-S Self," wrote Brand. "And you can identify both ways and then try to accommodate both of those selves."[47] At one level, the notion of transcendental planning echoed the communitarian ideals of the time: in its practice, Brand could imagine his own interests to be deeply in synch with the energies and interests of those around him. And in part to model these egalitarian ideals, Brand paid everyone who worked on the *Catalog* the same hourly wage. At another level, though, the rhetoric of transcendental management masked the material distinctions between Brand's own interests and his place at the *Catalog,* and those of the people he worked with. At the end of the day, Brand made all key editorial decisions on the *Catalog* and determined what to do with the profits it generated.

Tools for Transformation

Even as it reached toward a more egalitarian, less combative mode of leadership, Brand's notion of transcendental planning set the stage for the celebration of leaders who had mastered the forces of the "system" and whose own interests could be depicted as those of a revolution. In the 1990s, *Wired* magazine would proclaim the CEOs of telecommunications and software firms to be those leaders. In the late 1960s and early 1970s, though, the young social vanguard at which the *Whole Earth* was aimed was preoccupied with reclaiming the products of government and industry and transforming them into "tools." In every edition of the *Catalog,* directly above the statement of purpose, there appeared the following statement of the *Catalog's* function:

> The WHOLE EARTH CATALOG functions as an evaluation and access device. With it, the user should know better what is worth getting and where and how to do the getting.
>
> An item is listed in the CATALOG if it is deemed:
>
> 1. Useful as a tool,
> 2. Relevant to independent education,
> 3. High quality or low cost,
> 4. Not already common knowledge,
> 5. Easily available by mail.
>
> This information is continually revised according to the experience and suggestions of CATALOG users and staff.

On its face, this statement of function seems as plainspoken and straightforward as L. L. Bean's introductions to his own catalog. Yet a complex series of attitudes toward technology were embedded both within both the statement and the pages of the *Catalog*. These attitudes were developed in the networks linked by the *Catalog* and would go on to shape popular perceptions of networked computing in the 1990s.

Although they were surrounded by a down-home, do-it-yourself design sensibility on every page, the items listed in the *Catalog* took on a strongly informational caste. First, many of them were simply information goods. In keeping with the New Communalist emphasis on the importance of changing one's mind, the great majority of the "tools" offered by the *Whole Earth Catalog* were books and periodicals. Some of them, such as catalogs of mechanical devices or periodicals devoted to communal living, provided access to more material means of transformation, but most were simply books in the conventional sense. That is, they offered their readers the chance to encounter information and perspectives that might change their thinking or behavior. The books tended to speak to the reader at one or both of the levels of self suggested by the *Catalog's* statement of purpose. Some, like Buckminster Fuller's writings, or books of maps and landscape pictures, or even the mystical fiction of Carlos Castañeda, tended to depict the world as a whole system governed by invisible laws and so to address their readers as if they had a godlike ability to see the world from above. Others, such as manuals for Volkswagen repair or catalogs of military surplus gear, spoke to the reader in his or her local context. That is, they offered ways to manipulate local systems such as car engines, or to transform the products of the military-industrial complex, such as army jackets and boots, into individualistic statements of personal identity. In both cases, though, they acted first on the reader's *mind*.

The same was true of the devices and other material goods the *Catalog* offered. Like books, these items engaged readers in practices that could help them see the material world as a whole information system in its own right. In the context of the *Whole Earth Catalog,* as on the rural communes of the time, a backpack or a tent did not simply offer a means of escape into the woods. It offered readers a chance to join an invisible community of nomads, to act in accord with the ancient energies of nature, and to become a more "whole" person in the process. That is, these goods would help transport the reader into an environment in which she or he might be able, at the global level, to spot the laws of nature and, at the local, personal level, to act in accord with them. In this way, tents and backpacks, like calculators and books, could aid in "independent education." In the "whole systems" context of the *Catalog,* as on many communes, to be educated meant to be conscious of the energy flowing through the natural world and of the fact that the material world was nothing more than a patterning of that energy. This was the essential insight of the Trips Festival, too, and of the LSD and multimedia experiences as interpreted by the Pranksters and USCO: we are all one.

Even as they opened windows onto the universal order of things, the items in the *Catalog* promised to be "personal" technologies as well. First, within the New Communalist context, they aimed to transform the consciousness of an individual user. Second, they tended to be small-scale and to engage readers in practices in which no more than a few people could take part at any one time. Books had to be read alone or to small groups. Only two or three people could share in the paddling of a canoe. Even the largest devices depicted in the *Catalog,* school buses and geodesic domes, could hold only tens of people at a time. In listing after listing, the *Catalog* took items designed or built by industrial engineers working in a mass-production context and offered them as tools for individuals and small groups. Third, the *Catalog* emphasized that its products belonged to the do-it-yourself tradition of frontier elites: the cowboys and Indians of American myth, and now the commune keepers of the New Communalist movement. They were not simply tools to do a job; they were mechanisms that transformed their users into actors in the dramatic myths of American individualism. The readers of the *Catalog,* the nature of these items hinted, might be exceptional individuals, might be part of a vanguard, might in fact be able to merge consumption and technology with the dream of pre-industrial community.

The "tools" of the *Whole Earth Catalog* also linked multiple networks and institutions. Some items embodied their allegiances in their material components. For instance, the September 1970 *Supplement* featured a "Birch Bark Crib."[48] The walls of the crib were constructed of birch bark, into which the builders had inserted Plexiglas windows for the baby. The mattress was made of polystyrene. With its back-to-the-land allegiance to birch bark and its easy appropriation of industrial plastics, the crib neatly linked the world of the commune to the world of the high-technology factory. Other "tools," however, drew readers into performing actions within which they could link the insights of multiple networks. As he fixed a Volkswagen, for instance, the *Whole Earth* reader could perform the role of the amateur engineer, managing a technological "system" from above, and, once the car was running, perform the role of traveling hippie nomad. The user of the *I Ching* likewise could throw his coins and find himself imitating the ancient Chinese and the Merry Pranksters, and, in his attempt to read the *I Ching's* sayings as clues to a set of otherwise invisible probabilities, he could also act in concert with the probabilistic outlook of information theory. He could become a Comprehensive Designer, using the informational energies of the world to transform the "system" that was his life and, according to New Communalist dogma, the world itself. At the same time, he could experience the ancient and the new, the Eastern and the Western, the literary and the technological, as mutually legitimating elements of his "whole" experience.

Not all items listed in the *Catalog* performed this linking function. But many did. Among the most prominent of the linking items were geodesic domes. By the late 1960s, these emblems of America's cold war inventiveness and will to survive a nuclear attack had been transformed into symbols of a holistic way of life. Buckminster Fuller had built one for his own home in 1963. By 1965 Ken Kesey was rhapsodizing over building one in which to hold an Acid Test. In 1967 the two dozen founders of Drop City attended a lecture by Fuller in Boulder, Colorado, and promptly set out to build their homes to Fuller's blueprint. In 1968 Drop City's lead designer, Steve Baer, published his construction recipes in his *Dome Cookbook* and set off a small building boom across the counterculture.[49] Two of the communes that Stewart Brand visited most often, Libre and the Lama Foundation, soon appeared with domes of their own. And in 1970 and 1971, Lloyd Kahn, a co-editor with Brand of several editions of the *Catalog;* Jay Baldwin; and several other *Catalog* staffers, used the *Catalog's* own production gear to turn out Kahn's own how-to manuals, *Domebook One* and *Domebook Two.*

These books became staples of the *Catalog's* "Shelter and Land Use" section. Depicted there and deployed on the communes, domes, like the *Whole Earth Catalog* itself, became prototypes of a new way of being. If white-collar man was a "square," domes and their users were well rounded. If the ministrations of hierarchically organized governments and corporations had thrown the earth's energies out of balance, the dome's ferociously efficient management of surface tension modeled a world restored to energetic homeostasis. Although domes could be quite large, they could never become the towering skyscrapers of Manhattan or Chicago. They could never dominate a landscape, nor could they be broken up into cubicles. Instead, they could channel the energies of physics into creating glorious "whole" spaces. In their ability to distribute structural tension evenly across a wide area and in their refusal to concentrate it in pillars and pinnacles, Fuller's domes modeled the sorts of collaborative, distributed power arrangements that characterized the New Communalist ideal. They also modeled a holistic state of mind. *Domebook One,* for instance, recounts the history of one Swami Kryananda and his search for the proper structure within which to meditate. After trying rectilinear buildings and conventional domes, he concluded that "a geodesic dome is by far the best. It is truly an extension of the mind and resembles . . . our seventh chakra located at the top of our heads."[50]

The dome was also an extension of cold war industrial engineering. The Cowboy Nomads of the communes may have lit out for new frontiers, but they did it carrying materials developed within middle-class consumer culture and its military-industrial complex. Lightweight aluminum tubing, plastic sheeting, even the blueprint for the dome itself—all had first been created or put to use in the sorts of industrial and military institutions the back-to-the-landers were fleeing. At one level, this pattern serves as an example of appropriation. As Kesey and the Pranksters had taken a bus away from schools and used it to "educate" mainstream Americans, or as the members of USCO had transformed the oscilloscopes of industry into tools for the production of mystical multimedia theater, the builders of domes were appropriating a cold war military shelter and redeploying it in a communal context. At another level, though, the communards' deployment of domes serves as an example of legitimacy exchange. Domes appealed to their builders and users not only for their connotations of holism, but also for their scientism. With their interlinked triangles, each apparently identical to every other but in fact sized slightly differently, domes were futuristic, space-age shelters. They looked nothing like the square shelters of the American past and everything like the sorts that might eventually appear on Mars. The process of building those structures required measuring the various surface parts of the dome to very precise tolerances (without such care, and often even with it, domes leaked). To build and inhabit a dome was not only to enter into contact with mystical systems, or to come closer to personal or transpersonal communion; it was also to play at being an engineer, a scientist, a master of technology.

Domes, then, like backpacks and calculators and many of the other "tools" carried by the *Catalog,* became terms in a contact language of sorts that was evolving for communication between the world of high technology and the tribes of the New Communalist movement. Domes embodied the counterculture's critique of hierarchical politics and the celebration of distributed "energy" common to the mythos of LSD and multimedia theater, but also the celebration of form, system, and homeostasis common to cybernetics, population biology, and information theory. In this way, like the *Catalog* itself, they bridged high science and counterculture. In the *Catalog,* the products of these worlds might be juxtaposed on a page and the reader might be left to link them as best she could. But in the image of the dome, the reader could see a material example of how such a linking might work. In this sense, the dome was a socio-technical hybrid not unlike Wiener's anti-aircraft predictor; it was a material device that not only performed some function but also represented an emerging social system. In the case of Wiener's predictor, that system had brought together soldiers and engineers, the military and industry. In this case, the dome brought to life a system in which representatives of science and the counterculture could congratulate one another for being so forward-thinking. Like other "tools" in the *Catalog,* the domes represented in Baer's and Kahn's books allowed members of the counterculture to claim some of the force of science for their own pursuits. Think, for instance, of Brand's description of the *Whole Earth* as a "research organization." And they served as important examples of how the products of American science and industry—from camping gear to calculators—could be reconfigured as small-scale devices essential to individual and collective transformation.

Domes also served as sites for face-to-face meetings between members of these communities. Throughout the time he published the *Catalog,* Brand continued to migrate among the networks it linked. Representatives of some of those groups came together in their own right as well. In March 1969 dome magnate Steve Baer and his colleague Berry Hickman brought together 150 "World thinkers" and "drop outs from specialization" at an abandoned tile factory in the dry hills of New Mexico.[51] As Brand pointed out in that month's *Supplement,* the factory was strategically located halfway between the nuclear test site at Alamogordo and a Mescalero Apache Indian reservation. Like its location, the gathering, called "Alloy," was to blend the global perspectives demanded by the nuclear age with the neotribal ethos of the communes. Over the course of three days, conferees gathered in a large white dome and conversed on a series of themes not far from the categories of the *Whole Earth Catalog*: materials, structure, energy, man, magic, evolution, and consciousness. "If I had to point at one thing that contains what the *Catalog* is about," wrote Brand soon after the fact, "it was Alloy."[52]

What the Alloy gathering shared with the *Whole Earth Catalog* was an ability to bring together multiple networks of people, to model an emerging, collaborative way of living and working together, and to do it in a simultaneously high-tech and tribal context. Participants came from Libre, Drop City, and Pacific High School, and from New York, Washington, D.C., and Canada as well. The event was filmed by Robert Frank. In the March 1969 *Supplement,* Brand devoted eight pages to the conference. In keeping with the *Whole Earth*'s allegiance to juxtaposition, he mingled comments made by participants with photographs of speakers at the microphone and conferees climbing the uncovered aluminum ribs of the dome. In the pictures one could see the men and women of the New Communalist frontier—young, white, decked out in the jeans and boots that used to mark the working class. One could also see them working with tools—some old, such as hammers and nails; others new and electronic, such as microphones; others futuristic, such as the dome itself. Across these pictures, one could witness a tribe of Fuller's Comprehensive Designers, taking a global view and acting as local engineers.

Likewise, the comments posted around these pictures made up a collage of rhetoric drawn from systems theory, communal construction projects,

and the countercultural critique of technocracy. "Evolution is any dynami-
cally self-organizing system," intoned one anonymous commentator. "The
process improves itself without external influence." Another asked, "Am I
this 6-foot body or am I something else that could exist beyond it? If we
could get enough information maybe we could go beyond the flesh enve-
lope."[53] These comments represented a linking of institutions as well. As
Brand pointed out in the *Supplement,* the speakers quoted included dome
builders Kahn and Baer, Dave Evans from SRI, Steve Durkee of the Lama
Foundation, and, of course, Brand himself. At Alloy, as in the pages of the
Whole Earth Catalog, counterculture and technological culture came together. In the *Supplement,* the coming together was presented in bits of prose
and photography. Like the items offered in the *Catalog,* these fragments of
the Alloy experience were tools for the reader to use as he or she liked. Individually, they offered readers the opportunity to change their minds and
to act differently at a local level. Taken together, they offered a textual emblem of a whole, if temporary, system, created for three days in New Mexico. And in that system, readers could glimpse the possibility of an entirely
new world system, one in which American industry supplied tools that
could be appropriated for purposes of transformation. The tools would be
deployed first by an elite and later by the whole population.[54]

What Wasn't in the *Catalog*

But what kind of world would this new elite build? To the extent that the
Whole Earth Catalog serves as a guide, it would be masculine, entrepreneurial, well-educated, and white. It would celebrate systems theory and the
power of technology to foster social change. And it would turn away from
questions of gender, race, and class, and toward a rhetoric of individual and
small-group empowerment.

   Although it was published in the heyday of the Black Panthers and the
American Indian Movement, for instance, the *Catalog* left questions of race
unaddressed. Occasionally an African American would peer out from a photograph in the *Catalog* or the *Supplement,* but the first attempt to deal with
race explicitly did not come until the January 1970 *Supplement,* with the
printing of a "Black Reading List" from Robin's Distributing Company.[55]
Few similar items followed. In the fall of 1974, not long after the *Catalog* had
officially ceased publication, Brand did turn over an issue of the magazine
that grew out of the *Supplement* called *CoEvolution Quarterly* to the Black Panthers to edit as a special issue. The magazine they created simply copied the
format of their newsletters, and none of the editors or authors of that issue
became regular contributors to Whole Earth productions in later years.

Likewise, for all the talk of cowboys and Indians in the *Catalog*, real Native Americans were virtually invisible in its pages. Represented by buckskin shirts and moccasins, Indians remained little more than symbols for the tribal, wandering hippies.

Women fared only slightly better. The Women's Liberation Movement had begun to pick up steam by 1968, but it wasn't until a series of readers raised the issue of women's places on rural communes in the July 1970 *Supplement* that the *Whole Earth* began to take notice. Even then, its few depictions of women in a politically empowered context were often undercut by their framing. The *Last Whole Earth Catalog* of 1971, for instance, listed the book *Women and Their Bodies* (the precursor to *Our Bodies, Ourselves*) by the Boston Women's Health Collective. Alongside Diana Shugart's sensible, straightforward review, it ran two pictures: one of a naked young woman on her back, seen from three or four feet above, and the other, a close up of a child latched onto a young mother's breast. As his only selection from the book, Brand chose a long passage in which the authors tell women how to masturbate and then enjoined men who might read the passage not to use it "as a marriage manual."[56] Although *Women and Their Bodies* and Diana Shugart's review addressed a wide range of women's health issues, the *Catalog*'s editors focused narrowly on women's sexuality.

A similar pattern marred the *Catalog*'s few references to the Vietnam War. Despite the fact that the years of its publication overlapped the peak of American involvement in Southeast Asia, the *Catalog* almost completely ignored the conflict. Like Ken Kesey at Vietnam Day in 1965, it turned away from the war and the protestors alike. Only in 1971, long after the Tet Offensive and the My Lai Massacre had undercut the war's legitimacy, and nearly a year after the National Guard had shot antiwar protestors dead at Kent State, did the *Catalog* finally list a handful of publications related to left politics, such as Saul Alinsky's *Rules for Radicals* and *The Organizer's Manual*. What few references to the war appeared before then did little to bring the conflict home to readers. In the spring 1970 edition of the *Catalog*, for instance, Brand listed *Strategy and Tactics* magazine and printed an outtake ad for "VIET-NAM"—a board game. "I was once an umpire at a huge war game at Camp Drum, New York, and had a wonderful time," wrote Brand in his review.[57] In the fall 1970 edition, a press photograph of an American combat soldier with the words "MAKE WAR NOT LOVE" penned on his helmet was used to illustrate a review of places where readers could buy government surplus gear. For working-class American men, going to fight in Vietnam was a real possibility; judging by these listings, for the editor and readers of the *Whole Earth Catalog*, it was not. The faraway war was of primary interest only insofar as it generated new "tools" for their personal transformation at home.

Occasionally, and particularly in its last two years, the *Catalog*'s readers and even staffers took the *Catalog* and the communities it served to task. In the July 1969 *Supplement,* Brand printed a letter critiquing Buckminster Fuller for allowing only two classes in his work: elite designers and mass consumers. In the same issue, Brand reprinted an article from the *San Francisco Good Times* describing how commune dwellers in the Southwest had taken advantage of impoverished locals. A year later, Brand printed a letter calling for the *Catalog* to deal with the social impact of industrialization and capitalism.[58] In the January 1970 *Supplement,* under the headline "Staff Gripe Page," Brand printed a letter from former *Whole Earth* staffer Jay Bonner, critiquing the *Catalog*'s politics from top to bottom.[59] "Once," wrote Bonner, "while working with him on the catalog, I asked Mr. Brand if he would not carry any of a various number of politically oriented underground newspapers. Upon reply he told me that three of the first restrictions he made for the catalog were no art, no religion, no politics." Bonner then pointed out that *Catalog* offered all three: the art was fine art or craft; the religion, Eastern; the politics, libertarian. "From all the 128 pages of the *Whole Earth Catalog* there emerges an unmentioned political viewpoint," wrote Bonner. "The whole feeling of escapism which the catalog conveys is to me unfortunate."[60]

Brand responded with a defense of local action and of his personal experience:

The capitalism question is interesting. I've yet to figure out what capitalism is, but if it's what we're doing, I dig it. Oppressed peoples: all I know is that I've been radicalized by working on the *Catalog* into far more personal involvement with politics than I had as an artist. My background is pure WASP, wife is American Indian. Work I did a few years ago with Indians convinced me that any guilt-based action toward anyone (personal or institutional) can only make a situation worse. Furthermore the arrogance of Mr. Advantage telling Mr. Disadvantage what to do with his life is sufficient cause for rage. I ain't black, nor poor, nor very native to anyplace, nor eager any longer to pretend that I am—such identification is good education, but not particularly a good position for being useful to others. I am interested in the *Catalog* format being used for all manner of markets—a black *Catalog,* a Third World one, whatever, but to succeed I believe it must be done by people who live there, not well-meaning outsiders. I'm for power to the people and responsibility to the people. Responsibility is individual stuff.[61]

On the one hand, Brand's response resonates with the countercultural critique of hierarchical politics and with elements of systems theory.

In keeping with Reich's "Consciousness III," Brand suggests that top-down politics (i.e., the kind where Mr. Advantage tells Mr. Disadvantage what to do) is bankrupt. The center of change must be the individual, acting with other likeminded individuals. This emphasis on local action echoes the notion of the individual's local role in maintaining universal systems. By acting on a small scale, the individual can imitate Norbert Wiener's gunner, adjusting his fire, or Buckminster Fuller's Designer, turning the energies of the universe to his own purposes. He can thereby change the large-scale system of which he is both a small part and a tiny model. On the other hand, Brand's response offers a glimpse of the political consequences of this point of view: Indians must work with Indians, the Third World with the Third World, blacks with blacks, and so on. No group should count on help from any other. Everyone is on his own.

Such segregation might seem to conflict with the *Whole Earth Catalog*'s celebration of "whole" systems. After all, the essence of the *Catalog* would seem to be the notion that "everything is related."[62] Yet the *Catalog* is not a collection of everything. Rather, it is a collection of ideas and artifacts then circulating among a limited number of networks, virtually all of whose members were white and relatively young, with a high level of education and easy access to social and financial resources. What relates those items to one another in the *Catalog* and, to some extent, within the networks concerned, are the universal rhetorical strategies of cybernetics. In the *Catalog*, local systems mirror global systems, and to act locally is to act as if one had a view of the whole earth. In other words, to master the "system" of one's Volkswagen engine or to take in the "system" that is the *Catalog* itself through reading is to imitate the activities of those with command of other, larger systems. It is in fact to act as if one occupied the pinnacles of social, economic, and political power currently dominated by the same technocrats to whose world the New Communalists aimed to find an alternative. Moreover, for the readers of the *Catalog*, it is to act with the aid of "tools" created by and appropriated from the very technocracy under attack by both the New Communalists and the New Left. In this way the *Catalog* celebrates not only the counterculture but also the mainstream technocratic culture from which it emerged. And the *Catalog* replicates mainstream hierarchies of social distinction: from the pages of the *Catalog*, as from the halls of corporate and government power at the time, people of color, women, and the poor remain largely absent.

Brand's call for "responsibility to the people," as well as his *Catalog*'s turn away from the poor and people of color, reemerged in the Republican political agendas of the late 1980s and early 1990s. The *Catalog*'s technocentric attitude toward social change, its systems orientation, its preoccupation with information, and even the cluster of networks it brought together—all became central features of the 1990s debates about networked computing and the "New Economy." So too did the figure of the Long Hunter. Reconfigured as the hacker, he stepped away once more from the "Mother" country of middle-class life and headed out onto a new technological frontier. That frontier ultimately became incarnated in the term *cyberspace,* but even then, it continued to look a great deal like the communal frontiers of the late 1960s. Once again, the electronic products of American (and international) industry were taken out of the large institutions in which they first appeared. They were miniaturized, made "personal." And like the backpacks and calculators of the *Whole Earth Catalog,* they were claimed as sources of personal and collective transformation.

Brand himself came to have enormous authority in this world, in large part because of the networks and networking practices he developed across the 1960s. By entrepreneurially linking countercultural and technological communities, first in his own travels and later in the pages of the *Whole Earth Catalog,* Brand allowed the members of those communities to synthesize the ideals and insights of the two worlds. This synthesis generated a social vision in which small-scale informational technologies could be imagined to transform individual minds and, through them, the world. The *Whole Earth Catalog* presented an informational genre—the network forum—that exemplified that vision. The network forum in turn dramatically amplified the social legitimacy of its founder, Stewart Brand. By 1971 he had been profiled in *Time* magazine, lauded at the National Book Awards, and celebrated nationwide as a socio-technical visionary. Like P. T. Barnum, he had gathered the performers of his day—the commune dwellers, the artists, the researchers, the dome builders—into a single circus. And he himself had become both master and emblem of its many linked rings.

With the exception of Dave Evans at SRI, and perhaps Bob Albrecht, running his computer education project from the offices of the Portola Foundation, the technologists of the personal computer revolution to come were not core performers in Whole Earth circles. But they were watching, some very closely. On June 21, 1971, Stewart Brand threw a "Demise Party" to celebrate what he thought would be the final edition of the *Catalog* and the end of the *Whole Earth Catalog* publishing project. He invited five hundred *Whole Earth* staffers, readers, and friends to San Francisco's Palace of Arts and Sciences. He also promised them a "surprise educational event." At about nine-thirty that evening, a procession of entertainers appeared: clowns, trampoline jumpers, belly dancers, and a band called the Golden Toad that played "Irish jigs and Tibetan temple music."[63] The six-foot Brand moved through the crowd barefoot, wearing a black monk's cassock. At ten-thirty, he approached the event's master of ceremonies, Scott Beach, and handed him $20,000 in $100 bills. Beach stepped up to the microphone and explained: "About fifteen minutes ago, Stewart Brand gave me one of the tools that the *Whole Earth Catalog* has used. This is $20,000, and he gave it to the people here to be used as a tool. . . . Use this as a seed. The *Whole Earth Catalog* ceases. The seeds have been planted already. Your consensus will decide what will be done with this money. There are microphones, there are causes, there are lots of possibilities."[64] Over the next hour, more than fifty people stepped to the microphone, proposing an equal number of solutions. Brand stood on stage in his monk's robes, writing down each suggestion on a blackboard. As the evening wore on, the crowd gradually dwindled and so did the cash. By early the next morning, more than $5,000 had simply disappeared. The audience seemed no closer to a solution. Finally, the audience voted to give the remaining $14,905 to one Frederick L. Moore, who promised to put the money in a bank and reconvene the last twenty people at the party in a month to decide what to do with it.

What ultimately became of the money remains unclear, but Moore's fate does not. In the spring of 1975, along with Gordon French, he founded the Homebrew Computer Club.

CHAPTER 4

Taking the Whole Earth Digital

In a 1995 special issue of *Time* magazine entitled "Welcome to Cyberspace," Stewart Brand wrote an article arguing that that the personal computer revolution and the Internet had grown directly out of the counterculture. "We Owe It All to the Hippies," claimed the headline. "Forget antiwar protests, Woodstock, even long hair. The real legacy of the sixties generation is the computer revolution." According to Brand, and to popular legend then and since, Bay area computer programmers had imbibed the countercultural ideals of decentralization and personalization, along with a keen sense of information's transformative potential, and had built those into a new kind of machine.[1] In the late 1960s and the early 1970s, Brand and others noted, computers had largely been mainframes, locked in the basements of universities and corporations, guarded by technicians. By the early 1980s, computers had become desktop tools for individuals, ubiquitous and seemingly empowering. One had only to look at the machines themselves to see that the devices through which the leaders of government and industry had sought to manage the world had been wrested from their hands. The great machines of empire had been miniaturized and turned over to individuals, and so transformed into tools with which individuals could improve their own lives.

Like many myths, this one contains several grains of truth. The 1970s did in fact witness the rise of a new form of computing, and Bay area programmers, many with countercultural leanings, played an important part in that process. And as they were distributed, some of the new computers—particularly the 1984 Apple Macintosh—were explicitly marketed as devices one could use to tear down bureaucracies and achieve individual intellectual freedom. Yet, the notion that the counterculture gave rise to personal computing and computer networking obscures the breadth and complexity of the actual encounter between the two worlds. As Stewart Brand's migrations across the 1960s suggest, New Communalist visions of consciousness and community had become entangled with the cybernetic theories and interdisciplinary practices of high-technology research long before computers were miniaturized or widely interlinked.

In the 1970s, the same rejection of agonistic politics that had fueled the rise of New Communalism undermined the day-to-day governance of all but the most rule-bound communes, and the movement itself melted away. Yet, Stewart Brand and the *Whole Earth Catalog* continued to link information technology and cybernetics to a New Communalist social vision. This linking proceeded in three stages. In the first phase, between 1968 and 1972, two communities began to mingle within blocks of the *Whole Earth Catalog* offices in Menlo Park. One, centered around the Stanford Research Institute and composed primarily of engineers, was devoted to the ongoing pursuit of increased human-computer integration. The other, clustered around the *Catalog* and the countercultural communities it served, focused on the pursuit of individual and collective transformation in a New Communalist vein. Stewart Brand positioned himself between these worlds and, in a variety of ways, brokered their encounter. In the second phase, which spanned the middle of the 1970s, Brand turned away from the computer industry per se and toward the cybernetics of Gregory Bateson. Drawing on Bateson's vision of the material world as an information system, Brand and others began to imagine a new kind of home for themselves—space colonies. Fifteen years later, such fantasies of technologically sustained communities would reappear in celebrations of "cyberspace," but in the late 1970s, they marked the dissolution of the back-to-the-land movement's rustic technophilia, and with it the collapse of New Communalism as a social movement. Finally, confronted by this collapse and by the increasing presence of desktop computers, Brand turned back toward the computer industry and its founders in the early 1980s. Computer engineers, he argued, and not the failed back-to-the-landers, were the true heirs of the New Communalist project. By that time the New Communalist movement had vanished from the scene. Yet, thanks in large part to Brand's entrepreneurship, its ideals seemed to live on in the surging computer industry, and Brand himself became a key spokesman for this new and ostensibly countercultural group.

Making the Computer "Personal"

When Brand turned back toward the computer industry, he leaned on a legitimacy that he had established a decade earlier. With the *Whole Earth Catalog,* Brand offered a generation of computer engineers and programmers an

alternative vision of technology as a tool for individual and collective transformation. In the late 1960s and early 1970s, he also moved back and forth
between the Bay area's burgeoning counterculture and its centers of computer research. Between his networking and his publishing efforts, Brand
helped synthesize and legitimate multiple visions of "personal" computing.
In the process, he established himself as a voice for an emerging technological community, as he had done with the back-to-the-landers.

As historian Paul Ceruzzi has detailed, the 1960s witnessed a transformation in computing equipment.[2] Between 1959 and 1969, the computer industry managed to shrink the room-sized mainframes of the early 1950s into
minicomputers that could fit beneath a desk. In the late 1950s, computers
processed information in batches of punched cards; a computer user had to
prepare those cards and submit them to the managers of the machine for
processing. A decade later, users could find their way to time-sharing
machines like Digital Equipment Corporation's PDP-10, where they could
store files on tape and access their own files without the intervention of
other personnel. Perhaps most importantly, they could now feel as if they
had the machine to themselves even as other users might be logged on from
terminals elsewhere. As Ceruzzi has shown, many of the technical features
that we now associate with "personal" computing, including small computers, microprocessors, keyboard-based interfaces, individual usability, and
the sensation of interactivity, were all in place by 1972.[3]

These technological developments, however, did not in and of themselves spawn the ethos of personalness to which small computers have since
become attached. Before the early 1970s, small computers suitable for individual use were usually called *mini-*, *micro-*, or *desktop* computers. The word
personal had been used for some time to describe small-scale consumer technologies such as radios and televisions, and by the early 1970s it was occasionally applied to computers and calculators as well. But when it was, it
retained its earlier connotations: a "personal computer" was a calculating
device made small enough for use by a single person.[4] The notion that computers might empower individuals and so transform their social worlds did
not simply grow up alongside shifts in computing technology; rather, it had
to be linked to the machines themselves.[5] Scholars have offered two dominant accounts of how this happened. Many have argued that shifts in the
computing interface facilitated shifts in use patterns, which in turn allowed
users to imagine and build new forms of interfaces. Thus, Thierry Bardini
has suggested that computers have seen the development of a "dynamic of
personalization" since the 1940s, in which both computers and computer
users have become progressively more individualized. Paul Ceruzzi has
claimed that "personal" computing emerged when time-sharing computers

made it possible to imagine giving public users direct access to computers. Against these accounts, others have argued that the notion of the computer as a tool for personal and communal transformation first came to life outside the computer industry, among an insurgent group of hobbyists with countercultural loyalties. Members of this group, they point out, built the Homebrew Computer Club and ultimately not only Apple Computer, but a number of other important personal computer companies as well.[6]

A close look at the computing world of the Bay area in the late 1960s and early 1970s reveals that both of these accounts are true but that neither is complete. As journalist John Markoff has shown, industry engineers and hobbyists lived and worked side-by-side in this period, and both were surrounded by countercultural activities and institutions.[7] Two of the most influential of these groups in the region maintained offices within a few square blocks of each other and of the offices of the *Whole Earth Catalog* in Menlo Park. One of the groups consisted of the researchers associated with Douglas Engelbart's Augmentation Research Center (ARC) at the Stanford Research Institute (SRI) and later Xerox's Palo Alto Research Center (PARC), and the other was made up of computer hobbyists affiliated with the *People's Computer Company* and, later, the Homebrew Computer Club. Stewart Brand moved back and forth between these communities, and the *Whole Earth Catalog* served as inspiration to members of both. In the Bay area in this period, the dynamic of personalization that had long been at work within some parts of the computer industry and the ideals of information sharing, individual empowerment, and collective growth that were alive within the counterculture and the hobbyist community did not so much compete with as complement each other.

In Douglas Engelbart's ARC group, computers had long seemed to be natural tools with which to expand the intellectual capacity of individuals and their ability to share knowledge. This vision had grown out of the research cultures of World War II and the early cold war. In 1946, for instance, while stationed in the Philippines as a Navy radar technician, Engelbart had read Vannevar Bush's now-legendary *Atlantic Monthly* article "As We May Think." In it Bush argued that the same scientists who had just helped win World War II would now have to harness the power of the cheap electronics they had invented to develop a new form of information management. Having built the nuclear weapons that might destroy mankind, scientists should now turn to building technologies with which to "encompass the great record" of human activity and so facilitate a growth "in the wisdom of race experience."[8] By way of example, Bush described a hypothetical desktop machine he called the Memex. Designed for individual use, the Memex featured a keyboard, a translucent screen, microfilm inputs, and the ability to call up reams of stored data by means of a few keystrokes. This machine would turn the ordinary office into a site at which the whole of human history might in theory be called up. The executive equipped with this new knowledge base would not only expand his own intellectual capacities but also enhance his ability to control the world around him.

Bush's article helped interest the young Engelbart in working with computers.[9] During the war, Engelbart noted, following Bush, the American military had developed technologies with which it might destroy the world. In its wake, scientists and technologists had begun to fan out around the globe, seeking to use their knowledge to eradicate disease and increase food production, often in an effort to win the cold war loyalties of Third World nations. Engelbart had read about these efforts and saw that they often backfired. Rapid food production led to the depletion of the soil; the eradication of insects led to ecological imbalances. In Engelbart's view, humans had begun to face extraordinarily complex problems, and they needed to solve them urgently. They would need to improve the management of information and the control of human organizations in order to do so. During World War II, in the airplane-tracking projects of Norbert Wiener, the integration of man and machine had presented a way to win the war. Now the battlefield had shifted to the workplace. Like Wiener, Engelbart would go on to pursue questions of man-machine integration. And like the weapons researchers of the war era more broadly, he would conceive of his work in world-saving terms. To augment the mind of the individual office worker was not only to improve his or her efficiency, but also to expand his or her ability to serve the human race.

Engelbart joined the Stanford Research Institute in 1957. Over the next decade, he and his staffers at the Augmentation Research Center invented some of the most ubiquitous features of contemporary computers, including the mouse. Between 1966 and 1968, the group developed a collaborative office computing environment known as the On-Line System, or NLS. The NLS featured many of the elements common to computer systems today, including not only the mouse, but a QWERTY keyboard and a CRT terminal. More importantly, the system offered its users the ability to work on a document simultaneously from multiple sites, to connect bits of text via hyperlinks, to jump from one point to another in a text, and to develop indexes of key words that could be searched. The NLS depended on a time-sharing computer, yet it functioned within the office environment much like a contemporary intranet. At a time when many inside and outside the industry still thought of computers as massive calculating machines, the NLS offered a vision of computers as text processors and tools for collaboration. Unlike their cold war ancestors, the computers of Engelbart's ARC group were communication devices and, in that sense, direct antecedents of the personal computers to come.

The NLS and Engelbart's understanding of the social potential of computers also owed a great deal to World War II research culture and to cybernetics in particular. Engelbart described the NLS as a system that would augment human intellectual capacities, but the system itself demanded a high degree of integration between the user and the machine. Like the Memex, each terminal served as a tool that would allow the person it served to call up and manage information. Beyond that, it would recursively leverage the knowledge of other workers on the system. In Engelbart's view, each individual's comprehension would be increased by the participation of others through a process of collective feedback facilitated by the computer.[10] Within the ARC group, this process of collective feedback was elevated to a principle of social organization. At the level of technological engineering, Engelbart promulgated a philosophy of "bootstrapping," in which each experimental transformation of the socio-technical system that was the NLS would feed back into the system itself, causing it to evolve (and presumably to improve). At the level of the group's social life, Engelbart worked to create an environment in which individual engineers might see themselves as both elements and emblems of a collaborative system designed to amplify their individual skills. Engelbart saw the individual and the computer, like the group and the computer system, as complementary elements in a larger information system—a system that would use cybernetic processes of communication and control to facilitate not only better office communication, but even the evolution of human beings.

This cybernetic framework aligned the ARC mission with the goals of two seemingly antithetical communities: the defense establishment and the counterculture. Starting in 1963, much of the ARC group's work was funded by the Defense Department's Advanced Research Projects Agency (ARPA). ARPA was founded in 1958 with the aim of sparking new research into defense-oriented technologies. In 1962 it established the Information Processing Techniques Office, headed by Joseph C. R. Licklider; this was the office that would ultimately drive the development of the Internet. In many ways, ARPA marked an extension of the defense-oriented military-university collaborations that began in World War II. Likewise, Licklider's vision of computing grew out of the cybernetic ideal of human-machine integration. After World War II, Licklider became a professor of psychology at MIT, where he worked on a variety of projects descended from MIT's wartime commitments. He was steeped in the cybernetic theories of his colleague Norbert Wiener, and it showed. In a highly influential 1960 paper entitled "Man-Computer Symbiosis," Licklider imagined a form of human-machine collaboration that surpassed even Vannevar Bush's vision for the Memex: "The hope is that, in not too many years, human brains and computing machines will be coupled together very tightly, and that the resulting partnership will think as no human brain has ever thought and process data in a way not approached by the information-handling machines we know today." Licklider, like Bush and Engelbart, envisioned the computer becoming a communications device; along with the user and as part of a whole information system, it might, properly deployed, be of use to humanity as a whole. "Man-computer symbiosis," he suggested, should produce "intellectually the most creative and exciting [period] in the history of mankind."[11]

At one level, then, Engelbart's vision for the NLS owed a great deal to the work of Bush and Licklider and to the research culture of World War II and its cold war offshoots. Engelbart's own allegiance to that community was strong: by 1969 SRI had become one of the first four nodes on the ARPANET, which would develop into the Internet, and Engelbart's own ARC group, hoping to spark widespread adoption of the NLS, had become hosts to the ARPANET's Network Information Center. At another level, Engelbart's humanitarian ideals and his group's emphasis on the augmentation of human intellectual capacities resonated well with the New Communalist emphasis on transforming human consciousness. Engelbart's group bore a strong resemblance to groups like USCO and the Merry Pranksters. Like those groups, the Augmentation Research Center featured a relatively leveled community led by a visionary. Also like those groups, ARC was devoted to changing the prospects for humankind by using small-scale technologies to augment human consciousness. Moreover, individual members of ARC maintained substantial connections to various elements of the counterculture. In the late 1960s, Engelbart and others experimented with LSD and visited several communes; in 1972 they attended sessions of Werner Erhard's Erhard Seminar Training (EST) movement. As Engelbart later recalled, he was "very empathetic to the counterculture's notions of community and how that could help with creativity, rationality and how a group works together."[12]

Brand had met various members of the ARC group through Dick Raymond at the Portola Institute and through parties at the house of Bill English, ARC's chief engineer and builder of the first computer mouse.[13] As members of the ARC group became more intrigued by the burgeoning commune movement, Brand helped bring the two communities together. Steve Durkee, of USCO and the Lama Foundation, began to visit the ARC offices. Doug Engelbart and Bill English later traveled to New Mexico and the Libre commune, where they met with Steve Baer, the Whole Earth Catalog's foremost authority on geodesic domes. In the fall of 1969, Dave Evans, a member of the ARC group, staged a three-day event called Peradam in the woods near Santa Barbara, in which he brought together technologists and members of the New Communalist movement. Participants represented research institutes such as SRI and the Ecology Center and countercultural organizations such as Zomeworks (builders of domes), Portola, and the Hog Farm commune. They also included high school students (from Pacific High) and office designers (from Office Design). Stewart Brand, who also attended the event, featured it in the January 1970 supplement to the *Whole Earth Catalog*.[14]

Even as Brand was helping introduce the members of ARC to the commune-based readership of the *Whole Earth Catalog,* his connections to the group introduced him to the future of computing. In 1968 Dave Evans recruited Brand to serve as a videographer for an event that would become known as the "mother of all demos."[15] On December 9 of that year, at the Association for Computing Machinery / Institute of Electrical and Electronics Engineers (ACM / IEEE)–Computer Society's Fall Joint Computer Conference in San Francisco, Engelbart and members of the ARC team demonstrated the NLS system to three thousand computer engineers. Engelbart sat on stage with a screen behind him depicting both himself and the text he was working on. His system was linked via telephone lines and microwave channels to a terminal at SRI. In the course of the presentation, Engelbart demonstrated the key features of the personal computer interface to come—including the mouse-keyboard-screen combination we now take for granted—for the first time ever in public. Moreover, he showed that computers could be used for complex group communications over long distances and for the enhancement of individual and collective learning. By all accounts, the audience was electrified.[16] For the first time, they could see a highly individualized, highly interactive computing system built not around the crunching of numbers but around the circulation of information and the building of workplace community.

Stewart Brand later remembered his role on that day as "just a gig, a one-shot deal."[17] Yet the *Whole Earth Catalog,* which Brand had started only months before, would ultimately embody many of the ARC group's assumptions about the ideal relationship between information, technology, and community. Like the NLS, the *Catalog* would link multiple, geographically distributed groups and allow them to collaborate—albeit not in real time. And like the hyperlinked texts of Engelbart's system, the *Whole Earth Catalog* presented its readers with a system of connections. In the *Catalog,* no text stood apart from every other; each was part of an informational or social system, and each offered a doorway through which the reader could enter one of those systems.

In the early 1970s, the *Catalog* came to model the potential integration of New Communalist ideals and information technology for researchers at Xerox PARC and for the leaders of the region's emerging computer hobbyist culture. Founded in 1970 primarily to serve as a research laboratory for a recently acquired computer subsidiary, Xerox PARC substantially extended the trajectory of human-computer integration outlined by Bush and Licklider and pursued by Engelbart's ARC group. Within ten years, researchers there had designed a computer for individual use (the Alto), an internal network with which to link these computers together (the first Ethernet), a graphical user interface, and the laser printer, among many other innovations. For the most part, these innovations grew out of a technical tradition associated with the ARPA community and with Engelbart's ARC group. One of the very first hires at Xerox PARC was Robert Taylor, who had led ARPA's Information Processing Techniques Office since 1966. Taylor in turn recruited Bill English and a dozen other members of Engelbart's ARC group, hoping that they would bring their understanding of the NLS with them.[18] Along with members of the ARC team, Taylor recruited a number of talented young programmers and engineers whom he had met in a series of graduate student symposia sponsored by ARPA. One of the most prominent of these was Alan Kay. In 1969 Kay's PhD dissertation at the University of Utah had described an interactive desktop computer; as early as 1967, Kay had proposed a portable variation on that computer that he called the Dynabook. Kay's Dynabook would soon provide a guiding vision for Xerox PARC's pursuit of its own individualized computer, the Alto.

Within the various teams concerned with developing the Alto, two communities emerged. One group, based in PARC's Computer Science Laboratory and including designers Butler Lampson and Charles Thacker, focused on developing the architecture of the Alto and the Ethernet and on pushing the limits of computer design. The other, housed in the Systems Science Laboratory and including Alan Kay, Bill English, and software engineer Larry Tesler, concentrated on questions of how and why a computer might be used. By all accounts, Kay was among the most devoted to making computers into user-friendly tools for communication and creative expression.[19] Much of his drive in that direction came from within the world of computer research. In his first weeks in graduate school, for instance, the professor who recruited him handed him a copy of Ivan Sutherland's 1963 MIT PhD dissertation, "Sketchpad: A Man-Machine Graphical Communications System." In it Sutherland described how to use a light pen to create engineering drawings directly on the CRT screen of a computer. In 1968 Kay met with Seymour Papert and encountered Papert's LOGO programming language, a language so simple that it could be used by children. In both cases, Kay discovered visions of interactive, creative computing that had developed within the centers of technological research, far away from the Bay area's counterculture.

But Kay had also found the *Whole Earth Catalog*. He first saw a copy in 1969, in Utah. "I remember thinking, 'Oh yeah, that's the right idea,'" he explained in 2004. "The same way it should be easier to do your own composting, you should have the ability to deal with complicated ideas by making models of them on the computer." For Kay, and for others at Xerox PARC, the *Catalog* embodied a do-it-yourself attitude, a vision of technology as a source of individual and collective transformation, and a media format—all of which could be applied to the computers on which they were working. As Kay explained, he had already begun to think of the computer as a "language machine where content was the description of things." When he saw the *Catalog,* it offered him a vision of how an information system might organize that content. He and others at PARC saw the *Catalog* as an information *tool* and, hence, as an analogue to the computer; at the same time, they saw it as a hyperlinked information *system*. In that sense, remembered Kay, "we thought of the *Whole Earth Catalog* as a print version of what the Internet was going to be." Kay and his colleagues in the Systems Science Laboratory paid particular attention to the *Catalog*'s design. In the *Last Whole Earth Catalog* of 1971, for example, they came upon *Divine Right's Trip,* a novel by Gurney Norman that Stewart Brand had decided to print one page at a time on each page of the *Catalog*. This was "one of the best user interface ideas we had ever seen," Kay recalled.[20] Most users of information systems tend to browse in areas they are already interested in, said Kay. Brand had found a way to lead users through the system and expose them to its full range of offerings.

For Kay and others at PARC, the *Catalog* was a conceptual resource book and a legitimator of their own work. As Kay put it, "a lot of good ideas were had by idling through the *Catalog* when you didn't know what you were looking for." Larry Tesler agreed. "I looked through every page," he explained. "It was a big event to get [a new copy of the *Catalog*]."[21] When Xerox PARC established its own library, the new librarian asked Kay to help stock its shelves. He took her to the Whole Earth Truck Store, and together they bought a copy of every book there. The PARC library thus became something of a three-dimensional *Catalog* for PARC engineers, a place where they could relax and browse, but also a place whose terms had been set in part by the browsing Stewart Brand had already done. For the engineers at PARC, the *Catalog* represented much of what was most exciting about the countercultural world outside their laboratory walls. It did so, however, in terms that celebrated the elite, technocentric, self-sufficient ethos that characterized PARC itself. Although PARC researchers did not couch their work in countercultural terms, many did see themselves as explorers on the edge of a technological frontier. In Palo Alto they found themselves working in a self-sufficient group, far from the company's home base in Rochester, New York, and via their machinery inventing new tools for communication and collectivity. At a time when the Vietnam War had widely discredited the military establishment, the *Catalog* offered them a way to imagine their own research not only as an extension of the academic-military-industrial collaborations that had spawned the ARPA community, but as a variation of the New Communalist project of working in small, forward-thinking groups to develop new forms of consciousness and community with the aid of small-scale technologies.

The *Catalog* performed similar ideological work within two other groups that would play an important role in imagining the use of computers in countercultural terms: the *People's Computer Company* and Resource One. The *People's Computer Company* got its start at the Portola Foundation, alongside the *Whole Earth Catalog*. Bob Albrecht, a former engineer for the Control Data Corporation and Honeywell, had been teaching computing in public schools since the early 1960s. In 1968 he set up an office at the Portola Institute, and over the next few years, his office came to house both the computers he used in the schools and a technical-writing business called Dymax (after Buckminster Fuller's Dymaxion principle). As a result of his work in the schools, Albrecht had long imagined computers as tools that could be used by individuals to enhance their own learning. In the course of his work at Portola, however, this vision took on a countercultural cast. In 1972 he and his wife Mary Jo, several staffers from Dymax, and Lois Brand, as bookkeeper, founded a more or less bimonthly newspaper, the *People's Computer Company* and, shortly thereafter, a storefront center called the People's Computer Center that offered public access to computers. Over the next five years, the newspaper became one of the first and most important information sources for hobbyists and others hoping to personalize their experience of computing. With a circulation of eight thousand copies, the *People's Computer Company* (PCC) printed articles about BASIC programming language and how to use it, discussions of various hardware technologies, reviews of books, and pointers to various user groups. In 1976 it spun off another influential computer publication that continues to this day, *Dr. Dobb's Journal of Tiny BASIC Calisthenics and Orthodontia* (now known simply as *Dr. Dobb's Journal*).

One look at the *PCC* alerted the reader that this was not a mainstream computer-industry publication. Laid out in blocky, letterpress text and illustrated with neo-Victorian borders and funky line drawings, it looked more like an underground newspaper than an organ of the high-technology industry. In large part, this look reflected the *PCC*'s debt to the *Whole Earth Catalog*. The first issues of the *PCC* were laid out using the *Whole Earth Catalog*'s equipment. In later editions, the *PCC* reprinted whole pages of the *Catalog*. And throughout its existence, the *PCC* advertised and sold books by *Catalog*-connected authors. As Bob Albrecht put it some years later, "I was heavily influenced by the *Whole Earth Catalog*. I wanted to give away ideas."[22] By borrowing the look and the feel and sometimes the contents of the *Catalog*, the *PCC* directly linked the hobbyist pursuit of BASIC code to the New Communalist search for tools of personal and collective transformation. In January of 1975, for example, the editors of the *PCC* decided to put the first widely available hobbyist computer—the Altair—on their cover. But rather than depict the machine alongside other machines, or even with technology-savvy users, the *PCC* displayed an Altair set out in a desert. Much like the backpacks and handsaws of the *Whole Earth Catalog*, the *PCC*'s high-tech Altair appeared to be a tool with which to get back to the land.

In this way, the *Catalog* provided a framework within which engineers and hobbyists could link their own desires for both certain forms of information processing and countercultural legitimacy to the shifting capacities of new computing machines.[23] The *Catalog* offered new ways to imagine the possibilities of computers and also legitimated the use of computers in nontraditional settings such as classrooms and public storefronts by linking those uses to a New Communalist ethos. This was particularly true for people seeking to use time-sharing computers for peer-to-peer public computing. Lee Felsenstein, for example, was a former computer engineer, a participant in the Free Speech Movement, and an antiwar activist. He had written for the underground newspaper the *Berkeley Barb,* and he would go on to help found the Homebrew Computer Club. Felsenstein remembers the *Whole Earth Catalog* as a sort of Bible of countercultural technology. At that time, he explains, technology was a "secular religion" in mainstream America; with the *Catalog,* in contrast, Stewart Brand "set up an alternate temple of the same religion, of the church of technology, telling people in technological society that people needed to learn to use tools." For those who, like Felsenstein, were both trained engineers and participants in the youth movements of the 1960s, this new religion offered a way forward. In Felsenstein's words, the *Whole Earth Catalog* reminded its readers that "you don't have to leave industrial society, but you don't have to accept it the way it is."[24]

In the summer of 1971, Felsenstein joined Resource One, a gathering of former staffers from a volunteer switchboard and computer programmers who had left the University of California at Berkeley in protest of the invasion of Cambodia; Resource One was also a project partly funded by several thousand dollars Fred Moore had taken home from the *Catalog*'s Demise Party. At Resource One, Felsenstein and others sought to establish public computing terminals at several locations in the Bay area, with an eye toward creating a peer-to-peer information exchange. Ken Colstad, a member of the project, described its aims in a 1975 issue of the *People's Computer Company* thus: "Such a horizontal system would allow the public to take advantage of the huge and largely untapped reservoir of skills and resources that resides with the people. . . . [It would] counteract the tendencies toward fragmentation and isolation so visible in today's society." On the next page, in an article entitled "A Public Information Network," Efrem Lipkin made a similar point: "People must gain a sense of understanding of and control over the system as a tool. . . . [Computer] intelligence should be directed toward instructing [the user], demystifying and exposing its own nature, and ultimately giving him active control."[25]

The concept of building a peer-to-peer information system and the idea that individuals needed to gain control over information and information systems had been features of both the New Communalist movement and the New Left for some time. Yet, the notion of doing these things with computers was relatively new, at least outside the walls of SRI and Xerox PARC. For those who hoped to turn computing machines toward populist ends, the religion of technology espoused by the *Whole Earth Catalog* offered an important conceptual framework and source of legitimation. In the early 1970s, for example, Lee Felsenstein began to design the Tom Swift Terminal—a freestanding, easy-to-use terminal that would be as easy to repair as a radio. Although it was never built precisely to Felsenstein's first specifications, the Tom Swift Terminal design ultimately drove the creation of an early personal computer known as the Sol. Felsenstein envisioned the Tom Swift Terminal "as something that could be printed in the *Whole Earth Catalog*." As he saw it, the Terminal would be "a way to do things in line with the *Whole Earth Catalog* way to do things."[26] It might be built with technologies developed in the centers of American industry, but it could be used by individuals for their own purposes. With the *Catalog* and Brand himself as models, the Tom Swift Terminal offered Felsenstein the chance to see himself not simply as a trained engineer, but as a Fulleresque Comprehensive Designer.

In 1975 Felsenstein, along with several members of the *People's Computer Company* staff, would help create the Homebrew Computer Club. Many of the other early members of the club would be recruited from a list of people who had inquired about the People's Computer Center; Fred Moore compiled the list and passed it on to the club's first host, Gordon French.[27]

Within Homebrew, as within the *People's Computer Company* and Resource One, there was an ethos of information sharing, of peer-to-peer collaboration, and of information technology as something around which to build a community. That ethos would ultimately help drive the creation of Apple Computer and a number of other ventures, yet it was not the exclusive property of the Homebrew hobbyists. It belonged as well to the engineers of the ARPA community and Xerox PARC. Stewart Brand had entrepreneurially linked the two communities, and in the *Whole Earth Catalog,* he had offered key members of both a reflection of their technological ideals. He had also legitimated those ideals as elements in a larger New Communalist project.

Although the *Catalog* bridged cybernetics and the back-to-the-land movement, however, Brand himself had done little to address computers per se. That began to change in 1972, when, in the pages of *Rolling Stone* magazine, he gathered together the descendants of midcentury military research on computing and the members of the emerging countercultural hobbyist community. Not long after the *Catalog's* Demise Party, the editor of *Rolling Stone,* Jann Wenner, commissioned Brand to investigate the Bay area computer scene. Brand produced one of the first (and still one of the most widely quoted) pieces of journalism to link corporation- and government-funded computer research to New Communalist ideals: "Spacewar: Fanatic Life and Symbolic Death among the Computer Bums."

As its title suggests, the piece focused on the legendary computer game Spacewar. In October 1972 Brand and *Rolling Stone* photographer Annie Liebowitz slipped into the Stanford Artificial Intelligence Laboratory, convened a crew of programmers and researchers, and staged their own "Intergalactic Spacewar Olympics." Long-haired graduate students clustered around a PDP-10 time-sharing computer, entered a few commands, conjured up tiny triangular spaceships on the computer's monitor, and proceeded to blast each other out of the sky. In his story, Brand recorded not only the commands, but also the frantic delight of the players. He then turned their pleasure into evidence of the countercultural force of Spacewar, of computers, and of the freewheeling collaborative culture that surrounded them. "Ready or not, computers are coming to the people," Brand explained in the article's first lines. "That's good news, maybe the best since psychedelics." Stanford's AI lab was "the most bzz-bzz-busy scene I've been around since the Merry Prankster Acid Tests." The Spacewarriors themselves were "out of their bodies" in the game, not unlike high-tech versions of the turned-on dancers of the Trips Festival.[28]

In Brand's rhetoric, the Spacewarriors of the AI Lab became countercultural pioneers. And they were not the only ones. Leaving the stuffy Stanford basement, Brand took his readers to Xerox PARC, where he introduced them to Alan Kay and his Dynabook, and to the ARPANET as well. He then traveled to the offices of Resource One, where he presented the group's founder, Pam Hart. Both PARC and Resource One, he suggested, hoped to take computers out of their military, industrial, and academic contexts and turn them into tools for individuals to use as they saw fit. In that sense, both were making computers into tools for transformation in the *Whole Earth* tradition. They were also inventing a new, collaborative, play-oriented culture. The programmers and engineers at PARC and Resource One had long distinguished between "hackers" (those who figured things out as they went and invented for pleasure) and "planners" (those who pursued problems according to a set and less flexible strategy). Brand picked up on this distinction and mapped it onto the larger, New Communalist critique of technocracy. Hackers, he wrote, were not mere "technicians," but "a mobile newfound elite, with its own apparat[us], language and character, its own legends and humor. Those magnificent men with their flying machines, scouting a leading edge of technology which has an odd softness to it; outlaw country, where rules are not decree or routine so much as the starker demands of what's possible." For Brand, Stanford's AI Lab and the Defense Department–funded research rooms of Xerox PARC were the equivalent of what he and others, following Buckminster Fuller, had lately called "outlaw zones." The hackers were Comprehensive Designers. Like the builders of geodesic domes, they drew on the funding and technology emanating from the center of the American military-academic-industrial triangle in order to build new, playful, emotionally and intellectually satisfying forms of collaboration. In Brand's report, planners stood for bureaucrats everywhere, and hackers became not mere technicians, but cultural revolutionaries. The computer became a tool for the establishment of a better social world: "The hackers made Spacewar, not the planners. When computers become available to everybody, the hackers take over. We are all Computer Bums, all more empowered as individuals and as co-operators. That might enhance things . . . like the richness and rigor of spontaneous creation and of human interaction . . . of sentient interaction."[29]

In "Spacewar," Brand brought together two visions of personal computing and linked them in terms set by the New Communalist technological vision. The user-friendly, time-sharing vision of Xerox PARC and the politically empowering, information-community vision of Resource One were two sides of the same coin, Brand implied. Both groups, he suggested, were high-tech versions of the Merry Pranksters, and the computer itself was a new LSD. Drawing on the rhetorical tactics of cybernetics, Brand offered up Xerox PARC, Resource One, and the Merry Pranksters as prototypical elites for the techno-social future. He allowed each to claim some of the cultural legitimacy of the others: in his feature, Resource One appeared to be not a fringe group of ex-hippies but a central player in a new computer movement. Xerox PARC, while still a child of the military-industrial complex, took on the cool of the Pranksters. And the Pranksters and Brand himself, six years after the Trips Festival, demonstrated that they had survived the Summer of Love and should still be regarded as harbingers of social change.

This coming together fed back into the organizations involved. At the People's Computer Center, where members of Resource One and the hobbyist community often dropped by, the "Spacewar" article was posted on a bulletin board. At Xerox PARC—if not at Xerox headquarters in Rochester, New York—the article was much loved.[30] Xerox executives resented the depiction of their elite research team as a bunch of long-hairs and restricted press access to them for years afterward. But the young programmers loved it: by appearing in *Rolling Stone,* they had in effect been compared to rock stars. For both groups, the article served as a mirror in which they could see themselves reflected as technologically savvy and counterculturally cool. They could imagine that to pursue the development of individualized, interactive computing technology was to pursue the New Communalist dream of social change. In the pages of *Rolling Stone,* the local work of individual programmers and engineers became part of a global struggle for the transformation of the individual and the community. Here, as in the *Whole Earth Catalog,* small-scale information technologies promised to undermine bureaucracies and to bring about both a more whole individual and a more flexible, playful social world. Even before minicomputers had become widely available, Stewart Brand had helped both their designers and their future users imagine them as "personal" technologies.

The End of Self-Sufficiency and the Rise of Coevolution

By 1972 Stewart Brand had become one of the most visible representatives of the New Communalist wing of the counterculture, and the *Catalog* was one of its most widely disseminated documents. The *Last Whole Earth Catalog* had sold more than a million copies and won the National Book Award. Brand himself was receiving invitations to speak around the world. Yet, both the New Left and the New Communalist movement had begun to dissolve. Between 1969 and 1971, antiwar protests had turned violent. The FBI had infiltrated the antiwar movement; the SDS had spawned the Weathermen. In 1970 a group of Weathermen accidentally set off a bomb they were building in a Manhattan townhouse. A few months later, members of the National Guard shot four students dead at Kent State University in Ohio. The

New Left came apart. Todd Gitlin recalls, "Anxiety and despair were most of what I knew. . . . The revolutionary mood [of the late 1960s] had been fueled by the blindingly bright illusion that human history was beginning afresh because a graced generation had willed it so. Now there wasn't enough life left to mobilize against all the death raining down."[31]

Members of the New Communalist movement were no more immune to the political winds howling around them. Although some communes— particularly those with a strong religious bent—still flourished, many had lasted only a year or two. In 1970, for example, sociologist Hugh Gardner had visited some thirty rural and urban communes; in 1973, when he returned to see how they were faring, he found most on the verge of collapse, if not gone already. This was true of the particular communes Stewart Brand had visited as well. In 1972 two New Mexico communes with strong links to San Francisco, Morning Star East and the Reality Construction Company, were thrown off their borrowed land; in 1973 Drop City was disbanded; the Lama Foundation continued, but by 1973 the Durkees and many of the original founders had left. Most communes collapsed for lack of sufficient political organization. The libertarian tribalism of Drop City was fun for a while, but the New Communalist emphasis on consciousness transformation rendered intentional communities vulnerable to charismatic leaders and, in their absence, anarchy. Moreover, few communes succeeded in generating sufficient income to keep going after gifts from family members and friends ran out. To survive, communities needed structures of governance and structured ways of making a living—the very institutional elements of social life that many New Communalists had hoped to avoid.[32]

In the coming years, many former New Communalists would turn toward the emerging New Age movement and toward a minor religious revival in the mid-1970s.[33] In the early part of the decade, though, many of those who had sought to live outside mainstream American culture found themselves forced to return to it and to confront its many failings head-on. The economy that had been so strong in the mid-1960s had turned sour: by 1970 unemployment was running at 6 percent, interest rates had reached new heights, and the economy as a whole found itself pinched between inflation and recession.[34] The resulting "stagflation," as it was called at the time, led the Nixon administration to institute wage and price controls. In early 1973 inflation picked up steam again, and in the fall of 1973 the Organization of Petroleum Exporting Countries established an oil embargo in response to America's support for Israel during the Yom Kippur War. By the time the embargo was lifted in the spring of 1974, oil prices had risen some 300 percent.

In 1973 the Nixon administration removed the last of America's combat troops from Vietnam. The war that had provoked a decade of demonstrations was ending, for Americans at least. But the end of the war did not provide an end to the sense of crisis among young Americans, or many of their elders. In addition to economic and energy concerns, Americans faced what many believed to be an imminent ecological disaster. Three best sellers—Paul Ehrlich's *The Population Bomb* (1970), Barry Commoner's *The Closing Circle* (1971), and the Club of Rome's *The Limits to Growth* (1972)—predicted that without substantial shifts in man's relationship to the earth, the earth as we know it might disappear. In 1974 a housewife from Chicago spoke for many Americans when she told a reporter from *Newsweek,* "You always used to think in this country that there would be bad times followed by good times. Now maybe it's bad times followed by hard times followed by harder times."[35]

For Stewart Brand, the early 1970s led to a brief period of wandering. After the Demise Party, Brand turned away from publishing for nearly three years. Rather than keep the profits from the *Last Whole Earth Catalog,* he used them to establish the Point Foundation, from which he and members of the *Whole Earth* circle, including Xerox's Bill English, doled out some eight hundred thousand dollars in small grants to a wide variety of cultural entrepreneurs. "There are coming to be Private Statesmen," Brand wrote in his journal in August 1971. "I seem to want to be one, and visualize an instrumentality to encourage them." Over the next few years, he helped manage Point, wrote articles for *Rolling Stone* and *Harper's,* and established an annual "New Games Tournament," in which individuals and teams dueled with foam rubber swords and tossed "earth balls" back and forth. In 1972 his marriage to Lois fell apart. Gradually, Brand began to find himself busy but with no single, overarching purpose. Like others in the New Communalist movement and, for that matter, the New Left, he had entered his early thirties without a clear picture of what adulthood might look like. "Most of my contemporaries were either blurred out or settling down to long-term work," he later wrote. "We no longer had any remnant of a Generational Story to sustain us from without."[36]

Under these pressures Brand returned to the *Whole Earth Catalog* and to cybernetics. In 1974 he published the *Whole Earth Epilog*—the first of a half dozen versions of the *Catalog* that would appear over the next twenty years—and turned its old *Supplement* into a new quarterly magazine that he edited for a decade, the *CoEvolution Quarterly* (commonly called *CQ*). Now that the New Communalist movement had faded away, the *Catalog* began to offer new, more broadly consumer-oriented items, such as guides to mountain bikes and macramé, while retaining its traditional look and feel. In *CQ,* however, Brand explicitly repudiated the *Catalog's* New Communalist origins. In a 1975 article, he put it this way:

> "Self-sufficiency" is an idea which has done more harm than good. On close conceptual examination it is flawed at the root. More importantly, it works badly in practice.
>
> Anyone who has actually tried to live in total self-sufficiency—there must be now thousands in the recent wave that we (culpa!) helped inspire—knows the mind-numbing labor and loneliness and frustration and real marginless hazard that goes with the attempt. It is a kind of hysteria. . . .
>
> . . . self-sufficiency is not to be had on any terms, ever. It is a charming woodsy extension of the fatal American mania for privacy. . . . It is a damned lie. There is no dissectable self. Ever since there were two organisms life has been a matter of co-evolution, life growing ever more richly on life. . . .
>
> We can ask what kinds of dependency we prefer, but that's our only choice.[37]

For Brand and the readers of *CQ*, the fading of the New Communalist dream and the entry into middle age posed a dilemma: Having just repudiated the mainstream adult world, how could they join it? And if they did find a way in, how could they bring with them their entrepreneurial habits and their celebration of small-scale technology and spiritual community? In the late 1960s, the elevation of consciousness into a principle on which to found communities had helped justify a mass migration to the rural wilds. In the early 1970s, many were seeking a view of consciousness that might justify a return to civilization.

In the pages of *CQ*, as in the *Whole Earth Catalog* before it, Brand supplied that view by turning to systems-oriented ecological theory and cybernetics. He explained in the first issue that the magazine took its name from the biological theory of "coevolution," in which two species evolved symbiotically. Brand traced the origin of this idea to a 1965 study of the relationship between certain predatory caterpillars and the plants they ate, conducted by his old teacher Paul Ehrlich and Peter Raven.[38] The first issue of *CQ* prominently featured an article by Ehrlich outlining his conceptual framework, entitled "Coevolution and the Biology of Communities." Yet, Brand considered coevolution to be more than a biological theory. It was a metaphor—derived from and carrying the legitimacy of science—for a new way of life. That metaphor depended not so much on Brand's reading of contemporary biology as it did on his reading of the mystical cybernetics of a former anthropologist, psychiatrist, and biological researcher, Gregory Bateson. Much as the ideas of Buckminster Fuller and Norbert Wiener had presided over the *Whole Earth Catalog*, Bateson's cybernetic vision permeated *CQ*. In the late 1960s, Fuller and Wiener had offered a vision of tool use that accorded well with youthful migrations back to the land; in the early and mid-1970s, Bateson offered a vision of the world itself as a system and of its inhabitants as potentially influential elements of that system, a view that neatly supported the New Communalists' return to mainstream America. In Bateson's vision, as in Brand's, former counterculturalists and the society around them would have to coevolve.

At one level, the turn toward coevolution marked a return to the systems orientation of the *Whole Earth Catalog*. At another, it represented a shift both in information theory and in its relationship to the New Communalist critique of technocracy. To the communities among which Stewart Brand moved in the 1960s—USCO, the downtown Manhattan art world, the communards of the back-to-the-land movement—cybernetics meant primarily the writings of Norbert Wiener. As Katherine Hayles has pointed out, Wiener represents the "first generation" of cyberneticians. This generation, which gathered during and immediately after World War II, understood cybernetics as the study of communication and control systems that could be observed from a position outside the systems themselves. A second wave emerged in 1960 with the publication of *Observing Systems,* Heinz von Foerster's collection of essays.[39] There von Foerster, who later became a charter subscriber to the *Whole Earth Catalog* and a friend of Stewart Brand, attempted to include observers as elements in the systems they observed. Within von Foerster's vision and later, within the work of a number of other cyberneticians, observer and system were inseparable.

Chronologically, Gregory Bateson belonged to the first wave of cybernetics. In 1942, not long after carrying out field work in the South Pacific and marrying fellow anthropologist Margaret Mead, he attended a meeting in New York City convened by the Macy Foundation with an eye to discussing hypnosis and conditioned reflexes. There he met Warren McCulloch and Arturo Rosenblueth, and he heard Rosenblueth present the concept of feedback that he had lately developed with Norbert Wiener and Julian Bigelow. As Steve Heims has pointed out, both physical and social science had up until that time focused on linear models of causality. Despite the appearance of circular models in Einstein's general theory of relativity, most scientists believed that circular patterns of causality could not be modeled or verified mathematically, and so could not be studied. Rosenblueth's version of causality, however, was both genuinely new and open to study with traditional mathematical methods. In 1946, as soon as World War II had ended, the Macy Foundation convened the first of ten meetings to explore these and other insights of cybernetics. These meetings went on until

1953 and served as the principal site where the cyberneticians of MIT and elsewhere met social scientists and psychologists like Bateson and Mead and, through them and others, exported the cybernetic vision from the laboratory into the social sphere.[40]

Bateson's encounter with cybernetics informed his work for the rest of his life. In the twenty years following World War II, he transformed cybernetic principles into communication-based theories of alcoholism, schizophrenia, and learning. By the late 1960s, he had embraced the insights of second-wave cybernetics and developed a global, communication-based theory of being and evolution. In a series of essays published in a 1972 best seller entitled *Steps to an Ecology of Mind,* Bateson outlined a vision of the natural world as a set of information systems in interaction with one another. Individuals were both elements of this larger system and systems in their own right: "The individual mind is immanent but not only in the body. It is immanent also in pathways and messages outside the body; and there is a larger Mind of which the individual mind is only a sub-system. This larger Mind is comparable to God and is perhaps what some people mean by 'God,' but it is still immanent in the total interconnected social system and planetary ecology." Through cybernetics, Bateson explained, humans could finally recognize that the individual was no more than "a servosystem coupled with its environment." The notion that the individual "mind" somehow stood apart from the body or even from the larger world was simply a relic from the industrial and even pre-industrial eras of human civilization. Thanks to the work of the cyberneticians, he believed, citizens of the late twentieth century could finally recognize mind as a property of the aggregate interactions of individuals with their surroundings.[41]

Bateson's theory of immanent mind held enormous appeal for counterculturalists in the early 1970s, in large part because it echoed the New Communalist focus on shared consciousness. Yet, whereas the New Communalists had pursued the experience of collective transcendence, Bateson rejected transcendence entirely. Bateson taught that mind existed here and now, as the property of local collaboration between individuals and the social and natural systems of which they were a part. Mind could no more be separated from the material world than communes built on transcendent consciousness could survive beyond the reach of material forms of governance. In this way, Bateson's theory allowed New Communalists to reject the doctrines of self-sufficiency they had associated with transcendence, which had clearly failed in the field. With Bateson's second-wave cybernetics, they could accept their own increasing need to collaborate with mainstream society as a variation on the truth that no one could live outside "the system." To try—as many so recently had—was simply to court disaster.

Yet, Bateson's theory of immanent mind also offered those who took it up a way to recover their sense of themselves as world-savers. In *Steps to an Ecology of Mind*, Bateson proposed that although the immediate causes of what appeared to be an impending ecological crisis might be technological and social, the ultimate cause was epistemological. He pointed out in an essay entitled "Effects of Conscious Purpose on Human Adaptation" that individual consciousness was always engaged in processes of individual learning and cultural change. These processes shaped man's relationship to the natural world and so offered the individual an opportunity to change that world. At the moment, Bateson argued in 1972, what the natural world needed most was preserving. Over the previous century, certain "self-maximizing entities," such as corporations and governments, had turned the individual human being into "a dehumanized creature."[42] By recognizing the degree of their integration into the natural and social systems around them, he suggested, individuals could simultaneously restore their individual humanity and act more humanely toward the planet as a whole.

Bateson's vision clearly echoed the New Communalist critique of technocracy. Like the former commune dwellers, Bateson offered a new consciousness as an alternative to the destructive, mechanistic forces of bureaucratic America. Yet he did not call for the establishment of alternative communities. For Bateson, mind was simply present in all social and natural relations. To recognize that immanence and to act in accord with it (and thereby possibly save the world from ecological disaster), individuals need not join an alternative community; they could simply work to influence whatever local "system" in which they found themselves involved. In this way, Bateson offered a generation that had set out for the woods fully believing that they could save the world a chance to make their way back with their faith in their own importance still intact. Although the individual could not stand outside the "system," Bateson's epistemology implied, he or she could save the system from within.

Throughout the 1970s, Bateson exerted a substantial intellectual influence on *CQ*. After profiling Bateson for *Harper's* magazine in 1972, Brand introduced him to readers of *CQ* in 1974. In a series of articles and interviews over the next seven years, Brand presented Bateson to his readers much as he had presented Buckminster Fuller some years earlier. Brand's Bateson was an intellectual seeker, an autodidact and polymath possessed of an orphic speaking style and a childlike curiosity. Just as his theories of mind gave *CQ*'s readers a way to rationalize their return to society, Bateson himself served as an emblem of a possible adulthood. Like Fuller and, for that matter, like McLuhan and Wiener, Bateson had found a way to bridge high technology and communitarian idealism and to build a flexible career around their intersection.

Moreover, he had become an emotionally whole person. In 1980 Bateson died at the San Francisco Zen Center after a brief illness. His daughter, Mary Catherine, penned a long recollection of his death for *CQ*, in which she celebrated his affection for his children and grandchildren and described their visits to his bedside. After Bateson's life force had left his body, she recalled, she and a number of monks washed and tended his corpse and prepared it for cremation. In every way, her article suggested, this had been the end of a life well lived—perhaps even the life of a saint.

For a generation that had grown up in fear of cold war technocracy and the mechanistic adulthood it seemed to portend, the figure of Bateson, like that of Fuller before him, offered a way to celebrate the high-technology world of cybernetics without forgoing the full range of emotional and spiritual experience. And like the *Whole Earth Catalog, CQ* served as a forum for the discussion and integration of science, technology, mysticism, and right living. In its pages a reader might find an article on sanctuary in Cuba set next to a piece on neighborhood preservation or perhaps a technical discussion of a potentially useful but neglected metal alloy. At its peak, *CQ* had around thirty thousand subscribers, many, though by no means all, from northern California. Sized slightly smaller than a standard glossy magazine and printed on the familiar plain paper of the *Catalog, CQ* contained a mix of lengthy feature articles followed by briefer pieces and an assortment of *Catalog*-style reviews. Apart from the front feature section, it retained the categories of the *Catalog* and many of its contributors. Heavy on text and hand-drawn illustrations, light on photographs, and completely without advertising, *CQ* brought a do-it-yourself feel to the magazine genre.

CQ carried forward the down-home style of the *Whole Earth Catalog*, but it also made visible the disintegration of the *Catalog*'s characteristic techno-social ethos. In the *Catalog*, as in the back-to-the-land movement, small-scale technologies were depicted as tools to be used by individuals to construct communities. By dint of these individuals' efforts, their communities and their own lives would be more closely integrated into the landscape itself and the natural forces that governed it. Geodesic domes, for instance, may have been born in the world of cold war high technology, but, put to use on the plains of Colorado, they offered a way for communities to come closer to one another and to nature. They represented what would later be called "appropriate technology" or, in the language of the Whole Earth publications, "soft technology."[43] Although they emerged out of high-tech research and smokestack industrial processes, they could serve the local needs of their users and, ultimately, planetary health.

In *CQ* this tool-based, back-to-nature view of technology began to confront a different view, one in which technology served not as a tool with

which to build new communities, but as the host to communities themselves. In part, this vision derived from the work of Gregory Bateson. Bateson explicitly attacked mechanistic visions of the social and natural worlds,[44]
and his understanding of mind bore a mystical cast, but his vision of the
world as a set of interconnected information systems strongly echoed cold
war visions of the world as a mirror of the computer. In 1975 this implied
computational metaphor became attached to a specific technology: the
space station. That fall, Brand introduced *CQ* readers to Gerard O'Neill, a
Princeton physics professor. In 1969 O'Neill and his students had begun to
imagine a massive colony in space.[45] Powered by the sun, floating near the
vast mineral deposits of the moon and passing asteroids, O'Neill expected
this imaginary space colony to house a million people by the year 2000.
It would consist of two concentric, six-mile-long metal cylinders spinning in
opposite directions to generate gravity, and it would house a veritable Eden.
Each inhabitant would have five acres of land, and humans would coexist
with plants and animals in homeostatic harmony. In a much-circulated
painting by Don Norman, an illustrator who often worked for NASA, the
inside of the space colony bore a striking resemblance to the San Francisco
Bay area: colorful, clean, full of trees and water. Only the dome over the sky
and the slight curvature in the land itself revealed the technology on which
the colony depended.

By the mid-1970s, O'Neill's ideas had received widespread attention in
the press and a grant from the Point Foundation. When *CQ* wrote up
O'Neill's work in the fall of 1975, though, it sparked intense debate within
the Whole Earth community about the proper ways in which humans and
technology should coevolve. O'Neill's vision generated so many angry letters to the editor that Stewart Brand invited both members of his extended
network and the readership at large to mail in their opinions of the colony
for the next issue of the magazine. Close to two hundred responded, and
their letters, printed across seventy-five pages of the spring 1976 *CQ*, mark a
deep split in countercultural approaches to technology. On the one hand,
many regular contributors to *Whole Earth* publications remained wedded
to a small-is-beautiful view of technology. Essayist Wendell Berry made
their case vociferously. "The Fall 1975 issue displays a potentially ruinous
split between what I at least have thought to be coevolution and what I think
the energy lobby would unhesitatingly recognize as Progress," he wrote.
As far as Berry was concerned, O'Neill's project was nothing more than a
boondoggle for big business and big government. It was a "moral escape
valve," he wrote, and "yet another 'new frontier' to be manned by an elite
of experts."[46] Berry and those associated with soft technology were repelled
by the notion of living inside a closed technological system. Berry was a

small-scale farmer in Kentucky, and he and others like him sought to live in contact with the earth, not cut off from it.

On the other hand, many of *CQ*'s readers had lately confronted the harsh realities of rural living and the failure of their own communal experiments. For these readers, the chance to live inside a six-mile-long machine—at least in fantasy—offered a way to revivify the New Communalist dream. "I see the main issue of space colonies as religious," wrote Gurney Norman. He hoped that space colonies might become hippie cathedrals:

> I want the connection between the Indian Coyote tales and the Space colonies to be very direct and clean. I want the building of the colonies to encourage folk life and country music and old time religion, not discourage it. . . . I want there to be places for Neal Cassady and Nimrod Workman, and Merle Haggard. . . . In my head, I'm against all this space stuff. But in my heart, if they're goin' to build 'em, I want to be on one. I want to get to heaven, by hook or by crook.[47]

According to Stewart Brand, outer space could serve some readers "as a path, or at least a metaphor, for their own liberation." It was "free space"— never occupied and never inhabited. Its lack of oxygen and gravity were not so much hardships as opportunities. They opened space to settlement in ways that the materiality of the lands actually occupied by communes a decade before had always resisted. If the communes had collapsed, and with them the chance to imagine alternative ways of living, space colonies might offer the New Communalists a second chance. After all, as Brand put it, space was an "Outlaw Area too big and dilute for national control."[48]

Over the next few years, the debate about space colonies faded from view. However, its intensity in the pages of *CQ* marks an important change in the relationship of technology, and particularly information technology, to New Communalist ideals. For the readers of *CQ*, space colonies served as a rhetorical prototype. They allowed former New Communalists to transfer their longings for a communal home to the same large-scale technologies that characterized the cold war technocracy they had sought to undermine. Fantasies of a shared, transcendent consciousness gave way to dreams of technologically enabled collaboration in friction-free space. Within a decade, these fantasies would reappear in the rhetoric of cyberspace and the electronic frontier, and as they did, they would help structure public perceptions of computer networking technology. But in the late 1970s, they marked the final breakdown of the New Communalist movement. The communes of the late 1960s were almost all long gone.

And neither the soft-technology wing of *CQ*'s readership nor those who dreamed of traveling to space would see their socio-technical visions survive the decade. By 1979 space colonies remained little more than an elaborate fantasy. The soft-technology movement left a more widespread legacy. By the end of the decade, even urban Americans tried to conserve energy and to recycle their waste.[49] Even as many of the movement's conservationist ideals persisted, though, the hope that small-scale technologies might lead their users into utopian communion with one another vanished from public view.

Software, Hackers, and the Return of the Counterculture

In the early 1980s, former communards found themselves confronting both middle age and a changed political landscape. The buttoned-down, square-jawed former governor of California, Ronald Reagan, had assumed the presidency and promised to restore America to what he saw as its former military and economic greatness. A new era was coming into being, and in the pages of *CQ*, the shift was palpable. The magazine continued to run articles on ecology and reviews of books on topics such as voluntary simplicity and home remedies. But it also covered books on how to buy mutual funds, get a job, and manage grants. In 1980 Paul Hawken, cofounder of the garden tools company Smith & Hawken and a Point Foundation board member, began a series of articles on small business and the "new" economy that would be one of the most popular series in the magazine's history.[50] In the late 1960s, Stewart Brand and the first readers of the *Whole Earth Catalog* had set out to build an alternative America; little more than ten years later, most had returned to the mainstream, where, with varying degrees of success, they were trying to fit in.

In 1980 Brand tried to explain to a reporter from *Newsweek* what had changed. "It used to be back-to-basics. . . . Now it's mostly onward and up-ward," he said. Brand no longer described himself as serving a grand social experiment. Instead, he explained, "I'm a small-business man who is hit with the same kind of problems that face any small entrepreneur."[51] Throughout the interview, a sense of the counterculture's failures hung in the air. "We were the 'now generation' because we figured there would be no then," Brand told *Newsweek*.

> We were completely apocalyptic. The sky was falling, the population was exploding, people were starving, yet we went on. When the energy crisis finally happened in '73, we said, "Aha, it's here, the end of the world." It turned out we were wrong again. . . .

We were all outlaws who became responsible citizens—one of us [Jerry Brown] even governs California. We were looked at as the guiders of the culture. But we were also over-rewarded children. Can you imagine anything more boring than getting stoned all the time and bumping into each other?[52]

While Brand was lamenting the failure of the counterculture, the engineers and programmers he had inspired and celebrated in the early 1970s were enjoying extraordinary success. As Paul Ceruzzi has pointed out, the 1970s witnessed two waves in the development of the personal computer. The first, running roughly from 1972 to 1977, saw the rise of miniature computer technology, along with a variety of new interfaces, in parallel with the growth of a hobbyist community and, within it, new companies such as Apple and Microsoft devoted to producing minicomputers and software for public use. The second, which Ceruzzi dates from 1977 to 1985, saw the mass distribution of minicomputers into homes and offices nationwide. These computers bore the technological stamp of Xerox PARC and, in the case of Apple and its marketing campaign, at least, the cultural stamp of the Bay area hobbyists. By January 1983 minicomputers had become so ubiquitous and their effects on daily life so pronounced that *Time* magazine named the computer its "Machine of the Year."[53]

Since 1972 Brand had had almost nothing to do with computers. Nevertheless, in the early 1980s his cultural legitimacy, his networking skills, and the fame of the *Whole Earth Catalog* itself allowed him to broker a second encounter between the computer industry and the now much-faded counterculture. Ten years earlier, Brand had granted engineers and programmers a countercultural cachet. Now the computer industry returned the favor. In 1983 Brand's literary agent and friend from his forays into the Manhattan art scene in the early 1960s, John Brockman, proposed that Brand put together a *Whole Earth Software Catalog*. It would do for computing what the original had done for the counterculture: identify and recommend the best "tools" as they emerged. To Brockman and Brand, the timing looked right. The year before, Brockman had bought his own IBM PC and had begun to represent software makers, as well as authors of conventional books. And he had begun to make a lot of money. As *Wired* magazine later reported, he claimed that his clients had sold some $20 million worth of books, most of them computer-related, in 1983 alone.[54]

For his part, Brand had recently been recruited to join the faculty of an online educational project called the School of Management and Strategic Studies, sponsored by the Western Behavioral Sciences Institute in La Jolla, California. The School of Management employed the Electronic Information Exchange System (EIES) and had given Brand a modem-equipped

Kaypro II computer with which to access it. The students at the School of Management included representatives from business, academe, and government; the faculty included futurist Herman Kahn, climatologist Walter Orr Roberts, and anthropologist Mary Douglas. Brand was hired to teach a course called "Benign Social Genres"—that is, a course in understanding the organization of groups like Alcoholics Anonymous and others that Brand perceived as having a benign social impact.

What really excited Brand was the computer conferencing system itself. In the early 1980s, most commercial conferencing systems, such as CompuServe and the Source, focused on providing information for their customers to download. EIES, in contrast, emphasized conversation. Founded in 1975 by Murray Turoff, a former government official who had experimented in the 1960s with online group decision-making processes, EIES offered a series of private conferences that included representatives from industry, government, and academe. For seventy-five dollars a month plus the cost of phone calls, users could log on, enter their favorite conferences, and discuss whatever interested them. Brand felt that EIES represented a clear technological extension of the editorial world in which he was already living. The Whole Earth publications, he explained, depended on a "keyboard-enabled universe of people; electronic tools made easier what was already going on." Brand especially appreciated the system's ability to provide immediate feedback. Whereas the correspondence surrounding the *Whole Earth Catalog* and *CQ* had taken days in transit, e-mail on EIES moved at just under the speed of light. "I'm impressed," Brand told the readers of *CQ* in 1983: "By EIES, by computer conferencing, which I am reveling in, by the conferences I'm in, and by the Kaypro. Mind, it's like learning to drive in about 1924 with a Model T Ford, a big deal, and you get a flat tire every five miles, but it's adventurous. Word processing is technology I've been waiting half a lifetime for."[55]

Soon thereafter, John Brockman persuaded Doubleday to make a preemptive bid of $1.3 million for the rights to publish a *Whole Earth Software Catalog*. From a business point of view, the catalog was a failure. Like the original *Whole Earth Catalog*, the book was due to appear at least once a year and to be supplemented by a quarterly magazine that would update the book. Yet, for all of Doubleday's cash, the catalog appeared only twice and released only three of its quarterly reviews. For one thing, it had come too late to the party. By the fall of 1984, when the first *Software Catalog* appeared, the market for publications devoted to evaluating software was becoming crowded. For another, it was expensive to produce: writers knowledgeable about computing could command higher wages than the ten dollars per hour paid to most *CQ* staffers at that time, and, unlike the original *Whole*

Earth Catalog, much of the Software Catalog was to be printed on glossy paper. More importantly, the print-based catalog format, with its comparatively slow production process, simply could not keep up with the speed at which new software titles were being released. Of all his cultural interventions, Brand reports, "that was the time I felt most off the beat."[56]

Although it failed as a business, the Software Catalog succeeded in introducing new networks of technology journalists and technology developers to the Whole Earth community and in turning the Whole Earth network's collective gaze toward the digital horizon. Rather than establish new offices for his new project, Brand brought production of the Whole Earth Software Catalog—and the computer industry journalists he had recruited—into the offices of CoEvolution Quarterly. There the emerging culture of personal computing and the long-standing culture of the holistic counterculture mingled daily. The editor of the Software Review, for instance, was Richard Dalton, an experienced computer writer who went on to write a column for Information Week and to serve as an information technology consultant for a number of Fortune 500 companies. The Review's managing editor was Matthew McClure, a former head typesetter for the Whole Earth Catalog who had recently returned to the Bay area, broke, after ten years in a commune.

In addition to the offices of CQ, Brand and Art Kleiner, then editor of CQ, created a second cultural mingling point, online. Using the EIES system, they established a private conference through which software reviewers from around the country could submit their work for the Catalog. One of these reviewers was Kevin Kelly, the future executive editor of Wired magazine. The son of an executive for Time magazine, Kelly had spent years backpacking in Asia. Through his father, who had employed systems analysis techniques in his work, he had developed an interest in cybernetics. While traveling in the Middle East, he had also had a conversion experience and had become a born-again Christian. By the time he began contributing freelance pieces to CQ in 1980, Kelly was living in Athens, Georgia, writing freelance travel articles, editing a start-up magazine of his own called Walking Journal, and working in an epidemiology laboratory to support his writing.

Art Kleiner invited him to join the Software Conference on EIES. Once there, Kelly heard about an upcoming software industry gathering and decided to attend in the hope of meeting Stewart Brand. At the conference, Kelly pitched Brand the notion of producing an Essential Whole Earth Catalog, with Kelly himself as editor. Brand was noncommittal. He had liked Kelly's work on Walking Journal and his contributions to the Whole Earth Review, but he already had his hands full with his software-related projects. Soon after the conference, though, Brand replaced Richard Dalton as editor of the *Software Review* with Art Kleiner, and, logging on to EIES, offered Kleiner's editorship of *CoEvolution Quarterly* to Kelly—by e-mail. When Kelly flew out at Brand's invitation to meet and discuss the offer, he sported a long beard, and Brand was nervous: "I realized I'd hired a Christian fundamentalist to run my science magazine," he recalled. For his part, Kelly, a long-time reader of the *Whole Earth Catalog,* was delighted. "Here was an offer to do the only job I ever wanted," he later recalled.[57] He promptly returned to Georgia, quit his jobs, sold his business, and moved to Sausalito, where he rented a houseboat several hulls down from Brand's own.

In 1985 the *Software Catalog* folded and the *Software Review* merged with *CoEvolution Quarterly* to form the *Whole Earth Review.* By that time, Brand had taken several key steps toward integrating the ideas and people of the Whole Earth into the emerging world of networked computing. Having had a foot in both worlds himself, he had linked the two communities off-line, in person, in the shared offices of the *Whole Earth Software Catalog* and the *CoEvolution Quarterly,* and online, on EIES. With an eye for the sort of synergy that had once characterized the *Whole Earth Catalog,* he had created the conditions within which a network of conversations could move fluidly across the boundary between the online and off-line worlds. Brand had once again placed himself and the Whole Earth publications at the intersection of multiple communities—here, the residual countercultural and the flourishing technical—and offered a project within which they could collaborate. He had also engaged those communities in simultaneous conversations in several media: electronic, face-to-face, and print. Although the *Software Catalog* failed, the types of conversations it facilitated—and the multiple media forms within which those conversations took place—would become key features of the Whole Earth group's influence in the years to come.

So too would the new networks it created. In the middle of 1984, Brand and the staffs of *CQ* and the *Whole Earth Software Catalog* reached out to core members of the personal computing movement: hackers. They created a forum in which hackers could get to know one another—the first Hackers' Conference—and in the process, they put hackers and their concerns at the center of the Whole Earth community. That year, a handful of self-described computer hackers had been working with Art Kleiner, Kevin Kelly, and others to help generate ideas for the *Software Catalog.* But hackers as a group came to Brand's attention only when one of the *Catalog's* reviewers, a Bay area freelancer named Steven Levy, finished his book *Hackers: Heroes of the Computer Revolution.* In the book, Levy traced the origin of "hacking" back to the 1940s and the campus of MIT. There, at least a decade before the school began to teach computer programming to its undergraduates, the term referred to a particular style of work. According to Steven Levy, a "hack" was "a project undertaken or a product built not solely to fulfill some constructive goal, but with some wild pleasure taken in mere involvement."[58] The first *computer* hackers emerged at MIT in 1959. They were undergraduates who clustered around a giant TX-0 computer that had been built for defense research and then donated to MIT. Within several years, these undergraduates were joined by a variety of Cambridge-area teenagers and MIT graduate students and began working with a series of computers donated by the Digital Equipment Corporation (DEC). By 1966 most of these young programmers gathered on the ninth floor of Technology Square, in Marvin Minsky's Artificial Intelligence (AI) Laboratory (just two blocks away from Norbert Wiener's old Rad Lab).

Within the AI Lab, wrote Levy, echoing Stewart Brand's 1972 piece for *Rolling Stone,* there were two kinds of workers: planners and hackers. The planners were theoreticians, usually of the mind, who thought of computers as tools that could be used to generate or model information. The hackers focused on the computer systems themselves and on seeing what they could do. Within the lab, a culture clash emerged. Theory-oriented graduate students, equipped with well-funded and well-organized careers but not necessarily with computer programming expertise, resented the hackers' claims for computer time, as well as their freewheeling style. David Silver, for instance, was then a fourteen-year-old hanger-on at the lab who solved a seemingly impossible problem in designing a robot insect. He recalls that his work "drove [the AI theoreticians] crazy . . . because this kid would just sort of screw around for a few weeks and the computer would start doing the thing they were working on that was really hard. . . . They're theorizing all these things and I'm rolling up my sleeves and doing it . . . you find a lot of that in hacking in general. I wasn't approaching it from either a theoretical point of view or an engineering point of view, but from sort of a fun-ness point of view."[59]

According to Levy, this point of view characterized the work of two subsequent generations of innovators. The first comprised the "hardware hackers" of the 1970s. Clustered in and around the San Francisco Bay area, they included the young founders of Apple Computer, Steve Jobs and Steve Wozniak, as well as early proselytizers for personal computing such as Lee Felsenstein, Bob Albrecht, and Ted Nelson, a programmer who had authored a volume loosely based on the *Whole Earth Catalog* entitled *Computer Lib: You Can and Must Understand Computers Now.* For this generation, Levy suggested, computing was a form of political rebellion. Computers may have always been large and centralized, they may have always been guarded by institutionalized experts, and they may have been used to organize the war in Vietnam, but this generation would put them to new uses.

The second generation to follow the AI hackers of MIT knew little of this countercultural legacy. They were the "young game hackers" of the early 1980s.[60] They had grown up working with the minicomputers that the previous generation had struggled to invent, and they had turned them to a new purpose: fun. This generation worked in the shadow of Atari, maker of the game PacMan; but unlike Atari, which was infamous among computer designers for its organizational hierarchy, they also aimed to maintain an open management structure within their organizations. According to Levy, their designers would be "hackers"—semi-independent, creative individuals—not drones.

Levy argued that although they had not met, members of all three generations shared a single set of six values, a "hacker ethic":

> Access to computers—and anything which might teach you something
>   about the way the world works—should be unlimited and total. Always
>   yield to the Hands-On Imperative! . . .
> All information should be free. . . .
> Mistrust Authority—Promote Decentralization. . . .
> Hackers should be judged by their hacking, not bogus criteria such as
>   degrees, age, race, or position. . . .
> You can create art and beauty on a computer. . . .
> Computers can change your life for the better.[61]

As Levy suggests, this ethic emerged at a time when the sharing of information allowed everyone to profit. Throughout the 1960s, MIT hackers made whatever programs they designed available to one another. In fact, one common way to become a member of the hacker elite was to take one of these programs, improve on it, and make it available once again. Such improvements clearly benefited everyone in the AI Lab. Yet this sharing of information also characterized relationships between the hackers, MIT, and local corporations such as DEC and Bolt, Baranek, and Newman— corporations that were to play a leading role in the development of the personal-computer industry and the Internet. For example, when one hacker needed a particular subroutine to help create a local version of Spacewar, he simply drove over to DEC and took it; likewise, when DEC salesmen wanted to show off their computers to potential clients, they did so by demonstrating a borrowed copy of Spacewar. As Levy explains, MIT and DEC had "an easy arrangement," since "the Right Thing to do was make sure that any good program got the fullest exposure possible because *information was free* and the world would only be improved by its accelerated flow."[62]

This ethic also accorded well with the values espoused in the *Whole Earth Catalog*. Like the *Catalog,* the hacker ethic suggested that access to tools could change the world, first by changing the individual's "life for the better" and, second, by creating art and beauty. In keeping with the *Catalog's* habit of systems thinking, the hacker ethic characterized the tools themselves as prototypes: the computer was a rule-bound system that could serve as a model of the world; to study computers was to learn something about the world at large. Like the *Catalog,* the hacker ethic suggested that work should be organized in a decentralized manner and that individual ability, rather than credentials obtained from institutions, should determine the nature of one's work and one's authority. Finally, it insisted that access to both machines and information should be complete. Like the mystical energy that was supposed to circulate through the communes of the back-to-the-land movement, binding its members to one another, information was to circulate openly through the community of hackers, simultaneously freeing them to act as individuals and binding them in a community of like minds.

The hacker ethic helped make hackers particularly appealing to Stewart Brand and Kevin Kelly. Soon after Levy had shown them his book, Brand and Kelly got in touch with members of the hacking community, including Lee Felsenstein; Bill Budge, a software author; Andy Hertzfeld, a key member of Apple's Macintosh development team; and Doug Carlston, founder and president of Broderbund Software Inc. Together they invited some four hundred self-described hackers to pay ninety dollars each to join them, the Whole Earth crew, and about twenty mainstream journalists for a three-day weekend in November 1984 at Fort Cronkhite, a former army base in the Marin Headlands just across the Golden Gate Bridge from San Francisco.

At one level, the event was a master stroke of networking. Having been alerted to the existence of a new and potentially influential community by a member of their own Whole Earth network (Levy), Brand and Kelly reached out to that community and entrepreneurially extended and diversified their own networks. In that sense, Brand and Kelly bridged what sociologist Ronald Burt would call a "structural hole" between their own, largely countercultural, network and the networks that governed production within key parts of the computer and software industries. Steven Levy, of course, had made the first connection, along with Whole Earth staffers such as Art Kleiner, who had been talking with hackers like Lee Felsenstein about directions for the *Software Catalog.* Now Brand, Kelly, and others were building on these connections and opening a much broader road between the two communities. This outreach turned out to be of more than a little short-term use as they worked to start up the *Whole Earth Software Catalog* and the *Review*. At another level, organizing the conference was an act of deep cultural scouting. As Kelly later recalled, he and Brand wanted to see whether hacking was "a precursor to a larger culture." In particular, he suggested, they wanted to "witness or have the group articulate what the hacker ethic was."[63] Brand and Kelly aimed to explore via the conference whether hackers might constitute the sort of cultural vanguard for the 1980s that the back-to-the-land and ecology crowds had hoped to be for the decade before.

Something like 150 hackers actually arrived. Among others, they included luminaries such as Steve Wozniak of Apple, Ted Nelson, free software pioneer Richard Stallman, and Ted Draper—known as Captain Crunch for his discovery that a toy whistle he found in a box of the cereal gave just the right tone to grant him free access to the phone system. Some of the hackers worked alone, part-time, at home; others represented such diverse institutions as MIT, Stanford, Lotus Development, and various software makers. Most had come to meet others like themselves. Their hosts offered them food, computers, audiovisual supplies, and places to sleep— and a regular round of facilitated conversations.

By all accounts, two themes dominated those conversations: the definition of a hacker ethic and the description of emerging business forms in the computer industry. The two themes were, of course, entwined. The hacker ethic that Levy described—the single thread ostensibly running through all of the participants' careers—had emerged at a moment when sharing products and processes improved profits for all. By the mid-1980s, however, the finances of computer and software development had changed radically. As Stewart Brand pointed out, in what would soon become a famous formulation, information-based products embodied an economic paradox. "On the one hand," he said, "information wants to be expensive, because it's so valuable. The right information in the right place just changes your life. On the other hand, information wants to be free, because the cost of getting it out is getting lower and lower all the time. So you have these two fighting against each other."[64]

Throughout the conference, hackers discussed different ways they had managed this dilemma. Some, like Richard Greenblatt, an early and renowned MIT hacker, argued that source code must always be made freely available. Others, like game designer Robert Woodhead, suggested that they would happily give away the electronic tools they had used to make products such as computer games, but they would not give away the games themselves. "That's my soul in that product," explained Woodhead. "I don't want anyone fooling with that."[65] In discussion Bob Wallace said he had marketed his text editor PC-WRITE as shareware (in shareware, users got the software for free but paid if they wanted documentation and support), whereas Andrew Fluegelman indicated that he had distributed his telecommunications program PC-TALK as freeware (users voluntarily paid a small fee to use the software). Others, including Macintosh designer Bill Atkinson, defended corporate prerogatives, arguing that no one should be forced to give away the code at the heart of their software.

The debate took on particular intensity because, according to the hacker ethic, certain business practices—like giving away your code—allowed you to claim the identity of hacker. In part for this reason, participants in a morning-long forum called "The Future of the Hacker Ethic," led by Levy, began to focus on other elements of the hacker's *personality* and to modify their stance on the free distribution of information goods. For instance, participants agreed that hackers were driven to compute and that they would regard people who impeded their computing as bureaucrats rather than legitimate authorities. By and large, they agreed that although the free dissemination of information was a worthy ideal, in some cases it was clearly only an ideal. If they could not agree on proper hacker business practice, they could agree that being a hacker—in this case, being the sort of person who was invited to the Hackers' Conference—was valuable in its own right. Lee Felsenstein explained, "That little bit of cultural identity [was] extremely important." In the popular press, hackers had been characterized as machine-obsessed, antisocial, and potentially criminal loners. Gathered in the stucco halls of Fort Cronkhite, hackers could recognize themselves as something else. Lee Felsenstein recalls feeling empowered: "Don't avoid the word Hackers. Don't let somebody else define you. No apologies: we're hackers. We define what a hacker is . . . nobody else."[66]

In the end, the group did not come to any consensus on the right approach to take toward the emerging challenges of the software industry. But they had begun to reformulate their own identities, partially in terms of Whole Earth ideals. In the Hackers' Conference, Brand and company provided computer workers with a venue in which to develop and live a group identity around the idea of hacking and to make sense of emerging economic forms in terms of that identity. This work had the effect of rehabilitating hackers in the public eye, but it also explicitly and securely linked Whole Earth people and the Whole Earth ethos to the world of computing. Virtually all of the journalistic reports that came from the Conference echoed John Markoff's comments in *Byte* magazine: "Anyone attending would instantly have realized that the stereotype of computer hackers as isolated individuals is nowhere near accurate."[67] Some of those same reports picked up on another theme as well, however. Several either quoted or paraphrased Ted Nelson's exclamation "This is the Woodstock of the computer elite!"[68] One listed Stewart Brand among the "luminaries of the personal computer 'revolution.'" Another described Brand as a "long-time supporter of hackers."[69] Quietly, almost without noticing it, the invited reporters had begun to intertwine the countercultural play of Woodstock, and countercultural players such as Brand, with an industry and a work style that had emerged within and at the edges of such culturally central institutions as MIT, Stanford, and Hewlett-Packard. Hackers were not simply highly individualistic and innovative engineers; they were cultural rebels.

In his introduction to a transcript of the Hacker Ethic forum hosted by Levy that he published in *Whole Earth Review,* Brand celebrated the hackers as simultaneously technical, economic, and cultural pioneers:

> I think hackers . . . are the most interesting and effective body of intellectuals since the framers of the U.S. Constitution. No other group that I know of has set out to liberate a technology and succeeded. They not only did so against the active disinterest of corporate America, their success forced corporate America to adopt their style in the end. In reorganizing the Information Age around the individual, via personal computers, the hackers may well have saved the American economy. High tech is now something that mass consumers do, rather than just have done to them. . . . The quietest of the '60s sub-subcultures has emerged as the most innovative and most powerful—and most suspicious of power.[70]

Much of Brand's account, of course, is true. Some hackers, most famously perhaps Wozniak and Jobs, did confront uninterested corporations (in their case, Hewlett-Packard). At a local level, some of the early AI hackers did indeed set out to "liberate" MIT's giant mainframes from the "planners," if only during overnight programming sessions. Yet, when set against the history of the Whole Earth publications, Brand's remarks seem less like an accurate, if somewhat hyped, history of several generations of computer engineers than a recasting of that history in terms of the Whole Earth's own countercultural concerns and intellectual trajectory. After all, wasn't it the *Whole Earth Catalog* that had set out to liberate technology from its corporate and governmental contexts? And wasn't it the *Catalog* that had promoted the notion that the right tools, properly used, could help reform society? Could perhaps even save the "mass" economy by "personalizing" it?

However, Brand was not simply rewriting history to his liking here. Something much subtler was going on. Brand had gathered a normally geographically dispersed community under a single roof and literally given it voice. That community shared something of an ethic from the start, as Levy had shown, but it had other concerns as well—concerns with new working conditions and new digital technologies. Both Brand and the invited journalists built their accounts of those concerns on older symbolic foundations. That is, they linked the particular issues facing hackers to the broad themes of countercultural work generally and of the Whole Earth group in particular. They did not "report" a consensus generated by the invited hackers themselves so much as they melded the voices heard within the events' various forums with the principles along which those forums were organized and with the experience of unity within the forums. At the Hackers' Conference, Brand and his colleagues translated the individual experiences of three generations of hackers into a shared experience, an experience organized by Whole Earth people according to Whole Earth norms in the *Catalog*'s hometown.[71] In the post-event reporting, the concerns of conference-goers and the culture of the conference itself—the Whole Earth culture—became one, and Stewart Brand, rather than any of the hackers, arose as this fused culture's spokesman.

In the process, the New Communalist critique of technocracy was transformed into a tool with which to legitimate computer technologies and collaborative work styles that in fact emerged at the intersection of military, industrial, and academic research. As early as 1972, Brand had suggested that computers might become a new LSD, a new small technology that could be used to open minds and reform society. During the Super Bowl of 1984, Apple Computer introduced its Macintosh with a like-minded suggestion. Its mouse and monitor might have first been designed in research institutes funded by the Defense Department, but in the ad, a lithe blonde woman in a track suit raced up a theater aisle through row after row of gray-suited workers and threw a hammer into the maw of Big Brother on the screen. Thanks to the Macintosh, a voice then intoned, 1984 would *not* be like *1984*. Like the Merry Pranksters in their bus, the ad implied, the executives of Apple had unleashed a new technology on Americans that would, if they only embraced it, make them free.

By 1984 the New Communalist movement had disappeared. Nevertheless, thanks in large part to the entrepreneurship of Stewart Brand and the networks he assembled, its ideals lived on. In press accounts at least, the Long Hunter of the *Whole Earth Catalog*, the cultural adventurer who sought to inhabit an outlaw area, had become the Hacker. Equipped with the digital tools of his trade, he had converted the basements and back offices in which he worked into new, collaborative communities, from which he and his fellows would transform society. The world of the

New Communalists—the small-scale tools they treasured, the intense feelings of small-group camaraderie, and, above all, the faith that they were going to change the world—seemed to have come to life again. This time, though, the new world was being built not in the woods or on the open plains, but in the office, around the computer.

PLATE 1. Computing's state of the art in 1964, the IBM System/360. Courtesy of IBM Corporate Archives.

PLATE 2. Free Speech marchers at Berkeley wear computer cards as signs of protest, December 1964. Photograph by Helen Nestor. Used by permission of the photographer and by courtesy of the Helen Nestor Collection, the Oakland Museum of California.

PLATE 3. A photo collage of the USCO art group in front of their Garnerville, New York, church sometime in the mid-1960s. Stewart Brand and his first wife, Lois, stand farthest to the right. Courtesy of Gerd Stern.

PLATE 4. Stewart Brand around the time of the Acid Test Graduation, October 1966. He is wearing a button that reads, "Why haven't we seen a photograph of the whole earth yet?" Photograph by Gene Anthony, © wolfgangsvault.com. Used by permission.

PLATE 5. A handbill for the Trips Festival. Note the oscilloscope at the center of the image. For many at the festival, both LSD and small electronic devices served as technologies for the transformation of consciousness.

PLATE 6. Early residents of the Lama Foundation commune dance under a half-completed geodesic dome. Photograph © Dennis Stock. Used by permission of Magnum Photos.

PLATE 7. The cover of the first *Whole Earth Catalog.* Courtesy of Stewart Brand and Stanford University Special Collections.

WHOLE EARTH CATALOG

access to tools

Fall 1968

$5

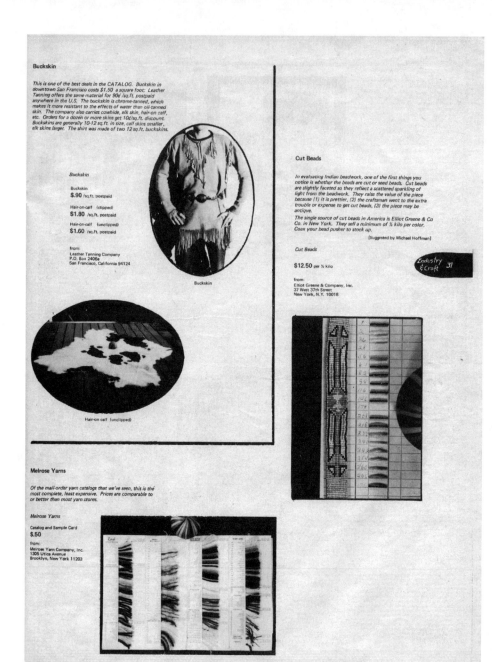

PLATE 8. Some of the items presented in the first *Whole Earth Catalog* suggested frontier handicraft. Courtesy of Stewart Brand and Stanford University Special Collections.

9100A Calculator

The best of the new table-top number crunchers is this Hewlett-Packard machine. It is programmable, versatile, and silent—more so than its competition. Portola Institute currently is using the 9100A to help kids gain early mastery over computers—it is a superb inquiry machine.

Specs: 9100A can do addition, subtraction, multiplication, division, square root, $\log x$, $\ln x$, e^x, $\sin x$, $\cos x$, $\tan x$, $\sin^{-1}x$, $\cos^{-1}x$, $\tan^{-1}x$, $\sinh x$, $\cosh x$, $\tanh x$, $\sinh^{-1}x$, $\cosh^{-1}x$, $\tanh^{-1}x$, polar to rectangular and vice versa co-ordinate transformations. Number range is 10^{-99} to 10^{99}. The magnetic core memory has 19 registers: 3 display and 16 storage. Display is decimal or floating point. Program capacity is 196 steps. Programming is done by pressing keys in proper sequence (no special language required). Programs may be stored on wallet sized magnetic cards. Typical operations take 2-280 milliseconds. Weight of the machine is 40 lbs, dimensions 8"x16"x19"deep. Reportedly the following accesories will be available soon: printer, xy plotter, input/output interface.

[Suggested by Robert Albrecht]

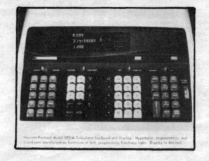

Hewlett-Packard Model 9100A Calculator keyboard and display. Hyperbolic, trigonometric, and coordinate transformation functions at left, programming functions right. Display is decimal.

HP 9100A

$4900.00 65 lbs shipping weight

from:
P.O. Box 301
Loveland, Colorado 80537

34. Communications

Cybernetics

McLuhan's assertion that computers constitute an extension of the human nervous system is an accurate historical statment. The research and speculation that led to computer design arose from investigation of healthy and pathological human response patterns embodied in the topological make-up of the nervous system. Insights here soon expanded into generalizations about communication that permitted the building of analgous electronic devices physically separate from the Central Nervous System. But they're just one artifact of these new understandings about communication. Society, from organism to community to civilization to universe, is the domain of cybernetics. Norbert Wiener has the story, and to some extent, is the story.

To predict the future of a curve is to carry out a certain operation on its past.

The central nervous system no longer appears as a self-contained organ, receiving inputs from the senses and discharging into the muscles. On the contrary, some of its most characteristic activities are explicable only as circular processes, emerging from the nervous system into the muscles, and re-entering the nervous system through the sense organs, whether they be proprioceptors or organs of the special senses. This seemed to us to mark a new step in the study of that part of neurophysiology which concerns not solely the elementary processes of nerves and synapses but the performance of the nervous system as an integrated whole.

The feedback of voluntary activity is of this nature. We do not will the motions of certain muscles, and indeed we generally do not know which muscles are to be moved to accomplish a given task; we will, say, to pick up a cigarette. Our motion is regulated by some measure of the amount by which it has not yet been accomplished.

I have spoken of the race. This is really too broad a term for the scope of most communal information. Properly speaking, the community extends only so far as there extends an effectual

transmission of information. It is possible to give a sort of measure to this by comparing the number of decisions entering a group from outside with the number of decisions made in the group. We can thus measure the autonomy of the group. A measure of the effective size of a group is given by the size which it must have to have achieved a certain stated degree of autonomy.

Thus small, closely knit communities have a very considerable measure of homeostasis; and this, whether they are highly literate communities in a civilized country or villages of primitive savages. Strange and even repugnant as the customs of many barbarians may seem to us, they generally have a very definite homeostatic value, which it is part of the function of anthropologists to interpret. It is only in the large community, where the Lords of Things as They Are protect themselves from hunger by wealth, from public opinion by privacy and anonymity, from private criticism by the laws of libel and the possession of the means of communication, that ruthlessness can reach its most sublime levels. Of all of these anti-homeostatic factors in society, the control of the means of communication is the most effective and most important.

The mongoose begins with a feint, which provokes the snake to strike. The mongoose dodges and makes another such feint, so that we have a rhythmical pattern of activity on the part of the two animals. However, this dance is not static but develops progressively. As it goes on, the feints of the mongoose come earlier and earlier in phase with respect to the darts of the cobra, until finally the mongoose attacks when the cobra is extended and not in a position to move rapidly. This time the mongoose's attack is not a feint but a deadly accurate bite through the cobra's brain.

In other words, the snake's pattern of action is confined to single darts, each one for itself, while the pattern of the mongoose's action involves an appreciable, if not very long, segment of the whole past of the fight. To this extent the mongoose acts like a learning machine, and the real deadliness of its attack is dependent on a much more highly organized nervous system.

To use a biological analogy, the parallel system had a better homeostasis than the series system and therefore survived, while the series system eliminated itself by natural selection. We thus see that a non-linear interaction causing the attraction of frequency can generate a self-organizing system.

Cybernetics — or Control and Communication in the Animal and the Machine

Norbert Wiener
1948,1961: 212 pp.

$1.95 postpaid

from:
The M.I.T. Press
Cambridge, Mass. 02142
or
WHOLE EARTH CATALOG

PLATE 9. Other items represented the state of the art in high technology. Courtesy of Stewart Brand and Stanford University Special Collections.

PLATE 10. In 1968 Brand manned a video camera for Douglas Engelbart's team at the Fall Joint Computer Conference held in San Francisco. The team demonstrated for the first time ever in public a computer system with the mouse-keyboard-screen combination interface that we now take for granted. Pictured here are Mary Church (*back to camera*), Marin Hardy, Dave Evans, Ed Van de Reit, Dan Lynch (?), Stewart Brand (*behind the camera*), Roger Bates, and Bill English (*sitting*). Courtesy of Douglas C. Engelbart and The Bootstrap Institute.

PLATE 11. The MITS Altair, one of the first minicomputers for hobbyists, depicted on the cover of the *People's Computer Company* as if it were a tool with which to return to nature. Courtesy of the *People's Computer Company*.

Plate 12. Apple cofounder Steve Wozniak (*right*) and Macintosh software designer Andy Hertzfeld help do the dishes at the first Hackers' Conference in 1984. © 1984 Matt Herron / Take Stock. Used by permission.

Plate 13. Cliff Figallo and John Coate, former members of the Farm commune, became early managers of the Whole Earth 'Lectronic Link, or WELL. They brought with them a deeply countercultural understanding of community. Photograph by Kevin Kelly. Used by permission.

PLATE 14. In the late 1980s, Stewart Brand cofounded a corporate consulting firm, the Global Business Network. The founders are (*left to right*) Jay Ogilvy, Peter Schwartz, Lawrence Wilkinson, Brand, and Napier Collyns. Photograph by Mary Gribbin. Courtesy of the Global Business Network.

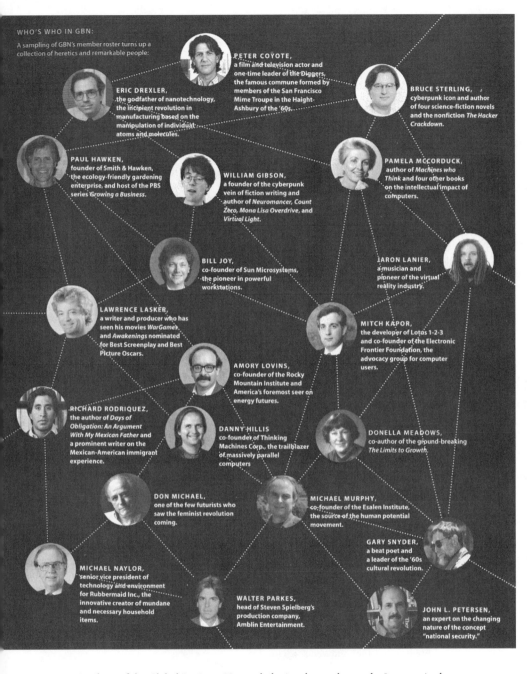

PLATE 15. Members of the Global Business Network depicted as nodes on the Internet in the pages of *Wired* magazine in November 1994. Those shown here include leading figures of the 1960s counterculture, such as poet Gary Snyder and actor Peter Coyote, cyberpunk authors William Gibson and Bruce Sterling, pioneer resource analyst and ecological advocate Amory Lovins, and leading technologists such as Jaron Lanier and Bill Joy. Courtesy of *Wired*, Condé Nast Publications Inc., and Global Business Network.

PLATE 16. By 1997 computers had been transformed into emblems of countercultural revolution, and a digitized version of the globe that had once graced the cover of the *Whole Earth Catalog* now appeared on the cover of *Wired*. Courtesy of *Wired*, Condé Nast Publications Inc., and Micha Klein.

CHAPTER 5

Virtuality and Community on the WELL

In 1985, nearly twenty years after it first served the back-to-the-land movement, the *Whole Earth Catalog* became a model for one of the most influential computer networks to date—the Whole Earth 'Lectronic Link (or WELL). Founded by Stewart Brand and computer entrepreneur Larry Brilliant, the WELL was a teleconferencing system within which subscribers could dial up a central computer and type messages to one another in either asynchronous or real-time conversations.[1] In its hardware and software it differed little from the many such systems that had begun to appear around the world by this time. But in its membership and its governance, the WELL carried forward a set of ideals, management strategies, and interpersonal networks first formulated in and around the *Whole Earth Catalog*. Within the WELL's electronic confines, Stewart Brand brought together former counterculturalists, hackers, and journalists—the same groups he had lately convened at Fort Cronkhite and at the offices of the *Whole Earth Software Catalog*. These groups collaborated within a network forum that had been shaped by New Communalist and cybernetic ideals. And as they worked together, they established a sense of geographically distributed community much like the one that once united the scattered communes of the back-to-the-land movement.

They did so, however, under radically new economic and technological conditions. In the late 1970s and 1980s, the professional communities of the San Francisco Bay area, where the WELL was located, and especially those associated with digital technology, witnessed an extraordinary rise in networked forms of economic organization and in freelance patterns of employment. For the Bay area's engineers and symbolic analysts, the WELL became a place to exchange the information and build the social networks on which their future employment depended.[2] In this new climate, notions of consciousness, community, and the socially transformative possibilities of technology associated with the counterculture became key tools with which WELL users managed their economic lives. To its users, the WELL became not simply a computer conferencing system but a way to recreate the countercultural ideal of a shared consciousness in a new "virtual community." That community in turn was located on what many WELL users imagined to be the digital descendant of the rural American landscape pioneered by the communards of the 1960s, the "electronic frontier." On the WELL, such terms kept alive a New Communalist vision of sociability and at the same time facilitated the integration of new forms of social and economic exchange into the lives of WELL members. Ultimately, thanks to the work of the many journalists on the system, and particularly the writings of Howard Rheingold and John Perry Barlow, *virtual community* and *electronic frontier* became key frames through which Americans would seek to understand the nature of the emerging public Internet.

What Was the WELL?

The WELL got its start when Larry Brilliant, founder of Network Technologies International, a company that sold computer conferencing systems, approached Stewart Brand with the notion of putting the *Whole Earth Catalog* online. Brilliant was looking for a ready-made user community on which to test his latest system, and he believed that in the *Whole Earth* network, Brand had one.[3] Brilliant proposed a partnership: Brilliant would supply a computer and the conferencing software it required. Brand would allow Brilliant to post all of the items in the most recent *Whole Earth Catalog* online as topics for discussion and let people respond. Whatever profits the system made would be split fifty-fifty with the Point Foundation, nonprofit owner of the *Whole Earth* publications. Brand accepted the financial arrangement and took day-to-day responsibility for the system. He did not, however, agree to post sections of the *Catalog*. He argued that, instead, users should be allowed to create their own conversation topics. As he had with the *Whole Earth Catalog,* Brand hoped to allow the system's users to converse with one another and to market that conversation back to its participants.[4]

Although he did not agree to put the *Catalog* online, Brand did bring two of its essential features to the project: a rich mix of technical, countercultural, and journalistic communities and a management ethos derived from a blend of New Communalist idealism and systems theory. In addition to readers and staff of the *Whole Earth* publications, including the *Software Catalog,* the WELL's several hundred users in its earliest years comprised a large number of computer technologists (most of them drawn from the Hackers' Conference).⁵ There were also staff writers and editors for the *New York Times, Business Week,* the *San Francisco Chronicle, Time, Rolling Stone, Byte, Harper's,* and the *Wall Street Journal,* as well as numerous freelancers. Some of these journalists, such as the then husband-and-wife team of John Markoff and Katie Hafner, or the *Chronicle's* Jon Carroll, were already well known in the Bay area and the *Whole Earth* community. Others heard about the system and logged on in part to keep an ear to the ground. All of them were offered free accounts on the system—a move that in the long term greatly increased the WELL's impact on public perceptions of networked computing. Finally, in 1986, disc jockey and Grateful Dead maven David Gans joined the WELL. He brought with him congeries of "Dead Heads," paying subscribers whose constant conversations about the band were a primary source of income for the WELL for several years.

These multiple, overlapping communities came together, as the readers of the *Whole Earth Catalog* had before them, in a text-based forum that was designed to be both a business and a community, one that would be governed in a nonhierarchical manner. In 1993 Kevin Kelly, an editor of *CoEvolution Quarterly* when the WELL was founded and, later, executive editor of *Wired,* recalled that the WELL team had seven design goals at the start:

1. That it be free. This was a goal, not a commitment. We knew it wouldn't be exactly free but it should be as free (cheap) as we could make it. . . .
2. It should be profit making. . . . After much hard, low-paid work by Matthew and Cliff, this is happening. The WELL is at least one of the few operating large systems going that has a future.
3. It would be an open-ended universe. . . .
4. It would be self-governing. . . .
5. It would be a self-designing experiment. . . . The early users were to design the system for later users. The usage of the system would co-evolve with the system as it was built. . . .
6. It would be a community, one that reflected the nature of *Whole Earth* publications. I think that worked out fine.
7. Business users would be its meat and potatoes. Wrong . . .⁶

As Kelly's list suggests, the WELL's early developers built both a countercultural conception of community and a cybernetic vision of control into the system. These were reflected in both the system's software and its business model. Although today the WELL can be found on the World

Wide Web, when it first went online in 1985, it was a bulletin board system (BBS) running on a finicky, Unix-based program called PicoSpan. Housed on a single computer located in the Sausalito offices of the *Whole Earth Software Review,* it allowed people to dial in with a modem. Once connected, users typed in their login names and a password and called up a long string of conference names.[7] Grouped into broad categories, such as "Arts and Letters" and "Entertainment," the conferences dealt with themes ranging from books and cooking to computing and the Grateful Dead. The user could then type a single command and the name of the conference; once "inside," she would find a series of numbered "topics," each created by a user and each representing an ongoing, asynchronous conversation. She could then post her own comment in the conversation or, if she liked, start another topic. From a technical point of view, PicoSpan was not unique. Like other conferencing software of the time, it mapped a tree of information in a hierarchy extending from the system level down through the conference level to individual topics. Yet, to its users, the system seemed to offer an extraordinary and familiar flexibility. Just as readers of the *Whole Earth Catalog* skipped from "Whole Systems" to "Nomadics," linking their reading as they went, so the users of the WELL could move from topic to topic, jumping in and out at will, creating their own conversations if they wished.

Like the *Whole Earth Catalog,* the WELL marketed its users' contributions back to those same users, but it did so under very different terms than the ones used by competitors such as Prodigy or General Electric's GEnie system. For commercial systems of the mid-1980s, computer conferencing was only one of a number of services offered. These companies saw themselves as information utilities, and they saw computer networks less as a site for peer-to-peer communication than as a new medium for the delivery of information. In 1985, for instance, the largest such system, CompuServe, offered its more than two hundred thousand subscribers access to e-mail, special-interest discussion groups, and a real-time chat network designed to emulate Citizens' Band radio, which was then popular. Such communication features were heavily outnumbered, however, by the system's facilities for the delivery of news and information. In CompuServe's databases, users could access news from the Associated Press, an array of electronic newspapers, health information written by doctors, and all sorts of up-to-the-minute financial news.[8] On CompuServe and elsewhere, developers largely treated information as a commodity to be exchanged and users as consumers of information goods.

When their users did produce information goods, commercial systems often tried to capture whatever value they might have. Many commercial systems in the mid-1980s claimed copyright on every word posted to them.

On the WELL, in contrast, the first log-in screen one encountered reminded users: "You own your own words. This means that you are responsible for the words that you post on the WELL and that reproduction of those words without your permission in any medium outside of the WELL's conferencing system may be challenged by you, the author." As he told Katie Hafner, Brand established this policy largely to prevent the WELL from being held liable for its users' postings.[9] But the policy also reflected the WELL's origins in the *Whole Earth Catalog* and the New Communalist movement. Even as it marked the fact that users' words could be transformed into commodities for exchange, it also suggested that the information they provided belonged to them in a more essential way. Information on the WELL was not merely an object of exchange, but a representation of its creator's consciousness.

The WELL's early managers sought to govern their emerging network in terms set by the countercultural critique of hierarchy and the *Whole Earth Catalog*'s trust in the power of tools. They refrained from intervening in fractious debates whenever possible. Although the WELL's member agreement gave conference hosts and the system's owners the power to remove members from the system, managers used that power only three times in the system's first six years, and each time they later allowed the member they had removed to return.[10] Rather than assert their authority directly, the WELL's early managers chose to give users the power of self-rule through information technology. Members who did not like one another's postings, for example, could erase them from their own screens—though not from the community as a whole—by using a "Bozo filter" program within PicoSpan. Likewise, members who later regretted their own postings could return to the system and erase them wholesale using a "Scribble" feature.

This technocentric form of management brought together the New Communalist preference for nonhierarchical forms of social organization with a cybernetic vision of control. The WELL's subscription rates, for instance, remained substantially below those of their commercial competitors not simply for commercial reasons, but because they served as a way for Brand and others to shape interpersonal relations on the WELL. Brand knew that the high cost of other systems had caused their users to post long, carefully crafted messages and to quickly exit the system. He worried, though, that if the WELL cost "nothing per hour" to use, "then the rap dominators would be motivated to really take over." As a result, he decided to charge users an eight-dollar subscription fee and two dollars per hour to log in—far less than the twenty-five dollars per hour of use that other systems were charging at the time. "Subscription, I knew, was a model of pay for free-seeming information that really worked," Brand later told Katie Hafner. "At that rate people could forget they were WELL members and not be stricken when they noticed their bill six months later. Often it would revive their interest in getting their money's worth."[11]

As he set subscription rates, Brand was helping to lay down boundary conditions for a self-governing system. Like a communard of the late 1960s, he was working to establish a forum in which individuals could express themselves and form an alternative community of kindred souls. Like a cybernetician, however, he was also designing a recursive, self-sustaining experiment. The WELL was to be the socio-technical equivalent of a homeostat. Once set in motion by its creators, it was to learn as it went, to find its ideal temperature, so to speak, through the actions of its constituent parts. In this sense, like the soldiers operating Wiener's anti-aircraft system, and like the fantasy citizens of O'Neill's space colonies of 1975, the users of the WELL were to become simultaneously themselves and circuits in a self-regulating biotechnological system. Machine and man would coevolve, to the benefit of each and of the system as a whole. That coevolution would take place simultaneously in the interpersonal, electronic, and economic realms. At the social and electronic levels, the system itself would be part of the circuit. That is, archived in bits, arrayed in conferences and discussion threads, the WELL, like the *Whole Earth Catalog,* would serve as a record and a map of community interactions. Like elements of a homeostat, individuals could monitor that text and reshape it by means of future interactions. This process would also serve as a business model. As Cliff Figallo, one of the WELL's early hosts and leaders, explained, "The discussion and dialog contained and archived on the WELL are its primary products. The WELL 'sells its users to each other' and it considers its users to be both its consumers and its primary producers."[12]

Throughout the WELL's early years, these systemic embodiments of the Whole Earth ethos, coupled with the lived countercultural experience of many WELL members, suggested that computer networks might bring back to life the New Communalist dream of a community of shared consciousness. Ramón Sender Barayón, who had helped Stewart Brand dream up the 1966 Trips Festival, joined the WELL early on, he said, in part because "I felt the energies on the WELL. It reminded me of the Open Land communes I'd been to in the 1960s. The tribal need is one our culture doesn't recognize; capitalism wants each of us to live in our own little cubicle, consuming as much as possible. The WELL took that need and said, 'Hey, let's see what happens if we become a disembodied tribe.'" This was especially true for the WELL's first managers. Soon after he and Brilliant established the WELL, Stewart Brand turned over day-to-day management of the system to the *Whole Earth Catalog*'s former typesetter, Matthew McClure. McClure hired John Coate as the WELL's marketing director, and when

McClure left the WELL in 1986, he hired Cliff Figallo to join Coate in directing the system. McClure, Coate, and Figallo were all long-time veterans of the Farm, a commune set on 1,750 hardscrabble acres in Summertown, Tennessee. The Farm had been founded by Stephen Gaskin, a former professor of English at San Francisco State University who, in the late 1960s, preached in an open forum known as Monday Night Class. His lectures there focused on psychedelic drugs and world religion and included a heavy dose of mysticism. When he and about 250 followers established their commune in 1971, they hoped to create a community of total interpersonal openness. As Coate remembered it, the Farm was a "mental nudist colony." Members were encouraged to work toward a state of transpersonal union of the kind some had felt on LSD. Figallo recalled that "extending the visions of the psychedelic world into the straight everyday world was one of the foundations of Stephen's teachings." In that context, members were encouraged to challenge one another, to "get into" one another's "thing," so as to make it possible to drop their personal defenses and become part of a transcendent collective. "We were trying to be tribal," Coate explained. "To get back to something that white Euro/American culture had lost. . . . That's what all that 'getting straight' and 'sorting it out' was about. Trying to get real close real fast, so we can get on with the trip."[13]

Although some of its members still live there, the Farm as McClure, Coate, and Figallo knew it collapsed in 1983. Burdened by debts and no longer comfortable with the extraordinary authority exerted by Stephen Gaskin, its members voted that year to stop pooling all their resources communally and to reorganize as a cooperative to which individual members paid dues.[14] Less than two years after the Farm ceased to be structured as a commune, its ethos of disembodied community found a home on the WELL. Like the Farm, and like the *Whole Earth Catalog,* the WELL was a community held together by talk, the textual mirror of a physically dispersed tribe that felt itself linked by a shared invisible energy. As Figallo explained, "We [veterans of the Farm] were conditioned to respond to the Community Imperative—the need to build and maintain relationships between people and to preserve the structure that supported those relationships. I also became aware . . . that those relationships were the only 'product' we had to sell."[15]

At the same time, even for the former citizens of the Farm, the WELL became a system to be managed according to a mix of cybernetic principles. On the WELL, human and technical systems existed simultaneously in interaction with one another and, at a theoretical level at least, as mirrors of one another. The manager, like the scientist in a first-generation cybernetic experiment, was to set the boundary conditions for the system and then to stand back and observe its operation. Within the framework of second-generation cybernetics brought into the Whole Earth network by Gregory Bateson, however, the observer was always part of the system being observed. On the WELL, McClure, Figallo, and Coate balanced both traditions, playing the roles of designer, observer, and participant simultaneously and drawing on both cybernetic and communal models in their management practice. Cliff Figallo explained: "Principles of tolerance and inclusion, fair resource allocation, distributed responsibility, management by example and influence, a flat organizational hierarchy, cooperative policy formulation and acceptance of a libertarian-bordering-on-anarchic ethos were all carryovers from our communal living experience."[16] Yet these principles were also key elements in the management of a pseudobiological system. The WELL, according to Figallo, was "like a small balanced social ecology"; it was a "pond" that "seems to renew itself in spite of continuing technical and interpersonal difficulties."[17] The first job of the managers was to set the conditions of the "environment." "My main emphasis," recalled Figallo, "was in preserving and supporting the exercise of freedom and creativity by the WELL's users through providing an open forum for their interaction." McClure agreed: "I don't think we had an a priori knowledge of exactly what it was going to turn out to be, but we had a pretty good idea about what its potential was and how to manipulate it into realizing that potential. And a lot of that manipulation was by staying the hell out of the way at the right time. The WELL didn't just evolve, it evolved because we designed it to evolve."[18]

In both its original business plan and its day-to-day management, then, the WELL owed a great deal to the legacy of the *Whole Earth Catalog* and its synthesis of New Communalist and cybernetic ideals. The WELL as described by Kelly, McClure, Figallo, and Coate was a little, self-contained world, and its managers, like scientists, were "as gods"—designing that world, channeling its disembodied "energies" through talk, creating settings in which individuals could simultaneously build their new community and transform themselves by using a new set of digital "tools" to which the WELL had given them access. They and the WELL carried the *Catalog*'s countercultural critique of hierarchical government and its celebration of cybernetic forms of collaborative organization forward from the counterculture into what was quickly becoming a world of individuals and organizations linked by networks of computers—a cyberculture.

New Technological and Economic Networks

That cyberculture depended on a new set of economic and technological arrangements, however. In the 1960s, mainstream economic life had been dominated by hierarchically organized corporations; it was that world that members of the New Communalist movement had set out to escape. By the time the WELL was created, the world had changed dramatically. As a variety of economic sociologists have noted, the mid-1980s saw hierarchical firms in many industries and several nations reorganize themselves as project-oriented networks.[19] They laid off workers, broke component elements of firms into semi-independent project teams, and decentralized their management structure. Out of this process emerged what Walter Powell has described as a new, networked logic for the organization of production, a logic characterized by a shift in the basis of employment from long-term positions to shorter-term projects, by the leveling of corporate hierarchies, and by the integration of activities across multiple industries. Within this logic, the boundaries that had previously surrounded firms and jobs became porous and flexible. Companies became collections of internal networks even as their constituent units reached out and joined networks that reached across traditional lines between firms, industries, and nations. For an increasing number of workers, employment meant not only performing particular tasks within the company, but helping to build and maintain interfirm networks.[20] In part, this networking helped to build alliances for one's firm. For some employees, though, it also helped mitigate the new insecurity of their jobs. Corporations were coming increasingly to the view expressed by James Meadows, vice president for human resources at AT&T, in 1996: "People need to look at themselves as self-employed, as vendors who come to the company to sell their skills. In AT&T, we have to promote the concept of the whole work force being contingent, though most of our contingent workers are inside our walls. Jobs are being replaced by projects and fields of work, giving rise to a society that is increasingly 'jobless but not workless.'"[21]

This situation was particularly true for the early users of the WELL. As Manuel Castells has pointed out, the electronics industry and its geographical hubs, including the San Francisco Bay area, were among the industries and regions most dependent on network patterns of organization.[22] In Silicon Valley, these networks had been coming together for decades. It is tempting to ascribe the rise of network organizations to the rise of networked communication technologies, but in the case of Silicon Valley, at least, it would be inaccurate to do so: there, the increase in networked forms of doing business preceded and in fact helped drive the development of the technologies on which systems like the WELL depended.[23] The Valley had been a center for electronics research since the early twentieth century. After World War II, much of that research was supported by contracts from the Defense Department. For example, virtually every integrated circuit made in the Valley in the early 1960s was installed in a Polaris or Minuteman missile system, and through much of the 1960s, the Valley's largest employer was Lockheed Missiles and Space (now Lockheed-Martin). Nevertheless, much of the region's technological innovation was driven by collaborations between local technology firms and Stanford University. During World War II, Stanford's future dean of engineering, Frederick Terman, had headed the Radio Research Laboratory, a spin-off from MIT's Rad Lab. In Cambridge, he had caught a glimpse of the possibilities for military, industrial, and academic collaboration, and when he returned to Stanford, he brought that vision with him. Throughout the late 1940s and 1950s, Terman worked to integrate the region's engineering culture with the academic aims of the university and to coordinate both with the tactical goals of the Defense Department.[24]

By the early 1970s, Terman's collaborative style had become a Valley-wide norm. As AnnaLee Saxenian has shown, the technical industries of the Valley at that time enjoyed a uniquely integrated culture. Social distinctions and institutional hierarchies common to other regions played little role in Valley life. This was especially true within the firms that would define the Valley's computer industry. In 1957, for instance, Robert Noyce, the first CEO of Fairchild Semiconductor, did away with many of the privileges characteristic of more hierarchical firms. He and his fellow managers decreed that the parking lot would be first-come, first-serve, that dress codes would not include coats and ties, and that engineers who found themselves in meetings with their formal superiors would be encouraged to speak their minds. Engineers from Fairchild went on to form more than fifty companies in the Valley, most all of which retained Noyce's antihierarchical social style.[25] Thanks largely to the absence of such distinctions, social and professional networks extended across local institutions, industries, and corporations. Over the next decade, as the personal-computer industry grew and the role of military sponsorship of electronics declined, those networks became increasingly important. By 1984 Silicon Valley's economy had become the fastest-growing and wealthiest in the United States. Between 1986 and 1990, the region saw the value of its electronics firms grow by $25 billion; by contrast, the Route 128 area of Massachusetts, a region endowed with similar industries but more hierarchical patterns of social and professional life, saw growth of just $1 billion.[26]

Within the Bay area's computer industries, the rapid growth, coupled with the constantly changing demands of technical work in this period, helped drive extraordinary professional mobility. Job tenure for Silicon Valley engineers and managers in the early 1980s averaged two to three years; turnover among manual laborers was even more rapid. In such a fluid employment environment, individuals cultivated professional and interpersonal networks as key sources of future employment. "A company is just a vehicle which allows you to work," explained one engineer. Even though individual employers came and went, strong networks allowed the engineers and managers of Silicon Valley to keep working steadily over time.[27] Throughout its early years, the WELL population included large numbers of users from the growing computer industry. Most of its members hailed from the San Francisco Bay and Silicon Valley areas. Moreover, its contributors included a substantial number of professionals from other industries that had long depended on networks, including academe, journalism, and consulting. For these users, the WELL offered an electronic forum in which they could meet, exchange information, build reputations, and collaborate.

This sort of exchange was nothing new to the *Whole Earth* network. The *Whole Earth Catalog* had long served as a site where members of various local communities could speak up, either by writing letters or by reviewing products, and in so doing they contributed to and asserted their own membership in the geographically distributed network of counterculturalists. The *Catalog* had appeared no more than twice a year, however, with two supplements per year published in the interim. As a paper-and-ink publication, it cost a great deal of time, labor, and money to produce and distribute. The digital forum of the WELL, in contrast, allowed for instantaneous postings. If the *Catalog* had *represented* a community in print, the WELL's digital technology allowed it to *become* an interactive collectivity in real time. This fact shaped the roles individuals could have in regard to the system. At the *Catalog,* individuals could review products, write letters, and perhaps join the editorial staff. But because of the production technologies involved, they could assume only one role at a time, a role that would be permanently fixed in the pages of the *Catalog.* At the WELL, individuals could adopt one persona in one conference and another elsewhere. They could post in several places, serve as a host to a conference, and start a new topic—all within a single hour. The WELL therefore often became intertwined with its users' daily lives in a way that no paper-bound catalog could. Maria Syndicus, an early and prominent WELL member, explains: "I'd be in the office, working, and at the same time, posting in conferences, sending email, and having a conversation in Sends [an early instant-messaging feature on the WELL]. I'd be at home, cooking dinner, and logging on to check what was new. Relationships developed fast and furious, ideas spread like wildfire. I never laughed so hard, argued so passionately, soaked up so many new ideas. The WELL made me run on high."[28]

As Syndicus's post suggests, the WELL's digital networks also offered women a prominence that that they had generally not enjoyed in the counterculture or at the *Whole Earth Catalog*. On the rural communes of the late 1960s, women had often been confined to support roles: cooking, cleaning, and the raising of children. On the WELL, they could and did slide across such gender divides. In the late 1980s, some 40 percent of WELL users were women.[29] Although top managers of the system in its earliest years were male, as were a number of the most frequent users of public forums, women also played strong leadership roles, establishing conferences, starting topics, and participating in a wide range of discussions.

These expanding roles of women reflected the rise of feminism throughout American culture, of course. Yet they also marked the empowerment felt by women on the WELL. In 1993, for example, scholar Susan Herring circulated a paper in which she argued that men and women displayed different online communication styles and that these differences tended to put women at a disadvantage online. When the paper made its way to the WELL, it helped spark a two-year debate on the experiences of women online.[30] In the course of that debate, women mentioned that they had at times received harassing e-mails and unwanted sexual approaches from men on the WELL. But on the whole, they rejected Herring's contention that a distinctly female posting style existed and its implication that women endured the same pressures online that they encountered elsewhere. Many argued that an aggressive verbal style of the kind Herring ascribed to men would cause problems for any WELL user, male or female. And several pointed out that the WELL's many conferences and the system's ability to filter incoming messages, as well as the availability and sensitivity of its managers and conference hosts, made it relatively easy not only to avoid harassment, but to find congenial settings for conversation.

One of the most powerful of these forums was the women-only conference Women on the WELL. Started soon after the WELL itself began, the conference required prospective contributors to speak directly to one of its hosts to confirm their female identity before they were admitted. Once inside the conference, women discussed a wide range of topics. Elizabeth Reba Wiese, in her introduction to *Wired Women*, an early and influential collection of essays on the roles of women online, recalled that she joined Women on the WELL (WOW) soon after taking an isolating third-shift editorial job. When she logged on in the middle of the night, she found the discussions of the conference waiting for her "like a letter on the kitchen table":

> I came in to the community with a cry of pain, feeling alone and bereft, and
> these women I did not know sat down beside me and offered comfort, told
> their own stories of break-ups and partings, of finding their way in a new city,

of making a life where you did not have one before. . . . I learned a lot in my late-night sojourns to the WELL. I who had few heterosexual friends met happily married women. I listened in as women with experiences vastly different from mine discussed blending families, tax law, how much to tip in a hotel, what it had meant to come of age in the sixties and how to cope when one's parents died. . . . In a way, the WELL, and WOW in particular, was like being given the gift of an extended family.[31]

The WELL as Economic Heterarchy

Together, changes in media technology and in the economic landscape in which WELL users worked substantially changed the nature and value of both information and information-based interpersonal connection. During the late 1960s, when the *Whole Earth Catalog* first appeared, the American economy was strong and long-term employment prospects were good, particularly for the largely upper-middle-class, college-educated readership of the *Catalog*. Many of those who struck out for the woods in 1968 did so knowing full well they would have something to go back to if they had to. Moreover, although its recommendations certainly had value for its readers, and although its recommenders could build a reputation in part by reviewing for it, the *Whole Earth Catalog* was published too infrequently and at too great an expense to be a source of rapid information exchange. Reviewers were paid ten dollars for a published piece, but almost all of the financial value generated by the information contributed to the *Whole Earth Catalog* returned to the *Catalog*'s publishers.[32]

On the WELL, by contrast, it was possible to exchange smaller, time-sensitive pieces of information. They could range from data on a not-yet-announced technology to a bit of gossip about the computer or magazine industries. This sort of information could have a great deal of value to the many information professionals on the WELL. Furthermore, because the WELL facilitated numerous, rapid interactions—as opposed to the printing of single, carefully crafted letters in the *Whole Earth Catalog*—it also allowed individuals to get to know the working styles of one another's minds in a way that was not possible in a paper-and-ink forum. This feature added a new dimension to the ways in which the forum could enhance the reputations of its users. Whereas in the *Whole Earth Catalog*, regular reviewers could establish reputations for know-how and, to some extent, for prose technique and taste, on the WELL, contributors were able to build reputations for these things and, beyond them, for charisma, personality, and style. The *Whole Earth Catalog* concentrated a wealth of countercultural experiences into a single publication that could be purchased, with the purchase price returning to the publisher. The WELL tended to push value out to its users, to distribute and increase value throughout the system.

On the WELL, the boundary between public and private was extraordinarily fluid. As a result, any given contribution to a WELL conference might have value simultaneously in multiple domains—collective, interpersonal, and economic. For many users, these domains met in the exchange of information. Like the *Whole Earth Catalog,* the WELL made visible a wealth of interesting facts and a network of experts who supplied them. By making both facts and experts available in real time, however, the WELL substantially increased the value of each. Reva Basch, a former librarian and at the time a professional freelance researcher, offered a sense of this value when she explained how she used the WELL in 1991:

> Although it doesn't host any of the formal databases that I use for research, The WELL *is* the online hangout of choice for an incredible array of experts: multi-media artists, musicians, newspaper columnists, neurobiologists, radio producers, futurists, computer junkies. I can contact any of them directly, through email, or post a plea for information in a public conference and more often than not, be deluged with insights and informed opinions. Most compellingly, the conferences devoted to non-work issues and to fun and nonsense give me a chance to get to know these folks better, and vice versa.[33]

For Basch, as for the many other information professionals on the WELL, the system offered access to information and expertise that could be transformed into income elsewhere. Howard Rheingold, for instance, had been a freelance journalist and author for a half dozen years before he joined the WELL. He found that the WELL extended the range of his social networks and his ability to find information quickly. "An editor or producer or client can call and ask me if I know much about the Constitution, or fiber optics, or intellectual property," Rheingold wrote in 1992. "'Let me get back to you in twenty minutes,' I say, reaching for the modem." These rapid and diverse connections amplified Rheingold's income. In a WELL topic devoted to the ways in which the WELL had improved members' work lives, entitled "De WELL Been Beddy, Beddy Goot to Me," Rheingold wrote that the WELL had supplied him with important information and key collaborators. As a result, he said, "I probably make more money from work that I do with the help of the WELL and the WELL community than I made from all sources before I joined."[34]

The exchange of information was by no means the only source of economic value on the early WELL. Revisiting the accounts of other members reveals at least two other forms: performance value and reputation value.

Carmen Hermosillo, for instance, writing under the name humdog, contributed to the WELL for several years and, like many other members, engaged in several emotionally charged debates. Toward the end of her time on the system, she later wrote, she began to feel that she had been performing rather than conversing: "i have seen many people spill their guts on-line, and i did so myself until, at last, i began to see that i had commodified myself. . . . i created my interior thoughts as a means of production for the corporation that owned the board i was posting to, and that commodity was being sold to other commodity/consumer entities as entertainment." Even though the WELL never made much of a profit, and although its managers in fact struggled to keep the system in the black, Hermosillo's point has been echoed elsewhere. John Coate described the experience of writing on the WELL as "a new hybrid that is both talking and writing yet isn't completely either one. It's talking by writing." Despite being text-based, contributions to the WELL constituted a kind of vocal performance—a performance that many subscribed to the system in part to attend.[35]

The value to others of one's performance did not necessarily depend on one's reputation. Like users of many emerging media forms today, such as reality television or the World Wide Web, many WELL clients watched others act out their own lives online and paid the WELL's owners for the privilege. Yet (though it didn't have to) a well-managed performance could also enhance the performer's reputation. As Coate put it, "Freelancers, contractors, entrepreneurs, and others who, because they are always looking ahead to that next job, need to have their shingle hung out . . . With so many people moving from one job to another, online public forums are good places to run into others who may lead you to your next work opportunity." A journalist who wrote with flair in a conference unrelated to his professional specialty could be noticed and contacted for work elsewhere. Reva Basch recalled that Jon Carroll, a columnist for the *San Francisco Chronicle,* spotted her writing on the WELL. When he went on vacation, he suggested to his editors that Basch and several other WELL members fill in for him. Basch's affectionate description of her Apple PowerBook in the *Chronicle* led to a regular and high-paying column with a Ziff-Davis publication, *Computer Life.*[36]

This pattern was common on the WELL. Online contributions in social and special-interest conferences led to work for Howard Rheingold, for his equally well-known colleague on the WELL, John Perry Barlow, and in later years for many others. Nonjournalists benefited in the same way. A computer programmer who built a functional bit of software for the WELL could have his or her skills recognized within the group and later elsewhere too. According to Coate, these migrations of reputation occurred frequently in the late 1980s.[37] Such reputation work ultimately led to a number of collaborations that had a substantial impact on the early culture of the public Internet, including the founding of the Electronic Frontier Foundation, *Salon* magazine, and even *Wired*.

This is not to say that journalists who posted witty responses to queries or programmers who built new tools were doing so in pursuit of economic gain. On the contrary, it seems clear that many were acting from a mixture of motives and in a mixture of social contexts simultaneously. Sociologist David Stark has explained that such mixtures are characteristic of emerging forms of postindustrial economic activity. In an influential study of firms in post-Soviet Eastern Europe, Stark christened this sort of mixture "heterarchy."[38] Within a heterarchy, he explained, one encounters multiple, and at times competing, value systems, principles of organization, and mechanisms for performance appraisal: "Heterarchies create wealth by inviting more than one way of evaluating worth."[39] In the post-Soviet context, for example, if a particular unit of a firm could be characterized simultaneously as a "public" resource and as the "private" property of a newly deregulated company, it could attract funds from both the public and private sectors and share financial risks between them as well.[40]

On the WELL, users' abilities to characterize their postings as having value in both the social and the economic registers depended on both the computer technology of the WELL and the cultural legacy of the New Communalist movement. By allowing users to communicate in real time and by allowing them to start and end topics more or less at will, the technology of the WELL made it possible for individual communications to have meaning and value in registers that contributions to the *Whole Earth Catalog* never could, simply because of the mechanics involved in producing a bound paper document.[41] Alongside these technical affordances, however, the WELL depended on a set of cultural tools that it had inherited from the American counterculture, and specifically from the *Whole Earth Catalog*. In the *Catalog*, readers contributed letters and product reviews primarily because they supported and wanted to contribute to the geographically distributed alternative culture they saw emerging in its pages. No one could make a living— or even a substantial part of a living—writing for the *Catalog*. Readers offered contributions as gifts to the community that the *Catalog* made visible; the *Catalog* then retailed those gifts (albeit at a low per-unit cost) to readers.

Thanks to shifts in technology and in the San Francisco Bay area's economy, the nature and value of the information exchanged on the WELL was qualitatively different. Yet WELL members retained two conceptual frameworks from the *Catalog* era with which to explain their interactions online:

the "gift economy" and the notion of a community of linked minds. As Howard Rheingold explained it, the WELL's gift economy consisted of the constant exchange of potentially valuable information without expectation of immediate reward.[42] Individuals contributed information to such a system, wrote Rheingold, because those who contributed would ultimately be rewarded with information themselves over time. This pattern of giving without expectation of immediate reward had deep roots in the San Francisco Bay area counterculture; for Rheingold and others, it was this pattern that distinguished the sorts of information exchange happening in places like the WELL from those of ordinary, cash-and-carry markets.[43] As several generations of sociologists and anthropologists have pointed out, though, a gift economy is not simply a system for the exchange of valuable goods. It is also a system for the establishment of social order.[44] Marcel Mauss argued in *The Gift,* his classic study of exchange relations in pre-industrial societies, that there is no such thing as a "pure gift." Gifts entail obligations and generate cycles of exchange that serve to establish and maintain structural relations between givers and receivers. Moreover, as Mauss suggested, the gift itself never stands outside social or economic relations. The gift encodes multiple social and economic meanings. Pierre Bourdieu has argued that these multiple meanings are an "open secret" to participants in the system. Within the gift itself and within cycles of giving and receiving, the multiple meanings work to transform material wealth into social capital.[45]

Their power depends on the ability of the "gift" to connect the economic work being undertaken to other forms of social interaction. On the WELL, it was the rhetoric of community that allowed this connection to be made. Rheingold asserted that the success of the informational gift economy on the WELL depended not only on the expectation of ultimate reward, but also on an intangible feeling that one was working to construct a new sort of social collective. In a gift economy, "people do things for one another out of a spirit of building something between them, rather than a spreadsheet-calculated quid pro quo. When that spirit exists, everybody gets a little extra something, a little sparkle, from their more practical transactions; different kinds of things become possible when this mindset pervades. Conversely, people who have valuable things to add to the mix tend to keep their heads down and their ideas to themselves when a mercenary or hostile zeitgeist dominates an online community."[46] In Rheingold's terms, the felt existence of community allowed individuals to exchange information without fearing that they might never see a return for their gifts. But as David Stark saw it, the ability of an information giver to characterize his "gift" as a valuable piece of information (in the economic register), as a demonstration of personal style (in the interpersonal register), and as a contribution to the building of a community (in the social register) allowed the information exchange to go forward in the first place. Thus, the rhetoric of community provided the ideological cover necessary to transform a potentially stark and single-minded market transaction into a complex, multidimensional act. To the extent that they could describe themselves as the givers and receivers of informational gifts within a community, members of the WELL could simultaneously recognize and ignore the degree to which they were also exchanging financially valuable goods within a newly informational economy. As a result, they could increase their own social capital and their access to the informational and social resources on which their work off-line depended.

On the WELL, this heterarchical form of information work came together with the experience of interpersonal intimacy. Under the rubric of a New Communalist vision of a community of consciousness, this blend of emotional interconnection and informational labor gave rise to one of the most influential frames with which we have since understood the Internet: virtual community. Through PicoSpan's stark white-on-black, text-only interface, the early users of the WELL told jokes, congratulated one another on life events, and recounted long parts of their personal histories. Soon the conversation spilled over into face-to-face gatherings called WELL Office Parties (WOPs). The first WOP took place in the WELL's Sausalito offices, around the computer that hosted the conversations; later events were located across the Bay area.[47] The face-to-face meetings sealed emotional bonds formed earlier online. The resulting strong interpersonal bonds were further strengthened by the history so many WELL members shared. Often, WELL members addressed that history directly, establishing topics of discussion such as "Memories on Morning Star [commune] in 1967" or just "Communes," in which they recalled their experiences in the 1960s and 1970s.[48] Even when they turned to more contemporary subjects, users of the WELL in the late 1980s and early 1990s could assume a more or less shared set of experiences and interests with other WELL users. The Grateful Dead, sexuality, information work, parenting—all were the subjects of extensive conferences online, and all reflected the shared generational experiences of early WELL users.

These shared interests, experiences, and emotional interconnections helped drive the dissemination of the notion that WELL constituted a virtual community. Although some users insisted that the WELL could best be compared to a "pub" or a "virtual coffee house," both contemporary accounts and online archives suggest that the notion of "community" was the most commonly used metaphor with which WELL users tried to name the whole of their experiences on the system. At one level, the rhetoric of community summoned up the back-to-the-land movement as a way to name the emotional intimacy many had experienced online. At another, the vision of the WELL as a community of shared consciousness also embraced the vicissitudes of the newly networked economy in which members found themselves living. John Coate put the point succinctly: "Professional and personal interactions overlap" on the WELL. For that reason, he wrote, the WELL could be compared to a village, "because that's what a village is: a place where you go down to the butcher or the blacksmith and transact your business, and at night meet those same neighbors down at the local tavern or the Friday night dance."[49]

The WELL's membership included few if any butchers or blacksmiths. By describing the WELL as a village, however, Coate and others enabled WELL users to reflect on their shared countercultural history, to celebrate their intense interpersonal connection online, and to transform both into resources for the amplification of social and material capital. To the extent that its members could imagine the WELL as a community, they could speak within multiple registers simultaneously, building their reputations, their friendships, and their businesses. They could also do so in the comforting sense that they had not betrayed their youthful ambitions for alternative community. The communes of the 1960s had largely vanished, but in John Coate's description of a pre-industrial village, we can hear echoes of the kind of community the Farm hoped to be and the kind of community the *Whole Earth Catalog* aimed to speak to. This time, though, New Communalist ideals no longer offered an alternative to life in the economic mainstream. On the contrary, they provided a vision by which to steer one's way through the complex currents of the increasingly mainstream network economy.

Exporting the Virtual Community Frame

Not long after that vision emerged on the WELL, Howard Rheingold transported it into wider regions of public discourse. In 1987, in a brief article for the *Whole Earth Review,* successor to the by-then-defunct *CoEvolution Quarterly,* Rheingold deployed the term *virtual community* for what was almost certainly the first time in print. In a subsequent 1992 essay and in his 1993 book *The Virtual Community: Homesteading on the Electronic Frontier,* he described the new forms of interaction that computers made possible: Gathered together online, yet restricted to text-only interfaces, individuals could connect to one another without encountering body-based forms of prejudice. They could come together not in the random interactions that characterized life in the material world, but by choice, around shared interests. And within this space, they could engage in a new form of social interaction that was simultaneously intimate and instrumental.[50] Invoking both the countercultural ideals of cooperation and the cybernetic vision of humans and computers as collaborating information systems, Rheingold explained in 1987 that members of his "virtual community" acted as "software agents" for one another, becoming "effective filters for sifting the key data that are useful and interesting to us as individuals."[51]

Even as they helped one another perform information-oriented work, though, the members of the WELL were also working to restore the New Communalist dream of a rural community of like-minded souls, suggested Rheingold. "We need computer networks to recapture the sense of cooperative spirit that so many people seemed to lose when we gained all this technology," he wrote in 1993. In the disembodied precincts of computer-mediated communication, people could "rediscover the power of cooperation, turning cooperation into a game, a way of life—a merger of knowledge capital, social capital, and communion."[52] Rheingold's vision of a collaborative virtual community not only echoed the goals of commune builders from the late 1960s, but also represented a transformation in the countercultural critique of technocracy. Like early 1960s critics of the cold war military-industrial complex, Rheingold critiqued the loss of cooperative spirit and implied that technology itself had brought about that loss. And, not unlike the reversionary technophiles of the *Whole Earth Catalog*, Rheingold trusted in tools to restore the cooperative spirit and to put cooperation once again at the center of social life. He believed the computer was a tool that could transform the consciousness of its user and so allow the user to enter into new, alternative, and exemplary community with others. But, unlike the hammers and books of the *Whole Earth Catalog*, the computer network that was the WELL was not simply a hand tool. It was also a system, albeit one to which an individual computer could grant access. In keeping with Stewart Brand's celebration of space colonies, and with Gregory Bateson's view of the world as an all-inclusive information system, Rheingold represented the information network of the WELL as an all-inclusive, collaborative, emotionally and materially sustaining world.

Almost immediately after the publication of his 1993 book, just as the Internet was beginning to gain widespread public attention, scholars, journalists, and businessmen alike took up Rheingold's vision and transformed it into a model for thinking about new forms of computer-mediated sociability.[53] Following his lead, scholars debated the authenticity of interpersonal connections online and explored the impact of disembodiment on the expression of the self. Although many critiqued the notion of virtual community, most did so within terms set by the concept itself. Much as the dancers at the Trips Festival had imagined that LSD would allow them to escape their bodies and enjoy a new form of communion, scholars and reporters began to describe computer-mediated communication as a form of interaction in which bodies had ceased to matter. For many, the economic aspects of Rheingold's description simply fell away. So did memories of earlier communication technologies, such as the telephone or even letters: what was distinct about this new form of communication, they suggested, was the way in which it facilitated disembodied intimacy.

On the WELL, the rhetoric of virtual community had made it possible to turn economically valuable information into gifts in part by obscuring the economic nature of certain transactions and the power relations established thereby. As the term *virtual community* made its way into public circulation, its ideological valence made it particularly appealing to the corporate world. If a company could sponsor an online "community," and if it could convince its customers that they were engaging in social rather than economic activity (or if they could convince them that the social and the economic were always blurred in any "real" community), then they could increase customer allegiance and their own profits.[54] Throughout the mid-1990s, many corporations, including the Microsoft Network and America Online, looked to the WELL to see how to pull this off. In keeping with Rheingold's emphasis on the virtuality of his community, the executives of these companies tended to believe that it was digital technology rather than strong off-line, interpersonal networks or a shared countercultural idea set that made the establishment of community online possible.[55] If Coate and Rheingold thought that computer networks would return isolated, postindustrial workers to a state of pre-industrial communion, members of the corporate sector thought such networks might bring isolated, postindustrial consumers into a state of postmodern economic communion.

As several writers, including Howard Rheingold, have noted, online communities have struggled, in part because they lack the local roots and strongly intertwined networks of the early WELL. Rheingold himself ultimately stopped using the designation *virtual community* and instead began referring to "online social networks."[56] Nevertheless, in the late 1980s and early 1990s, just as computer networks were emerging into public view, the notion of virtual community helped translate the New Communalist ethos of the Whole Earth network into a ready-made language for understanding the social possibilities of those networks and of new, multivalent forms of networked labor as well. Having emerged as a contact language on the WELL, a language that helped coordinate activities there, it was exported, by Rheingold and other network members, until it had become a language that could coordinate the activities of scholars, businessmen, and far-flung journalists.

Turning Cyberspace into an Electronic Frontier

In 1990 the WELL's technology and management style, along with the networks that had gathered around the system and other Whole Earth–related organizations, became resources for the redefinition of cyberspace itself. In that year computer pundit John Perry Barlow became what most acknowledge to be the first person to apply the word *cyberspace* to the then-emerging intersection of telecommunications and computer networks.[57] Drawing largely on his experience of the WELL, he configured this new, computer-network-based cyberspace as an "electronic frontier." In the process, he transformed a formerly dystopian vision of networked computing into an imagined space in which individuals could recreate themselves and their communities in terms set by New Communalist ideals. Like the rural landscape of the 1960s, Barlow's cyberspace would stand beyond government control. And like a Happening or an Acid Test, it would provide a setting and tools through which individuals could establish intimate, disembodied connections with one another. By summoning up the image of the electronic frontier, Barlow transformed the local norms of the WELL, including its Whole Earth–derived communitarian ethic, its allegiance to antihierarchical governance, and its cybernetic rhetoric, into a universal metaphor for networked computing. By the mid-1990s, Barlow's version of cyberspace had become perhaps the single most common emblem not only for emerging forms of computer-networked communication, but for leveled forms of social organization and deregulated patterns of commerce as well.

When cyberpunk novelist William Gibson first coined the word in his 1984 novel *Neuromancer, cyberspace* conjured up not the rural American frontier, but the electronic undergirding of a dark, hyperindustrialized landscape. Cyberspace itself was a luminous electronic universe, but one inhabited by potentially vicious anthropomorphized computer systems and dominated by large corporations. Tough, computer-savvy freelancers like the novel's hero Case could "jack in" to this space—that is, they could wire themselves up and enter the electronic universe, leaving their bodies behind. Their disembodiment had little to do with entering a state of mystical union. On the contrary, it could kill. As Case discovered on several occasions, if you stayed too long in cyberspace, your heart could stop beating. For Gibson, cyberspace was a fictional tool with which to explore not only the emerging possibilities of digital technologies, but also the deeply dystopian tendencies of American life in the early 1980s. Case and his fellow inhabitants of "the Sprawl" struggled to survive in the shadows of a world where large corporations had ruined the natural environment, where government seemed to be breaking down and local Mafias taking over, and where physical suffering was routine.[58]

For people working in high technology, however, Gibson's vision of cyberspace held enormous appeal. As Allucquère Rosanne Stone has argued, for example, the idea of cyberspace allowed a geographically dispersed group of individuals working on three-dimensional imaging systems— systems that Jaron Lanier named "virtual reality"—to reimagine themselves as members of a coherent community collaborating on the construction of the future. This community had begun its work in the 1960s, developing flight-simulation gear for the air force. Its members had also developed computer-assisted design (CAD) technology, particularly at Nicholas Negroponte's Architecture Machine Group—forerunner of the Media Lab— at MIT. In the early 1980s, many of these people migrated to Silicon Valley. In 1982, for instance, Scott Fisher, of the Architecture Machine Group, joined Atari. When the Atari lab closed, he moved to the NASA-Ames View Lab. There engineers had developed a virtual reality helmet and a sensor incorporated into a glove that could give the computer information about a subject's hand movements. In 1985 NASA contracted to have this glove developed by Jaron Lanier's Sausalito-based firm VPL Research; they manufactured the first glove in March 1986.[59] Another East Coast engineer, Eric Gullichsen, arrived at about the same time. He ultimately joined Autodesk, a San Francisco Bay area maker of CAD systems. In 1988 Autodesk developed a "cyberspace" initiative (quickly dubbed "Cyberia") in which they tried to build "'a doorway into cyberspace' for anyone with $15,000 and a 386 computer."[60] In 1989 Gullichsen went so far as to register the word *cyberspace* as a trademark. In return, William Gibson trademarked the word *Gullichsen*.

Throughout the 1980s, *cyberspace* was used primarily to describe virtual reality of the kind these firms were working to develop. But even as technologists worked to build a sort of placeless space, that space quickly became linked to local, Bay area stories of LSD and countercultural transformation. Autodesk, for instance, hired famed acid guru Timothy Leary to appear in its promotional video for its cyberspace initiative. Various journalists and science fiction writers also collaborated to link virtual reality to LSD. Ultimately, this group included Kevin Kelly and Stewart Brand, but its earliest and most active members were the writers and editors of the magazine *Mondo 2000*, including John Perry Barlow.[61] In the fall of 1988, Alison

Kennedy (aka Queen Mu) and Ken Goffman (aka R. U. Sirius), publisher and editor-in-chief, respectively, used their first-ever issue to announce that digital technologies had inherited the transformational mantel of the counterculture:

> All the old war horses are dead. Eco-fundamentalism is out, conspiracy theory is demode, drugs are obsolete. There's a new whiff of apocalypticism across the land. A general sense that we are living at a very special juncture in the evolution of the species.
>
> Yet the pagan innocence and idealism that was the sixties remains and continues to exert its fascination on today's kids. Look at old footage of Woodstock and you wonder: where have all those wide-eyed, ecstatic, orgasm-slurping kids gone? They're all across the land, dormant like deeply buried perennials. But their mutated nucleotides have given us a whole new generation of sharpies, mutants and superbrights and in them we must put our faith—and power.
>
> The cybernet is the place . . . The old information elites are crumbling. The kids are at the controls.[62]

At one level, the notion that digital culture was growing directly out of the counterculture and the LSD scene reflected the editorial ancestry of *Mondo 2000*. Before coming to *Mondo 2000*, Goffman had edited a Bay area drug 'zine, *High Frontiers*, which he had subtitled "Psychedelics, Science, Human Potential, Irreverence & Modern Art." *High Frontiers* featured lengthy interviews with LSD adventurers like Albert Hofmann, Timothy Leary, and Terence McKenna. In 1988 Goffman retitled the now-biennial magazine *Reality Hackers*, to mark its new emphasis on technology. It soon began running articles on computer viruses, psychoactive designer foods, and high-tech paganism.[63] Later that year, *Reality Hackers* took up the cause of cyberpunk fiction and became *Mondo 2000*. Its first issue featured contributions by cyberpunk heroes William Gibson, Bruce Sterling, and John Shirley, as well as pieces on hackers and crackers and Internet viruses. As Timothy Leary put it, *Mondo 2000* soon became "a beautiful merger of the psychedelic, the cybernetic, the cultural, the literary and the artistic."[64]

At another level, though, the link between digital technology and hallucinogens reflected a shared dream of disembodiment. For those who had attended the Trips Festival some twenty years earlier, LSD seemed to offer a risky passage to an out-of-body experience, an opportunity to feel a psychic union with others in the crowd. For cyberpunk authors, digital prostheses offered their users the opportunity to escape their bodies and enter cyberspace. Even if that cyberspace was a dangerous, threatening zone—as it was in *Neuromancer*—it could be beautiful, strange, and enticing. In the pages of *Mondo 2000*, readers learned that this new space was being built *right here, right now*, and they learned it from at least one writer with solid counterculture credentials: John Perry Barlow. In the summer of 1990 he visited the offices of Jaron Lanier's VPL Research and donned a pair of VPL Eyephones and a VPL Dataglove. He published the following description of his experience in *Mondo*: "Suddenly I don't have a body anymore. All that remains of the aging shambles which usually constitutes my corporeal self is a glowing, golden hand floating before me like Macbeth's dagger. I point my finger and drift down its length to the bookshelf on the office wall. . . . In this pulsating new landscape, I've been reduced to a point of view. The whole subject of 'me' yawns into a chasm of interesting questions. It's like Disneyland for epistemologists." Barlow could as easily be describing an acid trip. For all the digital technology involved, in Barlow's account the experience clearly belongs as much to the 1960s as the 1990s. And in case the reader has missed the point, Barlow quotes Lanier: "I think this is the biggest thing since we landed on the moon."[65]

Barlow himself was a fairly recent convert to the power of digital technologies but an old hand with mysticism and LSD. He had been raised a Mormon and a Republican, the son of Wyoming ranchers. He had not been allowed to watch television until he reached the sixth grade, and when he did, he recalls, he mostly watched televangelists. At the age of fourteen, he was sent to a Catholic school, and, ironically, his religious feelings began to ebb. They changed again when he went to college at Wesleyan in Connecticut in the late 1960s and began to visit Timothy Leary's group in nearby Millbrook, New York. With his first acid trip, his religious inklings returned. "The sense that there was something holy in the universe was with me again," he later recalled. Yet that holy presence could not be contained within a particular dogma. Rather, Barlow began to move toward the mystical inclinations of a Catholic priest, Pierre Teilhard de Chardin, whose work he read in college, and Gregory Bateson, whose *Steps to an Ecology of Mind* he had read in the early 1970s. In their work, and later in the work of biologists and chaos theorists, Barlow began to see what he called "an underlying grammar to nature."[66] The material world had become, for him, a shape-shifting collection of forms, each penetrated by a certain energy. Although the forms themselves would come and go, the energy remained, permanently circulating, uttering the world. In this sense, for Barlow as for Bateson, "mind was a space"—that is, mind and material world were both systems constituted and maintained by the circulation of energy and thus were mirrors of each other. And in Barlow's experience, if not in Bateson's, LSD had served as a gateway to that understanding.

In the early 1970s, Barlow put his mystical imagination to work for the house band of the San Francisco acid scene, the Grateful Dead. He had met Dead guitarist Bob Weir in boarding school. Starting in 1970, Barlow penned a variety of Dead songs, including "Hell in a Bucket," "Picasso Moon," "Mexicali Blues," and "I Need a Miracle."[67] In the process, he entered a world in which technology—in this case, electric guitars, amplifiers, oversized speakers, and colored lights—were routinely used to create a state of ecstatic union. Whereas other bands might have played to an audience, the Grateful Dead saw themselves as playing for a community. Especially with the long, improvisational guitar riffs by their lead guitar player, Jerry Garcia, affectionately known as "Captain Trips," the band would take their audience of Dead Heads on the aural equivalent of an acid trip. To attend a Dead concert was to enter another world, one in which drugs and technology were simply means to a harmonious, communitarian end.

At the same time, Barlow was working on his family's cattle ranch in Pinedale, Wyoming. By the early 1980s, he had taken over the ranch and had begun writing a series of never-produced television scripts. He got a computer to help with formatting (computers were "a really smart form of white out," he thought), and gradually became more and more interested in the machine itself. "Here was another environment that I could put my mind in that was clean," he later remembered. "I wanted to kind of hide in there and I did."[68] What he wanted to hide from was the fact that the ranch was slowly failing:

> I enjoyed being in the physical world [i.e., working on the ranch] and I would be doing that still if I had been able to, but at a certain point I had to bow to the same historical inevitabilities which have reduced what was, at the turn of the century, fifty percent of the American work force in agriculture to less than one percent today. I became part of that statistic. I sold the ranch. I didn't know what I would do for sure after that. But it did occur to me that there was a lot more money in bullshit than there had ever been in bulls and I would get into information. And here I am.[69]

Barlow's shift from agricultural work to information work was abrupt, painful, and involuntary. "I did try my personal best to resist conscription as a Knowledge Worker," he writes, "but I was as culturally doomed as the Tasaday of New Guinea. . . . Yanked from the 19th Century, I found myself . . . tossed unceremoniously onto the doorstep of the 21st."[70]

For Barlow, this meant reaching out to his old friends in San Francisco. In 1986, while still in Pinedale, Barlow heard that David Gans, a Bay area disc jockey and connoisseur of the Grateful Dead, and hundreds of other Dead

Heads, were conversing on the WELL. In December 1986, Barlow joined. Over the next few years he became one of the system's stars. As Bruce Sterling remembered, Barlow was "a computer networker of truly stellar brilliance. He had a poet's gift of concise, colorful phrasing. He also had a journalist's shrewdness, an off-the-wall, self-deprecating wit, and a phenomenal wealth of simple personal charm."[71] Like Howard Rheingold, Barlow contributed to the system in multiple ways, often simultaneously. He engaged in furious and funny debates about the nature of intellectual property, told personal stories, and periodically appeared for face-to-face meetings in San Francisco. For Barlow, as for Rheingold, the WELL was a simultaneously professional and interpersonal community; and as a working journalist, Barlow, like Rheingold, was able to take full and complex advantage of the system. Within four years of joining, he was writing regularly not only for *Mondo 2000*, but also for the *Communications of the ACM*, a newsletter for computer professionals. Shortly his work would begin appearing in *Wired*. Moreover, thanks to his presence on the WELL, Barlow became a source for a number of journalists. As reporter, commentator, and source, he began to weld his own experience of Pinedale, Wyoming, his acid-driven mysticism, and his experience of the WELL first to virtual reality and then to computer-networked communication.

As Barlow's 1990 article on VPL for *Mondo* suggests, he had been thinking of cyberspace for some time as referring to virtual reality. At the same time, however, thanks to his participation on the WELL, he was beginning to think that it might refer to computer networks too. The shift in Barlow's views began in December 1989, when Paul Tough and Jack Hitt, editors at *Harper's Magazine*, hosted a forum on hacking on the WELL. Forums were a long-standing genre at *Harper's*. Usually, the magazine would gather a half dozen experts on a particular issue, invite them to sit down with one another, and tape the ensuing conversation. Editors would later sort through the conversation, identify its main themes, and print key portions in the magazine. In 1989 the editors had become interested in hacking largely thanks to the case of Robert Morris Jr., a computer science graduate student at Cornell. In November 1988, he had released a "worm" onto the Internet. Self-propagating and self-replicating, the worm clogged thousands of computers around the world and gave many people their first glimpse of the power of computer viruses. It also reinforced long-standing public fears of rogue computer programmers and the damage they could do.[72]

Paul Tough, who suggested the forum, recommended that instead of the usual face-to-face meeting, it should be an invitation-only conference on the WELL. Tough had been a member of the WELL for six months, and in recruiting the thirty or so participants in the forum, Tough leaned heavily on internal WELL networks.[73] He selected some contributors, such as Lee Felsenstein and John Draper, who were in fact accomplished hackers. Many of these participants had migrated to the WELL after attending the Hackers' Conference at Fort Cronkhite in 1984. Tough also selected many participants who could not have been described as hackers but who had been longtime, high-visibility participants on the WELL. These included Stewart Brand, Howard Rheingold, Kevin Kelly, and John Perry Barlow. Tough later recalled that he chose these participants in part for the fact that they had participated in debates about hacking on the WELL and in part because they wrote vivid prose.[74] Yet it also seems likely that a network dynamic was at work here. As at the first Hackers' Conference, those who helped host the discussion of a topic (in this case, on the WELL) had become visible to mainstream journalists (in this case, Tough) and had ultimately become part of the story themselves. In this way, their local legitimacy as WELL members served to validate their authority on the broader subject of hacking. Finally, in addition to WELL regulars, Tough included Emmanuel Goldstein, the editor of *2600*, a New York quarterly devoted to the how-to's of hacking, and, on Goldstein's recommendation, two young, practicing hackers who worked under the pseudonyms Acid Phreak and Phiber Optik.

When they joined the discussion on the WELL, Phreak and Optik immediately set off a culture clash. The conflict could be seen clearly in the edited version of the forum eventually printed in *Harper's*. Like the online forum, and like its predecessor, the Hackers' Conference of 1984, the conversation opened with a discussion of the hacker ethic. WELL regulars described the ethic in cybernetic and countercultural terms familiar to their online colleagues. Lee Felsenstein compared hackers to the "Angelheaded hipsters" of Allen Ginsberg's poem "Howl." John Perry Barlow described them as solitary inventors designing a system through which humans would acquire the simultaneous unity of other "collective organisms." Acid Phreak would have none of it. "There is no one hacker ethic," he wrote. "Everyone has his own. To say that we all think the same way is preposterous."[75] Among WELL regulars like Felsenstein and Barlow, hackers were cybernetic counterculturalists, creatures devoted to establishing a new, more open culture by any electronic means necessary. For Acid Phreak, hackers were break-in artists devoted to exploring and exploiting weaknesses in closed and especially corporate systems.

The conflict came to a head over John Perry Barlow's credit records. For some time, Barlow's contributions to the online conversation had been echoing the WELL's longstanding internal ethos of virtual community by comparing open computer systems to villages with unlocked doors. In his view, Phreak and Optik were failing to respect a village covenant.

Emmanuel Goldstein, however, pointed out that institutional computer systems bore little relation to small towns. Rather, they served as centers for the compilation of surveillance data. Thus confronted, Barlow turned away from the village metaphor and toward cybernetics. Institutions, he wrote, were organisms whose "blood is digital"; hackers needed to be "in their bloodstreams like an infection of humanity."[76] In keeping with the Whole Earth view of networked computing and the local ideologies prevalent on the WELL, Barlow continued to depict interlinked machines as representatives of interchangeable systems—small towns, organisms, digital networks. Ultimately, Acid Phreak lost patience with Barlow and, in a classic bit of *realpolitik*, used Barlow's Pinedale address information to download and publish Barlow's personal credit history.

For Acid Phreak, the distinction between a real small town and an institution-based network of computers was crystal clear. Small towns could be collaborative, democratic, and, in that sense, public places. Institutions like the company that had maintained Barlow's credit records, however, were surveillance machines, organizations devoted to wresting individuals' control of their personal information away from them and centralizing it elsewhere for profit. In the *Harper's* forum, Acid's views became entangled in a larger culture clash, however. On the one hand, with their flashy pseudonyms and steady-state irreverence, Phreak and Optik came closer to the dark public image of hacking suggested by Robert Morris. With their talk of cybernetics and "open" systems and rural villages, on the other hand, Felsenstein, Barlow and the WELL regulars offered a plausible, if imperfect, alternative vision of the Net.

In Paul Tough's view, it was this culture clash that allowed two notions to enter wide public debate. For one thing, he recalls, Phreak and Optik had made it clear that hacking could be a free-speech issue, as the editors of *2600* had long maintained. But in addition, particularly through Barlow's writings, the forum exposed the wider public to the "communitarian vision of the online world" popular at the WELL.[77] Even as Phreak and Optik confronted Barlow within the forum, the forum itself modeled the WELL's own vision of computer-mediated communication. In the pages of *Harper's*, Tough and Hitt created a paginated version of the WELL. Like the online world of PicoSpan, the forum offered a disembodied, text-based conversation, one in which members of multiple networks—early hackers, the *2600* crowd, Whole Earth staffers, WELL regulars—came together around a particular question. In the *Harper's* textual forum, as in its online version, and as in the face-to-face forum of the 1984 Hackers' Conference, the communitarian ethos of the Whole Earth network was not only deployed as a symbolic resource in discussions of the hacker ethic; it was embedded in the organization of the discussion itself. In each case, contributors took part in a seemingly nonhierarchical, disembodied conversation among equals, and they did so within the same computer "space" supposedly being attacked by these very hackers. It is this *form* of conversation, and the image of hackers participating in it, that *Harper's* made visible to its readers.

Not long after the conclusion of the online discussion, and before the story appeared in the magazine, *Harper's* invited John Perry Barlow to dinner with Phreak and Optik in Manhattan. "They looked to be as dangerous as ducks," he later wrote. By his own account, Barlow became their "scout-master" and, as a result, began receiving "'conference calls' in which six or eight of them would crack pay phones all over New York and simultaneously land on my line in Wyoming." On January 24, 1990, Barlow wrote, "a platoon of Secret Service agents entered the apartment which Acid Phreak shares with his mother and twelve-year-old sister. The latter was the only person home when they burst through the door with guns drawn. They managed to hold her at bay for about half an hour until their quarry happened home."[78] Acid Phreak, along with Phiber Optik and a third New York City cracker, nicknamed Scorpion, had been accused of causing a massive crash in the AT&T computer system ten days earlier. The Secret Service confiscated their computers, answering machines, notebooks, and computer disks.

For Barlow and other WELL regulars, these visits were just the latest steps in what had begun to look like a concerted government crackdown on hackers everywhere. In June 1989, for instance, the FBI had begun investigating a group calling itself the NuPrometheus League. Named for the Greek god Prometheus, the bringer of fire, the League had gotten hold of a proprietary patch of software code that helped control the screen display in the Apple Macintosh and had mailed copies of it to a number of prominent people in the computer industry. At Apple's behest, the FBI began to interview the recipients of the code. Not long afterward, the Secret Service launched Operation Sundevil. On May 8, 1990, 150 agents fanned out in a dozen cities, executed some twenty-seven search warrants, and made three arrests. As a press release put out by the U.S. attorney's office in Phoenix, Arizona, put it, the agents were out to stop "illegal computer hacking activities."[79] Hoping to counteract electronic fraud (including the cracking of phone systems), agents seized forty-two computer systems, twenty-five of which were running computer bulletin board systems that might have allowed for the sharing of information on cracking and hacking.[80]

To Barlow and others on the WELL, the government's various search-and-seizure missions looked like an assault not only on particular forms of electronic activity, but also on a hacker culture that had itself become intimately intertwined with WELL culture. Acid Phreak, for instance, had become a fairly popular presence on the WELL. When he was raided, WELL regulars tended to feel that his "crimes," even if they had occurred, had not caused any significant damage. John Perry Barlow had long been active in WELL discussions of hacking and free speech, and in 1990 he linked the two as central components of "cyberspace." In May of that year, as part of the NuPrometheus investigation, an FBI agent named Richard Baxter visited Barlow in Pinedale. Barlow's name had appeared on a list of attendees at a recent Hackers' Conference (by that time there were annual conferences descended from the 1984 event). According to Barlow, Baxter believed the Hackers' Conference was a collection of computer criminals, likely with links to the NuPrometheus League.[81] Baxter also harbored numerous varied misconceptions about the computer industry and computers themselves. As Barlow later recalled,

> Poor Agent Baxter didn't know a ROM chip from a Vise-grip when he arrived, so much of that time was spent trying to educate him on the nature of the thing which had been stolen. Or whether "stolen" was the right term for what had happened to it.
>
> You know things have rather jumped the groove when potential suspects must explain to law enforcers the nature of their alleged perpetrations.[82]

Soon after Baxter left, Barlow posted an account of his visit on the WELL, as an early draft of what would ultimately become the essay in which he first described cyberspace as an electronic frontier: "Crime and Puzzlement." Barlow's account stirred up a hornet's nest on the WELL. Some members even accused Barlow of serving as an FBI informant by attempting to educate Agent Baxter. One WELL member who read Barlow's story was Mitch Kapor, who had founded Lotus Development Corporation, an early and highly successful software company. He had also coauthored Lotus 1-2-3, an extremely popular spreadsheet program. Some years earlier he had sold the company for tens of millions of dollars and had become something of a traveling computer pundit, writing on the WELL and elsewhere about intellectual property, software design, and civil liberties. In addition to being a WELL user, Kapor was a lifelong fan of the Whole Earth publications and owned a complete collection of its catalogs.[83] He was also one of the people who had received a copy of Apple's code in the mail from NuPrometheus.

In early June, not long after reading Barlow's work on the WELL, and in a gesture that has since become a bit of cyberculture legend, Kapor found himself flying in his private jet near Pinedale, Wyoming. He called Barlow from the air and asked if he might stop by. They had met before both socially and professionally (Barlow had interviewed Kapor for a computer magazine) but were not well acquainted. That afternoon, they sat down in Barlow's kitchen and talked about the various government crackdowns then under way. Together they decided to found an organization called the Computer Liberty Foundation. As Barlow explained in a later draft of "Crime and Puzzlement," the foundation would raise and channel funds for lobbying and education on issues of digital free speech. It would also involve itself in then-ongoing cases with an eye toward showing that the Secret Service had exercised prior restraint on publications. The foundation would, in addition, work "to convey to both the public and the policy-makers metaphors which will illuminate the more general stake in liberating Cyberspace."[84]

The first and most influential of the metaphors Barlow referred to was the "electronic frontier."[85] Being master networkers, Kapor and Barlow quickly gained press coverage of their new organization as well as offers of funding from Steve Wozniak, cofounder of Apple, and John Gilmore of Sun Microsystems. They started a conference on the WELL, and they recruited Stewart Brand, among others, to serve on their new organization's board of directors. One evening in the early fall, Barlow convened a dinner in San Francisco attended by Brand, Jaron Lanier, Chuck Blanchard (who worked at VPL with Lanier), and Paul Saffo (head of the Institute for the Future, a Silicon Valley think tank). Barlow and Kapor wanted help renaming their organization. Everyone at the dinner agreed that networked computing was then in what Barlow called "a frontier condition." "I came up with Electronic Frontier Foundation over the course of that dinner," Barlow recalled, "and everybody seemed to like it."[86]

The Electronic Frontier Foundation would have a substantial impact on public discussions of computing and regulation throughout the 1990s. Already, though, even as Barlow's dinner looked forward to that work, the notion he articulated there, of cyberspace as an electronic frontier, capped a long process by which the countercultural and cybernetic ideas that had informed the Whole Earth publications for two decades had migrated into the digital arena. In the final text of "Crime and Puzzlement," which he posted to the WELL on June 8, 1990, for example, Barlow depicted cyberspace as a frontier, but his model for that frontier was the WELL. The WELL, he wrote, was "the latest thing in frontier villages," a "small town" whose "Main Street is a central minicomputer." The minicomputer was linked to others in a network that "extends all across the immense region of electron states, microwaves, magnetic fields, light pulses and thought which sci-fi writer William Gibson named cyberspace." This region, wrote Barlow, "has a lot in common with the nineteenth-century West. It is vast, unmapped, culturally and legally ambiguous, verbally terse . . . hard to get around in, and up for grabs."[87]

Like John Coate and other WELL users, Barlow transformed the difficulty of using PicoSpan software into evidence that the WELL resembled the rural frontiers favored by the back-to-the-land movement. But Barlow's account of cyberspace also mingled the countercultural critique of technocracy with a celebration of the mobility and independence required of information workers in a rapidly networking economy:

> I'm a member of that half of the human race which is inclined to divide the human race into two kinds of people. My dividing line runs between the people who crave certainty and the people who trust chance. . . .
>
> Large organizations and their drones huddle on one end of my scale, busily trying to impose predictable homogeneity on messy circumstance. On the other end, free-lancers and ne'er-do-wells cavort about, getting by on luck if they get by at all.[88]

The "free-lancers and n'er-do-wells," he explained, had found a home in cyberspace. As once members of the back-to-the-land movement had farmed the rural margins of the material American landscape in the hope of escaping the ostensibly dronelike lives of corporation men, so, in Barlow's account, freelancers now roamed an immaterial landscape, Long Hunters trusting chance.

What is more, the best of them, like the rebels of the 1960s, were engaged in dismantling the very organizations in which drones were concentrated. These were the cyberpunks, whom Barlow, shifting rhetorical gears, described as "viruses" attacking the body of "The Institution." For Barlow, the government's crackdown on hacking had reawakened an old memory. "I drifted back into a 60's-style sense of the government, thinking it a thing of monolithic and evil efficiency," he wrote in 1990.[89] In "Crime and Puzzlement," the countercultural rebellion of the 1960s and the cybernetic rhetoric of biosocial systems together offered a symbolic language in which to celebrate the activities of freelance technology workers. In the process, the notion of cyberspace emerged as an emblem of an idealized, forward-looking social system—and yet, the terms of that system had been set by debates that took place twenty years earlier.

Ultimately, Barlow argued that cyberspace offered what LSD, Christian mysticism, cybernetics, and countercultural "energy" theory had all promised: transpersonal communion. In Barlow's account, the technological limitations of the WELL gave rise to and became evidence for a mystical transformation of humanity. "In this silent world," he wrote, "all conversation is typed. To enter it, one forsakes both body and place and becomes a thing of words alone." To Barlow, writing before the advent of the World Wide Web and its graphical browsers, this was more than a simple function of computer conferencing technology; it was a Sign: "As a result of [the opening of cyberspace], humanity is now undergoing the most profound transformation of its history. Coming into the Virtual World, we inhabit Information. Indeed, we become Information. Thought is embodied and the Flesh is made Word. It's weird as hell."[90] Barlow suggested that computer networks had achieved what the communes and countercultural consumption of the 1960s could not. Framed as the disembodied, nonhierarchical, high-tech home of computer hackers and other independent types, cyberspace, and its prototypical system, the WELL, constituted fitting alternatives to corporate and government hives. In the cybernetic style familiar to readers of the *Whole Earth Catalog* and *CoEvolution Quarterly*, Barlow held out cyberspace as a simultaneously technological, biological, and social system. His cyberspace became part of a universal discourse, enfolding experiences in multiple domains, and his "electronic frontier" extended well beyond the electronic confines of linked computers.

Nevertheless, like the homegrown rhetoric of virtual community on the WELL, Barlow's universal discourse of cyberspace simultaneously modeled and masked a new and very personal economic reality. By the time he wrote "Crime and Puzzlement," Barlow's ranch had failed. His own material American frontier landscape had faded from view. Like other members of the WELL, Barlow had become an independent information worker. In his notion of cyberspace as an electronic frontier, he had transformed his personal experience of economic transformation into a universal forecast. As he wrote in 1994, Barlow had come to believe that "we must seek our future in the virtual world because there is no economic room left in the physical one."[91] In the 1960s, Barlow and others of his generation saw themselves as having been failed by the large institutions around them and, in response, attempted to form alternative communities. The *Whole Earth Catalog* had been both an emblem of and a resource for those communities. Twenty years later, Barlow suggested, he and others were failed by the traditional economy, and they had to once again constitute an alternative community. For this community, the frontier of cyberspace, and especially the village of the WELL, would have to be home.

CHAPTER 6

Networking the New Economy

In the late 1980s and the early 1990s, the same economic and techno-logical forces that had long shaped work lives in Silicon Valley swept across much of the industrialized world. Networked forms of produc-tion, contract employment, global outsourcing, and deregulated marketplaces all became common features of everyday economic life. So did the nearly universal use of computers and computer networks in business and, increasingly, in the home. Together, these develop-ments suggested to many at the time, and particularly to politicians and pundits on the right, that a "new economy" had appeared, one in which digital technologies and networked forms of economic organi-zation combined to liberate the individual entrepreneur. In a 1988 speech at Moscow State University, President Ronald Reagan became one of the first to make the case. "In the new economy," he explained, "human invention increasingly makes physical resources obsolete. We're breaking through the material conditions of existence to a world where man creates his own destiny."[1]

Such a vision was very congenial to many members of the Whole Earth network, and as the economic and technological whirlwinds of the late 1980s gathered speed, Brand and, later, Kevin Kelly, drew heavily on the intellectual and social resources of the group. Each cre-ated new network forums in which formerly distinct communities could come together, exchange legitimacy, and become visible, to one another and to outsiders, as a single entity. In Brand's case, these communities included representatives of MIT's Media Lab and the Stanford Research Institute and officers of such corporate giants as Royal Dutch/Shell, Volvo, and AT&T, as well as former New Com-munalists. In the late 1980s Brand helped turn these individuals into the principals and clients of a small but highly influential consulting firm, the Global Business Network. For his part, Kevin Kelly linked computer simulation experts affiliated with Los Alamos National Laboratory and its offshoot, the Santa Fe Institute, to prairie ecologists, Biospherians, and programmers at Xerox PARC. In a 521-page volume entitled *Out of Control: The Rise of Neo-Biological Civilization*, Kelly transformed these scientists and their projects into prototypical representatives of what he claimed was a new era in human evolution.

Many of these scientists, like many of the clients of the Global Business Network, represented organizations and worked with technologies that had grown directly out of the cold war–era military-industrial complex. Within the precincts of the Global Business Network and *Out of Control*, however, these organizations acquired a new political valence. They became models of a collaborative world, a world in which technologies were rendering information systems visible, material production processes irrelevant, and bureaucracy obsolete. Their executives and engineers also became visible stand-ins for an emerging corporate elect—entrepreneurial, technologically savvy, but socially and culturally conservative. Like the communards of New Mexico and northern California, the scientists, futurists, and entrepreneurs of the Global Business Network and *Out of Control* constituted a highly educated, mobile, and predominantly white elite. Like the contributors to the original *Whole Earth Catalog*, they mingled the rhetorical and social practices of systems theory with the New Communalist celebration of disembodied intimacy and geographically distributed communion. Yet, like the communards, they also largely turned away from those whose bodies, work styles, and incomes differed from their own. By the mid-1990s, the technocentric, networked social worlds of the Global Business Network and *Out of Control* had become widely looked-to examples of the flexibility and individual satisfaction promised by the New Economy. They would soon become emblems of the social possibilities of the Internet and the World Wide Web as well. As they did, they helped shape popular understandings of the New Economy in terms set not only by the New Communalist dream of social transformation, but also by the New Communalist practice of social segregation.

Back to the Future at MIT

By 1985, despite his founding interest in the WELL, Stewart Brand had begun to get restless. He had edited *CoEvolution Quarterly* for a decade; the *Whole Earth Software Catalog* was failing rapidly. "By the time I'd done a half a dozen versions of the book, ending with a *Whole Earth Software Catalog* in

1985," Brand later explained, "I had no idea whatever about futures and was operating strictly on reflex."[2] Since Kevin Kelly had taken over the editorship of the *Whole Earth Review*, and since the WELL seemed to be self-sustaining, Brand felt ready to leave Sausalito for a while. In 1984 he attended the first of Richard Saul Wurman's Technology, Entertainment, Design (TED) conferences and heard Nicholas Negroponte describe his plans for MIT's new Media Lab.

Brand was dazzled. Negroponte was very much a showman-intellectual in the style of Brand's earlier mentor Buckminster Fuller. A few months later, Brand wrote to Negroponte, asking for a short-term job. Negroponte offered Brand a three-month appointment at MIT's Media Lab. Starting in January 1986, Brand was to help out on a series of projects, including one being led by his old friend from Xerox PARC, Alan Kay, and to teach a class of his own design. That month, he moved to Cambridge, Massachusetts, and took up residence in Kay's house. Over the next year he taught at the Lab, met with its various scientists, attended classes and briefings, and ultimately began to draft a book about the Lab. Brand saw the Lab as an example of the sort of research group he had once hoped the *Whole Earth Catalog* crew could become. Surrounded by computer scientists, musicians, and artists, all linked together by e-mail, Brand began to imagine the Lab as an emblem of a techno-tribal future. In that future, as in the New Communalist past, independent interdisciplinarians would take up tools, transform their individual mind-sets, and establish new collectivities built on a shared delight in innovation.

They would also carry forward the legacy of MIT's own collaborative research culture. In 1987 Brand published his best-selling profile of the Lab, *The Media Lab: Inventing the Future at MIT*, in which he explained that the Media Lab was a direct descendant of the Rad Lab. In 1952, he wrote, Jerome Wiesner, an electrical engineer and a Rad Lab veteran, took charge of the Rad Lab's postwar incarnation, the Research Laboratory of Electronics (RLE). At the RLE, as formerly in and around the Rad Lab, natural scientists, computer scientists, and electronics engineers worked together in a multidisciplinary full-court press to understand all forms of communication—mechanical, electronic, and biological. Wiesner never believed, as Wiener did, that the human brain and the computer could model one another. Even so, the RLE, like the Rad Lab, offered a rich soup of information theory and rhetoric, much of it growing out of the cybernetic intuition that digital systems and natural systems might model one another. Over the next two decades, the RLE went on to spawn the field of artificial intelligence, with its own MIT Lab (the AI Lab), and the Architecture Machine Group, headed by Nicholas Negroponte. After seven years of fund-raising by Negroponte and

Wiesner, the Architecture Machine Group evolved into the Media Lab, and in 1985 it took up residence in a $45 million I. M. Pei–designed building in the heart of the MIT campus.

In *Inventing the Future*, Brand depicted the Media Lab not only as a bridge between the cybernetic past and the digital future, but as the institutional home of a new form of technocentric performance art. The Media Lab was a functioning institution and a metaphor, he explained.[3] As an institution, it sat at the hub of a wide corporate and academic network. With an annual budget of $6 million a year, the Lab had almost one hundred sponsors at the time of Brand's visit, each of whom had paid a minimum of two hundred thousand dollars to join. The sponsors were not allowed to demand that any particular research be done on their behalf. Rather, they were buying permission to watch as the eleven different subdivisions of the Lab went about exploring the possibilities of human-machine interaction and multi-media convergence; a sponsor could later act on any insights that emerged. Around the time of Brand's visit, the Lab employed a wide array of special-ists, including scientists, musicians, visual artists, and software engineers. Together they developed projects ranging from electronic newspapers to wearable computers and large-scale holograms. Media Lab personnel were never required to produce artifacts that could be mass-produced or that would feed directly into sponsors' lines of business per se. Instead, they were expected to produce "demos." In these famously flashy presentations, grad-uate students and faculty alike would show how digital technology might alter a particular social practice. Corporate sponsors joined the Lab more for the chance to watch these demos than to get assistance with their ongoing research needs.

The Media Lab demos marked the latest steps in a complex dance be-tween high-technology research culture and the American counterculture. To be sure, they represented a traditional feature of engineering culture, particularly its World War II incarnation. In the Rad Lab and later, across those disciplines linked by systems theory, scientists and engineers routinely demonstrated new technologies in order to make manifest not only their immediate applications, but also their broad ability to transform existing so-cial systems. Norbert Wiener's anti-aircraft predictor, Ross Ashby's homeo-stat, and numerous other cybernetic machines each served as a demonstra-tion of the ways that human life could be enhanced by human-machine integration. In the late 1960s, the New Communalist wing of the counter-culture had, in its own way, thoroughly embraced the "demo-or-die" ethos of the engineering world. In venues like the Trips Festival, the hippies of Haight-Ashbury sought to demonstrate the ability of technologies such as LSD, stereos, and stroboscopic lights to amplify human consciousness.

The communes of the Southwest, too, served as demonstrations, illustrating the powers of new forms of housing and new forms of cohabitation to model a new society. These various local demonstrations were connected by a far-flung network of interpersonal relationships, a network in which Stewart Brand was a key figure.

Fifteen years later, Brand symbolically integrated the Media Lab into this network, depicting the Lab as a living demonstration of an alternative society based on a shared and technologically amplified experience of consciousness. The Lab, he wrote, served as a "prefiguration of the wider evolution" of media and organizational systems. The counterculture may have faded away and its networks dissolved, but a new mechanism for transpersonal communion was emerging. "A global computer is taking shape, and we're all connected to it," Brand explained. "*How* we're connected to it is the Media Lab's prime interest."[4] The Media Lab, like the *Whole Earth Catalog* before it, served as both an emblem of this developing world and a mechanism through which to enter it. As a working laboratory at MIT, the Media Lab was actively building real digital artifacts and networks. Like the products Brand had once reviewed in the *Catalog*, the Media Lab's digital newspapers and Lego robots could be bought and used, so to speak, at least by corporate clients. And like the *Catalog* itself, the lab served to link representatives of relatively disconnected groups—in this case, corporate, academic, and technical—into a single functioning network.

Brand depicted in his book both those human networks and their relationship to information technologies as prototypes of a simultaneously cybernetic and New Communalist social ideal. Brand found the Media Lab to be an open, diverse, and nonhierarchical social system, much like the media it was inventing. "Mass media," wrote Brand, mixing his metaphors, were "a form of cultural monocropping." Citing Norbert Wiener, he depicted mass media as dangers to the health of society. The scientists of the Media Lab, in contrast, were "committed to making the individual the driver of the new information technologies rather than the driven."[5] With the individual in charge, a new "communication environment" was emerging—diverse, interconnected, complex, and presumably healthy. The Media Lab stood as a particularly magnificent prototype of this "environment." Its internal diversity of scientists, technologists, anthropologists, and so on mirrored the diversity of an ideal ecosystem and an ideal society. So too did the diverse digital technologies it was developing. They both reflected and triggered the development of a nonhierarchical society, highly individuated and linked by invisible—in this case, digital—forces.

If Brand's Media Lab seemed to model a digital version of a New Communalist political ideal, Nicholas Negroponte as Brand portrayed him resembled that era's heroes. Brand compared Negroponte to McLuhan, noting that both knew how to play to a crowd. "Indeed," wrote Brand, "this is no rumpled, tweedy, musing scholar. *Fortune* magazine observed that he 'looks more like a matinee idol than a walking paradigm of the state-of-the-art technologist.' Negroponte does look a bit like a young Robert Wagner. He's meticulously groomed and dresses sharp."[6] In addition to his sartorial splendor, Negroponte possessed another quality for which McLuhan might have been known: "handwaving." Negroponte and others in the Lab waved their hands as they moved "past provable material into speculation, anticipating and overwhelming objection with manual dexterity."[7] Like McLuhan, and perhaps even more like Buckminster Fuller, Negroponte could make an emerging way of life visible to Brand in his speech. Moreover, like Kesey, Negroponte seemed to live the life he preached for others. As LSD and a beat-up school bus had once freed Kesey to roam the American landscape with a tribe of friends, so digital technologies now allowed Negroponte to turn work into play. "Some of us enjoy a privileged existence where our work life and our leisure life are almost synonymous," he told Brand. "More and more people I think can move into that position with the coming of truly intimate technology."[8]

In Brand's account, then, the Media Lab became a link in two chains simultaneously: one the chain of cybernetics, strung from the Rad Lab of World War II to the Media Lab of the present, and the other the chain of countercultural revolution, strung from the communes of the 1960s to the computer labs of the 1980s. Brand's book was infused with the universal rhetorical logic common to both intellectual trajectories. That is, he depicted the Media Lab and its digital technologies, as well as Negroponte and the corporate and research cultures within which he worked, as prototypes of an emerging socio-technical world. Each element modeled every other: the Media Lab made digital-social hybrids; its culture was itself a hybrid of digital and cultural workers; the world that its research would produce would be infused with such hybrids. In this sense, the Lab not only made and sold "demos" but was a demo in its own right. So was the life of its leader. If the Lab demonstrated the way a "wired" world might look, then Negroponte was the image of the social possibilities such a world might offer. Mobile, wealthy, handsome, completely networked in both the technological and the political sense, Negroponte was a new kind of man. As an echo of Marshall McLuhan, though, he was also the reincarnation of an earlier generation of hero. Like the Media Lab he headed, Negroponte was the living bridge between the legacy of cybernetics and the legacy of countercultural experimentation.

Almost immediately after it was published in 1987, *Inventing the Future* became a best seller in the United States and abroad. The Media Lab itself became the subject of numerous magazine and newspaper stories, most notably a lengthy encomium in *Time* magazine.[9] Over the coming years, both the Media Lab and Nicholas Negroponte would become leading emblems of the techno-social future. They would also become touchstones for Brand's next venture, the Global Business Network.

Building the Global Business Network

Shortly before Brand took up residency at the Media Lab, he and his new wife, Patty Phelan, traveled to Africa (he had exchanged a stay on their tugboat in Sausalito for a stay on a twenty-thousand-acre game ranch). On his way home in the fall of 1986, he stopped in London to visit an old friend, Peter Schwartz. Brand and Schwartz had known each other since the early 1970s, when Schwartz worked as a futurist at the Stanford Research Institute (SRI) and served on the board of the Portola Foundation. Since early 1982, Schwartz had been employed in the Planning Group at Royal Dutch/Shell, and he had recently begun writing for the *Whole Earth Review* under the pseudonym Szanto. The Planning Group had an unusual reputation in business circles. Through the late 1960s, Shell had planned its future business activities using a highly quantitative procedure known as the Unified Planning Machinery. Around 1970, though, members of the Planning Group embraced a version of the scenario methodology developed by futurist Herman Kahn.[10] Using it, the group had predicted the oil crisis of 1973, allowing Shell to profit when other oil companies had not. In 1981 they repeated the feat, and Shell was able to sell off its oil reserves before an international collapse in oil prices occurred. In 1986 the group's head, Arie de Geus, had begun to reexamine the company's planning process. Knowing of Brand's long-standing interest in organizational change, Schwartz introduced the two.

As a result of that meeting, de Geus and Schwartz hired Brand to organize a series of networking events known as the Learning Conferences; those events in turn gave rise to a network organization that, like the Media Lab, would have a substantial impact on public perceptions of digital technology and the New Economy. Like the Media Lab, the Learning Conferences and the Global Business Network that grew out of them would bridge cybernetic theory and the countercultural critique of hierarchy. On the one hand, they would draw on the collaborative work styles and systems rhetoric characteristic of cold war research institutes. On the other hand, they would recreate the New Communalist turn away from politics and toward business and everyday life as sites of social change. Like the happenings of the New York art world or the communes that followed them, the Learning

Conferences offered their attendees an experience of intense interpersonal connection and at the same time presented that experience as a metaphor for an ideal, elite, and alternative way of living. At the height of the cold war, countercultural artists and communards had hoped to create alternatives to bureaucratic technocracy. Now, in the late 1980s, as the cold war wound to a close, Brand, de Geus, and Schwartz melded countercultural and cybernetic rhetoric, practice, and social theory to help corporate executives model and manage their work lives in a post-Fordist economy.

In keeping with Brand and de Geus's first discussions, the six semiannual Learning Conferences were designed to explore the dynamics of group learning. Brand staged the events in environments that he considered to be "learning systems" in their own right. One meeting took place at Biosphere 2 in the Arizona desert; another involved a visit to Danny Hillis's Thinking Machines Corporation in Cambridge, Massachusetts; a third brought participants to the Esalen Institute in Big Sur. Like the Media Lab, these sites were meant to be both material and metaphorical. That is, they would allow participants to simultaneously study and engage with a "system" as it learned. They would also allow new interpersonal networks to form. The conferences were jointly sponsored by Shell, AT&T, and Volvo. For each conference, Brand reached out to his extended network of contacts and sought to bring them together with representatives of the sponsoring corporations. Regular participants included Mary Catherine Bateson (anthropologist daughter of Gregory Bateson and Margaret Mead), Peter Warshall (ecologist and steady contributor to the Whole Earth publications), and Chilean neurobiologist Francisco Varela—all longtime friends of Brand— as well as MIT's Marvin Minsky (head of the AI Lab) and Seymour Papert (a researcher at the Media Lab) and senior executives from the sponsoring corporations. Between face-to-face meetings, participants were invited to participate in a private conference on the EIES network and, later, on the WELL.

Brand modeled the conferences on the Macy meetings that had done so much to promote cybernetics. Like the organizers of those sessions, he hoped to bring together representatives of various communities with an eye to generating not formal products so much as intellectual insights and new rhetorics and new social networks to support them. "The meetings did not 'work' in the sense of creating any tangible product," recalled Schwartz. "Rather, they led to understandings and collaborations, for both the corporate clients and the participants." In the context of the conferences themselves, these collaborations first emerged alongside a systems-oriented contact language. Brought together from a variety of disciplines and communities, the participants needed to find a common tongue. "One language that we found in common—even amongst our different disciplines—was the idea of distributed learning," Brand later remembered. The notion of distributed learning, in which individuals learn together as elements in a system, was simultaneously congenial to Shell executives ("because that's pretty much how they do their administration"), to cyberneticians such as Francisco Varela (because it seemed to describe his notion of "awakening systems"), to computer engineers like Danny Hillis (because it was a conceptual element of massively parallel computing), and to Brand's own "'access to tools' approach to life."[11] Gradually, Brand later remembered, this rhetoric of distributed learning appeared to offer the answer to the questions that the founders of the conferences had first hoped to address: "We came to feel that the question of how you accelerate learning or adaptivity has already become answered—by distributed adaptivity or learning. That wasn't even discussed as such—it just emerged as a common language among the people at the Learning Conferences."[12]

The common language also closed a universal rhetorical loop. To the participants in the Learning Conferences, it served as both an answer to the question of how groups learn best and a tool with which to keep their particular, emerging network working. "In a sequence of conferences with mostly the same people, they become friends," Brand explained. "Gradually their professional lives intersect, and they visit each others' homes. . . . It's a family affair. Then it affects the work they choose to do."[13] In the Learning Conference model, the members of a nascent, interdisciplinary network were in fact geographically distributed collaborators. They were getting to know not only a shared body of ideas, but one another as well. Over time, their experience supplied a language of distributed learning that modeled that experience and offered answers to the analytical questions they had brought to the group. In effect, the social network itself became the answer to its members' questions as to the nature and effects of group learning. If the future of group learning was "distributed adaptivity," then the members of the Learning Conferences, huddled together in the Arizona desert or out on a cold Norse sea, were its vanguard. They were a human "system," the biological mirror of the digital networks through which they communicated and of the geographically distributed network of "learning systems" they visited twice a year. And, of course, they were also a model of the sort of "learning system" that the corporations that funded the conferences hoped to become.

In 1987 the networks and cybernetic thought style of the Learning Conferences became the basis of the Global Business Network (GBN). Peter Schwartz, together with Jay Ogilvy, whom he had hired at SRI and who was now director of research for the SRI Values and Lifestyles Program (a marketing research team), wanted to design a consulting firm that could take advantage of the networks and networking mind-set that had begun to emerge around the Learning Conferences. They recruited as cofounders Brand, Shell veteran Napier Collyns, and Lawrence Wilkinson, a Bay area financier and media producer who was serving at the time as president of Colossal Pictures, a film and television production company. As Schwartz put it, the founders hoped that GBN would do three things for their clients: "plug them into a network of remarkable people, . . . include them in a highly focused and filtered information flow, and . . . reorganize their perceptions about alternative futures through the scenario method."[14]

Like the Learning Conferences, the Global Business Network was designed to consist of overlapping networks of people, events, and information media. First, the company gathered up a network of individuals from a variety of fields: computing, ecology, anthropology, biology, and journalism, among others. It then created various forums in which corporate clients could interact with this network. Some were face-to-face, others took place online, and still others consisted of newsletters and lists of books suggested by members. Second, the company offered narrowly targeted consulting services, mainly grouped around scenario planning. In this way, GBN drew on the organizational structure and forecasting tools of cold war–era research culture and blended them with the countercultural turn toward business and social networks as sites of social change. GBN itself became both a model and a source of symbolic and rhetorical resources for corporate executives and government officials looking to understand post-Fordist forms of economic activity. In its meetings, its publications, and its presentations, GBN offered those individuals a vision of the New Economy as a networked entity, open to management by elite social groups and charismatic leaders and linked by interpersonal and informational networks, an entity whose laws could be made visible through a mix of systems theory, collaborative social practice, and mystical insight.

GBN's particular blending of countercultural and techno-cultural organizational styles depended on its roots in two organizations, the Stanford Research Institute and Royal Dutch/Shell. In the 1950s and 1960s, SRI and Shell represented the apogee of the military and the industrial worlds. SRI had been founded in 1947 to offer business consulting for the oil industry, but, along with the RAND Corporation, it very quickly became one of the two leading American think tanks for the U.S. military. Royal Dutch/Shell was a multinational behemoth devoted to extracting and refining oil. Yet, elements of both organizations had embraced countercultural practices. GBN cofounders Jay Ogilvy and Peter Schwartz, for instance, both worked at SRI just as the military-industrial consulting firm found itself coming to grips with the counterculture around it. As Art Kleiner has pointed out, SRI was the first university-based research institute to offer consulting services for business, the military, and scientific organizations, and to mingle operations research, economics, and political forecasting in the process. In the late 1960s and 1970s, with offices just down the road from Stanford in Menlo Park, SRI was permeated with a sense of what Kleiner calls "the sheer, pragmatic, exalting *usefulness* of system-centered, holistic faith." Much of that faith had first grown up in the heart of the cold war research establishment, around Jay Forrester's research in systems dynamics at MIT. But some of it had also come out of the Bay area's psychedelic scene. In 1967 SRI hired Willis Harman, cofounder of the Institute for Advanced Study, where Stewart Brand had first taken LSD. Harman brought with him a conviction that the psychological and social barriers of the white-collar, corporate world needed to be broken down so that executives and engineers might have insight not only into their own minds, but into the true nature of the world around them. LSD, which was now illegal, had been one tool for that purpose; perhaps, he thought, futures research could be another.[15]

By 1972 Harman was heading the Futures Group at SRI; in 1973 he hired Peter Schwartz. Only a few years out of college, Schwartz quickly absorbed both planning methodology and countercultural politics. At SRI he had the chance to work on contracts for both corporate and government clients. He soon came to believe that of the two, the corporate sector was more flexible and more open to change and, in particular, that businesses, unlike governments, could be decentralized. This impression was reinforced by his participation in the San Francisco Bay area's countercultural business scene. Schwartz happened to live near Paul Hawken, founder of the organic grocery chain Erewhon Trading Company and later cofounder of the gardening tools company Smith & Hawken. Together they became involved in the Whole Earth Truck Store, and in the mid-1970s they joined the board of the Portola Institute, home of the *Whole Earth Catalog*. Schwartz went on to be an early investor in Smith & Hawken. Standing outside governmental and corporate organizations, these enterprises worked very much in synch with the precepts of the countercultural critique of bureaucracy. Each sought to support individual lifestyles that their staffers believed would, in aggregate, lead to collective change; and all stood against the hierarchical organization and psychological fragmentation they thought characteristic of large-scale American industry.[16]

From their work at SRI and their connections with Hawken and the Whole Earth community, Ogilvy and Schwartz brought to the Global Business Network a deep faith in business as a site of social change and a habit of working in an informal, networked way. They also came with extensive experience in scenario planning. Like Norbert Wiener's cybernetics, the scenario method had its roots in World War II, when American military planners tried to model the possible behaviors of their enemies.[17] Paul Edwards has pointed out that in its earliest efforts, World War II operations research gathered up and quantified many different kinds of data about observed enemy actions so as to predict enemy behavior in the future. Systems analysts then aimed the quantitative methods of operations research toward developing cost-benefit analyses of potential missions. After World War II, however, analysts confronted an array of nuclear weapons for which, of course, no combat data existed. As Sharon Ghamari-Tabrizi has argued, "Atomic weapons brought about a colossal shift in authority. They swallowed up the personal wisdom of senior officers rooted in combat experience in favor of intuitions arising from repeated trials of laboratory-staged simulations of future war."[18] Under conditions of nuclear uncertainty, analysts had to *imagine* the data to which they might apply the mathematical formulas, game theories, and computer technologies they had developed for earlier forms of combat. In short, they had to simulate the future.

At the RAND Corporation and later, at his own Hudson Institute, Herman Kahn, perhaps the most well-known analyst of this period, began to present his simulations in the form of scenarios—narrative scripts of possible futures. These included his infamous scenarios for nuclear Armageddon, in which he tried to convince policymakers that nuclear warfare was a real possibility and one for which they should prepare, and his equally well-known visions for America in the year 2000.[19] On the one hand, Kahn's work on nuclear war seemed to many to be the epitome of American technocratic hubris. Even today, many remember Kahn primarily as the model for Stanley Kubrick's Dr. Strangelove. Rather than acknowledge the utter futility of a nuclear war, Kahn seemed to revel in planning for its aftermath. He once told a reporter, "We [scenario writers] take God's view. The President's view. Big. Aerial. Global. Galactic. Ethereal. Spatial. Overall. Megalomania is the standard occupational hazard." At the same time, however, particularly as the 1960s progressed, Kahn embraced the American counterculture. "I like the hippies," he explained to a reporter in 1968. "I've been to Esalen. I've had LSD a couple of times. In some ways I'd like to join them." The Whole Earth community reciprocated. In 1976, during a brief stint as an adviser to California governor Jerry Brown, Stewart Brand brought Herman Kahn to Brown's office to talk with the governor and energy conservationist Amory Lovins. He printed their conversation, as well other writings by Kahn, in *CoEvolution Quarterly*.[20]

In 1971 two futurists, Ted Newland and Pierre Wack, began using Kahn's analytical techniques at Shell's Group Planning Office in London. When these still largely quantitative modeling methods began to suggest that oil prices might rise very rapidly in the early 1970s, Shell's managers ignored them. In response, Wack led Newland and the planning team to shift rhetorical gears.[21] In his college days, during World War II, Wack had attended weekly salons at the Paris home of the mystic philosopher Georges Ivanovitch Gurdjieff. During his time there, Wack began to develop a deep preoccupation with "seeing"—that is, with perceiving the hidden order of events and the inner natures of individuals. At about this time as well, Gurdjieff was writing a book that would later be published as *Meetings with Remarkable Men*. In Gurdjieff's account, a "remarkable man" was someone who "stands out from those around him by the resourcefulness of his mind" and who conducts himself "justly and tolerantly towards the weakness of others."[22] Throughout his life, Wack would seek out "remarkable men"— apprenticing himself, for instance, to an Indian guru and a Japanese Zen gardener—with an eye to increasing his own insight into human nature and the structures of world affairs.

At Shell, Wack used Gurdjieff's mystical orientation to reorient the corporate planning process. In the early 1970s, for example, rather than present charts and figures, he drew on Gurdjieff's narrative style and began telling stories about the future. His stories were sufficiently compelling that Shell's managers did in fact prepare for the price rise that took place in 1973. This experience led Wack to believe that in order to make the corporate future visible, he had to change executives' mental maps of the world. In Wack's view, the minds of managers were a microcosm of the world outside. To change that world, he would first have to change the microcosm.[23] Wack turned to scenarios as tools for changing executive mind-sets and, with them, the direction of the corporation. By the mid-1970s, his scenarios had welded the quantitative modeling of wartime operations research and the fantastic futurism of cold war atomic forecasting to the experiential, insight-oriented practices of the mystics and gurus favored by the hippies. Scenarios became a form of corporate performance art; in Wack's form of scenario planning, two traditions, corporate and countercultural, merged.

In the 1970s Peter Schwartz absorbed that form of planning, and in 1982 he took the retiring Wack's place at Shell. At the Global Business Network, scenario planning retained its countercultural and systems-theoretical connotations. "Essentially," Schwartz later recalled, "we wanted to create a new type of company which would do for many clients what Pierre Wack had done for Shell."[24] The Global Business Network, like the Learning Conferences—and like SRI, RAND, and the Planning Group at Shell—constantly entwined the formation of interpersonal networks and the modeling of network systems. When it was formally founded in 1987, GBN charged clients twenty-five thousand dollars per year.[25] In return for their annual dues, clients were invited to gatherings called WorldView Meetings two to four times a year; enjoyed subscriptions to a series of in-house reports; received a new book every month, chosen by Stewart Brand; and were granted a membership to the WELL and access to a private GBN conference on it. For an extra fee, they could hire GBN to work with their home organizations to create site-specific scenarios. The GBN founders had pegged their rate to the going salary for an executive research assistant, promising to deliver more in the way of information and insight collectively than any individual re-searcher could alone.[26] Much like the *Whole Earth Catalog*, GBN aimed to grant its members "access to tools" for changing their social worlds, and like the *Catalog*, GBN included among those tools not only information and technique, but new social networks as well.

The founders quickly extended the GBN networks to include the former leaders of the cold war military-industrial complex. Over the next ten years, GBN listed as clients not only multinational corporations such as Xerox, IBM, BellSouth, AT&T, Arco, and Texaco, but also the Joint Chiefs of Staff and the Defense Department. To some members of the Whole Earth com-munity, GBN's embrace of such clients seemed to mark a strategic forget-ting of earlier commitments to local economics and small-scale technolo-gies. Paul Hawken, for example, though still a member of GBN, pointed out that the *Whole Earth Catalog* was full of examples of the "small scale working and large scale not working." When Brand and GBN decided to take on large corporate and government clients, he argued, "the scale question was rationalized: 'Well, yes, but they're awfully nice people and they mean well.'" Moreover, by the mid-1980s there was a sense in Whole Earth circles that "they [big corporations] are here and we've got to talk." In Hawken's view, as in the views of many in the 1970s who objected to Stewart Brand's support of space stations, it was not so much the turn toward working with business or even the government that rankled; rather, it was the turn to large organizations. Such organizations were hard to hold accountable, Hawken explained, and their executives had a low tolerance for truths that challenged the mission or the profits of the company. However, he said the founders of the Global Business Network had made an important discovery: "Under the guise of very conservative planning, you could talk about radical ideas."[27]

Peter Schwartz later recalled that the founders had hoped clients would explore those ideas within a network that felt "convivial, like a club that people could join." To that end, they kept administrative staff at a mini-mum. In 1994, for instance, GBN had some 30 employees while serving 55 corporate and governmental clients and earning $4.5 million in annual revenues.[28] But in addition to the five founders and the staff, GBN's promotional materials reminded prospective clients, the firm included a loose group of about 90 affiliates, known as "network members." These members had been brought together over a number of years through the entrepreneurial bridging of structural holes by the principals, particularly by Stewart Brand. Early members, such as Douglas Engelbart, Mary Catherine Bateson, biologist Lynn Margulis, and ecologist Peter Warshall, represented Brand's time at the *Whole Earth Catalog* and *CoEvolution Quarterly* and his journeys to SRI and Xerox PARC. Others, such as computer scientist Danny Hillis and sociologist Sherry Turkle, suggested Brand's links to MIT. Together, the network members represented a handful of groups: computer technologists, economists and financial analysts, corporate executives, natural scientists, journalists, and technology-oriented artists. They also had a distinctly male and, as journalist Joel Garreau put it with consummate tact, "Anglo-American cast." Of the 90 network members in place in 1994, only 15 were women, and only 3 were non-Caucasian.[29]

Although a few network members quietly complained about the lack of diversity at GBN, Brand later suggested that it was both a product and a productive feature of the network organizational form. When the founders sought network members, Brand recalled, they looked for "people we knew and liked and respected" who could "inform and titillate." On the one hand, much like the New Communalists, Brand and the founders hoped to found a nonhierarchical, collaborative alternative to mainstream, vertical bureaucracies. To that end, they turned away from the rigid hiring practices and clear employment boundaries that characterized mainstream firms and toward network entrepreneurship as an organizing force. On the other hand, like the back-to-the-landers, they ended up drawing new members from their own social and cultural communities of origin. Within GBN, this shared cultural affinity took the place of other forms of management. Like the Merry Pranksters, the network members of GBN were a loose group, able to come and go as they pleased. Yet they were also subject to what Brand called "second-order accountability." As Brand put it, "Nepotism works so long as the whole system isn't corrupt. Your cousin better deliver or he's going to hear about it."[30]

The social and cultural homogeneity of the GBN network worked hand in hand with an ethos of openness to allow GBN clients and members to engage in interpersonal and for-profit forms of interaction simultaneously. GBN, like the WELL, functioned as a heterarchy within which a member's or a client's contribution could have value in multiple domains. Consider the criteria for network membership, for instance. Joel Garreau later explained it this way: "'Membership' is a tricky word at GBN; there is no initiation ritual. One simply gets more and more tangled in its swirling mists. I was first asked to join a discussion on the network's private BBS [on the WELL]. Then I started receiving books that members thought I might find interesting. Then I got invited to gatherings at fascinating places, from Aspen to Amsterdam. Finally, I was asked to help GBN project the future regarding subjects about which I had expertise. By then, the network seemed natural." As Garreau's experience suggests, an individual's social style worked together with her or his access to and command over new forms of information to make a member "interesting." Network members were never paid simply to be listed as members of the network. Once recognized as a "remarkable person," though, the member might be hired for specific consulting projects. In the meantime, he or she gained access to a carefully selected and highly accomplished network of individuals and organizations in a semisocial manner. A member could participate as much as she or he liked, contributing and profiting accordingly. Likewise, corporate clients could begin to think of themselves not only as paying consumers of information, but as members of an elite *social* group. Having recharacterized their relationship to GBN, having seen it as social as well as economic, clients could in turn become producers of value for one another. Peter Schwartz later wrote, "With our atmosphere of openness, clients began to contribute not just as information users, but as sources."[31] Like network members, clients could simply listen, they could contribute information, or they could contribute in ways that enhanced both collective access to information and their own reputations. Over time, they could and did begin to build new professional as well as interpersonal and intellectual networks. Through GBN meetings, many corporate clients encountered not only network members, but other paying customers with whom they could in turn build professional relationships outside GBN.

Many of those encounters took place at WorldView Meetings and at associated "Learning Journeys." As Brand and his colleagues had done for the Learning Conferences, the organizers of WorldView Meetings sought to maximize the relationship between the particular themes of a meeting and the place at which the meeting was held. Over its first ten years, GBN held more than thirty meetings. Some meeting themes, such as "Environmental Technology" (for a gathering held in 1991 at the Monterey Bay Aquarium) or "Business and Social Responsibility" (for one at The Hague in 1997), reflected long-standing countercultural concerns. Others, such as "Environment as Infrastructure" (held at Biosphere 2 in 1990) and "Complex Adaptive Systems" (at the Santa Fe Institute in 1991), reflected GBN's ongoing concern with the legacy of cybernetics. Most, however, brought elements of both those traditions to bear on questions of economic change.

"The Network Corporation," "The Future of Information Services," "Risk Within and Beyond the Organization," and "Restructuring the Global Economy" are just a few of the themes around which meetings were organized in the early 1990s. For GBN's corporate clients, WorldView Meetings became a prime site for exploring the dynamics of emerging economic forms in terms set by the synthesis of countercultural and cybernetic practices and ideals. By the same token, for network members with backgrounds in those traditions, the meetings became places where they could reorient their social and technological aspirations toward the resources and the needs of the corporate realm.

A close look at any one of these meetings suggests that they served as important forums for the construction of both new networks and a new rhetoric of networks. They also offered participants a chance to imagine themselves as members of a mobile elite, able to glimpse in the natural and economic systems around them the invisible laws according to which all things functioned. In July 1993, for instance, ecologist Peter Warshall led a small number of GBN network members and clients on a multiday rafting trip near Taos, New Mexico. Participants represented GBN's varied constituencies and included Mary Catherine Bateson; Brand's wife, Patty Phelan; former Grateful Dead manager Jon McIntire; anthropologist and network theorist Karen Stephenson; neurobiologist William Calvin; futurist Don Michael; consumer analyst Steve Barnett; and Paris-based vice-chairman of L'Oréal Robert Salmon. Guided by Warshall, they rafted down the Rio Chama, a tributary of the Rio Grande, examining local flora and fauna and pausing to visit villagers, sheep farmers, and a local fish hatchery.

In his report on the event for *Netview*, GBN's quarterly in-house magazine, Warshall later wrote, "It's hard for me to say just what others gained from the trip. My purpose was to open the 'nature book' and teach the reading of waterflow and landscape." Yet, as Warshall's report reveals, for many of the participants, the river itself and the people along it served as a source of metaphors by which the group could come together on the trip and by which they could later seek to understand the social, and especially the economic, world. At the start of the journey, Stewart Brand asked the group to keep notes in small, portable journals. Jon McIntire recorded the following in his journal: "New Words . . . from Bruce the boatman . . . *Keeper hole*: A current out of the mainstream that captures and holds water in a rapid circular motion. More dangerous than a keeper eddy. According to the boatman, it is nearly impossible to row or paddle out of a keeper hole; outside intervention is almost always necessary." Like a cybernetician, McIntire read the water as an emblem of social process, inadvertently echoing Norbert Wiener's words in *The Human Use of Human Beings*: "We are but whirlpools in a river of ever-flowing water. We are not stuff that abides, but patterns that perpetuate themselves." Similarly, Warshall reports that Don Michael transformed the survival strategies of local flowers into emblems of corporate survival tactics. Michael wrote, "A shooting star flower mimics penstemons but does not do the work needed to produce nectar. It cons the hummingbird into fertilizing it in the mistaken belief there is nectar to be had. Much advertising does the same."[32]

For the GBN travelers, as for the communards who had come to the same area twenty-five years earlier, the landscape of the West was a setting for ruminating on the proper way of living under conditions of increasing techno-social integration. For the 1993 event, local citizens of Las Truchas and Los Ojos, towns along the way, played a variation of the role Native Americans had played for the counterculture. On the one hand, they seemed to possess an enviable authenticity. As Warshall put it, "The huge contrast with the lives of most GBN members was a curious mirror: the cosmopolitan ambitions, the going into nature as a vacation, the globe trotting, the work place far away from home life. Can consultants or transnational cosmopolitans give practical advice to villagers?"[33] But on the other hand, the villagers seemed bogged down, unwilling to change or to acknowledge the new technological and social realities of their world. "There was a quiet 'post-modernist' skepticism among many [GBN] members," wrote Warshall. "Many of the villagers' decisions appeared suboptimal because they only thought one or two steps ahead of the moment."[34] For the GBN travelers, the local citizenry, like the landscape itself, was not so much a living entity in its own right as a text to be read for clues as to how GBNers ought to organize their lives in light of the various technological and social "systems" within which they lived.

For all the materiality of rivers and mud and boats, the Rio Chama journey, like the communal migrations of the back-to-the-landers, took participants into a deeply semiotic region, one in which the exigencies of everyday life assumed an informational cast and where being informed and thinking in cybernetic terms came to seem to be much the same thing. This pattern characterized GBN's scenario process as well. Like the Learning Conferences and the WorldView Meetings, scenario-building workshops aimed to make visible the hidden informational systems of their participants. In the process, as Schwartz and Brand wrote in 1989, GBN promised to allow corporations and their executives to "embrace uncertainty (by exploring alternative futures) and to navigate through complexity (by invoking the organizing power of storytelling)." To build scenarios, GBN consultants acted as network entrepreneurs within their client firms. They selected relevant players, brought them together, and had them engage in a series of guided discussions. Like GBN's various meetings, the sessions were designed to generate shared understandings of the group's strategic situation, a new shared rhetoric for articulating those understandings, and new social and (via computer systems such as the WELL and internal corporate systems) technological networks for disseminating and preserving those insights. Each workshop produced a series of stories, often three, about possible future trajectories of the issues at hand. Sometimes the stories would present a clear market opportunity. For AT&T, for instance, several of GBN's early scenarios suggested that mobile telecommunications such as cell phones would soon undergo rapid growth.[35] More often, though, the scenario planning process itself generated a shared rhetoric and social process around which managers could continue to plan for the future. To the extent that the scenario-building process, like other GBN events, built symbolic resources and social networks simultaneously, it modeled and imparted a networked style of working to GBN clients.

The network style could hit clients with the force of revelation. In 1995 Brad Hoyt, a senior project manager at Senco, a Cincinnati toolmaker, recalled a scenario-planning session with Stewart Brand: "He changed my whole life in one scenario planning session. He asked whether we'd heard about complexity theory. . . . Little did I know he's on the board of the Santa Fe Institute."[36] Over the next year, Hoyt reported reading another dozen books on complexity and came to use complexity theory as a guide to "thinking about the housing industry and other ecosystems affecting Senco." For executives like Hoyt, the systems-oriented rhetoric of complexity theory, buttressed by the cultural legitimacy of Stewart Brand, offered a compelling framework within which to understand the topsy-turvy economy of the late 1980s and early 1990s. Even at firms with more skeptical executives, GBN quietly brought into the corporate world people and publications that both promoted and modeled a networked sensibility. At Xerox, for instance, Brand introduced executives to the work of Richard Normann, author of the book *Designing Interactive Strategy* and a proponent of viewing individual firms not as stand-alone industrial competitors, but as elements within a web of economic relationships. In 1995 Robert Mauceli, director of strategic development and communications at Xerox, told a reporter for *Fortune* magazine, "We were very taken by Normann and invited him to speak to 500 of our executives this summer. We already use some of his stuff in work we've done. Now we're thinking of bringing him back." Tom Portante, cofounder of Andersen Consulting's technology assessment group, told the same reporter, "It's funny . . . you sometimes look at these books Stewart sends and think, 'What the hell am I supposed to do with those?' But they disappear, and we routinely have roundtable discussions on them."[37]

For executives like Mauceli, Hoyt, and Portante, the overlapping inter-personal, interinstitutional, and informational networks of GBN served as a channel through which the systems rhetoric that had emerged out of and helped to organize collaborative technological research during World War II and the cold war could once again enter the corporate sphere. This time, though, it came with the countercultural legitimacy of Stewart Brand. In keeping with the New Communalist turn away from government, GBN promoted the corporation as a site of revolutionary social change and inter-personal and information networks (including the computerized networks of EIES and the WELL) as tools and emblems of that change. Throughout the 1990s, until it was sold in 2001 to the Monitor Group, a strategic con-sulting firm (where it continues today), GBN's work reversed the counter-cultural antipathy toward industry and the military. In its consulting, the same corporate and military institutions that the New Communalists and the New Left had condemned became homes to the transformed states of mind and leveled bureaucracies that the counterculturalists had worked so hard to create.

Kevin Kelly as Network Entrepreneur

For the founders of GBN, computer networks were but one in a series of overlapping systems that included member networks, meeting series, sub-scriptions to newsletters and book clubs, and ongoing conversations on the WELL. Computers helped sustain GBN and, to that extent, helped give its members a glimpse into the role computer networks might play in the New Economy. The metaphor of the network within GBN referred not so much to digital technologies, however, as to a series of intersecting social and informational systems. For the founders of GBN, computers were only one of several forces driving the leveling of bureaucracies and the rise of net-worked patterns of organization.

For Kevin Kelly, in contrast, computers became the signal emblems of a new era in human development. In the late 1980s, Kelly extended the social and institutional networks Brand had first knit together, reaching deep into the technical communities of the Bay area and beyond. By the mid-1990s, he had transformed those networks into prototypes of what he believed to be a new social order: neobiological civilization.

Kelly signed on as the editor of *CoEvolution Quarterly* in 1984, just as Brand was developing the *Whole Earth Software Catalog*. Since the early 1970s, Kelly had immersed himself in the *Quarterly* and in the original *Whole Earth Catalog* ("I have that thing practically memorized," he later re-membered).[38] Yet, when he arrived in Sausalito, the various Whole Earth publications had begun a wholesale turn away from their down-home roots in the back-to-the-land movement and toward digital technologies. Within a year of his arrival, Kelly had helped host the first Hackers' Conference, joined the WELL, and seen *CoEvolution Quarterly* merge with the *Whole Earth Software Review* to become the *Whole Earth Review*. Over the next half dozen years, as he edited the *Review* and as he wrote his compendious 1994 volume *Out of Control: The Rise of Neo-Biological Civilization*, Kelly would attempt to apprehend the technological and cultural shifts around him by deploying the entrepreneurial networking and editorial tactics that Brand had earlier developed at the *Whole Earth Catalog*. These tactics enabled Kelly not only to link new forms of computing and commerce to the Whole Earth community's long-standing synthesis of cybernetic theory and countercultural politics, but also to transform both digital technologies and the New Economy into Darwinian variations on a New Communalist ideal.

When *CoEvolution Quarterly* became the *Whole Earth Review* in 1984, Kelly inherited a growing network of potential writers and sources, one that increasingly spanned countercultural and technical communities. Kelly soon began to publish writers who had first appeared on the WELL or in connection with either the Hackers' Conference or the *Software Catalog*, such as Steven Levy and Howard Rheingold. As Kelly began to travel in the Bay area's digital circles, and especially as he and other Whole Earth regulars became interested in the emerging technologies of virtual reality, he picked up new writers. In 1989, for instance, he published an interview with novelist William Gibson, as well as a "Cyberpunk 101" reading list. He also published a lengthy interview with virtual-reality entrepreneur Jaron Lanier, an article by computer maven Esther Dyson, and Stewart Brand's own description of his first immersion in virtual reality, "Sticking Your Head in Cyberspace." And in the fall of 1990, he published the WELL document "Crime and Puzzlement," in which John Perry Barlow first used the word *cyberspace* to describe a digital frontier.[39]

In all of these cases, Kelly relied on an editorial model that mingled the norms and genres of professional journalism with the network-building practices of the *Whole Earth Catalog*. Occasionally, Kelly aimed to produce the seemingly objective, balanced coverage of an issue that might characterize a more traditional magazine.[40] For the most part, though, he used the *Whole Earth Review* as a forum for particular Bay area networks of which he was becoming an increasingly visible member. Kelly brought together former counterculturalists, contemporary computer technologists, and writers who frequented the WELL with long-standing members of the Whole Earth community, including ecologists, small businessmen, and former communards. The *Review* looked much more like a mainstream magazine than like the *Catalog*: it carried feature articles as well as short reviews, and it did so in a standard, if visibly low-cost, magazine format. And, unlike the *Catalog*, the *Review* did not serve as a communication mechanism among its members. If you wanted to meet the networks depicted in or contributing to the *Review*, you didn't write in; you signed on to the WELL. But the *Review* did inherit the *Catalog's* reliance on interpersonal networks and its confidence that the members of those networks constituted an emerging avant-garde. Like the *Catalog* and like the later *Wired*, the *Review* mirrored the concerns of a series of communities linked first and foremost by the networking efforts of its editor.

The *Review* was not the only forum in which Whole Earth precepts and publishing patterns met the digital world, however. In 1988, four years after the *Software Catalog* had failed, Kelly edited *Signal*. Published by the Point Foundation, put together largely by Whole Earth regulars, and consisting almost entirely of brief product and book reviews, *Signal* looked very much like the *Whole Earth Catalog*. On page 2, readers could find the old statement of purpose ("We are as Gods, and might as well get good at it . . . "). And on page 3, they could find a picture of Stewart Brand, kicked back in his office chair, a Macintosh computer on his desk. The Macintosh was a tip-off: what the old *Whole Earth Catalog* had been to the back-to-the-land world of the countercultural revolution, *Signal* would be to the emerging landscape of the information revolution. In his introduction to the book, Brand explained that the computer on his desk was simply the descendant of the wood stoves and solar-energy systems of the earlier communards. The hairy old hippie-cowboy outlaws of twenty years before had been replaced by hackers. And the wholeness of the earth revealed in the NASA photographs on the covers of the old *Catalog* was no longer simply an image. Thanks to the "all-encompassing and planetary" nature of information, Brand wrote, people could now experience a sense of collective unity that the readers of the old *Catalog* could only imagine.[41]

Like the *Whole Earth Software Catalog*, *Signal* marked an attempt to embed emerging digital technologies within design frameworks and interpersonal networks developed in the Whole Earth community. Like the original *Whole Earth Catalog*, *Signal* was organized in categories that could be read as prototypes of one another. There were ten, each containing on average forty items.[42] The first category, "Prime Information," played the role of the former "Whole Systems" section. It featured books on cybernetics, information theory, and even "whole systems," as the earlier section had. But it also included reviews of newer work, such as Richard Dawkins's *The Selfish Gene* and James Gleick's *Chaos*. Likewise, the category "Network Societies" featured both news of the latest in networked communications—bulletin board systems, the WELL, teleconferences—and reviews of radio and film-making gear much like the ones that had run in the *Catalog* twenty years earlier. Within each category, elements long familiar to readers of the *Catalog* and the *CoEvolution Quarterly* shared space with the latest in computing and information technology. At the end of the book, Kelly printed the project's accounts, rendering the project's whole editorial and financial system visible to readers, just as Brand had always done.

Kelly had intended *Signal* to be a "prototype for a new kind of magazine."[43] But, like the *Software Catalog, Signal* was a commercial failure. In both cases, neither the look and feel of the old *Catalog* nor its editorial mechanics quite fit with the new social and technological environment. In the late 1960s, the *Whole Earth Catalog* had made an underground network of communitarians visible and available to one another and to mainstream America; by 1988 the computer culture of the San Francisco Bay area was national news. For communards and commune wannabes, the *Whole Earth Catalog* offered a unique collection of contacts and information sources. But by 1988 people interested in information technology had a wide array of resources they could consult. What *Signal* and other Whole Earth publications of the late 1980s did offer, though, was a way for their readers to see the new information technologies as extensions of an older countercultural revolution.

Over the next six years, Kelly went on to link that revolution to a new form of one of the defining practices of cold war military research: computer simulation. By the time Kelly published *Signal,* the availability and increasing power of desktop computers had led an increasing number of scientists to play with algorithms in ways that had once been restricted to the panjandrums of the RAND Corporation and SRI. As Herman Kahn and his colleagues had once simulated the end of life on earth, small groups of scientists, many based in and around Los Alamos National Laboratory in New Mexico, began to simulate the creation of biological life. During the same years, a number of economists and pundits, including members of the Global Business Network, began to apply biological metaphors to economic processes. Michael Rothschild, whose 1990 book *Bionomics: The Inevitability of Capitalism* attempted to turn these metaphors into a school of thought, spoke for many when he wrote, "In the biologic environment, genetic information, recorded in the DNA molecule, is the basis of all life. In the economic environment, technological information, captured in books, blueprints, scientific journals, databases, and the know-how of millions of individuals, is the ultimate source of all economic life." For many, though not all, adherents to the bionomic viewpoint, the economic environment was by definition capitalistic. As Rothschild put it, "Capitalism [is] the inevitable, natural state of human economic affairs. Being for or against a natural phenomenon is a waste of time and mental energy."[44]

Stefan Helmreich has shown that bionomic ways of thinking and desktop-based computer simulation came together nowhere more powerfully than at the Santa Fe Institute (SFI).[45] The institute was founded in 1984 by a group of scientists from Los Alamos National Laboratory who had come to believe that since World War II, the biological, physical, and social sciences had begun to converge.[46] Computers, they argued, had made this convergence possible in two ways: first, they had served as tools for examining and modeling the world, and, second, the algorithms with which they organized information mimicked the algorithmic patterning of life itself by means of biological "technologies" such as DNA.[47] In many ways, these arguments resuscitated the cybernetic visions of the cold war era. They did so at a very different cultural moment, though, one when the industrial bureaucracies of the 1950s were rapidly giving way to the globalized, flexible, and temporary work world of the post-Fordist era. Moreover, in the mid-1980s, executives worldwide were engaged in computerizing their firms, and many now had computers on their own desktops. To these executives, the neocybernetic perspective of the Santa Fe Institute held great appeal. Within two years of its founding, SFI had attracted a number of corporate sponsors, most notably Citibank/Citicorp. In 1986 Citicorp CEO John Reed asked SFI to sponsor a workshop that was titled "International Finance as a Complex System," and in 1987 another called "Evolutionary Paths of the Global Economy."[48]

In 1987 SFI joined Apple Computer and the Center for Nonlinear Studies at Los Alamos National Laboratory to sponsor the first workshop on artificial life. Hosted at Los Alamos by Christopher Langton, then a postdoctoral researcher at the laboratory, the conference brought together 160 biologists, physicists, anthropologists, and computer scientists. Like the scientists and technicians of the Rad Lab and Los Alamos in World War II, the contributors to the first Artificial Life Conference quickly established an intellectual trading zone. Specialists in robotics presented papers on questions of cultural evolution; computer scientists used new algorithms to model seemingly biological patterns of growth; bioinformatics specialists applied what they believed to be principles of natural ecologies to the development of social structures. For these scientists, as formerly for members of the Rad Lab and the cold war research institutes that followed it, systems theory served as a contact language and computers served as key supports for a systems orientation toward interdisciplinary work. Furthermore, computers granted participants in the workshop a familiar God's-eye point of view. For the defense analysts and futurists of the 1950s, computers had transformed the globe into an informational system that could be monitored twenty-four hours a day against the possibility of nuclear attack and the destruction of all human life. For the participants of the first Artificial Life Conference, computers served as windows onto life itself. Peering into their desktop screens, watching images change and grow in patterns made possible by algorithms they themselves had set, the scientists could and did imagine themselves, not unlike the early readers of the *Whole Earth Catalog*, "as gods."[49]

For Kevin Kelly, the 1987 conference on artificial life sparked a series of epiphanies. First, it validated the long-standing Whole Earth embrace of systems theory. If the counterculture had faded away, the vision of a world linked by invisible patterns had not. Small-scale technologies such as LSD had suggested the existence of those patterns to hippie adepts, but here were more than 150 scientists, working with the latest digital technologies, who seemed to be coming to the same conclusion. Moreover, like LSD, those computers seemed to make it possible to envision life itself as a *whole*. If the New Communalists had sensed that they were "all one," the computers of the Artificial Life Conference seemed to prove the point: The natural world and the social world really *were* all one system of information exchange. That vision of singularity in turn allowed Kelly to link his religious yearnings to the particular form of sociability common to both the cold war research world and the New Communalist wing of the counterculture: collaborative networks. On the one hand, the God's-eye point of view shared by the programmers at the conference suggested to Kelly that perhaps God himself had created the world as a set of algorithms, out of which he then let an efflorescence of life forms emerge.[50] On the other hand, it suggested that the scientists and sociologists at the conference, gathered in a forum, busily constructing new social networks, were themselves the vanguard of the future. Computers; collaborative scientists; invisible, informational patterns of interconnection—for Kelly, steeped as he was in the synthesis of cybernetic and New Communalist ideals common to the Whole Earth community, as well as his own idiosyncratic Christianity, each of these elements seemed to mirror the others, and all smacked of the Divine.

The Atom Is the Past, the Network Is the Future

Over the next five years, Kelly turned his experiences at the Artificial Life Conference into the basis of a book, *Out of Control,* that would translate the interpersonal networks and the ethos of the Whole Earth publications into symbolic resources for corporate executives and others seeking to make sense of the post-Fordist economy. Like Stewart Brand twenty-five years earlier, Kelly wanted to make visible a new mode of being that he himself

had discovered by migrating across the boundaries of various social, institutional, and technological networks. In his reporting, he brought together
representatives of four communities: descendants of the cold war research
world (including Los Alamos, MIT's Media Lab, and Xerox PARC), affiliates
of the Whole Earth (ecologists, writers from the WELL), designers and theorists of new forms of computing (artificial life, multiple-user dungeons,
Sim Earth), and corporations (Benetton, Pixar, Disney). With the exception
of the corporate world, all of these groups had had a long-standing presence
in the Whole Earth publications. In the pages of *Out of Control,* Kelly arrayed
his subjects one after another, as if they were samples in a catalog. In the
late 1960s, in the pages of the *Whole Earth Catalog,* the moccasins and backpacks of those lighting out for the woods had bumped up against the calculators and technical manuals of Bay area engineers. Now, in the early 1990s,
computer scientists met prairie ecologists, online gamers, and corporate
executives.

The book's catalog-like structure supported its cybernetic themes. Each
of its twenty-four chapters developed a topic that in some way illustrated
the intersection of the biological, the technological, and the social. Some
chapters, such as "Coevolution" and "The Structure of Organized Change,"
reflected long-standing Whole Earth concerns. Others, such as "Artificial
Evolution" and "Postdarwinism" dealt with issues arising at the intersection
of biology and informatics. Still others, such as "Network Economics" and
"E-Money" pointed to new, networked forms of enterprise and the role
played by computers in such systems. Yet, according to Kelly, any one of
these chapters might serve as a mirror for the others. As he explained
at the start of his book, "The apparent veil between the organic and the
manufactured has crumpled to reveal that the two really are, and have always been, of one being."[51] What had joined the two was information, especially the work of computer scientists at places like the Santa Fe Institute.
Technologists, he explained, had begun "extracting the logical principle of
both life and machines, and applying each to the task of building extremely
complex systems." Echoing the claims of artificial-life researchers, Kelly
argued that these systems were simultaneously "made and alive": "What
should we call that common soul between the organic communities we
know of as organisms and ecologies, and their manufactured counterparts
of robots, corporations, economies, and computer circuits? I call those examples, both made and born, 'vivisystems' for the lifelikeness each kind of
system holds."[52]

On the one hand, Kelly's account of "vivisystems" owed a substantial
debt to the legacy of Norbert Wiener's cybernetics. Kelly even went so far
as to suggest that "a short-hand synopsis of *Out of Control* would be to say it

is an update on the current state of cybernetic research." On the other hand, in keeping with Kelly's Whole Earth background, the book linked that research to a New Communalist social ideal. For instance, Kelly devoted an early chapter to a phenomenon that he called "hive mind." The chapter opened with a discussion of bees and beekeeping, in which Kelly described the hives he kept outside his house as single, collective organisms. The scene then shifted to the backyard of Kelly's friend and fellow beekeeper Mark Thompson. One day, Thompson saw a bee swarm forming up: "Mark didn't waver. Dropping his tools he slipped into the swarm, his bare head now in the eye of a bee hurricane. He trotted in sync across the yard as the swarm eased away. Wearing a bee halo, Mark hopped over one fence, then another. He was now running to keep up with the thundering animal in whose belly he floated."[53] Eventually, the unstung Thompson stumbled, and the swarm went on without him. For Kelly, the swarm served as an emblem of a new form of social organization. Although the hive had a queen, he pointed out, it was governed by the rule-driven behavior of its many members. In the hive one could see "the true nature of democracy and all distributed governance." One could also see the faded image of New Communalism. Leveled, collaborative, linked by invisible signals and shared feelings, Kelly's hive was a sort of natural commune. "It was a mob," he wrote, "united into oneness."[54]

As his friend's experience with the swarm suggested, the hive was also a social system, held together by information exchange, into which human beings could insert themselves. Immediately after describing beehives, Kelly conjured up a conference room in Las Vegas. There he described Loren Carpenter, a software developer, booting up an old game of Pong. He gave each member of the audience a lighted wand and then, with custom-designed software, engaged them in a process of keeping a ball moving back and forth across a computer screen projected at the front of the room. When the group had mastered that exercise, Carpenter had them use the same wands to create numbers on the screen and ultimately to pilot an airplane flight simulator. After a few dangerous pitches and rolls, the crowd managed to right the plane and turn it in a new direction. "No one was in charge," wrote Kelly, yet the crowd acted as if it was "of one mind."[55]

What had made visible the group's oneness was the power of collective computing. The computer had revealed a hidden order to collective action; at the same time, it had helped to create a collaborative social group. Kelly showed in this way that computers had fostered the creation of a New Communalist ideal. They had transformed the consciousness of the individuals in the room and, by doing so, made possible the destruction of political hierarchy, the elimination of psychological boundaries between the individual and the group, and the establishment of a powerful social whole. Moreover, Kelly preceded this story by the account of his neighbor's bees and followed it with a discussion of yet another "hive mind," in an anthill. For all its technological advancement, this ordering suggested, the computer was in fact deeply in accord with natural principles. Like the geodesic domes and camping gear favored by the New Communalists, the computer had in fact helped its users integrate their lives more closely with the "laws" of nature.

The new hive mind represented the sort of world-saving social revolution that many New Communalists had hoped to spark. According to Kelly, the Pong game, the bee swarm, and the anthill were all examples of "parallel operating wholes." These wholes could be called "networks, complex adaptive systems, swarm systems, vivisystems, or collective systems."[56] Whatever they were called, together they would overthrow the rigid, hierarchical logic of the old atomic era: "The Atom is the icon of 20th century science. . . . The Atom whirls alone, the epitome of singleness. It is the metaphor for individuality: atomic. It is the irreducible seat of strength. The Atom stands for power and knowledge and certainty. It is as dependable as a circle, as regular as round."[57] But now, thanks to new forms of computing and the new, collaborative forms of social organization that they both enabled and modeled, the atom had been driven away:

> Another Zen thought: The Atom is the past. The symbol of science for the next century is the dynamical Net.
>
> The Net icon has no center—it is a bunch of dots connected to other dots—a cobweb of arrows pouring into each other, squirming together like a nest of snakes, the restless image fading at indeterminate edges. The Net is the archetype—always the same picture—displayed to represent all circuits, all intelligence, all interdependence, all things economic and social and ecological, all communications, all democracy, all groups, all large systems.[58]

In *Out of Control,* however, Kelly took pains to show how the Net was above all the symbol of a post-Fordist economic order. One the one hand, Kelly implied, networked systems, and particularly computer systems, would lead humanity back toward a reintegration with nature—an ability to run with the bees, so to speak. On the other hand, he suggested, this reintegration would take place within the heart of the corporate world. Like the New Communalists thirty years earlier, Kelly turned away from any notion of political struggle and toward the commercial sphere as a site of social change. That sphere, he argued, was itself already a model of the natural world. Like hives of bees or anthills or computers, the economy was governed by an "Invisible Hand." Like the vivisystems of nature, the ideal corporation should be "distributed, decentralized, collaborative, and adaptive."[59] The firm, he explained, had become an organism, and through the proper deployment of technology, and especially information technology, it could return both workers and machines to a more natural way of being:

> Industrial ecology must grow into a networked just-in-time system that dynamically balances the flow of materials so that local overflows and shortages are shuttled around to minimize variable stocks. More net-driven "flex-factories" will be able to handle a more erratic quality of resources by running adaptable machinery or making fewer units of more different kinds of products.
>
> Technologies of adaptation, such as distributed intelligence, flex-time accounting, niche economics, and supervised evolution, all stir up the organic in machines.[60]

In the pages of *Out of Control*, Kelly transformed the New Communalist dream of a rural Eden, of an antitechnocratic reintegration with nature, into a celebration of information technology, post-Fordist production practices, and the entrepreneurial engineers, executives, and scientists who watched over both. Like Stewart Brand and his colleagues at the Global Business Network (of which Kelly was now a member), Kelly had created a series of overlapping networks: social, technological, informational, and natural. In keeping with the universal rhetorical principles of cybernetics, each network legitimated every other. For Kelly, the ability of computers to produce fractal shapes on their monitors served as evidence that fractal formations in the natural world had been produced by informational algorithms embedded in genes and DNA. The existence of ecosystems in nature and the struggles for dominance and position therein seemed to naturalize the increasingly fluid relations of a rapidly globalizing economic world and the struggles for power within it. Networked forms of commerce, and the integration of information technologies into them, quickly began to seem like stages in a natural, rather than a socio-technical, progression. Suddenly mankind had entered a new stage of *evolution*: the scientists of the artificial-life movement, wrote Kelly, had already shown that "evolution is not a biological process. It is a technological, mathematical, informational, and biological process rolled into one."[61]

Soon after the book was released, it became a well of symbolic resources for corporate executives looking to understand the technological and economic context in which they worked. Reviewers repeatedly took up Kelly's hive-mind analogies and applied them to the New Economy.[62] In 1994, for instance, a reviewer for the august *Harvard Business Review* argued that Kelly's "image of 5,000 passengers copiloting a jet neatly captures the promise of work and organization in the New Economy. In the 'company' created by Carpenter, everyone makes his or her own decisions, everyone has fun—and the enterprise doesn't crash and burn. It's the ultimate goal of building companies around networked computers, mobile communications, and self-managed teams: to marry the competitive demands of business with the desire for personal satisfaction and democratic participation; to achieve productive coordination without top-down control." In the pages of *Out of Control,* the Long Hunter of the *Whole Earth Catalog* had become an entrepreneur. Journalists picked up on the point too. "The renegade competitor," wrote the *Harvard Business Review,* "the lone knowledge worker equipped with a laptop, a modem, and an inspired idea—these are our heroes, the change agents who are reinventing industries, reshaping the economy, creating vast wealth."[63] Almost thirty years earlier, thousands of young, highly educated Americans had tromped off into the wilderness seeking to build an egalitarian, fun-loving world. Today, suggested Kelly, they should look to technology and the economy for satisfaction.

They should do so, he argued, because the world itself was an information system. In his view, to manipulate computers and to work with information was not simply to hold down a job; it was to gain access to a hidden world, to live by its laws, and to become in a sense a Comprehensive Designer of one's own fate. In that sense, Kelly's vision echoed the New Communalists' celebration of consciousness. It also resuscitated the commune-dwellers' disregard for the demands of the material world. In the 1960s, many had set out for rural America with little sense of the embodied labor that building their new society might take and little feel for the work already done by those among whom they settled. In the 1990s, as a number of critics have noted, Kelly's doctrine of cyberevolutionism gave a potent ideological boost to executives seeking to outsource labor, automate industrial processes, and decrease the stability of their worker's employment.[64] Throughout his book, Kelly underplayed the work of embodied labor, celebrated intellect and the collaborative styles associated with intellectual institutions, and so offered a model of a world inhabited exclusively by freelancing elites. In the early 1990s, as in the late 1960s, that turn away from the material world helped legitimate the authority of those who controlled information and information systems by rendering invisible those who did not.

At the same time, the turn toward imagining the world in terms of dematerialized networks of information helped assuage the increasing sense of helplessness among executives themselves. On the one hand, like scientists at the Rad Lab a half century earlier, executives could call on the rhetoric of cybernetics to justify the pursuit of their professional goals. Like the cold warriors who had long ago scanned their computer screens for signs of incoming bombers, they could imagine the world as an information system and themselves as monitors of that system. Thanks to the computers they were so rapidly installing in their firms, they could see farther, plan more effectively, and perhaps manage their firms "as gods." On the other hand, they could begin to accept that they lacked precisely the sorts of power that Stewart Brand and others of his generation imagined belonged to corporate leaders. In the late 1980s and early 1990s, despite the spike in executive incomes and the broad-based movement of wealth toward those at the top of the social ladder, many executives labored under a sense that they were surrounded by forces *beyond* their control.[65] In the cybernetic pages of his book, Kevin Kelly suggested that yes, in fact, they were—and that it was okay, even natural, to feel at sea.

Toward the end of the *Harvard Business Review*'s analysis of *Out of Control,* its author offered a single, pointed criticism. "The missing ingredient in biology," he wrote, "is values."[66] The most successful firms worked well together, he argued, not simply because they were efficiently organized, but because they shared a set of core beliefs. Yet, in the case of Kelly's book, and in the case of the Global Business Network, the turn toward biology did not reflect an abandonment of values and a simple embrace of rapacious capitalism. On the contrary, it marked the integration of the New Communalist ideals of egalitarian collaboration and spiritual interconnection with the scientific celebration of interdisciplinary work and unifying theory. It also pointed toward the increasing power of networked elites and of social norms, as opposed to formal organizational structures, in governing those elites. In the Global Business Network, social affinity became a key element of network coherence; in the pages of Kelly's book, it was simply an unspoken element linking his various scientific entrepreneurs. In both cases, Kelly and Brand offered up their own entrepreneurial, male, predominantly Anglo-American social networks as emblems of the technological and economic networks emerging around them.

In the coming years, Brand continued to stay involved with the Global Business Network and the Electronic Frontier Foundation, but he also turned to other projects. In 1994, for instance, he published a book on the ways buildings change over time (*How Buildings Learn*), and in 1995 he helped found the Long Now Foundation, a society devoted to building a clock that would keep time for ten thousand years, so as to encourage humans to focus on the long-term consequences of their actions.[67] Kevin Kelly became executive editor of *Wired* magazine. In that capacity, he helped turn the social networks that he and Brand had helped create into symbols of the rise of a newly networked social order and evidence for the countercultural potential of the Internet and the World Wide Web.

CHAPTER 7

Wired

In *Wired*'s March 1993 inaugural issue, founder and editor-in-chief Louis Rossetto proclaimed that a cultural transformation was under way. "The Digital Revolution is whipping through our lives like a Bengali typhoon," he announced, bringing with it "social changes so profound their only parallel is probably the discovery of fire."[1] The magazine itself seemed to illustrate his point. Tricked out in a cacophony of type faces, swimming in a sea of Day-Glo orange and chartreuse, *Wired* was explicitly designed to conjure up the multimedia possibilities of digital convergence. To readers of that first issue, long accustomed to the traditional aesthetics and consumer orientation of the mainstream computer press, *Wired* aimed to herald the arrival not only of a new era in computing machinery, but a new era in social life. "There are a lot of magazines about technology," wrote Rossetto. "*Wired* is not one of them. *Wired* is about the most powerful people on the planet today—the Digital Generation. These are the people who not only foresaw how the merger of computers, telecommunications and the media is transforming life at the cusp of the new millennium, they are making it happen."[2]

Almost immediately, readers began to believe that *Wired* and the executives and engineers it profiled might in fact be harbingers of the future. Over the next five years, the magazine became a touchstone for CEOs, politicians, and, above all, other journalists. It won two National Magazine Awards, saw its readership grow to more than three hundred thousand a month, developed a book publisher (HardWired) and a variety of online ventures (HotWired, Suck), and helped spawn a clutch of magazines focused on the Internet and the New Economy, including *Fast Company, Business 2.0,* the *Industry Standard,* and *Red*

Herring. Thanks in part to a confluence of extraordinary economic, techno-logical, and political currents, its technocentric optimism became a central feature of the biggest stock market bubble in American history. Its faith that the Internet constituted a revolution in human affairs legitimated calls for telecommunications deregulation and the dismantling of government enti-tlement programs elsewhere as well. And each month, its Technicolor pages of gadgets and gurus cataloged the delights awaiting information profes-sionals in the New Economy.

Yet, for all its forward-looking verve, *Wired*'s vision of the digital future also carried with it a particular version of the countercultural past. In its pages, desktop computers and the Internet became tools for personal and collective liberation in a distinctly Whole Earth vein. "The '60s generation had a lot of power, but they didn't have a lot of tools," explained Jane Met-calfe, cofounder and president of *Wired*, as well as Rossetto's wife. "And in many respects their protests were unable to implement long-term and radi-cal change in our society. We do have the tools. The growth of the Internet and the growing political voice of the people on the Internet is proof of that."[3] In the pages of *Wired,* the Internet, and digital communication gen-erally, stood as a prototype of a newly decentralized, nonhierarchical society linked by invisible bits in a single harmonious network. The builders of computers and telecommunications networks, suggested *Wired*—men like John Malone of TV cable behemoth TCI, Frank Biondi and Ed Horowitz of Viacom, and Bill Gates of Microsoft—were working to construct the high-tech infrastructure of a new and better world. So too were libertarian pun-dits and politicians. In the logic of *Wired,* they were simply social, as opposed to technical, engineers. Like their brethren in Silicon Valley, conservative author and media analyst George Gilder, futurist Alvin Toffler, and Repub-lican Speaker of the House Newt Gingrich were working to bring about in-dividual liberation and government by contract and code. Together, *Wired* seemed to suggest, these two communities had set about to free America and the world from the rigid, oppressive corporate and government bureau-cracies of the twentieth century.

In 1998 Richard Barbrook and Andy Cameron named *Wired*'s particular blend of libertarian politics, countercultural aesthetics, and techno-utopian visions the "Californian Ideology." As they pointed out, by the end of the de-cade, its tenets had become the day-to-day orthodoxy of technologists in Sil-icon Valley and beyond. But this ubiquitous set of beliefs did not in fact grow out of the legacy of the New Left, as Barbrook and Cameron suggested. Rather, a close look at *Wired*'s first and most influential five years suggests that the magazine's vision of the digital horizon emerged in large part from its intellectual and interpersonal affiliations with Kevin Kelly and the Whole

Earth network and, through them, from the New Communalist embrace of the politics of consciousness.[4]

Although Louis Rossetto and Jane Metcalfe founded *Wired,* and although Rossetto's libertarian politics exerted a substantial influence on the magazine, Rossetto and Metcalfe also drew heavily for funds and, later, for subjects and writers, on the Whole Earth world. In 1992, while Kevin Kelly was finishing up *Out of Control,* Rossetto hired him to serve as executive editor of the magazine. Kelly brought with him the simultaneously cybernetic and New Communalist social vision of the Whole Earth publications and their networked style of editorial work. Together with Rossetto and managing editor John Battelle, Kelly turned *Wired* into a network forum. Within it, writers utilized the computational metaphors and universal rhetoric of cybernetics to depict New Right politicians, telecommunications CEOs, information pundits, and members of GBN, the WELL, and other Whole Earth–connected organizations as a single, leading edge of countercultural revolution. Together, *Wired* suggested, this digital generation would do what the New Communalists had failed to accomplish: they would tear down hierarchies, undermine the sorts of corporations and governments that had spawned them, and, in the hierarchies' place, create a peer-to-peer, collaborative society, interlinked by invisible currents of energy and information.

By the end of the decade, theirs would be the governing myth of the Internet, the stock market, and great swaths of the New Economy.

Founding *Wired*

For all his magazine's countercultural rhetoric, Louis Rossetto saw the digital revolution as an extension of a long-standing, if not widely acknowledged, American libertarian tradition. After growing up in suburban Long Island, Rossetto had arrived at Columbia University in 1967. By that time, the Vietnam War was nearing its apogee, as were antiwar protests and domestic violence. In April 1968, less than three weeks after the assassination of Martin Luther King, a group of students occupied buildings on Columbia's main quad to protest the university's involvement in military research and its mismanagement of relations with the local African American community. Columbia's president responded by calling in more than one thousand police in the middle of the night. They arrested 692 strikers and cleared out the buildings. As Todd Gitlin has pointed out, the occupation at Columbia marked a turning point for the SDS and the New Left generally.[5] In the years to come, antiwar protests turned increasingly violent, with bombings by young leftists and attacks by police on marchers becoming common.

To Louis Rossetto, this shift suggested the futility of agonistic politics as a whole. Rossetto had served as the president of the Columbia Young Republicans, campaigned for Nixon, and celebrated Nixon's election in 1968 with other Republicans at New York's Waldorf-Astoria Hotel. By his junior year, though, he had begun to think of himself as a libertarian anarchist. That year, he gathered a group of like-minded friends into a loose confederation they called the Freedom Conspiracy. He read psychologist Wilhelm Reich's calls for sexual freedom and Marshall McLuhan's multimedia collage books, and at the same time discovered Ayn Rand. In his senior year, he wrote a long paper on the libertarian stream in American thought, in which he chronicled the work of long-forgotten figures such as Benjamin Tucker, a turn-of-the-century editor of the magazine *Liberty* and an ardent follower of social Darwinist Herbert Spencer, and Lysander Spooner, an abolitionist and the operator of a private postal service that he created to challenge the government's monopoly on the mails. In 1971 Rossetto and his friend Stan Lehr published a lengthy article in the *New York Times Magazine* entitled "The New Right Credo—Libertarianism." In it they argued that "liberalism, conservatism and leftist radicalism are all bankrupt philosophies. The only question at issue among their adherents is which gang of crooks and charlatans is to rule society, and for what noble purpose." As Rossetto recalled nearly thirty years later, "it wasn't a Buckleyite conservatism that got me—it was the individualist, anti-statist conservatism that got me." At about the same time that Ken Kesey and the Merry Pranksters were rejecting the politics of the New Left and the hippies of the Haight were heading back to the land, Rossetto was coming to a similarly antipolitical position. In his work with the Young Republicans, he later remembered, he had come to believe that "in order to influence [the political world] you had to become it. The best way to change things was to walk away. . . . You had to start with yourself."[6]

In 1973 Rossetto earned an MBA from Columbia. Over the next decade, though, he drifted. He wrote a novel entitled *Takeover* about an American president who avoids impeachment by faking a national security crisis; the novel appeared a week before Richard Nixon resigned, and it received little attention. Some years later, he found himself in Rome, working on the set of the film *Caligula*. He decided to use the orgies he had seen on the set as a metaphor for the sexual revolution and penned a book called *Ultimate Porno*. Like *Takeover*, it vanished quickly. Finally, in the mid-1980s, Rossetto found his way to Ink, an Amsterdam-based translation firm that served high-tech companies. He produced a magazine for them in which the company could advertise its translation software. Gradually, he began to cover other technologies, including desktop publishing, CD-ROMs, and the like. In 1986 the magazine became *Language Technology,* and in 1988, *Electric Word.* Jane Metcalfe, whom Rossetto had met during a stint in Paris several years earlier, joined Rossetto and became marketing director for the magazine.

For Rossetto and Metcalfe, the magazine provided a vehicle with which to build the networks on which *Wired* would later depend. In 1988 Rossetto read *Time* magazine's report on the Media Lab and sought out Nicholas Negroponte for an interview. He later found his way to hypertext guru Ted Nelson and to Richard Saul Wurman, the host of one of the most important networking events in the computer industry, the soon-to-be-annual Technology, Entertainment, and Design (TED) Conference. In 1988 Kevin Kelly gave *Electric Word* an enthusiastic review in *Signal,* thus alerting a number of San Francisco Bay area technology journalists to its existence.

Around the time when the *Signal* review appeared, Rossetto began visiting the United States in the hope of bringing the magazine there. New York City journalist Michael Wolff met with Rossetto as a favor to a friend. "I opened the door to a Christ-like figure with dramatic hair and a rucksack over his shoulder," Wolff later recalled. "He had watery eyes, a caring, 'I have been hurt' voice, and an otherworldly presence. . . . I thought he was a lost soul."[7] Rossetto and Metcalfe also made a trip through California at about this time and met with Kevin Kelly as well. Kelly was not much more interested than Wolff had been, at least at first.[8] By 1991, though, *Electric Word* had gone out of business and Rossetto and Metcalfe had moved to New York. They brought with them the idea for a new lifestyle-and-technology magazine, to be called first *Millennium,* and later *Wired.* In February 1992, they attended Wurman's TED conference and carried with them a prototype of their new magazine to show one of the conference's speakers, Nicholas Negroponte. Unlike Wolff and Kelly, Negroponte was impressed. He arranged meetings for them with a series of media moguls, including Henry Kravitz, S. I. Newhouse Jr., Michael Eisner, Ted Turner, Rupert Murdoch, and Christy Hefner, and all declined their requests for funding.[9] Later that year, Negroponte himself became the magazine's first investor, ponying up $75,000 in return for a 10 percent stake in the magazine and promising to write a monthly column as well. He also persuaded Charles Jackson, CEO of Silicon Beach Software, to invest another $150,000 in the magazine.

With this, Rossetto and Metcalfe, together with the magazine's designers, John Plunkett and Barbara Kuhr, moved to San Francisco, started a conference on the WELL, and began seeking staff for the magazine. On the financial side, they created a series of business plans and began showing them to potential contributors. When they met with Bruce Katz, then head of the WELL, he referred them to Peter Schwartz. Schwartz in turn passed them to Global Business Network cofounder Lawrence Wilkinson. Wilkinson invested both his own money and that of the Global Business Network in the magazine and introduced Rossetto and Metcalfe to bankers at the firm of Sterling Payot, who ultimately provided several hundred thousand dollars in funds. Wilkinson went on to become the magazine's chief financial strategist. On the editorial side, Rossetto and Metcalfe created another, more fully developed prototype of the magazine, complete with a glossy look and feel, flashy graphics, and actual stories. Up until he saw this prototype, Kevin Kelly had been watching Rossetto and Metcalfe from a distance, expecting them to fail. But, says Kelly, "The minute I saw the [new] prototype I knew it was going to work."[10] For Kelly, *Wired* marked a logical extension of the work he had been doing at the *Whole Earth Review* and that others had been doing at *Mondo 2000*. Both of those publications had begun to merge lifestyle issues and technology, but always with the low-rent production values of underground periodicals. Finally, Kelly thought, here was a magazine that would get the attention that the *Whole Earth Review* and *Mondo* had both deserved. Kelly signed on as executive editor, and in June of 1992 he joined Rossetto, Metcalfe, and Wilkinson on the board of the newly formed Wired Ventures.

New Technology, New Economy, New Right

Even before they published their first issue, then, Rossetto and Metcalfe had stitched *Wired* into the social fabric of the Whole Earth world. They had found their financial strategist in the Global Business Network and a key editor in the *Whole Earth Review;* as the magazine ramped up, they would find many writers and ideas for stories in their conference on the WELL. Over time, these connections would link Rossetto's own long-standing antistatism to the New Communalist vision of an ideal social order born from the transformation of consciousness.

They would also connect both intellectual traditions with a series of extraordinary transformations in computing technology, the American economy, and American political life. By the time *Wired's* first issue appeared in March of 1993, desktop computers had become common features of homes and offices nationwide. The cost of computing was plummeting. According to one economist, between 1987 and 1995, the price of computing power decreased an average of 14.7 percent a year; from 1996 to 1999, it fell 31.2 percent a year. Thanks to their licensing practices, Microsoft and Intel supplied software and hardware, respectively, for a rapidly expanding array of computer manufacturers, including Dell, Compaq, and Gateway. By 1995 Microsoft's Windows operating system had become a global standard.[11]

The increasing availability of powerful small computers coincided with the privatization of the Internet backbone, a flowering of commercial networks, and a dramatic increase in public computer networking. In the early 1980s, the Internet backbone was government property. Managed by the Defense Department's Advanced Research Projects Agency (ARPA), it joined a set of operational and research networks, most of them connected to military projects. In the late 1980s, the number of academic users increased, and in 1990 ARPA transferred control over the Net to the National Science Foundation (NSF). ARPANET and NSFNET prohibited commercial traffic; but in the 1980s a series of commercial and alternative networks had also sprung up, such that by the late 1980s, millions of Americans were e-mailing one another, participating in online discussions, and posting information. Finally, in April 1995, the NSF relinquished control of the Internet backbone, facilitating the interlinking of commercial, alternative, and government-sponsored networks and the mixing of for-profit and not-for-profit uses across the system.[12]

By that time, another phenomenon had appeared on the Internet: the World Wide Web. Created in 1990 by Tim Berners-Lee and his colleagues at the Centre Européenne pour la Recherche Nucléaire (CERN), the Web took advantage of the Internet's information transfer protocols to create a new system of information exchange. Thanks to hyperlinks embedded in documents, as well as the new Universal Resource Locator (URL) system, users could navigate information in new and complex ways. For many, the Internet had long served as a system for the exchange of text messages. With the arrival of the Web, it became a way to publish information, to incorporate multimedia formats, and to quickly and easily connect previously discrete clusters of information.

At first, CERN distributed its Web software principally within the scientific community and Web use grew very slowly. Then, in 1993, a team led by Marc Andreesen, a staffer at the National Center for Supercomputing Applications (NCSA) at the University of Illinois, developed a new Web browser called Mosaic, which allowed users to embed hyperlinks in images for the first time and also permitted users to post color images within their Web pages. The NCSA made Mosaic available to the public in November 1993, just as *Wired* magazine's fifth issue was arriving on newsstands. Users downloaded forty thousand copies of Mosaic in the first month; by the spring of 1994, more than a million copies were in use. The rapid distribution of Mosaic in turn drove growth in the Web itself. In April 1993, the Web featured only 62 servers; by May of 1994, that number had ballooned to 1,248.[13] In 1994 Andreesen left the NCSA to found a commercial browser manufacturer, Netscape. The Netscape browser, which was faster, more secure, and easier to use, helped drive the rise of e-commerce, and in August of 1995, Netscape went public. Its shares doubled in value on the first day of trading.

Over the next five years, use of the Internet and the Web would grow astronomically, and as it did, speculators would bid up the share values of Internet-related stocks to extraordinary heights. Between 1995 and 1999, companies with limited (if any) actual profits saw their stock values grow by as much as 3,000 percent. By the end of the decade, shareholders would witness the inflation of the largest speculative bubble in American economic history. When the bubble first began to grow, Americans did in fact have reason for economic optimism. Just as the Internet and the World Wide Web were coming online, the American economy was enjoying a major expansion. From 1993 to 2000, Americans saw rapid growth in manufacturing output, investment, and worker productivity; at the same time unemployment and inflation sank to levels close to those of the prosperous 1950s.[14]

However, the growth did not derive from productivity increases brought about by the increasing use of computers and computer networks in business. Most growth was concentrated in the 12 percent of the American economy devoted to manufacturing durable goods, including computer hardware and peripherals. Although an increase in the manufacturing of computer hardware certainly boosted the economy overall, the deployment of computers per se did not. By the year 2000, 76.6 percent of all computers used in business were being used in retail and service firms; yet, though such firms accounted for about 75 percent of all business-oriented computer use, this sector of the economy had seen little in the way of productivity gain. Conversely, within the manufacturing sector that was almost exclusively responsible for economic growth in this period, the use of computers—as distinct from the manufacture of computer hardware—had very little measurable effect on productivity.[15]

Nevertheless, by the end of the decade, computers, telecommunications, and the Internet in particular had seized the public imagination. In part, some have suggested, this came about naturally, as individual users encountered the Internet for the first time. As Nigel Thrift has shown, however, by the end of the 1990s an entire circuit of stock analysts, journalists, publicists, and pundits had also emerged. They spun out a series of self-reinforcing prognostications, and as they did, analysts and investors appeared to come to a consensus: computers were bringing about a New Economy and perhaps even a long economic boom. New, more entrepreneurial forms of corporate organization, rapid investment in high technology, and the ability to corral the intangible knowledge and skills of employees—all seemingly made possible by the suddenly ubiquitous computer and communication networks—were transforming America and perhaps even bringing an end to the business cycle itself. In 1999 even the exceptionally sober-minded chairman of the Federal Reserve, Alan Greenspan, had come on board. With his inimitable diction, he explained to an audience of bankers in Chicago that "a perceptible quickening in the pace at which technological innovations are applied argues for the hypothesis that the recent acceleration in labor productivity is not just a cyclical phenomenon or a statistical aberration, but reflects, at least in part, a more deep-seated, still developing, shift in our economic landscape."[16]

This vision of a New Economy was accompanied by an ongoing swing to the right in American corporate and political life. Although Bill Clinton, a centrist Democrat, occupied the White House from 1993 to 2001, the era witnessed an extension of Reagan-era calls for the rollback of government entitlements and the deregulation of industry; there was also an increase in the visibility of the Christian right. The elections of 1994 ushered in the first Republican majority in both houses of Congress for forty years. Led by Newt Gingrich, the House of Representatives in the mid-1990s pushed for the downsizing of government and widespread deregulation—especially in the telecommunications sector. Together with Alvin Toffler, George Gilder, and technology journalist and entrepreneur Esther Dyson, Gingrich argued that America was about to enter a new era, one in which technology would do away with the need for bureaucratic oversight of both markets and politics. As Gingrich and others saw it, deregulation would free markets to become the engines of political and social change that they were meant to be.

Thomas Frank has termed this vision "market populism," and as he has indicated, in the 1990s it depended on a particular reading of the Internet. If the market was to be a deregulated mechanism of political as well as economic exchange, the recently privatized circuits of the Internet, with their free-flowing streams of commercial and noncommercial bits, made a perfect rhetorical prototype of the market-populist ideal. By the end of the decade, the libertarian, utopian, populist depiction of the Internet could be heard echoing in the halls of Congress, the board rooms of Fortune 500 corporations, the chat rooms of cyberspace, and the kitchens and living rooms of individual American investors. At its most extreme, Frank suggested, this ever-present ideology depended on a cybernetic understanding of information. By the end of the decade, he wrote, more than a few Americans agreed: "Life is in fact a computer. Everything we do can be understood as part of a giant calculating machine. . . . the 'New Economy,' the way of the microchip, is writ into the very DNA of existence."[17]

The Whole Earth at *Wired*

Frank and others understood the integration of computing, biology, and economics and its links to a rhetoric of political liberation as quintessentially 1990s phenomena. Yet, a close look at the history of *Wired* suggests that this rhetorical constellation emerged not simply alongside new communication technologies, nor exclusively among those who made and marketed those technologies, nor even in the 1990s. Rather, this particular version of what Kevin Kelly called the "computational metaphor" had been coming together for decades. Since the late 1960s, Stewart Brand and others associated with various Whole Earth publications had been linking information technologies to a New Communalist politics of personal and collective liberation. On the communes of the late 1960s, on the WELL of the 1980s, and even on Global Business Network retreats, information networks and social networks, biological systems and economic systems had seemed to mirror one another. It had all been "one," so to speak, for some time. In the 1990s, however, the editors and writers of *Wired* transformed the long-standing Whole Earth synthesis of cybernetics and New Communalist social theory into a means of embracing figures such as Gilder and Gingrich. In the process, they legitimated calls for corporate deregulation, government downsizing, and a turn away from government and toward the flexible factory and the global marketplace as the principal sites of social change. And they did so using the collaborative editorial tactics, universal rhetoric, and interpersonal networks of the Whole Earth.

Editorially, *Wired* made no pretense of pursuing balance in either its point of view or its sources. At one level, Rossetto simply aimed to distinguish the magazine from its competitors. As he told a reporter for *Upside* magazine in 1997, "The mainstream media is not allowing us to understand what's really happening today because it's obsessed with telling you, 'Well, on the one hand' and 'on the other hand'"; under conditions of digital revolution, Rossetto believed that a magazine could tell the truth—and achieve distinction—only by "not being objective." At another level, though, *Wired*'s editorial practices grew out of its integration into the Whole Earth world. John Battelle, the magazine's managing editor, had worked for two years at *MacWeek* and joined *Wired* after earning a master's degree in journalism at the University of California, Berkeley. He later recalled the editorial process at *Wired* thus: "It was about networks, and everyone brought their own. I was on the WELL. Kevin was on the WELL. I was in the trade magazine world, so I brought that whole world over with me, all the writers, all the people, all the knowledge and all the players who I knew from that world. Kevin knew all the players from the Whole Earth world and the

WELL. And Louis brought in Europe and the global perspective, tying it all together."[18]

Kevin Kelly agreed. When he was at *Wired,* he later said, he thought of himself as a "nonjournalist." Kelly meant for *Wired* to be a forum for the various networks in which he circulated, as the *Whole Earth Review* had been. He thought of himself as "a convener of interesting ideas"—much like a conference host on the WELL.[19] His job, he thought, was to stir up conversations and print them. For this reason, Kelly often allowed traditional professional boundaries to dissolve. As part of the editing process, for instance, he routinely allowed writers to share drafts of their stories with their sources. And when the magazine ran stories by and about members of the editors' personal and professional networks, those relationships often went unacknowledged. For one example, although Peter Schwartz regularly contributed articles to *Wired,* and although the Global Business Network was the subject of a feature story, the fact that GBN had helped fund the magazine was never reported in its pages.

At the same time that they were working to break down the traditional journalistic wall between writers and their sources, the editors of *Wired* were using the WELL to break down barriers between the magazine and its audience and potential contributors. From the time Rossetto and Metcalfe established a *Wired* conference on the WELL, they used it to build interest in the magazine and a sense of ownership in it on the part of WELL regulars, and, ultimately, as a way to identify writers for the magazine. As the magazine's paper issues hit the stands, the WELL hosted regular forums to discuss *Wired* articles, as well as forums for *Wired* contributors. Soon, *Wired* opened forums on other services, including Mindvox, Onenet, and AOL. The magazine also began distributing other articles online for free. In the early years particularly, contributors to these online forums often felt as though they part of the magazine.[20] And many were. Almost immediately, some of the WELL's most prominent members, including Stewart Brand, Howard Rheingold, and John Perry Barlow, began writing for *Wired.*

To Rossetto and Metcalfe this made sense, since they saw WELL users as living the sort of forward-thinking, technocentric lives their magazine celebrated. Rossetto was fond of comparing *Wired* to *Rolling Stone.* "Rolling stone held a window up to this group [of rock musicians] for the rest of the world to see how innovative, smart and powerful this group was," Rossetto explained. At the same time, "it held a mirror up to the group itself." *Wired,* he said, wanted to do the same with the citizens of the WELL and others like them. Rossetto's claim in this regard masks a somewhat more complex process, though. In a 1992 business plan, Rossetto and Metcalfe had described their target audience to potential investors as "Digital Visionaries." With annual incomes averaging $75,000 a year, this group represented "The top ten percent of creators, managers, and professionals in the computer industries, business, design, entertainment, the media and education."[21] In the coming years, *Wired* reached this group with extraordinary success. Less than three years after the first issue appeared, for instance, when *Wired* was selling 300,000 copies a month, its readers were 87.9 percent male, 37 years old on average, with an average household income of more than $122,000 per year. In a reader survey, more than 90 percent of subscribers identified themselves as either "Professional/Managerial" or "Top Management."[22]

Even though a number of WELL users certainly fell into this category, *Wired* was not, by and large, opening a window on the world of the WELL per se. Rather, its editors were using their links to the WELL and to a variety of other Whole Earth networks and organizations in order to conjure up and legitimate a particular social vision. In the pages of *Wired,* Whole Earth–affiliated organizations such as the WELL served as prototypes of a new and ideal form of networked sociability to which their readers might aspire. Over the course of its first five years, *Wired* ran lengthy features not only about the WELL, but also about the Electronic Frontier Foundation, the Global Business Network, and the Media Lab. The stories often focused on individuals who were also regular contributors to *Wired,* such as John Perry Barlow in the case of the Electronic Frontier Foundation and Peter Schwartz in the case of the Global Business Network. In addition to legitimating *Wired*'s own writers, such stories presented the organizations as prototypes of the sort of life that digital technologies were ostensibly bringing about for society at large. That life, in turn, represented the fulfillment of a revolution begun in the 1960s.

In June 1994, for instance, *Wired* ran Joshua Quittner's profile of the Electronic Frontier Foundation (EFF), entitled "The Merry Pranksters Go to Washington." The headline streamed across a full page, in one-and-a-quarter-inch hot pink type; underneath it, a little dotted arrow directed the reader to turn the page. There, filling the next two pages, stood the eight principals of the EFF, including Mitch Kapor, John Perry Barlow, Stewart Brand, and Esther Dyson. Across the image ran a single line of text, drawn from the article: "The EFF does something that Mitch Kapor has wanted to do for three decades—'find a way of preserving the ideology of the 1960s.'" Never mind that only one of the assembled group—Brand—had actually been a Prankster. To Quittner and his editors, the analogy was clear: "Older and wiser now, they're on the road again, without the bus and the acid, but dispensing many similar-sounding bromides: Turn on, jack in, get connected." Quittner centered much of the article around Barlow and Kapor and several times quoted them as they suggested that their current work was an extension of the 1960s consciousness revolution, undertaken with grown-up sobriety. As Kapor put it, "John and I are refugees from the 1960s, trying to make it as adults in the 1990s, understanding that transforming consciousness takes some doing."[23]

For the New Communalists, transforming consciousness had meant stepping outside party politics. To Kapor and Barlow in the 1990s, it meant heading to Washington. Quittner asserted that the EFF had developed an "Open Platform" proposal (essentially, a multipoint plan to facilitate interconnectivity across media) that had become a central element in Vice President Al Gore's 1993 Information Superhighway plans. For the leaders of the EFF, Quittner implied, creating a highly interconnected digital network open to all was a way to create a countercultural ideal: the leveled, harmonious community, linked by invisible signals. In that sense, the EFF had taken up where the Whole Earth publications had left off. As Quittner put it, "The *Whole Earth Catalog* was a tool catalog. The EFF is about empowering people through the tool of networking."[24] In a long passage pulled out of the text and stretched across two pages, EFF board member Esther Dyson explained, "The fundamental thing (the Net does) is to overcome the advantages of economies of scale . . . so the big guys don't rule." On the Net, she argued, people could "organize ad hoc, rather than get stuck in some rigid group." Quittner summed up her argument this way: "The Net, the very network itself, is merely a means to an end. The end is to reverse-engineer government, to hack Politics down to its component parts and fix it."[25]

The urge to "hack" politics by bringing governance down to a manageable local level and by basing social integration on technologically facilitated forms of consciousness was one of the driving impulses behind the New Communalist movement. Now, however, the old hammer-and-saw-wielding, do-it-yourself ethos of the back-to-the-landers had been fused to the craft ethic of computer programmers. Much as Stewart Brand and his Whole Earth colleagues had done at the Hacker's Conference of 1984, Quittner and Dyson joined the cultural legitimacy of the counterculture to the technological and economic legitimacy of the computer industry. Married to a libertarian longing for the reduction of government, Dyson's Internet became an idealized political sphere in the image of the forms of organization pursued by the Merry Pranksters, USCO, and many communes—forms in which authority was distributed, hierarchies were leveled, and citizens were linked by invisible energies. The Internet became both a metaphor for such a system and a means to bring it into being.

In Quittner's article, the global Net also called to mind the local network of relationships in which the leaders of the EFF found themselves enmeshed. Quittner organized the piece around several miniature portraits of key EFF people. At each stage, he carefully emphasized their extraordinary mobility, their access to people in power, and their material success. In *The Electric Kool-Aid Acid Test,* Tom Wolfe took readers inside the garage where the Merry Pranksters painted their psychedelic bus. Quittner here took readers inside San Francisco's Bistro Rôti—"a cozily upscale place overlooking the bay . . . woodburning stove . . . valet parking . . . white Jaguar in front . . ."—for the EFF's quarterly board meeting. Diners included Bill Joy, founder of Sun Microsystems; David Liddle, head of Interval Research Corporation; *Wired*'s own Jane Metcalfe; and a handful of other Silicon Valley luminaries alongside the current board members. Like the Merry Pranksters in Wolfe's account, this new elite inspired a hush in onlookers: "Waiters and waitresses quietly remove the uneaten shrimp and satay and whisper to each diner: *Chicken, steak or fish? Hot from the wood stove . . .*" And like the Pranksters, the diners celebrated their historical importance. When Kapor introduced Barlow, Esther Dyson shouted, "Tell them how you travel, John!" Barlow replied, "Well . . . sometimes I travel by bicycle, sometimes by computer, and sometimes—like the day before yesterday—I travel by Air Force Two."[26] The other diners cheered, knowing that the vice president had invited Barlow on board to talk about Internet policy.

In the context of Quittner's story, Barlow's introduction represented a measure of the EFF's power to influence contemporary politics and, at the same time, a vision of a future world in which social life, technological life, and political life had been completely intertwined. Barlow's comments demonstrated that his material and immaterial networks overlapped. He traveled by computer and by Air Force Two, and his ability to do so modeled the mobility and flexibility of life in the leveled society that Esther Dyson argued digital networks were bringing about. Gathered in the warmth of the woodstove, the leaders of Silicon Valley and of the EFF also modeled the sort of informal politics said to take place on the Net. In fact, their obvious success and easygoing camaraderie seemed to mark the effects those politics could have on the rest of the world. Highly individual, smart, fun, they had come together in a room where, like master planners overlooking a map, they could view the landscape (or, in this case, seascape) far below. They were a new kind of elite, born out of the antihierarchical ethos of the 1960s and powerful in a manner that matched that ethos. And if readers simply went online, the article seemed to suggest, they too could share in that world.[27]

The prototypical elements of "The Merry Pranksters Go to Washington" reappeared in *Wired*'s profiles of the Global Business Network, the Media Lab, and the WELL. In November 1994, for instance, journalist Joel Garreau, himself a member of GBN, described the Global Business Network as "a cause, a club, a conspiracy, and a collection of highly energetic particles aimed at bumping up against huge organizations with positive results." Seen from one angle, Garreau's GBN was simply a group of interdisciplinary and interpersonal networks that specialized in the promotion of group learning. Seen from another, it was an information system, a collection of people who were themselves little packets of information colliding with one another and with "huge organizations." Perhaps, Garreau implied, the Global Business Network would work like Esther Dyson's Internet and would transform its client organizations into inventive, problem-solving ad-hocracies. His sources reinforced this notion, as did the article's cybernetic tropes. GBN staffer Eric Best, for instance, described the organization thus: "It's a convention of curious kids. They want the opportunity and license to explore anything with the smartest people they can find. At a time of macro change, it's a collection of magpies and blue jays that set up the screeching when a big animal moves in the forest—because the forest needs that."[28] In Best's view, GBN would play the role once assigned to the communes of the back-to-the-land movement. It would become an elite example of the sorts of organizations the world needed, a collection of magpies who might save the economic and social ecosystem in the face of rapid technological change.

These parallels between Whole Earth–related interpersonal networks, emerging digital networks, and "systems" more broadly construed, as well as the echoes of the cold war–era world-saving impulse of the New Communalists, also appeared in Katie Hafner's 1997 portrait of the members of the WELL and in Fred Hapgood's 1995 account of MIT's Media Lab. After quoting leading WELL citizens describing the WELL as an "ecology" and as a "disembodied tribe," Hafner slipped into nature metaphor herself.[29] Conflicts, she wrote, "seemed a necessary force of nature, like a periodic brushfire that works its destruction to seed nutrients into the soil." Online system, disembodied community, the WELL's interpersonal networks—in Hafner's account, each mirrored every other, and together they were a self-contained system akin to the natural systems of the earth itself. Likewise, in a feature pinned to the Media Lab's tenth anniversary, Fred Hapgood argued that the Lab's "cultural variety gave it the outline of a complete society" and that "the relentless flood of projects made the place feel as if wherever it was going, it was getting there without losing a beat."[30] As Hapgood pointed out, the Media Lab had missed two of the most important developments in computer networking, HTML code and Web browsers. Yet, he argued, like the WELL, the Global Business Network, and the Electronic Frontier Foundation, the Media Lab was a prototype of an emerging world:

> A decade after its inception, the lab serves as a model for the organization of technical research and the relation of research to industry. It is also a model for education, in which art and engineering are combined in a project-centered curriculum where students' work is reviewed by real-world experts instead of academic professionals. No doubt this model has limitations, but we live at a time when the old ideas on these issues are simultaneously rusting out. Perhaps the single biggest achievement of the last 10 years will turn out to be the Media Lab itself.[31]

The New Communalists Meet the New Right

In each of these articles, the writer depicted a networked organization that seemed to be living out a contemporary version of the tribal countercultural ideal and appeared to forecast the social potential of the digital networking technologies of the 1990s *in terms of* that model. These groups served as prototypes not only of ways to coordinate research or online conversation, but of ways to organize a life. In addition, they helped to legitimate calls for telecommunications deregulation and smaller government. *Wired* served not only as a platform on which Whole Earth–related organizations could be displayed as prototypes, but also as a forum in which New Right pundits and politicians, proffering a highly libertarian version of the social impact of digital technologies, could be integrated into the Whole Earth's story of world-saving countercultural revolution.

This role can be seen most clearly in *Wired*'s complex relationship with Esther Dyson, libertarian telecommunications analyst George Gilder, and House Speaker Newt Gingrich. Over the magazine's first two years, these figures became involved in a cycle of mutual legitimation. At *Wired,* Gilder and Dyson served variously as sources, subjects, and authors of stories, and in August 1995 Dyson interviewed Gingrich for a *Wired* cover story. These appearances in *Wired* took place, however, against a background of other collaborations. In August 1994 Gilder invited Dyson to Aspen, Colorado, for a conference sponsored by the Progress and Freedom Foundation, a think tank closely linked to Newt Gingrich. There, along with Ronald Reagan's former science adviser, George Keyworth, and Alvin Toffler, Gilder and Dyson lent their names to a document featuring what was arguably the decade's most potent rhetorical welding of deregulationist politics to digital technologies, "Cyberspace and the American Dream: A Magna Carta for the

Knowledge Age."[32] A year later, while Gingrich's portrait graced the cover of *Wired*, Dyson and Gilder returned to the Aspen conference, taking with them John Perry Barlow, Kevin Kelly, and Stewart Brand, as well as bionomist Michael Rothschild and representatives from Microsoft, America Online, and Sun Microsystems.

In keeping with the Whole Earth's editorial tradition, *Wired* magazine simultaneously facilitated and celebrated these encounters. As members of the Whole Earth network, the computer industry, and the Republican right began to meet in person, they also began to appear in the magazine. In and of themselves, these appearances conferred legitimacy on members of each group. *Wired* also served as a site where representatives of each of these communities could lend members of other communities elements of their own public standing. The technical community could declare Gingrich to be a "wired" politician; the highly visible Gingrich could declare the technical community to be central to the national interest and on the cutting edge of politics. The countercultural community, represented in person by Brand, Barlow, and to some extent Kelly (and, in the pages of *Wired*, represented graphically by the magazine's neo-'60s layout and design), worked to legitimate the rising forces of technology and New Right politics as signs of the coming of a countercultural revolution.

This process took place over several years and depended for its success on editorial tactics first developed in the Whole Earth publications. George Gilder's relationship with *Wired*, for instance, began when Kevin Kelly interviewed him in the magazine's fourth issue. At first glance, Kelly and Gilder would seem to be an odd match. During the same decades when Kelly was wandering Asia with his backpack, Gilder was establishing a reputation as a right-wing pundit. In 1973 he wrote an article for *Harper's* magazine in which he declared that "the differences between the sexes are the single most important fact of human society" and that "the drive to deny them—in the name of women's liberation, marital openness, sexual equality, erotic consumption, or homosexual romanticism—must be one of the most quixotic crusades in the history of the species." In 1974 the National Organization for Women declared him the Male Chauvinist Pig of the Year for the book that grew out of that article, *Sexual Suicide* (later republished as *Men and Marriage*). In 1981, just a few years before Kelly came to work for Stewart Brand, Gilder published a defense of supply-side economics entitled *Wealth and Poverty*. Critics and supporters alike called the book "the bible of the Reagan revolution," and it shortly reached number four on the *New York Times* best-seller list.[33] Over the coming years, Gilder served up a volume of worshipful portraits of entrepreneurs (*The Spirit of Enterprise*, 1984), a celebration of technological miniaturization (*Microcosm*, 1989), and studies of digital technologies as forces for the enhancement of individual liberty (*Life after Television*, 1990, and *Telecosm*, 2000). By the end of the 1990s, he would become famous as a promoter of telecommunications stocks, most notably Global Crossing—a company that went public in 1998 at nineteen dollars a share, saw its share price nearly triple within a year, and, only four years later, became the largest telecommunications company to go bankrupt in American history.

In the early 1990s, though, Gilder and Kelly were moving in the same high-tech circles. Both, for instance, had served as keynote speakers at the annual conferences on bionomics that Michael Rothschild had started in 1991. These conferences attracted executives from Silicon Valley as well as libertarians of various stripes (including John Perry Barlow, who spoke at one in 1992).[34] As an intellectual framework, bionomics offered a natural meeting point for representatives of the New Right, such as Gilder, and of the Whole Earth's cybernetic tradition, such as Kelly. For Kelly, the notion that natural and social systems could model one another had long made sense. For Gilder and others on the right, the notion that markets were "natural"—in the sense of inevitable and right—was virtually a mantra. For each, it was a small step to integrate computers into the analogy.

In his interview with Kelly, Gilder took this step with aplomb. "The Internet," Gilder explained, "is an exciting kind of metaphor for spontaneous order." That is, the Internet might model a biological or a social system, but wherever set, that system would be governed from within and would be well organized. According to Gilder, the Internet was also a trigger for a libertarian reorientation of government. As opposed to "top-down technologies" such as TV and telephones, digital technologies "put you in command again." Government had no role to play in this process: "The government always discovers a technology after its moment is passing," he intoned. "If you're a winner you don't go to the government."[35]

By the middle of the interview, Gilder had begun to suggest that the Internet might be both a metaphor for a libertarian, free-market system and a sign of that system's inevitability. Kelly then picked up Gilder's thread and linked it explicitly to his own recently completed research on artificial life. Kelly suggested that the idea that the Internet would "eliminate hierarchy" might be a "myth, a utopian hope." Experiments with computers had shown that what appeared to be peer-to-peer systems in fact depended on "nested hierarchies." Gilder finessed the point: "The complexity of digital systems requires a hierarchical organization," he explained. "You need nested hierarchies. . . . So hierarchies do indeed exist. But they are ubiquitously distributed, which renders them an egalitarian force." In Gilder's comments, the hierarchical elements of computers became evidence for their *anti*hierarchical social effects. And those effects could be mind-boggling. Simply having access to a workstation granted a person "the power that an industrial tycoon commanded in the industrial era."[36]

By the end of their conversation, Kelly and Gilder had come together around the computational metaphor and used it to link several previously distinct ideas and social positions. Digital networks, which depend on all sorts of logical and electronic hierarchies to function, had become the emblems of the theoretically "level playing field" of the ideal free market. At the same time, the "nested hierarchies" of the machines served as symbolic stand-ins for local tycoons. The material power of tycoons had been virtualized; in Gilder's account, to control information was to control the world. This sort of statement could make sense only if one assumed, in keeping with the universal rhetoric of cybernetics and its social Darwinist cousin, bionomics, that the biological and social worlds were no more than information and that humans were, in the words of Norbert Wiener, not "stuff that abides but patterns which perpetuate themselves." And it was a very short step from the notion that the control of information makes one an industrial tycoon to the notion that the tycoons of the information industries should naturally control other systems. In his interview with Kelly, Gilder had set up an array of rhetorical mirrors. Biological, economic, and digital systems reflected one another; each should ideally be decentralized, deregulated, and ruled by a series of information tycoons; each of the tycoons in turn should be the master of his own local, temporary, nested hierarchy.[37]

In *Wired*'s view, Gilder himself was both such a tycoon and something of a cultural revolutionary. In March 1996 Rossetto and Kelly put Gilder on the magazine's cover. For the newsstand, the editors framed Gilder's face in a cool neon dance-floor green; inside the magazine, they depicted him as a cyber-age Peter Pan, flying across a green sky, hair waving. Gilder was hip, young, and maybe a bit countercultural, even if he did wear a tie. He was also in touch with the machine. In his profile, Po Bronson compared the social and economic systems within which Gilder made his living as a consultant to the digital systems he studied. Much as other *Wired* writers had celebrated the members of the Electronic Frontier Foundation or the Global Business Network for their social connections, Bronson dwelled at length on Gilder's hectic schedule of appearances, his migrations from tech company to tech company, and his twenty-thousand-dollar speaking fees. Gilder appeared to be a pattern of information, shuttling from node to node along a web of elite institutions. In case the reader missed the point, Bronson depicted Gilder literally speaking in the machine language of zeros and ones. When he met a new engineer, Bronson explained, Gilder and the engineer would "go through this sort of cascade of language syntax, negotiating like two modems, trying to find the most efficient level of conversation they can hold." In Bronson's sample conversation, the engineer was named Steve:

GEORGE: Hi, nice to meet you. Hey, that's a sweet access router over there.
  Wow, both Ethernet and asynchronous ports?
STEVE: Yeah, check this baby out—the Ethernet port has AUI, BNC, and RJ-45 connectors.
GEORGE: So for packet filtering you went with TCP, UDP, and ICMP.
STEVE: Of course. To support dial-up SLIP and PPP.
GEORGE: Set user User_Name ifilter Filter _Name.
STEVE: Set filter s1.out 8 permit 192.9.200.2/32 0.0.0.0/0 tcp src eq 20.
GEORGE: 00101101100010111001001101100001010101000111111001.
STEVE: . .. .
GEORGE: Really? Wait, you lost me there.[38]

Read in the context of Kelly's earlier interview and alongside Gilder's own frequent contributions to the magazine in later issues, Bronson's turning Gilder into a speaking computer represents a new level of legitimation for Gilder and his views. When Kelly interviewed Gilder, the conversation had revolved around the "computational metaphor" of cybernetics, and it linked that metaphor, and the Internet more generally, to a deregulated marketplace. Bronson's profile placed Gilder himself *inside* the computational metaphor. By the end of the piece, it was hard to escape a cascade of conclusions: the Net modeled an ideal social, biological, political, and economic sphere; computers were the latest stage in the evolution of those spheres; computers also served as tools and analogies for a new and more highly evolved type of leader; George Gilder was one of those leaders. As in its profile of the Electronic Frontier Foundation, *Wired* had offered the freelance lifestyle of a high-profile consultant as a model of the independent lifestyle ostensibly becoming available to the digital generation as a whole.

A month after Kelly's first interview with Gilder appeared in *Wired*, Paulina Borsook published a similar profile of Dyson. The story moved swiftly through Dyson's biography—child of physicist Freeman Dyson, childhood friend of Alice Bigelow (daughter of Julian Bigelow, John Von Neumann's engineer), former *Forbes* reporter and Wall Street stock analyst, later editor of the newsletter *Release 1.0* and hostess of the annual PC Forum conference. When it came to Dyson's present career, however, the story slipped into information-system metaphors like those that appeared in Bronson's profile of Gilder. Like Bronson's Gilder, Borsook's Dyson moved from company to company, "assimilating new ideas and retelling them to those who can turn them into wealth." She was a human node in an invisible network of information exchange. According to Borsook, she was somewhat singular and emotionally mechanical in her pursuits: "She often calls people 'friendly' or 'nice,'" wrote Borsook, "meaning they have interesting ideas and are willing to share them."[39] Like a computer, Dyson was "constantly cross-referencing and time stamping" her encounters: "What Esther does, in short, is provide a salon bound neither by time nor by space. Most of its habitués will never meet, but they all know Esther."[40]

Borsook's notion of Dyson as a cross-referencing, time-stamping information system neatly blurred the distinctions between Dyson's professional networks and the emerging digital networks of the Internet. Dyson appeared to be a computer; her invisible salon, a sort of cyberspace. In Borsook's story, Dyson's life as an entrepreneurial information worker and the emergence of digital networks became mutually legitimating mirrors of each other. Both were signs and products of the digital revolution under way. Borsook reminded her readers that this revolution was an extension of the countercultural revolution of thirty years before: "In spite of her libertarian leanings and her identification with the capitalist class, [Dyson] is in some ways the ultimate hippie. She has constructed a life that adheres to the '60s credo 'Follow your bliss and the money will come.'"[41]

By the time she appeared in *Wired,* Dyson had become well integrated into the extended Whole Earth network. She was one of the earliest members of the Global Business Network, joining in 1988. Brand, a long-time admirer, later recalled that "She brought to business a sharp analytical mind, no end of energy, intelligence and a somewhat libertarian political frame but an extreme public service inclination." Through the Electronic Frontier Foundation, Dyson had remained in close contact with Brand, Barlow, Kelly, and others. In 1995 she would go on to become chairman of the board of the Electronic Frontier Foundation, and in 1998 she would become chairman of ICANN, the international nonprofit corporation responsible for assigning domain names and addresses on the Internet. At the same time, however, Dyson was finding her way into the center of Republican power. In 1994 George Gilder arranged for Dyson to be invited to a conference in Atlanta entitled "Cyberspace and the American Dream," sponsored by the Progress and Freedom Foundation (PFF). "I didn't know much about the foundation," Dyson later explained. "But they mentioned that, along with George, Alvin and Heidi Toffler would be there. That was good enough for me. Oh yes. And Representative Newt Gingrich, too." In the summer of 1994, Dyson flew to Atlanta. At a small planning meeting for the conference, she met Gingrich for the first time. He impressed her with his poise, his knowledge of the Net, and most of all with the way in which he saw the

Net not so much as a way to make current government structures more efficient, but as an agent of political change in its own right. These views accorded well with her own, but the political terrain felt new and a little strange. "I walked into a world I didn't understand," she later recalled. "I discovered that the document I was to help draft was to be a manifesto."[42]

The manifesto that Dyson went on to coauthor extended the cybernetic and countercultural analogies current in the social worlds of the Whole Earth and *Wired*, linked them to a libertarian political agenda, and ultimately used them as symbolic resources in support of the narrow goal of deregulating the telecommunications industry. The "Magna Carta for the Knowledge Age" represented the combined efforts of four authors: Esther Dyson, George Gilder, Alvin Toffler, and George Keyworth, who was Ronald Reagan's former science adviser and a current PFF staffer. The document's preamble opened with a grand flourish: "The central event of the 20th century is the overthrow of matter. . . . The powers of mind are everywhere ascendant over the brute force of things." On the one hand, this triumph of the immaterial reflected Alvin Toffler's claim that a "Third Wave" of socioeconomic change was sweeping the world. In the first wave, farming and manual labor dominated the economy; in the second, machines and mass production ruled the land. Now, the authors wrote, echoing Daniel Bell and other theorists of postindustrial society, "the central resource is actionable knowledge."[43] On the other hand, the preamble linked Toffler's framework to the countercultural revolution of three decades before. After all, what had LSD users hoped to accomplish, if not the "overthrow of matter" by the "powers of mind"? This hope also reflected Norbert Wiener's older, early cold war hope that somehow the powers of mind represented in computers could contain the "brute force" then represented by the massed armies of East and West.

As the manifesto progressed, so did the rhetorical commingling of these historical streams. Cyberspace, the authors explained, was "more ecosystem than machine"; it was "a bioelectronic environment that is literally universal." Systems metaphors collided apace: like Gilder's first interview at *Wired*, or like Kevin Kelly's book *Out of Control*, the "Magna Carta" argued that computer systems and ecosystems modeled and interpenetrated one another. They also modeled the land of America itself: "The bioelectronic frontier is an appropriate metaphor for what is happening in cyberspace, calling to mind as it does the spirit of invention and discovery that led ancient mariners to explore the world, generations of pioneers to tame the American continent, and, more recently, to man's first exploration of outer space. . . . Cyberspace is the land of knowledge, and the exploration of that land can be a civilization's truest, highest calling. The opportunity is now before us to empower every person to pursue that calling in his or her own way." This invocation of the "frontier" mythos linked the cybernetic and countercultural rhetoric of the preamble to two constituencies: the lawmakers of Washington, D. C., and the back-to-the-landers of three decades earlier. In Washington, the metaphor of the frontier had long been used to justify political action—particularly the disposition of military force and the development of new technologies. In the wake of World War II, Vannevar Bush himself had justified the pursuit of science and technology as a quest to explore an "endless frontier."[44] In the 1960s, of course, many now-middle-aged lawmakers had grown up with John F. Kennedy's celebration of the New Frontier. For former New Communalists, this frontier rhetoric suggested that the computer and telecommunications industries represented an extension of their own youthful efforts. Thirty years earlier, the commune-based subscribers to the *Whole Earth Catalog* had dressed up in the archaic cowboy hats and ankle-length dresses of the nineteenth century and headed out into the Southwest to build their encampments. Today, the "Magna Carta" suggested, echoing the postcountercultural rhetoric of *Wired* magazine, John Perry Barlow, and the Electronic Frontier Foundation, they need only boot up their computers and head out into cyberspace.

This frantic mingling of biological, digital, and frontier metaphors marked not only a collision of ideas, or even of historical thought-streams, but of communities of interest. Thrown together in Atlanta, the four authors of the "Magna Carta" had pooled the symbolic resources of the various communities they represented and created a contact language. Broadly speaking, this language served to facilitate collaboration across the groups it interconnected. Having agreed that computing was a "new frontier," for instance, former hippies, young computer technologists, and government regulators could claim a common rhetorical ground on which to pursue their individual interests.

In the "Magna Carta," though, this contact language quickly came to serve a much narrower agenda. As Richard Moore has pointed out, the "Magna Carta" argued that digital technologies would enhance individual liberty, only to then confuse individual freedom with corporate deregulation. Cyberspace belonged to "the people," argued Dyson, Toffler, Gilder, and Keyworth, and as such, should be governed by them. Yet, thanks to the rhetorical confusion of cyberspace and the marketplace and, particularly, of cyberspace with the computing and telecommunications industries, the notion of returning cyberspace to its owners took on an entirely new connotation. "The most pressing need," explained Dyson and her colleagues, "is to revamp the policies and programs that are slowing the creation of cyberspace. . . . Indeed, if there is to be an 'industrial policy for the knowledge age,' it should focus on removing barriers to competition and massively deregulating the fast-growing telecommunications and computing industries."[45] What is more, it should allow "much greater collaboration between the cable industry and phone companies." In a twist of logic reminiscent of George Gilder's comments to Kevin Kelly on "nested hierarchies," the document went on to argue that "obstructing such collaborations"—and, presumably, the near-monopolies that could result—"is socially elitist."[46] With a spectacular mix of hubris and hyperbole, the authors asserted that since digital technologies drove egalitarian empowerment, by definition, to restrain their technological development (and the empowerment of telecommunications and cable companies) would be to resist the forces of history, nature, technology, and American destiny all at once.

These arguments helped set the stage for the first major rewriting of American telecommunications policy in sixty years. By the end of 1994, Newt Gingrich and his insurgent Republicans had seized control of the Congress; almost immediately they launched a campaign to deregulate the telecommunications industry. With the *Telecommunications Act of 1996*, they succeeded. As the act was being developed, the "Magna Carta" helped make clear the House Speaker's own position and offered a justifying logic for the deregulation of the largest players in the industry. Although the act would ultimately reach out in a number of ways to noncorporate stakeholders, retaining universal service provisions, for instance, and including provisions in support of small entrepreneurs, it also freed massive telecommunications firms and cable companies to expand their operations dramatically. Moreover, as Patricia Aufderheide has explained, it enshrined in law the notions that undergirded the "Magna Carta." In the *Telecommunications Act of 1996*, as in the "Magna Carta," technologies—particularly communication technologies and the Internet—were seen as models of open markets and an open political sphere and at the same time as tools with which to bring them about. In that sense, the act treated the interests of the marketplace and those of the public as if they were fundamentally synonymous.[47]

Though she may have felt somewhat awkward when she first entered Gingrich's realm, Dyson returned for a second conference the following year. Entitled "Aspen Summit: Cyberspace and the American Dream II," this meeting took place in Aspen, Colorado, and was again sponsored by the PFF. This time, the PFF extended invitations not only to Dyson, Toffler, and Keyworth, but also to John Perry Barlow, Stewart Brand, Kevin Kelly, and executives from Microsoft, America Online, and Sun Microsystems. Corporate sponsors of the event paid $25,000 to attend (other visitors paid $895), and many were unhappy. "If these people are opinion leaders, maybe I'm stuck in a Second Wave paradigm," griped Christopher C. Quarles III, manager for emerging markets at AT&T.[48] Brand found himself on a panel reminding fellow spokesmen of the government's central role in developing the digital technologies that they claimed the government should now step away from.[49] If the "Aspen Summit" was intended to unite the technology industry, representatives of the San Francisco Bay area counterculture, and Republican Washington, it failed.

Nevertheless, though that meeting of the minds did not take hold in the mountains, it found a home in *Wired*. While the summiteers were meeting in Aspen, the August 1995 issue of *Wired* convened an interview between Esther Dyson and Newt Gingrich. In it they engaged in many of the rhetorical flourishes that characterized the "Magna Carta." Together they depicted the Internet as a model of an ideally decentralized and in many ways degovernmentalized society, and as a tool with which to bring that society about. As Dyson and her coauthors had done in the "Magna Carta," Gingrich compared the digital revolution to the birth of the American nation. In the interview, however, he extended that vision to include the social agenda of his own, then-insurgent party. Gingrich and the House Republicans had come to power carrying with them a multipoint program called the *Contract with America*. The *Contract* offered a blend of conservative social politics (welfare reform, anticrime legislation, promarriage tax policies) and laissez-faire business policy (corporate deregulation and tax reductions). In his interview with Dyson, Gingrich linked the Internet to both. "This is a society permeated by a belief that we have a mission, that our mission relates to God, and that our powers relate to God," he declared.[50] To settle the "bioelectronic frontier" he seemed to imply, was a divine mission, not unlike the settling of America some two hundred years earlier. And if that was true, then the Republicans themselves represented the vanguard of a new kind of society — one that would be more technologically savvy, but also more religious and more conservative. Toward the end of the interview, Gingrich hammered the point home by virtually restating the key points of the Republicans' *Contract with America*:

> We have to do nine things in parallel, which is complicated. We have to renew American civilization at a core-values level. We have to do everything we think we are doing to compete in a world market so we're economically sufficient. We have to make the transition to the information age. We have to replace welfare with a very different set of values and structures. We have to decentralize power out of Washington and ideally out of government to some extent. Everything we do at the federal level ought to be the best in the world, or we shouldn't be doing it. We need to balance the budget for fiscal long-term reasons that are very real in terms of baby boomers' retirement, in terms of

our kids' lives. We need to reestablish physical safety against drugs, violent crime, and foreign attacks. And finally we have to lead the planet. We're the only country capable of leading the human race. And we've got to do all nine of those simultaneously. Life's complicated.[51]

In her introduction to the interview, Esther Dyson expressed reservations about Gingrich's social politics, explaining, "I like his ideals—but not necessarily the people who espouse them. Or the society that will result from them."[52] But by the end of her interview, the doubts seemed to have washed away. Dyson and Gingrich clearly spoke the same language—the language of the "Magna Carta." Moreover, for regular readers of *Wired*, their encounter came at the end of a long series of articles in which the cybernetic, countercultural, and deregulationist strains of their rhetoric had already been legitimated. Their conversation and its rhetoric also reflected a series of earlier encounters between the Whole Earth community, the technological community, and the corporate community. By the time Dyson interviewed Gingrich, the notion of business as a source of social change, of digital technology as the tool and symbol of business, and of decentralization as a social ideal were well established in the pages of *Wired* and in its networks of contributors. So too was the idea that the digital revolution represented an extension of the countercultural revolution. From here, it took little imagination to guess that perhaps the Republican "revolution" of 1994 might itself be riding the same "Third Wave."[53]

The Internet as the New Millennium

In the end, Newt Gingrich's appearance on the cover of *Wired* signaled the high-water mark of the alliance between the techno-libertarians of the computer industry, the former counterculturalists of the San Francisco Bay area, and the social conservatives of the New Right. As the failure of the second "Cyberspace and the American Dream" conference suggested, the apparent similarity between Newt Gingrich's Republican agenda and Esther Dyson's vision of post-Internet politics hinged as much on shared rhetoric as on shared material interests. In the late 1990s, though, as the stock market began its final ascent toward its end-of-the-decade peaks and as investors clamored for shares in Internet stocks, that rhetoric reappeared. In 1997 *Wired* published two articles that together linked the cybernetic thought styles and countercultural social ideals of the Whole Earth world to millenarian claims for the emergence of a New Economy. Both articles would be developed into books, and both would be among the most widely cited documents to argue that thanks to the Internet, the laws of twentieth-century economics, not to mention the hierarchies of twentieth-century bureaucracy, had been left behind.

The first of these articles appeared in July 1997. The cover of *Wired* trumpeted the piece: the magazine's designers centered a picture of the earth against a bright yellow background, echoing the covers of the *Whole Earth Catalog*. Over the green continents and blue oceans of the globe, they drew an early 1970s smiley face, chewing the sort of daisy long-haired protesters had famously slipped into the rifle barrels of soldiers at the 1967 March on the Pentagon. Even as its iconography pointed back toward the counterculture, the cover's text suggested that a new revolution was afoot. "THE LONG BOOM," it proclaimed, was under way: "We're facing 25 years of prosperity, freedom, and a better environment for the world. You got a problem with that?"

The article itself claimed to be a "positive scenario" of the future.[54] Written by Global Business Network president Peter Schwartz and GBN staffer Peter Leyden and entitled "The Long Boom: A History of the Future, 1980 – 2020," the article argued that two long-term historical streams had merged. The first was technological. The computer and telecommunications networks of the 1990s were only the beginning. Soon biotechnology and nanotechnology would come online and, in their wake, a form of technology much sought after on the communes of the 1960s: alternative energy. The second stream was social. A new "ethos of openness" had taken root, wrote Schwartz and Leyden, in America and abroad. Characterized by "the relentless process of globalization, the opening up of national economies and the integration of markets," the new ethos spoke directly to the market populism of the late 1990s: in Schwartz and Leyden's view, deregulation of international markets represented the opening up of international politics.[55] Yet it also spoke to the dreams of those who had grown up in the 1960s. In their imaginary year 2000, they wrote, "Optimism abounds. Think back to that period following World War II. A booming economy buoyed a bold, optimistic view of the world: we can put a man on the Moon, we can build a Great Society, a racially integrated world. In our era we can expect the same." That era would meld the technological achievements of the New Frontier to the social ambitions of the New Communalists. In the year 2000, the bureaucracies of the cold war era would be "flattened and networked through the widespread adoption of new technologies."[56] In their place would arise "a new civilization, a global civilization, distinct from those that arose on the planet before." It would be a civilization marked by a singular understanding: "We're one global society, one human race."[57]

In Schwartz and Leyden's article, and in the book that grew out of it, the Internet became a tool with which to fulfill both the cultural ambitions of the New Communalists and the technological ambitions of the nation they sought to change. Like the space program of the 1960s, the Internet had revealed that the world was a single whole. And like the drugs of that era, it was linking the minds of individuals into a new, collaborative and geographically distributed civilization. Moreover, they wrote, the sudden rise of the Internet and the World Wide Web and, alongside them, the transformations in corporate life and the run-up in the stock market, were simply tastes of things to come.

Two months after "The Long Boom" appeared in *Wired,* Kevin Kelly amplified its conclusions and linked them to the social and intellectual networks he had brought together in his book *Out of Control.* In an article entitled "New Rules for the New Economy," and in a book of the same name shortly thereafter, Kelly argued that digital networks and networked forms of economic activity would open a new era in human life. Like contemporary pundits such as George Gilder and John Hagel, a corporate consultant and author of the widely read *Net Gain,* Kelly argued that the rise of the Internet was driving a shift toward networked forms of economic and social life. But he went on to embed the shift in a cybernetic rhetoric and to claim that it was evidence for the imminent fulfillment of a New Communalist dream.

Almost fifty years earlier, Norbert Wiener's vision of the world as an information system seeking homeostasis had offered cold war Americans a framework with which to imagine their own survival in a nuclear era. In Kevin Kelly's work, however, that vision offered readers a glimpse of a new and more turbulent renewal:

> Silicon chips linked into high-bandwidth channels are the neurons of our culture. Until this moment, our economy has been in the multicellular stage. Our industrial age has required each customer or company to almost physically touch one another. Our firms and organizations resemble blobs. Now, by the enabling invention of silicon and glass neurons, a million new forms are possible. Boom! An infinite variety of new shapes and sizes of social organizations are suddenly possible. Unimaginable forms of commerce can now coalesce in this new economy. We are about to witness an explosion of entities built on relationships and technology that will rival the early days of life on Earth in their variety.[58]

Mind and computation, economy and nature, the corporation and the individual—for Kelly, all mirrored one another, linked by the universal rhetorical logic of cybernetics and by the New Communalist hope that new, nonhierarchical social forms might arise thanks to technologies of consciousness.

In the late 1990s, Kelly also saw these new forms as a business opportunity: "Those who obey the logic of the net, and who understand that we are entering into a realm with new rules, will have a keen advantage in the new economy." By the end of the decade, millions of Americans were investing their savings in Internet companies, very much in the belief that the economy and perhaps even humanity as a whole had entered a new era. Young engineers were migrating to the hubs of digital innovation as fast as they could. In the industrial-era lofts south of Market Street in San Francisco and in the narrow corridors of Manhattan's Silicon Alley, twenty-something marketers pulled their six-hundred-dollar Herman Miller chairs around hand-hewn oak and redwood tables and plotted something called "web strategy." More than a few began to imagine themselves as bits of talent and information swirling in the currents of a knowledge economy, their own careers tied to their ability to divine its rapidly changing laws.[59] Corporations reconfigured offices to facilitate flexible work, programmers camped in their companies' open-all-night offices, and day after day, financiers, technologists, and ordinary Americans checked the financial pages for signs that the future was still dawning.

However, even as optimism peaked in its pages and among its readership, *Wired* magazine began to stumble. Since 1993 *Wired*'s investors had put up a total of $40 million. As of January 31, 1997, *Wired* and its associated ventures had lost some $50 million—despite taking in as much as $17 million in advertising in 1996 alone.[60] In part, these losses reflected Louis Rossetto's extraordinary ambition. No sooner had the magazine begun to appear on newsstands than Rossetto and his team began to expand into online ventures, book publishing, television production, and multilingual overseas editions of the magazine.[61] That ambition in turn led Rossetto and his team to try to capitalize on the magazine's reputation. In May of 1996, they did what so many Internet start-ups were doing: they hired Goldman Sachs to take them public. Most magazine and publishing companies typically sell at three times their book value. At this rate, *Wired* should probably have sold for between $6 million and $10 million.[62] Goldman Sachs floated an initial public offering that valued *Wired* Ventures at $447 million. Had it been accepted, Louis Rossetto alone would have pocketed $70 million. When they could not find enough takers at that price, Goldman Sachs withdrew the IPO. In September of 1996, they tried again. This time they valued the firm at $293 million. Even at this revised rate, *Wired* would have been valued more highly than 92 percent of the five thousand largest publicly traded companies in America at the time.[63]

Perhaps Goldman Sachs had been hoping that investors would mistake *Wired* magazine for the technological "revolution" it covered. After all,

Wired's editors had long conflated the success of their interpersonal networks with the power of emerging networking technologies. If so, they were out of luck. Goldman Sachs found itself forced to cancel the second IPO as well, for lack of interest. *Wired* continued to lose money, and in July 1997, just as *Wired's* cover heralded the arrival of the Long Boom, *Wired's* investors forced Louis Rossetto to step down as chief executive officer of Wired Ventures. Five months later, he left the staff of the magazine altogether; soon thereafter, Kevin Kelly followed suit.

Not long after this, the stock market's dot-com bubble began to leak and then suddenly burst. *Wired's* techno-libertarian optimism would live on, as would the magazine itself. But for most Americans, the "Long Boom" was over.

CHAPTER 8

The Triumph of the Network Mode

Looking back on the dot-com bubble's spectacular collapse, we can be tempted to dismiss the millenarian claims that surrounded the Internet in the 1990s as little more than the cunning hype of those who stood to profit from the building of broadband pipelines, the sale of computers, and the distribution of soon-to-be-worthless stock. But that would be a mistake. Although Kevin Kelly, Peter Schwartz, and *Wired* magazine certainly helped fuel the raging optimism of the period, their techno-utopian social vision in fact reflected the slow entwining of two far deeper transformations in American society. The first of these was technological. Over the previous forty years, the massive, stand-alone calculating machines of the cold war had become desktop computers, linked to one another in a vast network of communication that reached into almost every corner of the civilian world. This shift in computing technology took place, however, alongside a second, cultural transformation. In the late 1950s, Stewart Brand and others of his generation had come of age fearing that they would soon be absorbed into an unfeeling bureaucracy, a calculating, mechanical form of social organization that had brought humankind to the edge of nuclear annihilation. Over the ensuing forty years, their attempts to find an alternative to this grim vision of adulthood saw them push back the boundaries of public life and make room for styles of self-expression and collective organization that had been taboo in much of cold war America.

By the late 1990s, Brand and his Whole Earth colleagues had repeatedly linked these technological and cultural changes and in the process had helped turn the terms of their generational search into the key frames by which the American public understood the social possibilities of computers and computer networking. Thanks in no small part to Brand's work at the *Whole Earth Catalog* and later at *Rolling Stone*, desktop computers had come to be seen as "personal" technology. In keeping with the New Communalist ethos of tool use, they promised to transform individual consciousness and society at large. Thanks to the citizens of the WELL, computer-mediated communication had been reimagined in terms of disembodied, communal harmony and renamed virtual community. Cyberspace itself had been reconfigured as an electronic frontier. Finally, in the 1990s, the social and professional networks of the Global Business Network and *Wired* seemed to suggest that a new, networked form of economic life was emerging. Because of computer technologies, their example implied, it was finally becoming possible to move through life not in hierarchical bureaucratic towers, but as members of flexible, temporary, and culturally congenial tribes.

In all of these ways, members of the Whole Earth network helped reverse the political valence of information and information technology and turn computers into emblems of countercultural revolution. At the same time, however, they legitimated a metamorphosis within—and a widespread diffusion of—the core cultural styles of the military-industrial-academic technocracy that their generation had sought to undermine. In the imagination of the young Stewart Brand and others like him, and in the popular imagination even now, the middle-aged men who ran the corporations, universities, and governments of the cold war had found themselves locked into rigid roles. Their hands ached from years on the corporate ladder, and their souls had begun to wither beneath their suits. But during those same years, throughout the military-industrial-academic complex responsible for developing America's defense technologies, a far more collaborative style was emerging. Interdisciplinary, entrepreneurial, project-based, this new style thrived not only on government funding, but on the rhetoric of information and systems theory as well. By the late 1990s, both the highly flexible, networked cultural style of this research world and its dependence on informational metaphors had migrated far from the weapons laboratories and planning institutes of the cold war defense establishment. Like computers themselves, the culture and rhetoric of collaborative cold war research had become standard features of corporate and governmental life, and they remain so today.

In that sense, Stewart Brand and the Whole Earth network not only reconfigured the cultural status of information and information technologies as they moved from the government-funded, military-industrial research world into society at large; they also helped legitimate a parallel migration on the part of that world's cultural style. Moreover, they did so by embracing the cybernetic theories of information, the universal rhetorical techniques, and the flexible social practices born out of the interdisciplinary collaborations of World War II. Like the designers of that era's weapons-research laboratories, Brand and his colleagues created network forums in which members of multiple social and technical communities could come together, collaborate, and, in the process, build shared understandings of their collective interests. Expressed first in local contact languages, these understandings were repeatedly exported from the forums themselves, either by forum members or by professional journalists in attendance. Like the laboratories that first gave rise to cybernetics, however, the forums produced more than new bits of rhetoric. They also produced new social networks and, in Brand's case, new information systems, such as catalogs, meetings, and online gatherings. These systems in turn hosted and helped to create new social and professional networks and at the same time modeled the networks' governing ideals.

By the 1990s, each of these elements had come to play an important role in building the rhetorical and social infrastructure on which the techno-utopianism of the decade depended. But they also represented a new, networked mode of organizing the production of goods, information, and social structure itself. Fifty years earlier, across the military, industry, and academe, the dominant mode of organizing work was bureaucratic. Universities, armies, corporations—outside their research laboratories and designated think tanks—all featured vertical chains of command, long-term employment prospects, clear distinctions between individuals and their professional positions, firm boundaries between the organization and the outside world, and reward systems based on some combination of merit and seniority.[1] By the end of the twentieth century, however, these bureaucratic organizations had begun to lose their shape. In many industries today, and in some parts of military and academic life as well, hierarchies have been replaced by flattened structures, long-term employment by short-term, project-based contracting, and professional positions by complex, networked forms of sociability.[2]

Even as they decoupled computers from their dark, early 1960s association with bureaucracy, then, Brand and the Whole Earth community turned them into emblems not only of New Communalist social ideals, but of a networked mode of technocratic organization that continues to spread today. In that way, they helped transform both the cultural meanings of information and information technology and the nature of technocracy itself.

The Counterculture That Wasn't

With this history in mind, it is time to revise our understanding of both the counterculture of the 1960s and its relationship to the rise of postindustrial forms of production and culture. Since the 1960s, scholars and journalists alike have tended to entangle the New Communalist movement and the New Left. Focusing on the fashions, music, and drug use common to both, critics have suggested that the two movements merged in one of two ways. Some have pointed to the New Left's embrace of new cultural styles in the late 1960s and suggested that that cultural turn helped corrode its political ambitions. Others have elided this moment and simply argued that the New Left was a particular manifestation of an otherwise unitary phenomenon called "the counterculture." In both cases, historians and sociologists, and particularly those interested in the relationship between the counterculture and information technologies, have tended to take the youth movements of the 1960s at their word and to argue that they did in fact represent an alternative to the military-industrial-academic culture of the cold war.

The history of Stewart Brand and the Whole Earth community suggests that this was not entirely the case. Even as the Free Speech Movement and the New Left explicitly confronted military, industrial, and academic institutions, the bohemian artists of cold war Manhattan and San Francisco, and later the hippies of Haight-Ashbury and the youthful back-to-the-landers, in fact embraced the technocentric optimism, the information theories, and the collaborative work style of the research world. Fully in keeping with the scientific ethos of the era, young members of the New Communalist wing of the counterculture, along with many in the New Left, imagined themselves as part of a massive, geographically distributed, generational *experiment*. The world was their laboratory; in it they could play both scientist and subject, exploring their minds and their bodies, their relationships to one another, and the nature of politics, commerce, community, and the state. Small-scale technologies would serve them in this work. Stereo gear, slide projectors, strobe lights, and, of course, LSD all had the power to transform the mind-set of an individual and to link him or her through invisible "vibes" to others. Thus changed, these new individuals could in fact complete the mission so long entrusted to the panjandrums of the military research community: saving the world. If twentieth-century bureaucracy had brought mankind to the edge of destruction, the commune-dwelling readers of the *Whole Earth Catalog* hoped their own example might return human beings to a new state of integration—psychological, techno-social, natural.

The New Communalist celebration of information, technology, and experimentation has two implications, one for our understanding of the roots of postindustrial society and another for our understanding of the counterculture's role in the spread of both computing and the networked mode of production. Since the early 1970s, a series of sociologists and geographers have chronicled the growth of a new, knowledge-based form of economic production.[3] Their descriptions of the forces driving this shift and of its likely consequences have varied, largely in synch with technological and economic developments occurring as they wrote. Yet, despite their differences, these scholars have tended to agree that, starting sometime in the late 1960s or early 1970s, a postindustrial mode of development emerged as a dominant force in society.[4] Within this mode, as Daniel Bell put it in his early and still-influential 1973 account *The Coming of Post-Industrial Society,* "theoretical knowledge" would serve as the "axial principle" of production.[5] Under the industrial regime, he argued, major technological innovations such as telegraphy and aviation had arisen from individual tinkering. By contrast, under the postindustrial system then emerging, new technologies such as chemical synthesis had come about as a result of systematic scientific research. In the future, he explained, this trend would accelerate. Scientists and researchers would work collaboratively to apply systematic knowledge to complex problems. They would produce both new goods and new knowledge, and as they did, their status in society would rise. As they acquired increasing social power, suggested Bell, bureaucratic hierarchies would begin to crumble, to be replaced by the leveled social structures of the research world.

Analysts have often argued that the shift to knowledge-based forms of production and flatter forms of organization either began or sped up dramatically at about the time Bell was writing. However, the history of Stewart Brand and the Whole Earth group serves as a reminder that many of the qualities associated with postindustrial society and its subsequent analytical incarnations in fact appeared earlier, in the military-industrial-academic research collaborations of World War II and the cold war.[6] As historians of science have demonstrated, the government-sponsored research projects first created to help win World War II also saw the deployment of systematic knowledge across disciplines on an enormous scale. Tinkers did not design radar technologies or atomic weaponry; these technologies grew out of the gathering of interdisciplinary teams of scientists, engineers, and administrators. Though housed and funded by a massive bureaucracy, these teams did not stand on status and position; rather, they worked collaboratively, within a relatively flat social structure. In part, that structure grew out of the need to take a comprehensive, systemic approach to weapons development, one that could see men and machines as twinned elements of a larger combat apparatus. And in part, that flexible, interdisciplinary mixing helped spawn a rhetoric of systematic knowledge (cybernetics) and the tools with which to model and manage such knowledge (computers).

In other words, by the time Daniel Bell wrote *The Coming of Post-Industrial Society,* theoretical knowledge had already been serving as the central principle of military research and military-industrial production for some thirty years. Perhaps partially for this reason, Bell argued that "the decisive social change taking place in our time . . . is the subordination of the economic function to the political order." As subsequent analysts such as David Harvey and Manuel Castells have convincingly demonstrated, Bell was wrong on this point. The theoretical knowledge, the collaborative work styles, and the information technologies associated with government-sponsored research and science have indeed become increasingly important elements of society. Yet they have acquired that importance first and foremost in the economic sector. Harvey and Castells have each confirmed that knowledge, broadly construed, has become a central element in the production of new goods and services. As computers and computer networks have come online, scholars have in turn increasingly shown how these technologies have amplified and accelerated the impact of knowledge and information on the production process.[7] A variety of sociologists have likewise confirmed Bell's suggestion that alongside the rise of knowledge and information as key elements in the production process, a corresponding corrosion of corporate bureaucracy would occur. In many industries, vertical chains of command with clear reporting structures have indeed given way to more leveled forms. Bureaucracies certainly still exist, but increasingly, and particularly within knowledge-intensive and high-technology industries, networks rather hierarchies are becoming key forms of organizing production.

Over the past fifty years, then, the knowledge-based principles of production, the organizational styles, and the information technologies of the military research laboratory have in fact proliferated. Stripped of their associations with military or even government roots, they have come to be seen as economic and cultural forces, and even, in the writings of Kevin Kelly and the *Wired* group, at least, as forces of nature. And it is here that the counterculture's contribution to the rise of postindustrial society begins to come into view. When Stewart Brand and his generation left home to attend college, they found themselves in the heart of a research world still devoted to fending off America's enemies. As Brand's diary entries of the time suggest, students in this era feared that the institutions devoted to winning the cold war might end their own lives in one of two ways: first, they might fight a nuclear war and destroy the world; and second, they might offer college-educated youth no choice but to enter what they imagined to be the psychologically deadening silos of bureaucratic careers. For Brand and others, these two threats were inextricably entangled. The Free Speech marchers who invaded Sproul Hall in 1964, for instance, imagined the university as both a factory and a giant computer. Like other engines of the militarized state, they suggested, the university was devoted to creating both knowledge and intellectual laborers with which to defend the nation. In the process, they argued, it would also annihilate the students themselves by turning them into bits of information. This critique of the military-industrial-academic complex as a mechanism, a machine, a technocratic device for the destruction of the world and for the crushing of souls, rang throughout the youth movements of the 1960s.

Nevertheless, even as they were protesting cold war research and the information technologies that supported it, students of Stewart Brand's generation were being immersed in the intellectual legacy of collaborative military research. Systems-oriented social theory, information-oriented biology and psychology, and, in cybernetics, an information-based theory that seemed to claim to link all of these domains—the waves of students entering America's universities in the late 1950s and the 1960s encountered them all. For Stewart Brand, as for the artists he met soon after graduation, and as for the New Communalist readers of the *Whole Earth Catalog* some years later, these systems theories promised a solution to the conundrums of their adolescence. On the one hand, as Norbert Wiener had argued as early as the late 1940s, cybernetics and related systems theories offered up a vision of the world in which each of its elements could be read as connected to, and to some extent a reflection of, every other. Human beings, the natural world, technological systems, institutions—all were both individual examples of and knit together within what Gregory Bateson would call "the pattern that connects."[8] If the atomic era had conjured up a nightmare vision of humankind broken into factions across invisible "iron curtains" and of all of humanity leveled in a single blast, cybernetics, and systems theory more generally, offered a vision of a world united, inextricably connected, and tending, at least in Norbert Wiener's view, toward the calm of homeostasis. It was this vision of a natural world engaged in constant, complex patterns of coevolution yet tending to stability that Stewart Brand first encountered among the butterflies of Stanford's Jasper Ridge. And it was this vision of the social world that the artists of USCO and the founders of communes such as Libre and the Farm invoked as they gathered to build alternative communities.

On the other hand, the technophilic orientation of cybernetics and information theory, together with the example of idiosyncratic technocrats such as Buckminster Fuller, offered the youth of the 1960s a solution to another dilemma as well. Although they had grown up under the shadow of the atomic bomb, Brand and his generation had also come of age in an era of extraordinary abundance. While the marchers of the Free Speech movement attacked the factories of American industry, those factories were bringing forth an unending stream of consumer delights for American youth. This presented college-aged Americans with a predicament: how could they reject the core institutions of American society and yet retain access to the products of that society and the pleasures they offered?

The New Communalists parsed this dilemma by fusing the technocentrism and celebration of knowledge and experimentation common to the cold war research world with their individual quests to create alternative communities. As they turned away from the agonistic politics of the New Left, the New Communalists turned toward what they imagined to be a world interlinked by invisible systems. Much as the information systems of cybernetics could be made visible and managed by computers, the artists of USCO and the communards of the back-to-the-land movement imagined that the invisible mesh binding the social and natural worlds could be accessed through the use of small-scale technologies. If, as Stewart Brand suggested, the military-industrial complex had introduced human beings to a state in which they really did have the power to destroy the world, a state in which they really were "as gods," then its products could also enable individual youths to become Buckminster Fuller's Comprehensive Designers. As Fuller suggested, and as Brand and the *Whole Earth Catalog* demonstrated, they could take up the goods of industrial society and transform them into tools for their individual and collective reformation.

The New Communalists made two especially important collective decisions in the late 1960s. First, they turned away from political struggle and toward social and economic spheres as sites from which to launch social change. Second, they brought with them the central faith of the military research world: that experimentation and the proper deployment of the right technologies could save the world. In the military world, computers stood among the most prominent of these technologies. To the extent that they transformed the landmasses of the globe into information subject to monitoring, they made visible patterns of enemy behavior and so, in theory at least, could forestall a potentially devastating attack. Likewise, for the New Communalists, small-scale technologies opened up a window on the hidden patterns that linked human beings to one another and to the natural world. Some of those technologies, such as the *Whole Earth Catalog*, were explicitly informational; others, such as slide projectors and electric guitars, were more broadly communication-oriented. Still others, such as geodesic domes and LSD, did not seem to have anything "informational" about them. And yet, these various technologies had all grown out of American industry, and all were turned into tools with which to make visible the comprehensive designs of human experience. Once apparent, like the intentions of the cold war enemy, these designs could be acted upon and could allow the evolution of the human race to go forward.

Thus, the back-to-the-landers of the New Communalist movement simultaneously turned their backs on the militarized bureaucracy of the state and embraced the systems theories, the technocentric orientation, the emphasis on mind, and the collaborative, experimental sociability that had grown up within it. In the process, they reintroduced many of the core principles of research culture into American society—but this time, as the intellectual foundations of a *counter*culture. In this sense, the New Communalists did not so much represent an alternative to mainstream cold war culture as an extension of one increasingly important element of that culture. At the time, this connection between the counterculture and military research culture remained largely unspoken, if it was acknowledged at all. Gazing out from his Harvard office on waves of antiwar protest and on the New Age movement that followed, for example, Daniel Bell read the youth movements of the era as many others at the time did: as a force devoted to tearing down the bourgeois solidity of cold war American culture. The counterculture, he thundered, was "antinomian," "anti-institutional," and "profoundly anti-bourgeois."[9] In retrospect, however, the example of Stewart Brand and the Whole Earth network suggests that even as the young communards criticized midcentury bourgeois life, the antinomian, anti-institutional impulses of the New Communalist movement were working to usher in a new form of that life: the flexible, consciousness-centered work practices of the postindustrial society.

To the extent that the *Whole Earth Catalog* serves as a guide to the movement and the era, it suggests that the New Communalists helped transform from occupational into cultural categories the notions of self and community, and the ideal relationship of information and technology to both, that had already emerged within the research culture of World War II. On the communes of the back-to-the-land movement and in the pages of the *Catalog*, the mobile, entrepreneurial scientist seeking to save the world from Armageddon through his research became the Long Hunter, the Comprehensive Designer, the mobile, entrepreneurial hippie who sought to save the world through his own research at the frontiers of consciousness and community. The commune itself became a social laboratory, and daily life an experiment. Social and intellectual boundaries collapsed; each woman or man became her or his own interdisciplinarian, seeking to build a whole self and a whole world. Within this process, information and information technologies played a role much like the one assigned to them within the research world, and especially within the part of it that had helped create cybernetics. In the pages of the *Catalog*, "information" linked and facilitated the communal work of saving the planet; and the information technology of the *Catalog* itself, as a network forum, made visible the underlying structure of the New Communalists' social world. Much as computers had allowed scientists and soldiers to monitor distant horizons, the informational tools of the *Whole Earth Catalog* turned readers into visionaries, scanning one another and the world around them for signs of Aquarian revolution.

These cultural categories outlived the protests of the era and shaped the waves of computerization to come. By the mid-1970s, the communes of the back-to-the-land movement had largely crumbled. Yet, holistic notions of self, the vision of technologies as tools for helping to create such selves, and the dream of a leveled, harmonious community linked by invisible signals remained. In the case of Stewart Brand and others associated with the *Whole Earth Catalog*, so too did a series of social networks, a set of reputations, and a series of social and rhetorical tactics for bringing communities together and facilitating the articulation of their interests. Over the next twenty years, Brand's cultural credibility and his networking skills allowed him to transform the lingering ideals of the New Communalists into ideological resources for the technologists of the computer and software industries in what had begun to be called Silicon Valley.

This process took place alongside two dramatic shifts in computer technology: miniaturization and networking. By the early 1970s, computing power that had formerly been available only to those with access to massive mainframes had been fit into desktop boxes. The machines were already "personal" in two senses: first, the technologies needed to render computers accessible to individuals, such as keyboards and television-sized monitors, had already been developed; second, thanks to time-sharing on existing mainframes, individual users had also begun to experience—and to long for more of—a feeling of complete control over their machines. The *Whole Earth Catalog*, however, offered to the computer technologists of Xerox PARC, the *People's Computer Company*, and the Homebrew Computer Club models of ways to link these existing technologies and visions of the user under the New Communalist rubric of "personal" tool use. As computer scientists such as Lee Felsenstein and Larry Tesler read the *Catalog*, they encountered a vision of technologies that could transform the individual consciousness and the world. So too did Alan Kay, first in the pages of the *Catalog* and later in the *Catalog*-derived library of Xerox PARC. As they developed their various microcomputers, some for the business world, some for hobby use, and later, in the case of Kay's work at Apple, for both, these computer scientists could imagine their work as an extension of the New Communalist social project. In his *Rolling Stone* article of 1972, Brand reinforced this impression. Xerox PARC might have emerged out of the intellectual, organizational, and technological legacy of cold war research; yet in Brand's depiction, its computer scientists, like the antiwar protestors of

Resource One, represented a cultural vanguard. They were "hackers"—versions of the Long Hunter of the *Catalog* and representatives of the experimental, exploratory ideals of the communards.

Over the next ten years, the cultural logic of New Communalism supplied key frames within which to market the new machines and granted them cultural legitimacy as well. Apple Computer, in particular, advertised its devices as tools with which to tear down bureaucracy, enhance individual consciousness, and build a new, collaborative society. The impact of the New Communalist legacy was felt well outside the boardrooms of computer and software manufacturers, though. In the 1980s Brand continued to bring together representatives of the technical world and former New Communalists, and to link computers to Whole Earth accounts of tool use. As he did, he steadily corroded the association of computers and computer technologists with the military-industrial-academic complex within which both had first appeared. By continuously depicting the desktop computer as a "personal" technology in a New Communalist sense, and by linking computer hacking to New Communalist attempts at Comprehensive Design, Brand helped build up and maintain a deep association between the ongoing migration of computers into society and New Communalism.

This association in turn helped shaped public perceptions of a second great wave of computerization: computer networking. When Brand cofounded the WELL, he helped create the socio-technical network out of which computer-mediated communication came to be publicly reimagined as virtual community and through which cyberspace was reconfigured as an electronic frontier. As bulletin board systems gave way to the public Internet and the World Wide Web, these terms became synonymous with the social effects of computer networking. In both popular and scholarly accounts of the mid-1990s, microcomputers appeared to be gateways to a new, exploratory, holistic understanding of the individual user's self, and to new forms of intimate, harmonious community. To many, these virtual communities—and the WELL prominently among them—seemed to offer alternatives to the hierarchical bureaucracies of a heavily institutionalized material world. As wider and wider streams of digital bits flowed around the globe, filling the glassy tunnels of more and more fiber-optic cables, many imagined their movements as the reincarnation of the American frontier, a place where the world could be remade—not through the agonistic struggles of confrontational politics, but through the technology-assisted construction of exemplary ways of life.

But as a closer examination of the appearance of virtual community on the WELL reveals, the new computer networks not only created new arenas for communication, they also helped to build a social and economic infrastructure for an increasingly common, networked form of production. For its citizens in the late 1980s, many if not most of whom worked in technology industries or journalism, the WELL offered a powerful form of economic as well as interpersonal support. Part of its power came simply from the social networks it summoned: Individuals seeking employment (at a time when job tenure for professionals in the San Francisco Bay area's technology industry averaged less than three years) could use the WELL to maintain many loose connections that could help them find work.[10] Those who traded information for a living, such as journalists, could use the WELL as a data mine, gathering and distributing the facts and opinions they gathered from the WELL's many professional experts. Finally, any member could use the WELL to build a reputation, to perform or play with a new identity, and to assess the credibility of his or her online colleagues. With an emphasis on sharing, intimacy, and leveled social hierarchies inherited from the New Communalist movement, to which many WELL members had once belonged, the rhetoric of virtual community offered a powerful ideological support for the multiple, heterarchical economic relations of the WELL. To the extent that they could imagine themselves as villagers on an electronic frontier, the members of the WELL could rewrite their ongoing integration into flexible economic practices as an extension of their youthful hope to found an alternative to a stultifying bureaucratic world. They could even begin to reimagine the emerging, networked form of technocracy as the antidote they had once sought to its bureaucratic forerunner.

In the 1990s both computer networks such as the Internet and the social networks of the Whole Earth community became emblems of what many claimed at the time was a new economic and political world. Thanks in large part to the example of the Global Business Network and to the writings of Kevin Kelly and Peter Schwartz, as well as to the work of *Wired* magazine as a whole, many began to imagine that the New Communalist dream of a nonhierarchical, interpersonally intimate society was on the threshold of coming true. Despite their libertarian orientation, the writings of Esther Dyson, John Perry Barlow, and Kevin Kelly in this period fairly ache with a longing to return to an egalitarian world. For these writers and, due to their influence, for many others, the early public Internet seemed poised to model and help bring into being a world in which each individual could act in his or her own interest and at the same time produce a unified social sphere, a world in which we were "all one." That sphere would not be ruled through the work of agonistic politics, but rather by turning away from it, toward the technologically mediated empowerment of the individual and the establishment of peer-to-peer agoras. For the prophets of the Internet, as for those who had headed back to the land some thirty years earlier, it was government, imagined as a looming, bureaucratic behemoth, that threatened to destroy the individual; in information, technology, and the marketplace lay salvation.

Cultural Entrepreneurship in the Network Mode

Between the founding of the *Whole Earth Catalog* in 1968 and the departure of Louis Rossetto, Jane Metcalfe, and Kevin Kelly from *Wired* magazine some thirty years later, then, Stewart Brand and the editors, writers, and entrepreneurs associated with the Whole Earth publications completely reversed the political valence of information and information technologies. As Brand and his generation reached the far side of middle age, the machines that had once stood for all the social forces that threatened to end their lives and perhaps even to destroy the world had become windows on a way of living and working that, according to key members of the Global Business Network and the editors of *Wired* at least, promised to fulfill their youthful dreams of an egalitarian utopia. Wedded to the aspirations of the New Communalists, computers and computer networks had become powerful ideological supports for the techno-libertarianism of the 1990s and the Internet bubble it helped spawn. Yet, they had become more than that as well. As Brand and the Whole Earth group realigned the cultural meanings of computing, they returned the technocentric, knowledge-oriented, collaborative social practices of the research world to the center of the culture at large. Stewart Brand and the back-to-the-landers of the New Communalist movement had come of age searching for an alternative to the bureaucratic mode of technocracy; some thirty years later, they had helped to substantially transform that mode, smoothing the way for the information theories and information technologies on which much of cold war technocracy depended to become ubiquitous and thoroughly integrated elements of social and economic life.

Moreover, they did so by using the social and rhetorical tactics by which the defense engineers of World War II and the cold war had organized and claimed legitimacy for their own work. Much like Norbert Wiener and the scientists of the Rad Lab, Stewart Brand had made a career of crossing disciplinary and professional boundaries. Like those who designed and funded the weapons research laboratories of World War II, Brand had built a series of network forums—some face-to-face, such as the Hacker's Conference, others digital, such as the WELL, or paper-based, such as the *Whole Earth Catalog*. Like the Rad Lab, these forums allowed members of multiple communities to meet, to exchange information, and to develop new rhetorical tools. Like their World War II predecessors, they also facilitated the construction and dissemination of techno-social prototypes. Sometimes, as in the case of the *Catalog* or the WELL, Whole Earth productions themselves would model the sorts of relationships between technology, information, the individual, and the community favored by network members. Other times, as in the case of the terms *virtual community* and the *electronic frontier*, Whole Earth forums would be summoned to support particular rhetorical constructions.

Finally, alongside network entrepreneurship and the creation and circulation of prototypes, Brand and the Whole Earth group turned to the rhetoric of cybernetics to facilitate a complex and long-lasting exchange of legitimacy between technological and countercultural communities. In the pages of the *Catalog* and later at the Hacker's Conference, on the WELL, in the meetings of the Global Business Network, and at *Wired* magazine, the notion that social, technological, and biological systems were in fact mirrors of one another provided a rhetorical pattern within which members of one community could imagine themselves as members of—and to that extent, enjoy the legitimacy of—another. As they read the *Catalog*, communards could think of themselves not as social dropouts, but as a neoscientific avant-garde in whose social experiments lay the fate of the world. As they camped with Stewart Brand, the programmers at the first Hacker's Conference and, later, the executives attending the Global Business Network's Learning Conferences, could think of themselves not as ordinary businesspeople and manufacturers, but as a countercultural elite. In the 1960s, these sorts of legitimacy exchange had allowed for the promiscuous mingling of information theory and other systems-oriented doctrines, particularly psychedelic mysticism and disciplines derived from Buddhism and other Eastern traditions. In the 1990s, they facilitated the fusion of the economic ambitions of corporate executives with the ecological ideals and tribal cultural sensibilities of the New Communalist movement. By imagining the world as a series of overlapping information systems, and by deploying that imagination in particular organizational and media forms, Brand and his Whole Earth colleagues ultimately preserved certain New Communalist ideals long after the movement itself had faded away. They did so by creating a series of forums within which those ideals, and the social networks in which they lived, could be linked to emerging technologies and new centers of economic power.

One effect of this linkage was to sustain Brand's own authority across a series of technological, economic, and cultural eras. In the mid-1960s, Brand was an obscure itinerant photographer. Only five years later, thanks to the *Catalog*, he had become an internationally recognized spokesman for the American counterculture. By the late 1980s, thanks to the WELL, the Hacker's Conference, and his book on MIT's Media Lab, he had become an oft-quoted source on the social potential of computing. Finally, by the mid-1990s, for the clients of the Global Business Network and the readers of *Wired*, he was both spokesman for and emblem of a networked mode of economic and social life. Although they attest to Brand's own entrepreneurial skill, these shifts also mark the power of the network mode of cultural entrepreneurship within which he worked. In Brand's case, the network mode has helped reshape public understandings of computing and create deep cultural categories with which to frame discussions of the proper relationship of the individual and the community to information technology. It has served as a way to preserve the social ideals of the New Communalist movement in the face of rapid technological and social change. And at the same time, it has helped to link new technologies, new patterns of labor, and new forms of sociability to the past, and so to offer the public familiar conceptual tools with which to confront their arrival.

For all of these reasons, the history of Stewart Brand and the Whole Earth network offers an important context in which to reconceptualize the process by which technologies take on symbolic meanings and in which to rethink the role of network entrepreneurship in the shaping of public discourse. To date, those who have studied the social work through which new technologies enter systems of representation have tended to focus on one of three ever-widening social circles: those closest to the technology itself, especially inventors and designers; those slightly farther out, including users and various related professional, technical, and legal communities; and the press.[11] In each case, scholars have shown how various actors have enabled a multitude of technologies to become widely used and thoroughly integrated into a society by establishing not only their material utility but also their semiotic fit with existing systems of discourse. In the case of Stewart Brand, no one of these categories adequately captures the nature of his entrepreneurial work or its effects on the cultural meaning of information technology. At various times across his career, Brand has helped design information technologies, has used them, and has reported on them for mainstream (and his own) publications. Over those same years, he has created a series of network forums within which members of all three of these circles could come together and collaboratively develop both local contact languages and, through them, key terms in which information technologies would later be understood.

Larry Tesler, a veteran of both Xerox PARC and Apple Computer, recalled encountering Brand's entrepreneurship this way: "The rest of us are just doing [something]. . . . it's our life. We don't try to put it in some other context. Stewart comes along and observes it as an anthropologist would or as a journalist. He creates some new organization . . . that leverages this through and maybe brings it to the world in a way that it wasn't before. He looks at a thing and sees a missing business or a missing publication. It's not always the same thing." The forums that Brand created brought a variety of benefits to the communities he linked. The first of these was his own cultural standing. As he became "immersed enough in a project to gain legitimacy" among its members, Tesler explained, Brand also "brought legitimacy from what he did before." Along with legitimacy, Brand brought a welter of loose connections, some in the technical world, some in the remnants of the counterculture, and some in the press. "A lot of researchers found ways to bridge fields," remembered Tesler, "but Stewart had the rare ability of knowing how you get the public to get wind of it, how to make it accessible, and get the media to cover it." Finally, Brand brought his own world-saving orientation to the construction of his forums, an orientation born out of the atomic-era fears that haunted his generation. Dennis Allison, a founding board member of the *People's Computer Company*, put it this way: "Stewart's a very moral guy. My every contact has been that he's trying to move people toward a better place. That's really the secret of Stewart."[12]

As Tesler and Allison suggest, Brand did not simply serve as a transmission channel between those networks. Instead, driven in part by the world-saving impulse of his youth, he collaborated with each community, absorbing and integrating its norms and practices. He then drew on those elements in order to establish and maintain the forums in which the networks themselves could meet. Like P. T. Barnum, he gathered performers from a variety of traditions into a series of multi-ring circuses. At the *Whole Earth Catalog*, as later at the Hackers Conference and on the WELL, these performers included technologists and counterculturalists, businessmen and journalists. Like Barnum, Brand not only hosted these multiple rings of activity, but also gave voice and meaning to the circus as a whole. While professional journalists such as John Markoff or Katie Hafner were transforming bits and pieces of the circuses into traditional newspaper and magazine accounts, Brand was working to create new forums in which the performers could collaborate with one another. As he coordinated those collaborations, Brand quickly learned to speak the contact languages developing around him. In this way, he and others like him, including most prominently Kevin Kelly and the writers of *Wired*, gave voice to an ongoing integration of ideas and practices that had first appeared in the New Communalist and high-technology research worlds. Having helped that synthesis to emerge in interpersonal collaboration among multiple communities, and having helped link it to new computing technologies, Brand, and later Kevin Kelly, Peter Schwartz, and others, found themselves in a unique position to "report" the synthesis as "news" to the rest of the world.

By means of their network entrepreneurship, then, Brand and his colleagues not only created new rhetorical and symbolic resources, but modeled the synthesis of counterculture and research culture in their own lives. For that reason, Brand and the Whole Earth network may offer important examples with which to think about the role of cultural entrepreneurship in public discourse, particularly in regard to journalism. Given the wide range of their activities, it is difficult to even think of Brand and his colleagues as journalists per se. Yet, even from a strictly professional point of view, they qualify. Over the years, they have founded and edited influential magazines, written popular books, and reported for outlets as mainstream as *Rolling Stone* and *Time*. They have done so, however, using tactics that fall well outside most analysts' descriptions of professional journalistic work or professional journalistic ethics.

Scholars of journalism, like journalists themselves, have tended to argue that those who report the news are distinct from those who make it and that, as a result, the power of journalists to shape public discourse derives primarily from their ability to represent the social world in media. In traditional accounts, journalists gather information, process it according to a series of professional, industrial routines, and distribute the finished product to a third group, the audience. Some have qualified this view, showing how journalistic norms are in fact historical constructions,[13] or demonstrating that reporters often use events to establish their own professional legitimacy. Yet even these scholars have tended to take as their starting point a notion of journalists as professionals "sandwiched between the audience and the event being reported."[14] In keeping with this view, many have suggested that journalists shape public perceptions of reality by acting as intermediaries. By choosing what to cover and how to frame what they see, it is argued, journalists constrain what the public can know—and often in ways that support the interests of those in power. These constraints in turn have ideological effects. For instance, as Todd Gitlin demonstrated in *The Whole World Is Watching*, his influential study of the effects of press coverage on the Students for a Democratic Society, coverage of SDS-led antiwar protests framed SDS activities in such a way as to minimize the importance of the organization's work. Simultaneously, simply by covering these protests, the press made youth across America aware of SDS and caused a sudden, massive swelling in SDS ranks.[15]

Such accounts work well to describe the activities of a highly professionalized press corps, but they leave little room for thinking about the ideological impact of Stewart Brand and his colleagues. Unlike full-time professional reporters, Brand and others associated with the Whole Earth network actively collaborated with what traditional journalism theory might call "newsmakers" in the construction of rhetoric, symbols, and narratives. In the case of the Hackers' Conference, for example, Brand created a forum within which hackers and former New Communalists could gather and imagine their individual projects as elements of a shared cultural mission. This work helped shaped the public image of hackers in three ways: through the reporting done by professional journalists who had attended the conference; through the writings of Brand, Kelly, and others in the Whole Earth network; and through the promotion of Stewart Brand himself as a proto-typical, if predigital, hacker. Out of the conference grew a statement that expressed a way of imagining information, one that would travel throughout public discourse in future years: "information wants to be free." Never mind that moments before he uttered those words Brand had pointed out that "information wants to be expensive because it's so valuable."[16] For the networks gathered at the conference, and later for the public at large, "information wants to be free" voiced an irresistible fusion of the cultural legitimacy of the research worlds that had brought forth computers and the countercultural communities that had tried to set the world "free."

In this example, as throughout Brand's career, frames emerged as elements in a collaborative social process. Whereas journalists are often thought to apply frames to events they witness and to represent those frames in media, Brand and the Whole Earth network in fact created the forums within which frames were constructed. Once developed, the frames could be and often were exported, by both professional journalists and network members. Moreover, within the process of their making and distribution, entrepreneurs such as Brand often took on multiple roles—founder, convener, reporter, publisher. Within the traditional professional norms of journalism, such multiplicity would be construed as conflict of interest. Yet for Brand, as for the citizens of the network forums he created, the simultaneous playing of multiple roles served as both a source and an amplifier of Brand's own authority. By creating network forums and by choosing carefully which individuals and which networks to gather in them, Brand and others effectively granted themselves access to a diverse array of newsmakers. By bringing them together, Brand and his colleagues came to be seen as important members of those networks in their own right. Finally, as they spoke the languages of the forum's guests and exemplified the social norms those guests had come to share, they ceased to be mere hosts and became instead representatives of the networks they had convened.

To the extent that these tactics first emerged in the research worlds of World War II, and to the degree that they invoke the systems-oriented, information metaphors of cybernetics, Brand's form of networked cultural entrepreneurship represents the migration into society at large of a cultural style that first grew up within a particular historical location. This migration marks a kind of cultural influence that remains invisible within contemporary accounts of journalism and public discourse. If professionalized journalists have ideological impact primarily by depicting events, Brand and the cultural entrepreneurs of his circle have had their impact in large part by transforming themselves into emblems of the social forces they have chronicled. In this way, they have framed the introduction of information technologies into American culture at two temporal levels, one short-term and one long-term. At the short-term level, they have helped synthesize and disseminate key terms on which the techno-utopianism and Internet bubble of the 1990s depended. At the long-term level, they have naturalized and legitimated the technologies, theories, and work patterns of the scientific research world as cultural rather than simply professional styles. Part of this work has involved shaping the representation of particular information technologies. But much more of it has involved building forums and social networks. Within the network forums of the Whole Earth publications and projects, Brand and his circle have created the key frames by which we have come to understand the social implications of digital technologies; at the same time they have produced the social infrastructure to support, legitimate, and disseminate those frames.

The Dark Side of Utopia

We have seen that between the late 1960s and the late 1990s, Brand and the Whole Earth network brokered a complex series of encounters between the traditions of the research world and those of the New Communalists. In the process, they helped shape visions of self and community, and of the proper relationship of work and technology to both, that became beacons by which others of their generation lived their lives. Those visions grew out of a deep distrust of the institutions that governed cold war politics and commerce and of rationalized social formations more broadly. In the late 1960s, many fled Haight-Ashbury for the hills of New Mexico hoping not only to found an alternative society but also to find a way to escape having their own lives shaped by the forces of society at large. Across the 1970s and 1980s, as the communes of the back-to-the-land movement crumbled and disappeared, Stewart Brand and the entrepreneurs of the Whole Earth group preserved these hopes by welding them to the computer technologies and flexible organizational practices of the rapidly emerging postindustrial economy. By the 1990s, it seemed to many as if the digital networks on which that economy increasingly depended would in fact bring to life the New Communalist dream of breaking the bonds of institutional power and freeing individuals to pursue their own holistic lives.

Even today, discussions of digital technologies and the network economy continue to invoke New Communalist ideals. Yet the legacy of the communes offers a warning. As they embraced the cybernetic vision of the world as an information system, Stewart Brand and the readers of the *Whole Earth Catalog,* like the libertarian promoters of the Internet thirty years later, began to imagine that the fluid play of embodied distinctions that characterizes the social world could be dissolved into an account in which all were equally patterns of information. To many in a generation who feared that their bodies would be destroyed by the mechanized armies and the massive missiles of the Soviet Union, this account was enormously appealing. If all could be imagined as one, and if bodies themselves were no more than "pattern-complex function[s]," as Buckminster Fuller put it, then individuals could do away with the formal governance structures that had lately caused so much trouble and restore global harmony by relying instead on tools available to everyone—impulse, feeling, small-scale technologies, and the shared intuition of a collective consciousness.[17]

When they tried to live these ideals, however, the communards discovered that embracing systems of consciousness and information as sources of social structure actually amplified their exposure to the social and material pressures they had hoped to escape. When the members of communes such as Drop City freed themselves from the formal structures of government, for example, they quickly suffered from an inability to attend to their own material needs and to form common cause with their neighbors. The first of these difficulties grew directly out of the New Communalist rejection of formal politics. In the absence of formal rule structures, many communes saw questions of leadership and power become questions of charisma. As a result, many suffered from the rise of hostile factions, and some from the appearance of nearly dictatorial gurus. The turn away from formal politics also gave norms that the communards had brought with them from mainstream society an extraordinary governing force. In the absence of institutions that might regulate the relations of men and women, many fell back on old customs. Under the guise of social experimentation, for example, many rural communes in particular witnessed the comparative disenfranchisement of women and children. Like the men of the suburbs whose lives they had rejected, the men of many communes left the cooking and the cleaning and the care of the children to the women.

By the same cultural logic, individual communes routinely ignored the local communities among whom they settled. Drawing on notions of shared consciousness and supported by documents such as the *Whole Earth Catalog,* they imagined themselves as members of a geographically dispersed elite bound together by means of invisible signals. The back-to-the-landers were in fact predominantly members of a particular social class, bound together by education and race and the ambition to change the world. Yet, by articulating their class identity in terms of consciousness and information networks, many found themselves unable to recognize their own dependence on others, particularly those of other classes. They ignored the degree to which their embodied lives depended on material support from distant parents and friends, and like residents of a segregated suburb, they effectively cut themselves off from the poor and the people of color among whom they often lived.

If the information workers of the postindustrial era buy into the notion that computers and the network economy will bring about a peer-to-peer utopia, as many still do, they run the risk of perpetuating the forms of suffering and exclusion that plagued the back-to-the-landers. For example, in her widely read 1997 memoir *Close to the Machine,* Ellen Ullman offered a cautionary depiction of the potential consequences of the New Communalist legacy. A forty-six-year-old freelance software engineer when she wrote her book, Ullman had been programming since 1971. Some years earlier, she had worked as an employee, but her company was bought out. Now, she wrote, "My clients hire me to do a job, then dispose of me when I'm done. I hire the next level of contractors then dispose of them." In keeping with the macroeconomic forces of the 1980s and 1990s, the pressures of rapid technological and economic change had driven Ullman into a network enterprise model of work. She explained that her clients expected consultants like her "to assemble a group of people to do a job, get it done, then disassemble. We're not supposed to invest in any one person or set of skills—no sense in it anyway. . . . The skill-set changes before the person possibly can, so it's always simpler just to change the person."[18]

Within their task-based networks, Ullman and her colleagues enjoyed a high-pressure form of emotional connection to one another, but no sooner was the project at hand completed than this now-intimate group had to disperse. These disruptions were painful—yet the distress they caused paled in comparison to Ullman's anxieties about her own obsolescence. The technologies with which she worked were constantly changing, and if she hoped to stay in business, she had to keep up. Since 1971, she wrote, "I have taught myself six higher-level programming languages, three assemblers, two data-retrieval languages, eight job-processing languages, seventeen scripting languages, ten types of macros, two object-definition languages, sixty-eight programming-library interfaces, five varieties of networks, and eight operating environments—fifteen, if you cross-multiply the distinct combinations of operating systems and networks. I don't think this makes me particularly unusual. Given the rate of change in computing, anyone who's been around for a while could probably make a list like this."[19] In her youth, learning these languages was a great deal easier than it had now become. In middle age, her body was tiring. "Time tells me to stop chasing after the latest new everything," she wrote. "Biological life does not want to keep speeding up like a chip design, cycling ever faster year by year."[20]

Ullman's predicament points up both the power and the perniciousness of New Communalist ideology for those who work within the technology-intensive precincts of the network economy. Despite its many stresses, Ullman's life seems to fulfill key elements of the New Communalist ethos. It is flexible and mobile, and it demands that she build small tribes around a shared mission and link them together with information and information technologies. To the extent that Ullman tries to change the world, she does so as Buckminster Fuller might suggest she should: by designing new technologies for the management of information and the transformation of society's resources into knowledge on which others can act. Yet, Ullman's turn toward technologies of consciousness and toward social and economic networks has hardly brought her into the community she seeks. On the contrary, like many rural settlers thirty years earlier, Ullman has found herself alone in an alien wilderness. Cut off from the civilizing effects of membership in permanent corporate and civic communities, Ullman hustles from employer to employer like a hired gunman in a real-life version of a late-night spaghetti western. Her power derives primarily from what knowledge of technological systems she can carry with her and secondarily from her networks of professional friends. Her personal links to her colleagues are tenuous and brief. She is lonely. And the situation is not likely to change anytime soon. As Ullman's example suggests, coupling one's life to the technologies of consciousness does not necessarily amplify one's intellectual or emotional abilities or help one create a more whole self. On the contrary, it may require individuals to deny their own bodies, the rhythms of the life cycle, and, to the extent that their jobs require them to collaborate with far-away colleagues, even the rhythms of day and night.[21] It may in fact result in every bit as thorough an integration of the individual into the economic machine as the one threatened by the military-industrial-academic bureaucracy forty years earlier.

Furthermore, it may cut individual workers off from participating in local communities that might otherwise mitigate these effects. To stay employed, Ullman and workers like her must move from node to node within the network of sites where computers and software are manufactured and used, and in order to pick up leads for new work, they must stay in touch with one another. As a result, programmers and others often find themselves living in a social and physical landscape populated principally by people like themselves. To succeed within that landscape, they must often turn their attention away from another, parallel landscape: the landscape of local, material things, of town boards and PTA meetings, of embodied participation in civic life. They must declare and maintain an allegiance to their own professional network, to its sites and technologies. And they must carry with them a handful of rules that Ullman trumpets with more than a little sarcasm: "Just live by your wits and expect everyone else to do the same. Carry no dead wood. Live free or die. Yeah, surely, you can only rely on yourself."[22]

For those like Ullman who have the education, the professional skills, and the lack of geographically binding social ties that allow a person to remain mobile and flexible, such libertarian nostrums can transform a series of personal losses—of time with family and neighbors, of connection to one's body and one's community—into a soothing narrative with which they can rationalize the limits of their own choices. As Richard Barbrook and Andy Cameron have argued, the antinomian and antistatist impulses of the American counterculture do in fact allow workers like Ullman to acknowledge the power of market forces in their lives and, paradoxically, to preserve a sense of their own autonomy.[23] However, to the degree that the libertarian rhetoric of self-reliance embraces a New Communalist vision of a consciousness-centered, information-oriented elite, it can also permit a deep denial of the moral and material costs of the long-term shift toward network modes of production and ubiquitous computing.

For Stewart Brand and, later, for the writers and editors of *Wired,* the mirror logic of cybernetics provided substantial support for this denial. For Norbert Wiener and those who followed his lead, the world consisted of a series of informational patterns, and each of those patterns in turn was also in some sense an emblem of every other. As taken up by the New Communalists, this vision produced two contradictory claims, one egalitarian and the other elitist. On the one hand, the fact that material phenomena could be imagined as part of a single, invisible whole suggested that an egalitarian order might obtain in the world. Human beings, nature, machines—all were one and each should coevolve with every other. On the other hand, though, in keeping with the vision's history as a universal rhetorical tool with which cold war researchers claimed authority for their projects, the fact that the social and the natural, the individual and the institutional, the human and the machine could all be seen as reflections of one another suggested that those who could most successfully depict themselves as aligned with the forces of information could also claim to be models of those forces. They could in fact claim to have a "natural" right to power, even as they disguised their leadership with a rhetoric of systems, communities, and information flow.

It was this claim that Stewart Brand and his colleagues modeled for their clients at the Global Business Network, and it is was this claim that the writers of *Wired* bolstered by depicting subjects such as Esther Dyson and George Gilder as people who spoke or acted like computers. As the communards of the back-to-the-land movement had once argued that they were forerunners of a new, more egalitarian society on the basis of their being in touch with a shared consciousness, the information consultants of the 1990s asserted that the Internet modeled not only an egalitarian future, but their own, existing lives. In touch with the flow of information, they could safely represent themselves as a "digital generation"—or, in a term much used at the time, as "digerati."[24]

The rhetoric of peer-to-peer informationalism, however, much like the rhetoric of consciousness out of which it grew, actively obscures the material and technical infrastructures on which both the Internet and the lives of the digital generation depend. Behind the fantasy of unimpeded information flow lies the reality of millions of plastic keyboards, silicon wafers, glass-faced monitors, and endless miles of cable. All of these technologies depend on manual laborers, first to build them and later to tear them apart. This work remains extraordinarily dangerous, first to those who handle the toxic chemicals required in manufacture and later to those who live on the land, drink the water, and breathe the air into which those chemicals eventually leak.[25] These tasks also continue to be the province of those who lack social and financial resources. In the mid-1980s, for instance, the Immigration and Naturalization Service estimated that 25 percent of the overall Silicon Valley workforce—approximately two hundred thousand workers—consisted of illegal aliens, many if not most of whom worked in manufacturing. In the same period, 75 percent of all Silicon Valley assemblers were women, many from the Third World. In recent years, both manufacturing and recycling have migrated overseas. And once again, women and the poor find themselves disproportionately engaged in high-risk work. Unprotected by American laws, factory hands in China and elsewhere labor eighteen hours a day at wages that often hover around thirty cents per hour building new computers. In China, India, Pakistan, and the Philippines, workers earn similar wages breaking apart computers with their bare hands to salvage the parts within.[26]

In the 1990s, all of this work was invisible to those who promoted the Internet and the network mode of production as evidence of a new stage in human evolution. Like the communards of the 1960s, the techno-utopians of the 1990s denied their dependence on any but themselves. At the same time, they developed a way of thinking and talking about digital technologies from within which it was almost impossible to challenge their own elite status. On the communes of the 1960s, the rhetoric of consciousness and community contained little in the way of language with which to describe, let alone confront, a less-than-egalitarian distribution of resources. The same was true of information theory and the universal rhetoric of cybernetics. In both cases, human power was an individual possession, born of the proper use of technologies for the amplification of awareness through access to information. In the writings of the *Wired* group in the 1990s, this model of power and the rhetoric on which it depended reappeared. Both persist today throughout discussions of computer-mediated communication. Even as they conjured up visions of a disembodied, peer-to-peer utopia, and even as they suggested that such a world would in fact represent a return to a more natural, more intimate state of being, writers such as Kevin Kelly, Esther Dyson, and John Perry Barlow deprived their many readers of a language with which to think about the complex ways in which embodiment shapes all of human life, about the natural and social infrastructures on which that life depends, and about the effects that digital technologies and the network mode of production might have on life and its essential infrastructures.

The End of the End of History

In that sense, for these writers, the arrival of the Internet marked not only the end of the industrial era, but the end of history itself. Forty years earlier, Stewart Brand and others of his generation had been among the first to come of age in a world that could, as a whole, be destroyed in a matter of minutes. As young adults, although they turned away from the war-making mind-set, the bureaucratic structures, and the partitioned psyches that they imagined characterized life in the military-industrial research establishment, many embraced its information theories, its collaborative, experimental orientation, and its underlying world-saving mission. Like the atomic scientists at Los Alamos, they would become Comprehensive Designers, of their own fates and, by vanguard example, of the fates of mankind. By 1968 more than a few communards believed, as Stewart Brand put it, that "We are as gods and we might as well get good at it."

In his 1968 volume *The Young Radicals,* Kenneth Keniston looked out on the fractures within the youth movements of the day and wondered how they might ultimately shape American society. "How and whether [the] tension between alienation and activism is resolved seems to me of the greatest importance," he explained. In the short term, Keniston feared that antiwar activists would become frustrated at the failure to stop the conflict in Vietnam and would retreat into academe and the professions. "The field of dissent would be left to the alienated," he wrote, "whose intense quest for *personal* salvation, meaning, creativity, and revelation dulls their perception of the public world and inhibits attempts to better the lot of others."[27] In recent years, Keniston's fears seem to have come true, particularly in discussions of the social potential of the Internet and the World Wide Web. To many, these technologies still seem to promise what the strobe lights and LSD of the Trips Festival once offered the hippies of the Haight: access to a vision of the patterns underlying the world, and by means of that vision, a way to join one's life to them and to enter a global, harmonious community of mind. As both information technologies and the network mode of production have spread across the landscape, they have been celebrated as sites of personal and collective salvation. And to that extent, they have rendered their believers vulnerable to the material forces of the historical moment in which they live.

And yet, they have preserved a deeper dream as well. As they set off for the hills of New Mexico and Tennessee, the communards of the back-to-the-land movement hoped to build not only communities of consciousness, but real, embodied towns. Most failed—not for lack of good intentions, nor even for lack of tools, but for lack of attention to politics. To the extent that Stewart Brand and the Whole Earth group have succeeded in linking the ideals of those whom Kenneth Keniston called the alienated to digital technologies, they have allowed computer users everywhere to imagine their machines as tools of personal liberation. Over the past thirty years, this reimagining has helped transform the machines themselves, the institutions in which we use them, and society at large. Yet, as the short life of the New Communalist movement suggests, information and information technologies will never allow us to fully escape the demands of our bodies, our institutions, and the times in which we find ourselves. Much like the commune-bound readers of the *Whole Earth Catalog,* we remain confronted by the need to build egalitarian, ecologically sound communities. Only by helping us meet that fundamentally political challenge can information technology fulfill its countercultural promise.

Notes

Introduction

1. Negroponte, "Being Digital—A Book (P)review," 182.

2. See, e.g., Mitchell, *City of Bits;* Negroponte, *Being Digital;* Rheingold, *Virtual Community;* Stone, *War of Desire and Technology;* Turkle, *Life on the Screen.*

3. Warshaw, *Trouble in Berkeley,* 99.

4. "FSM Newsletter"; for a full history of the phrase, see Lubar, "Do Not Fold, Spindle, or Mutilate."

5. For an overview of these changes, see Ceruzzi, *History of Modern Computing* (1998).

6. Zuboff, *In the Age of the Smart Machine.*

7. Burt, "Network Entrepreneur," 281–307. See also Burt, *Structural Holes.*

Chapter 1

1. Mario Savio quoted in Draper, *Berkeley,* 98.

2. Lubar, "Do Not Fold, Spindle, or Mutilate."

3. Kerr, *Uses of the University,* 20.

4. Ibid., 124.

5. Draper, *Berkeley,* 153; Savio, "California's Angriest Student," 100–101, quotation on 100.

6. Barlow, "Declaration of the Independence of Cyberspace."

7. For other examples of this phenomenon, see Mitchell, *City of Bits;* and Negroponte, *Being Digital.*

8. Dyson, *Release 2.0,* 286, 3; Barlow, "@home.on.the.ranch."

9. Kelly, *New Rules for the New Economy,* 2, 160.

10. Kelly, "Computational Metaphor."

11. For entry points into this literature, see Boyer, *By the Bomb's Early Light;* Kuznick and Gilbert, *Rethinking Cold War Culture;* May, *Homeward Bound;* Whitfield, *Culture of the Cold War.*

12. Edwards, *Closed World,* 94–107.

13. Ibid., 161, 1, quotation on 1.

14. For an introduction to this literature, and to the ways in which shifts in the organization of science during World War II helped shape the cold-war world, see Leslie, *Cold War and American Science,* 1–13.

15. Ibid., 2. For the specific case of physics, see Galison, "Trading Zone," 149–52. There were, of course, important exceptions to this pattern. For examples, see Seidel, "Origins of the Lawrence Berkeley Laboratory"; and Galison, Hevly, and Lowen, "Controlling the Monster," 46–77.

16. Leslie, *Cold War and American Science,* 8.

17. Ibid., 7.

18. Edwards, *Closed World,* 47.

19. Galison, "Trading Zone," 149.

20. Buderi, *Invention That Changed the World,* 98; Galison, "Trading Zone," 149; Guerlac, *Radar in World War II,* 233–48.

21. Buderi, *Invention That Changed the World,* 106; Galison, "Trading Zone," 152.

22. Leslie, *Cold War and American Science,* 20–43; Hughes, *Rescuing Prometheus,* 15–140.

23. Buderi, *Invention That Changed the World,* 254. See also Bryant et al., *Rad Lab.*

24. For a compelling examination of entrepreneurship at the Rad Lab, see Mindell, "Automation's Finest Hour." For a portrait of the social life surrounding the Rad Lab, see Buderi, *Invention That Changed the World,* 129–30. The freewheeling, collaborative life of the war years spilled over into the cold war as well. Louise Licklider lived in Cambridge with her husband, J. C. R. Licklider, whose work ultimately helped drive the development of the Internet, in the years immediately after the war. She later recalled that "Cambridge was like an anthill. Everybody was getting involved with everybody else—finding different challenges, taking up different ideas. I use the word *cross-fertilization* because there was an awful lot of that going on. And quite a lot of socializing, too." Quoted in Waldrop, *Dream Machine,* 66.

25. Galison, "Trading Zone."

26. Ibid., 138.

27. Ibid., 157. On the laboratory floor, this led to an egalitarian ethic of collaboration and a "hybrid of practices" in Galison's terms, known as "Radar Philosophy" (152).

28. As several historians have pointed out, the "systems" approach taken by cybernetics predated the invention of the term itself by a little more than a decade. In 1928, for instance, John Von Neumann published his "Theory of Parlor Games," thus inventing game theory. Heims, *John Von Neumann and Norbert Wiener,* 84. In the 1930s in England, Robert Lilienfeld has argued, the invention of radar led to the need for the coordination of machines and thus the invention of the "total point of view" characteristic of systems thinking. Lilienfeld, *Rise of Systems Theory,* 103. Cybernetics emerged as a self-consciously comprehensive field of thought, however, with the work of Norbert Wiener. For a fuller account of Wiener's career and the emergence of his cybernetics, see also Galison, "Ontology of the Enemy"; and Hayles, *How We Became Posthuman.*

29. Wiener, *Cybernetics,* 8.

30. Ibid., 9.

31. Heims, *John Von Neumann and Norbert Wiener,* 182–88. For a chronicle of Wiener's shifting relationship to the Rad Lab, see Conway and Siegelman, *Dark Hero of the Information Age,* 115–25.

32. Wiener, *I Am a Mathematician,* 251–52.

33. For a critical analysis of this choice, and especially its relationship to conceptions of the Other in contemporary cultural theory, see Galison, "Ontology of the Enemy."

34. Wiener, *I Am a Mathematician*, 252.

35. For Wiener, as Peter Galison put it, "Servomechanical theory would become the measure of man." Galison, "Ontology of the Enemy," 240.

36. Heims, *John Von Neumann and Norbert Wiener*, 184.

37. Rosenblueth, Wiener, and Bigelow, "Behavior, Purpose, and Teleology"; Galison, "Ontology of the Enemy," 247; Wiener, *Cybernetics*, 15, 21. Shannon published his theory in a 1948 article, "Mathematical Theory of Communication." Shannon's theories rose to public prominence through his 1949 collaboration with Warren Weaver in *The Mathematical Theory of Communication*. There is some controversy over the question of how much Wiener's theory of messages owes to Shannon's theory of information. For detailed, if differing, accounts of this question, see Waldrop, *Dream Machine*, 75–82; and Conway and Siegelman, *Dark Hero of the Information Age*, 185–92.

38. Wiener, *Human Use of Human Beings*, 49.

39. Wiener, *Cybernetics*, 164–65.

40. "Long before Nagasaki and the public awareness of the atomic bomb," he wrote, "it had occurred to me that we were here in the presence of another social potentiality of unheard-of importance for good or evil." Ibid., 36.

41. Heims, *John Von Neumann and Norbert Wiener*, 343. After World War II, Wiener became increasingly afraid of the ways science could be used to undermine human goals. For a particularly explicit example of his views, see Wiener, "Scientist Rebels."

42. Wiener, *Human Use of Human Beings*, 11.

43. By the mid-1960s, the systems orientation of cybernetics had spread throughout the natural and social sciences. In 1968 Ludwig von Bertalanffy, a biologist who promoted an organismic view in biology as early as 1940, tried to distinguish systems theory from cybernetics: "Systems theory also is frequently identified with cybernetics and control theory. This again is incorrect. Cybernetics, as the theory of control mechanisms in technology and nature and founded on the concepts of information and feedback, is but a part of a general theory of systems; cybernetic systems are a special case, however important, of systems showing self-regulation." Bertalanffy, *General System Theory*, 3. For Bertalanffy, cybernetics was only one root of systems theory, albeit an important one. Others included the servomechanisms of the nineteenth century, Claude Shannon's information theory, Von Neumann and Morgenstern's game theory, and the increasing need in the post–World War II world to monitor and control large systems for social functions such as traffic and finance. For a critical analysis of the relationship between cybernetics and other systems theories, see Lilienfeld, *Rise of Systems Theory*.

44. Rau, "Adoption of Operations Research," 57, 6. For a fascinating demonstration of the ways systems analysis helped set the aesthetic terms of planning for nuclear war, see Ghamari-Tabrizi, *Worlds of Herman Kahn*, esp. 54–57, 128–30.

45. Heims, *John Von Neumann and Norbert Wiener*, 302.

46. Bowker, "How to Be Universal," 108.

47. Ibid., 116.

48. Pickering, "Gallery of Monsters." For more on Ashby's homeostat, see Hayles, *How We Became Posthuman*, 65–66.

49. Hayles, *How We Became Posthuman*, 62.

50. See Lilienfeld, *Rise of Systems Theory*. For a fascinating study of the roles defense planners and cybernetics played in cold war attempts at urban renewal, see Light, *From Warfare to Welfare*.

51. Hayles, *How We Became Posthuman;* Heims, *Social Science for Post-War America*.

52. According to Hayles, these meetings ultimately helped bring into existence a new cultural category, the "posthuman." Within this view, she writes, the world consists of information patterns and the boundaries of the individual body and mind are highly porous, and because of these facts, the human being can be "seamlessly articulated with intelligent machines." Hayles, *How We Became Posthuman*, 3.

53. Paul Edwards has pointed out that in addition to researchers at MIT and government officials, SAGE involved heavy contributions from IBM (which built some fifty-six SAGE computers for approximately $30 million each) and the RAND Corporation (which wrote much of the computers' software). Edwards, *Closed World*, 101–2. Hughes, *Rescuing Prometheus*, 16, 4.

54. Air Defense Systems Engineering Committee, "Air Defense System: ADSEC Final Report," October 24, 1950, MITRE Corporation Archives, Bedford, MA, 2–3, quoted in Hughes, *Rescuing Prometheus*, 21.

55. Hughes, *Rescuing Prometheus*, 66.

56. As Sharon Ghamari-Tabrizi has noted, there were important exceptions to this trend. On May 11, 1959, for instance, *Life* magazine published a photo essay on the RAND Corporation. Although most of the images depicted "people doing something iconically scientific," the final image showed a group of analysts in suits, reclining together on the floor, surrounded by "the *mise en scene* for the modern intellectual," including "futuristic chairs and a Japanese paper kite dangling from the ceiling." Ghamari-Tabrizi, *Worlds of Herman Kahn*, 57. In this case at least, the photographer hinted, the scientific experts might be cool.

57. Mills, *Power Elite*, 3, quoted in Jamison and Eyerman, *Seeds of the Sixties*, 42.

58. Mills, *Sociological Imagination*, 168.

59. Ibid., 169, 171.

60. For a review of the critiques listed, see Winner, *Autonomous Technology;* Mumford, *Myth of the Machine*, 3.

61. See, e.g., Keniston, *Young Radicals*, 229–47.

62. Burner, *Making Peace with the 60s*, 136.

63. Galbraith, *New Industrial State*, 295. Galbraith also notes that in 1960 there were some 381,000 professors in America; by 1972 that number had risen to 907,000 (294).

64. Brooks, *Bobos in Paradise*, 26–34. See also Baltzell, *Protestant Establishment*.

65. May, *Homeward Bound*, 13–16; the young woman is quoted in Keniston, *Young Radicals*, 48.

66. Weart, *Nuclear Fear*, 133.

67. Quoted in Keniston, *Young Radicals*, 39.

68. The relationship between these two movements has been subject to extensive (and heated) investigation. For historiographies of the issue, see Rossinow, "New Left in the Counterculture"; and Gosse, "Movement of Movements." See also Breines, *Community and Organization in the New Left;* and Rossinow, *Politics of Authenticity*.

69. Frank, *Conquest of Cool*, 2–6, 8–9. Bell, *Cultural Contradictions of Capitalism*, 21; Gitlin, *Sixties*, 6, 206–35; Jamison and Eyerman, *Seeds of the Sixties*, 126–28.

70. Hugh Gardner, one of the most thorough commune analysts working in the early 1970s, estimated the number at slightly over 600, in *Children of Prosperity,* 3. Historian Foster Stockwell has estimated the number of communes established between 1663 and 1963 at 516. Stockwell, *Encyclopedia of American Communes.* See also Holloway, *Heavens on Earth;* and Miller, *American Communes.*

71. Miller, *60s Communes,* xx. For a comprehensive review of scholarly and journalistic attempts to establish the number of communes in this period, see ibid., xviii–xx.

72. Jerome, *Families of Eden,* 16–18, cited in Miller, *60s Communes,* xix–xx.

73. Miller, *60s Communes,* xiii–xiv. Sociologists at the time and since have been fascinated by the principles around which communes were organized. See Berger, *Survival of a Counterculture;* Case and Taylor, *Co-ops, Communes, and Collectives;* Gardner, *Children of Prosperity;* Jerome, *Families of Eden;* Kanter, *Commitment and Community;* Kanter, *Communes;* Zablocki, *Alienation and Charisma;* Zicklin, *Countercultural Communes.*

74. Miller, *60s Communes,* 13. There are many contemporary accounts of life on these communes, some written by journalists, some by residents. Journalists tended to wander from commune to commune, building a first-person narrative as they went. Work in this genre includes Fairfield, *Communes U.S.A.;* Hedgepeth, *Alternative;* and Houriet, *Getting Back Together.* The founders of communes and early residents often wrote vivid portraits of their communities as they lived in them. Books in this vein include Diamond, *What the Trees Said;* Gaskin, *Hey Beatnik!;* Gravy, *Hog Farm and Friends;* Mungo, *Total Loss Farm;* Rabbit, *Drop City.*

75. See, e.g., Barbrook and Cameron, "Californian Ideology."

76. See, e.g., Bey, *T.A.Z.,* 95–114.

77. For a persuasive attempt to locate the SDS and the youth movements of the 1960s within a broader New Left framework and a multidecade framework, see Gosse, "Movement of Movements." SDS, "Port Huron Statement," 163–72, quotation on 164. As historian Douglas Rossinow put it, "Whatever else it was, the New Left was a response to the deepening symptoms of life under advanced, bureaucratic capitalism." Rossinow, *Politics of Authenticity,* 20.

78. SDS, "Port Huron Statement," 166–67.

79. Rossinow, *Politics of Authenticity,* 162.

80. Sociologist Wini Breines has distinguished between two political modes within SDS, modes she calls "strategic" and "prefigurative." Strategic politics represented the work of changing traditional political structures by means of activism; prefigurative politics denoted the desire on the part of many in SDS to live out and exemplify their political ideals. See Breines, *Community and Organization in the New Left,* 7. Gitlin, *Sixties,* 107; Greg Calvert, "The Beloved Community," *New Left Notes,* November 25, 1966; quoted in Breines, *Community and Organization in the New Left,* 48.

81. *San Francisco Seed,* 1967, quoted in Breines, *Community and Organization in the New Left,* 36.

82. Roszak, *Making of a Counter Culture,* 208, 50, 240.

83. Reich, *Greening of America,* 78.

84. Ibid., 204, 204, 223.

85. Ibid., 272. Reich's statement bears an uncanny resemblance to Manuel Castells's words almost twenty years later: "There is not, sociologically and economically, such a thing as a global capitalist class." Castells, *Rise of the Network Society,* 474.

Chapter 2

1. Stewart Brand, "Notebooks," March 14, 1957.

2. Brand, interview, July 17, 2001.

3. Brand quoted by Katherine Fulton in interview notes for "Always Two Steps Ahead," Stanford University Library, Special Collections, Whole Earth Catalog Records, 1969–1986, box 24, folder 13.

4. Brand, "Notebooks," March 14, 1957.

5. Whyte, *Organization Man*.

6. Quotation in Kay, "How a Genetic Code Became an Information System," 463; Haraway, "High Cost of Information," 247.

7. Ehrlich and Holm, *Process of Evolution,* viii, 19.

8. Ibid., 279.

9. Brand, "Notebooks," September 17, October 15, 1958 (original emphasis).

10. Ibid., January 12, 1961; January 29, 1962.

11. Joselit, *American Art since 1945*, 33. In its August 8, 1949, issue, for instance, *Life* had profiled Pollock. In a series of bold, black-and-white images, the magazine showed him stooped over floor-sized canvases, a cigarette dangling from his mouth, carefully dripping paint in abstract patterns. Although audience members might not know what the patterns meant, *Life*'s images suggested that Pollock surely did. Likewise, on January 15, 1951, *Life* published a photograph of fifteen of the eighteen signatories to a 1950 letter protesting a resistance to modern art on the part of curators at the Metropolitan Museum of Art in New York. The eighteen artists were Jimmy Ernst, Adolph Gottlieb, Robert Motherwell. William Baziotes, Hans Hofmann, Barnett Newman. Theodoros Stamos, Clyfford Still, Richard Pousette-Dart, Ad Reinhardt, Jackson Pollock, Mark Rothko, Bradly Walker Tomlin, Willem de Kooning, Hedda Stern, James Brooks, Weldon Kees, and Fritz Bultman. For more on this point, see Guilbaut, *How New York Stole the Idea of Modern Art.*

12. John Cage and Robert Rauschenberg, quoted in Tomkins, *Bride and the Bachelors,* 5, 204.

13. Leonard B. Meyer quoted ibid., 5. By the mid-1960s, Cage and Rauschenberg had become leading figures in what critics termed a large-scale shift in American art away from formalism and the construction of objects and toward the use of technology and the embrace of information theory. Jack Burnham, an art critic and professor at Northwestern University, was perhaps the most articulate spokesman for this vision. In 1968, in "Systems Esthetics," he described the rise of a "systems esthetic" in American art. In keeping with the discoveries of cybernetics and information theory, he explained, artists had come to see themselves as engineers and scientists. At one level, they embraced the mission of scientific research, seeking to reveal the systems that organized the material world. At another, they adopted its interdisciplinary, technocentric practices. A systems perspective, wrote Burnham, required that artists "solve problems . . . on a multileveled, interdisciplinary basis. Consequently some of the more aware sculptors no longer think like sculptors, but they assume a span of problems more natural to architects, urban planners, civil engineers, electronic technicians, and cultural anthropologists" (34). See also Burnham, *Beyond Modern Sculpture;* and Chandler and Lippard, "Dematerialization of Art." For later assessments of this shift, see Woodward, "Art and Technics"; and Burnham, "Art and Technology." For a fascinating evaluation of 1960s art and its relationship to shifts in communication technology, as well as an incisive reading of Jack Burnham's criticism, see Lee, *Chronophobia.* For an account of post–World War II avant-garde art and literature and their relationship to cold war liberalism and, to some extent, science and technology, see Belgrad, *Culture of Spontaneity.*

14. For a fuller description of Cage's event, see Vesna, "Networked Public Spaces." "Happenings are events that, put simply, happen. Though the best of them have a decided impact . . . they appear to go nowhere and do not make any particular literary point. In contrast to the arts of the past, they have no structured beginning, middle, or end. Their form is open-ended and fluid; nothing obvious is sought and therefore nothing is won, except the certainty of a number of occurrences to which we are more than normally attentive." Kaprow, "Happenings in the New York Scene," 16. For photographs and examples of happenings in this period, see Kaprow, Kyokai, and Lebel, *Assemblage, Environments, and Happenings*. In 1966 Kaprow codified seven rules for happenings: "1. The line between the Happening and daily life should be kept as fluid and perhaps indistinct as possible. . . . 2. Themes, materials, actions, and the associations they evoke are to be gotten from anywhere except from the arts, their derivatives, and their milieu. . . . 3. The Happening should be dispersed over several widely spaced, sometimes moving and changing, locales. . . . 4. Time, closely bound up with things and spaces, should be variable and independent of the convention of continuity. . . . 5. The composition of all materials, actions, images, and their times and spaces should be undertaken in as artless and, again, practical a way as possible. . . . 6. Happenings should be unrehearsed and performed by nonprofessionals, once only. . . . 7. It follows that there should not be (and usually cannot be) an audience or audiences to watch a Happening." Kaprow, "Happenings Are Dead," 62–64.

15. Feigelson, "We Are All One," 74, quotation on 75.

16. Byerly, *Gerd Stern*, 354.

17. Feigelson, "We Are All One," 74; Dion Wright, personal communication, March 29, 2004.

18. Stern and Durkee quoted in Kostelanetz, "Scene and Not Herd," 71.

19. Stern, personal communication, September 15, 2005.

20. "Psychedelic Art," 65. The precise origins of the term *be-in* are unclear. By the late 1960s, however, it had become a prominent cultural form. On January 14, 1967, for instance, more than twenty thousand hippies gathered in San Francisco's Golden Gate Park, waving psychedelic banners, dropping the now-illegal LSD, and dancing to the sounds of Janis Joplin and the Grateful Dead, for what was billed as the first Human Be-In.

21. In 1950 Innis had published an epic study of the role communication had played in various empires since the time of ancient Egypt, entitled *Empire and Communications;* in 1951 he published a collection of essays, *The Bias of Communication.* Together, these works argued that the modes of communication constituted key forces shaping a society's structure and culture. But in fact, alongside Innis, McLuhan drew on an eclectic mix of thinkers, including Lewis Mumford, Saint Thomas Aquinas, and McLuhan's good friends Wyndham Lewis and the anthropologist Edmund Carpenter. For insights into McLuhan's intellectual biography, see Marchand, *Marshall McLuhan;* Gordon, *Marshall McLuhan;* Theall, *Virtual Marshall McLuhan;* Stamps, *Unthinking Modernity;* Horrocks, *Marshall McLuhan and Virtuality.*

22. Theall, *Virtual Marshall McLuhan,* 30.

23. McLuhan, *Gutenberg Galaxy,* 252, 31; McLuhan, *Understanding Media,* 3.

24. At several points in his writing, McLuhan described this electronic nervous system in explicitly cybernetic terms. "By continuously embracing technologies, we relate ourselves to them as servomechanisms," he wrote in *Understanding Media.* "That is why we must, to use them at all, serve these objects, these extensions of ourselves, as gods or minor religions" (46).

25. And in that sense, Fuller's public persona fit well within what Peter Braunstein has called a "culture of rejuvenation" in the 1960s. See Braunstein, "Forever Young."

26. Fuller quoted in Fuller and Snyder, *R. Buckminster Fuller*, 12.

27. Emerson quoted in Kenner, *Bucky*, 149–50.

28. Fuller, *Ideas and Integrities*, 35–43.

29. Ibid., 173.

30. Ibid., 176.

31. Ibid., 63.

32. Brand, "Buckminster Fuller," 3, 249.

33. Fuller quoted in Fuller and Snyder, *R. Buckminster Fuller*, 38. By the early 1960s, Fuller was traveling more than two-thirds of every year. Kenner, *Bucky*, 290.

34. Brand, "Notebooks," April 21, 1963, quotation in October 9, 1964 entry. For a rich analysis of the role played by Native American symbolism in the counterculture, see Deloria, *Playing Indian*.

35. Brand, "Notebooks," May 28, 1963.

36. Perry et al., *On the Bus*, 11. See also Lee and Shlain, *Acid Dreams*.

37. Lee and Shlain, *Acid Dreams*, 200.

38. Ken Kesey, "A Successful Dope Fiend," 4.

39. Brand, "Notebooks," December 18, 1962.

40. Wolfe, *Electric Kool-Aid Acid Test*, 13.

41. Lardas, *Bop Apocalypse*, 4.

42. Ginsberg quoted in Lardas, *Bop Apocalypse*, 10, 92–93; Ginsberg, "New Consciousness."

43. In this regard, as Daniel Belgrad has pointed out, they were part of a much larger move to embrace an aesthetic of "spontaneity" across the American art world. See Belgrad, *Culture of Spontaneity*, 196–221.

44. Stewart Brand, interview, July 17, 2001.

45. Wolfe, *Electric Kool-Aid Acid Test*, 195.

46. Ibid., 222.

47. Ibid., 138, quotations on 127.

48. Ibid., 230–49.

49. *America Needs Indians* was one of several multimedia pieces Brand pulled together in the mid-1960s. During this period, multimedia art served as the primary forum within which he sought to "comprehensively design" collaborative, immersive social experiences. Brand and the visitor quoted in Perry, *Haight-Ashbury*, 19, 47.

50. Kesey and Garcia quoted in Lee and Shlain, *Acid Dreams*, 143, 144. For more on the Trips Festival and the Haight, see Perry, *Haight-Ashbury*, 41–44.

Chapter 3

1. Brand, interview, July 17, 2001.

2. Roszak, *From Satori to Silicon Valley*, 8.

3. For a fascinating account of the intermingling of countercultural and technological communities in this area at the time, see Markoff, *What the Dormouse Said*.

4. Brand, *Last Whole Earth Catalog*, 439.

5. McClanahan and Norman, "*Whole Earth Catalog*," 95.

6. Star and Griesemer, "Institutional Ecology, Translations, and Boundary Objects," 505, 518–19, quotations on 505.

7. In this way, network forums can also serve as sites for and/or products of the collaborative meaning-making processes that Pablo Boczkowski has called "distributed construction," processes that scholars of science and technology have lately begun to analyze under the broad rubric of "co-production." Boczkowski, *Digitizing the News,* 165–69; Jasanoff, "Ordering Knowledge, Ordering Society." Other work on collaborative activity online echoes the conclusions of this tradition, while not necessarily building on it explicitly. Studies of virtual community, collaborative online work, and the open source software community in particular have emphasized the power of digital technologies to facilitate collaboration in and around communicative artifacts. As the example of the *Whole Earth Catalog* will show, though, the properties of interaction we often ascribe to digital media in fact predate the wide dissemination of those media.

For further reading in the research streams on which I am drawing here, see, in organizational studies, Orlikowski and Yates, "Genre Repertoire"; Yates, *Control through Communication;* and Bowker, *Science on the Run.* For work in cultural psychology, see Scribner and Cole, *Psychology of Literacy;* and Hutchins, *Cognition in the Wild.*

8. Brand, "Civilization and Its Contents," 5; Farber and Foner, *Age of Great Dreams,* 115; Marable, *Race, Reform, and Rebellion,* 92.

9. Gardner, *Children of Prosperity,* 243. Rosabeth Moss Kanter points out that communes in other eras tended to be organized according to one of four authority schemes: anarchism, organized democracy, charisma, or variations of local, traditional political forms. See Kanter, "Leadership and Decision-Making," 143.

10. Perhaps they had taken to heart John F. Kennedy's famous call to their generation: "I tell you the New Frontier is here," proclaimed Kennedy in 1960, as he accepted the Democratic presidential nomination. "Beyond that frontier are the uncharted areas of science and space, unsolved problems of peace and war, unconquered pockets of ignorance and prejudice, unanswered questions of poverty and surplus. I believe the times demand new invention, innovation, imagination, decision. I am asking each of you to be pioneers on that New Frontier." Kennedy, "Address Accepting the Nomination."

11. Gardner, *Children of Prosperity,* 36, Rabbit quoted on 42. In a strange countercultural echo of the American government's cold war policy of dispersion, this gathering of domes was to be a prototype of an emerging world: "Soon domed cities will spread across the world, anywhere land is cheap—on the deserts, in the swamps, on mountains, tundras, ice caps. The tribes are moving, building completely free and open way stations, each a warm and beautiful conscious environment. We are winning." Rabbit, quoted ibid., 37.

12. Rabbit, *Drop City,* 31; quoted in Hedgepeth, *Alternative,* 36.

13. Steve Durkee, quoted in Hedgepeth, *Alternative,* 84.

14. Steve Durkee quoted in Fairfield, *Communes U.S.A.,* 119; and Gardner, *Children of Prosperity,* 78.

15. Barbara Durkee quoted in Houriet, *Getting Back Together,* 366; Steve Durkee, quoted in Gardner, *Children of Prosperity,* 74.

16. Justin (no surname given), quoted in Hedgepeth, *Alternative,* 75.

17. For the role of feminism in the New Left, see Echols, *Daring to Be Bad;* and Evans, *Personal Politics.* For the rise of feminism within SDS, see Gitlin, *Sixties,* 363–74.

18. Kanter, "Family Organization," 300; Lois Britton, interview, May 21, 2004.

19. Hedgepeth, *Alternative,* 74.

20. Quoted ibid. For examples of similar attitudes on other communes, see Estellachild, "Hippie Communes"; and Davidson, "Hippie Families on Open Land."

21. Gardner, *Children of Prosperity,* 139, 117, Wheeler quoted on 139.

22. Even before the back-to-the-land migrations of the late 1960s, the establishment of New Communalist groups had sparked racial conflicts. In the early 1960s, for instance, the bohemians of Haight-Ashbury found themselves competing for cheap housing with local African Americans; by the late 1960s, comparatively few African Americans remained in the neighborhood. Likewise, on Memorial Day 1967, predominantly white hippies clashed with local Hispanics over the use of Tomkins Square Park on New York's Lower East Side. Gitlin, *Sixties,* 219.

23. Hedgepeth, *Alternative,* 72–78, quotations on 72.

24. Quoted in Gardner, *Children of Prosperity,* 113.

25. Brand, *Last Whole Earth Catalog,* 438, 439.

26. Quoted by Fulton, interview notes for "How Stewart Brand Learns," *Los Angeles Times Magazine,* October 30, 1994; transcription in Whole Earth Papers, Special Collections, Stanford University, M1045, box 24, folder 11.

27. Full details of Whole Earth Catalog finances between 1968 and 1971, with the exception of Lois Brand's contributions, can be found in Brand, "Money," 438.

28. By the time Brand had begun working on the *Catalog,* typesetting technologies had changed the face of publishing. Working with an IBM Selectric Composer typewriter, Brand could change the typeface of the *Catalog* simply by swapping out the daisy wheel on his machine. A Polaroid MP-3 camera allowed Brand and his staff to easily take pictures not only of the covers of the books they carried, but of pages of text within. Brand then cut and pasted these images into the pages of the *Catalog.* As a result, each page of the *Catalog* was a collage of images and texts derived from the items displayed, as well as bits of commentary, recommendations, and price listings from the *Catalog* itself, all arranged in a variety of fonts. By 1968 these techniques had become common throughout the alternative press. For contemporaneous accounts of the New Left and New Communalist presses and the effects of technological change on them, see Glessing, *Underground Press in America;* Leamer, *Paper Revolutionaries;* and Lewis, *Outlaws of America.*

29. By February 1969, Brand reported having sold 800 copies of the *Catalog* and having attracted 340 subscribers. Brand, "Money," 438.

30. For the first *Supplement,* Brand managed to attract some 500 subscribers; three months later, he printed four times that many *Supplements.*

31. Though Stewart and Lois Brand ceased to publish the *Catalog* twice yearly in 1971, Stewart Brand and/or the Whole Earth organization have gone on to publish a variety of new *Whole Earth Catalogs* sporadically over the last three decades. These include the *Whole Earth Epilog* of 1974, the *Whole Earth Software Catalog* of 1984, and the *Millennium Whole Earth Catalog* of 1994.

32. Branwyn, *Whole Earth Review.*

33. J. Tetrault and S. Thomas, *Country Woman: A Handbook for the New Farmer* (New York: Anchor Books, 1975), 97, quoted in Binkley, "Seers of Menlo Park," 299.

34. Brand quoted in McClanahan and Norman, "*Whole Earth Catalog,*" 118; Bowker, "How to Be Universal," 116.

35. Reich and Bihalji-Merin, *World from Above;* Royce, *Surface Anatomy.*

36. Members of Ant Farm worked closely with the *Whole Earth Catalog* crew in 1969, when they built an giant inflatable "pillow" in the Saline Valley, California. *Catalog* staffers used the pillow to house a temporary production facility for the *Catalog.* For a fascinating history of the Ant Farm collective, see Lewallen and Seid, *Ant Farm.*

37. Brand, Bonner, and Helmuth, *Difficult but Possible Supplement* (July), 17.

38. Norman, "On Heroes," 13.

39. Tomkins, "In the Outlaw Area," 35; and Brand et al., *Whole Earth Catalog $1*, 21.

40. Freeman Dyson, in the *Futurist*, December 1969, quoted in Brand et al., *Whole Earth Catalog $1*, 48.

41. Sociologist Thomas Streeter offers an intriguing take on this new sort of self in two important articles: "Romantic Self and the Politics of Internet Commercialization"; and "That Deep Romantic Chasm."

42. Brand et al., *Difficult but Possible Supplement* (March), 8.

43. Brand explained his editorial tactics thus: "I try to take as much stuff out of the way between the structure of what originally happened and the structure of the mind that's going to be looking at it, and let those two structures deal with one another without having to deal with me in the middle." Quoted in McClanahan and Norman, "*Whole Earth Catalog*," 118.

44. Although Lois Britton has reported contributing several thousand dollars of an inheritance she received in the early stages of developing the *Catalog*, most of publication's funding came from Brand. Lois shared in every aspect of making the *Catalog*, and she performed much of the administrative work on which it depended, but Brand retained ultimate editorial control. Britton, interview, May 21, 2004.

45. Brand, interview, July 17, 2001.

46. Brand, "How to Do a Whole Earth Catalog," 438.

47. Brand, quoted in McClanahan and Norman, "*Whole Earth Catalog*," 118.

48. Smith and Hershey, *Whole Earth Catalog One Dollar*, 32.

49. Wolfe, *Electric Kool-Aid Acid Test*, 232; Rybczynski, *Paper Heroes*, 90.

50. Alan and Heath [no surnames listed], "Centering," 46.

51. Brand et al., *Difficult but Possible Supplement* (March), 18.

52. Brand, quoted in Rybczynski, *Paper Heroes*, 96.

53. Brand et al., *Difficult but Possible Supplement* (March), 23.

54. Alloy was just one of the many gatherings attended by *Whole Earth* subscribers or staffers between 1968 and 1971 and reported on in *Whole Earth* publications. Others included Buckminster Fuller's World Game at Southern Illinois University (see Norman and Shugart, *Whole Earth Catalog $1*) and Brand's own experimental production of the *Catalog* from a city of temporary pillow domes constructed around hot springs in the California desert (see Brand, *Whole Earth Catalog One Dollar*). Each of these events, like Alloy, featured an attempt to fuse systems theory, new technology, and countercultural practice. One especially important gathering also attempted to fuse the technological and countercultural communities.

55. Brand et al., *Whole Earth Catalog $1*, 17.

56. Brand, *Last Whole Earth Catalog*, 221.

57. Brand, Kahn, and Kahn, *Whole Earth Catalog*, 74.

58. The letter, from Bradley H. Dowden, was printed in Ashby, *Whole Earth Catalog $1*, 10.

59. Explained Brand, "The gripe page is a peace-keeping device where *Catalog* staff can make personal statements which the editor may not edit. He may add a remark or two." Brand et al., *Whole Earth Catalog $1*, 47.

60. Bonner, quoted ibid.

61. Brand, quoted ibid.

62. Streeter, "That Deep Romantic Chasm," 52.

63. Albright and Perry, "Last Twelve Hours of the Whole Earth," 121, 122.

64. Beach, quoted ibid., 123.

Chapter 4

1. Brand, "We Owe It All to the Hippies," 54. Paul Freiberger and Michael Swaine, for example, describe one of the earliest home computers, the Altair, as a product of the "cultural revolution of the 1960s." *Fire in the Valley,* 111. In his foreword to Freiberger and Swaine's book, *New York Times* technology correspondent John Markoff explains that "it was a particular chemistry—not just greed and not just engineering, but also a strain of passionate political purity . . . that gave rise to the personal computer industry" (xiii). This notion guides Markoff's 2005 volume *What the Dormouse Said.* Even the most cautious historians have tended to accept this account. Thierry Bardini, in his thoroughly researched history of Douglas Engelbart's work, for example, argues that the personal computer was in part a product of the "generation of '68." *Bootstrapping,* 194.

2. Ceruzzi, *History of Modern Computing* (1998), 109–206.

3. Ibid., 143–206.

4. As late as May 1974, for instance, Hewlett-Packard identified its HP-65 calculator as a "personal computer" because it was portable, programmable, and designed for individual use. See Tung, "Personal Computer."

5. As scholars of other technologies have shown, engineers often draw on cultural resources to shape their machines and to define their meanings and potential uses. For an introduction to this literature, see Bijker, Hughes, and Pinch, *Social Construction of Technological Systems.* At the same time, this linking can be read as a species of a cultural process that Stuart Hall has analyzed under the rubric of "articulation." See Grossberg, "On Postmodernism and Articulation." See also Slack, "Articulation in Cultural Studies."

6. Bardini, *Bootstrapping,* xiii; Ceruzzi, *History of Modern Computing* (1998), 221; Pfaffenberger, "Social Meaning of the Personal Computer"; Freiberger and Swaine, *Fire in the Valley;* Levy, *Hackers.*

7. Markoff, *What the Dormouse Said.*

8. Bush, "As We May Think," quotation on 47.

9. Engelbart described how he became involved in computing, and his motivations, in an extensive interview by historian Thierry Bardini in 1996. See Bardini, *Bootstrapping,* 4–10.

10. For an exploration of Engelbart's debt to cybernetics, see ibid., 45–53. As Engelbart put it in 1988, "the workstation is the portal into a person's 'augmented knowledge workshop'—the [virtual] place in which he finds the data and tools with which he does his knowledge work, and through which he collaborates with similarly equipped workers." Quoted ibid., 219.

11. Ibid., 146; Waldrop, *Dream Machine,* 105–41, 18–23; quotations in Licklider, "Man-Computer Symbiosis," 74, 75.

12. For a complete history of Engelbart's role in the development of the ARPANET, see Bardini, *Bootstrapping,* 182–214. In 1966 Engelbart and his colleague Bill English participated in an experiment led by Willis Harman to test the impact of LSD on creativity. Like Stewart Brand, they were given the drug in a laboratory setting. For Engelbart, at least, the drug offered little of the sort of creativity enhancement he hoped computers would bring about. "The psychedelics took me so high that I was useless to the experiment," he recalled in 2004. "I ended up without the slightest inclination that it would help me be productive in what

I was trying to do." Interview, August 1, 2004. For an account of the ARC group's involvement with EST, see Bardini, *Bootstrapping,* 201–14; for a thinly veiled memoir of the period at SRI, see Vallee, *Network Revolution.* Quotation in text from Engelbart, interview, August 1, 2004.

13. Bill English, interview, July 27, 2004; Engelbart, interview, August 1, 2004.

14. Brand et al., *Whole Earth Catalog $1,* 52.

15. Andries Van Dam, quoted in Bardini, *Bootstrapping,* 138.

16. For accounts of audience responses to the NLS demo, see ibid., 138–42; and *Engelbart's Unfinished Revolution.*

17. Brand, interview, July 24, 2001.

18. Hiltzik, *Dealers of Lightning,* 67.

19. English, interview, July 27, 2004. For extensive accounts of PARC's internal politics, see Hiltzik, *Dealers of Lightning;* and Smith and Alexander, *Fumbling the Future.*

20. Alan Kay, interview, August 5, 2004. For more on the *Catalog's* influence at PARC, see Kay, "Turning Points."

21. Kay, interview, August 5, 2004; Larry Tesler, interview, July 26, 2001.

22. Bob Albrecht, interview, July 22, 2001.

23. Another influential figure who took advantage of the *Whole Earth Catalog* in this way was Ted Nelson. In 1974 he modeled his much-cited *Computer Lib: You Must Understand Computers Now!* after the *Catalog.* See Nelson, *Computer Lib; Dream Machines,* 6.

24. Felsenstein, interview, July 18, 2001.

25. Brand, "Spacewar," 56; Colstad, "Community Memory"; Lipkin, "Public Information Network."

26. Freiberger and Swaine, *Fire in the Valley,* 115; Felsenstein, "Sol"; Felsenstein, interview, July 18, 2001.

27. Keith Britton, personal communication, July 18, 2004.

28. For a history of Spacewar, see Lowood, "Biography of Computer Games"; and Lenoir, Lowood, and Stanford Humanities Laboratory, *How They Got Game;* Brand, "Spacewar," 50.

29. Brand, "Spacewar," 51, 58.

30. Dennis Allison, interview, July 26, 2004; Hiltzik, *Dealers of Lightning,* 156–62.

31. Gitlin, *Sixties,* 408.

32. Gardner, *Children of Prosperity,* 46, 91, 116, 240–41. For an analysis of the variance in governance strategies deployed on communes, see Kanter, "Leadership and Decision-Making."

33. For more on this transition, see Heelas, *New Age Movement;* and FitzGerald, *Cities on a Hill.*

34. Carroll, *It Seemed Like Nothing Happened,* 128.

35. *Newsweek,* March 4, 1974, quotation on 132.

36. The eight-hundred-thousand-dollar figure comes from Brand's "Notebooks," September 15, 1971. Quotations ibid., August 20, 1971; and Brand, "History," 752.

37. Brand, "Local Dependency."

38. *CoEvolution Quarterly* 1 (Spring 1974), inside front cover.

39. Hayles, *How We Became Posthuman,* 16, 10, quotation on 16.

40. Heims, *Social Science for Post-War America,* 14, 16. For a full account of the Macy Conferences and their effects, see Heims, "Bateson and the Mathematicians"; Heims, *Social Science for Post-War America;* Hayles, *How We Became Post-Human.* For a critical look at the legacy of systems theory and cybernetics, see Lilienfeld, *Rise of Systems Theory.*

41. Quotations in Bateson, "Form, Substance, Difference," 468; and Bateson, "Effects of Conscious Purpose on Human Adaptation," 448. For more extensive interpretations of Bateson's intellectual career, see Berman, *Reenchantment of the World;* and Harries-Jones, *Recursive Vision.*

42. In testimony to the State Senate of Hawaii in March 1970, for example, Bateson ascribed the ecological crisis to a combination of "technological advance; . . . population increase; and . . . conventional (but wrong) ideas about the nature of man and his relation to the environment." Bateson, "Roots of Ecological Crisis," 496. Quotations in text in Bateson, "Effects of Conscious Purpose on Human Adaptation," 451–52.

43. For a study of the Whole Earth network's links to the alternative technology movement, see Kirk, "Machines of Loving Grace"; and Kleiman, "Appropriate Technology Movement," 154–216. For more broad-brush analyses of the alternative technology movement and its achievements, see Rybczynski, *Paper Heroes;* Willoughby, *Technology Choice;* Winner, "Building the Better Mousetrap," 61–84.

44. Harries-Jones, *Recursive Vision,* 6, 73–75, 103.

45. Brand, "Space Colonies," 4; Kleiman, "Appropriate Technology Movement," 190–91. For a full account, see O'Neill, *High Frontier.*

46. Wendell Berry, letter, *CoEvolution Quarterly* 9 (Spring 1976), 8–9, reprint in Brand, *Space Colonies,* 36–37.

47. Gurney Norman, letter, *CoEvolution Quarterly* 9 (Spring 1976), 48, reprint in Brand, *Space Colonies,* 69.

48. Brand, "Sky Starts at Your Feet," 6.

49. Kirk, "Machines of Loving Grace," 374.

50. Kleiner, "History of *CoEvolution Quarterly,*" 335.

51. Quoted in Langway and Abramson, "Whole Earth Revisited," 100.

52. Ibid.

53. Ceruzzi, *History of Modern Computing* (1998), 207–80; *Time,* January 3, 1983.

54. St. John, "Agent Provocateur," 106.

55. Hiltz and Turoff, *Network Nation,* 18–27, 117–21; Kelly, "Birth of a Network Nation." Quotations from Brand, interview, July 24, 2001; and Stewart Brand, [untitled], *CoEvolution Quarterly* 37 (Spring 1983), 152.

56. Brand, interview, July 24, 2001.

57. Kelly, interview, July 27, 2001.

58. Felsenstein, interview, July 18, 2001; Levy, *Hackers,* 9.

59. Quoted in Levy, *Hackers,* 104.

60. Ibid., x.

61. Ibid., 27–33.

62. Ibid., 77 (original emphasis).

63. Burt, *Structural Holes;* Kelly, interview, July 27, 2001.

64. Schrage, "Hacking Away at the Future"; Markoff, Robinson, and Shapiro, "Up to Date"; Elmer-DeWitt, "Let Us Now Praise Famous Hackers"; Brand, "Keep Designing." Quotation in Brand, "Keep Designing," 49.

65. Quoted in Brand, "Keep Designing," 48.

66. Ibid.; Felsenstein, interview, July 18, 2001.

67. Markoff, Robinson, and Shapiro, "Up to Date."

68. Schrage, "Hacking Away at the Future"; Markoff, Robinson, and Shapiro, "Up to Date."

69. Markoff, Robinson, and Shapiro, "Up to Date"; Florin and New Dimension Films, *Hackers*.

70. Brand, "Keep Designing," 44.

71. As Michelle Callon puts it, "To translate is to displace. . . . But to translate is also to express in one's own language what others say and want, why they act in the way they do and how they associate with each other; it is to establish oneself as a spokesman. At the end of the process, if it is successful, only voices speaking in unison will be heard." "Some Elements of a Sociology of Translation," 223, quoted in Star, "Power, Technologies and the Phenomenology of Conventions," 45. In that essay Star offers an excellent account of how network benefits can redound to the perceived "executive" at the heart of that network—in this case, Brand.

Chapter 5

1. The WELL still exists; it now employs the "WELL Engaged" system, which has full HTML capabilities. This chapter focuses on the WELL from its inception in 1985 to 1992. In 1992 the last of the WELL's early managers, Cliff Figallo, left; the number of members had increased drastically; and the WELL's character had begun to change substantially. The Point Foundation sold its 50 percent ownership stake in the system to Bruce Katz in 1994.

2. For the importance of informal social networks to employment in the region in this period, see Saxenian, *Regional Advantage*. To get a glimpse of how important the WELL was to its members' employment, see the archives of the WELL's "Work" conference at http://engaged.well.com/engaged.cgi?c=work.

3. Hafner, "Epic Saga of the WELL."

4. Brand, interview, July 24, 2001. Brand was also influenced in this decision by the fact that he had recently begun participating on the EIES network. He had found the conversations there exciting, and he hoped to spark a similar use of the WELL.

5. No formal accounting of early WELL membership exists today. Howard Rheingold estimates that some 600 people were using the WELL when he joined in the summer of 1985. "Slice of My Life in My Virtual Community," 430. Marc A. Smith estimates that that number had grown to approximately 6,600 by 1992. "Voices from the WELL," 8.

6. Quoted in Rheingold, *Virtual Community* (1993), 43.

7. Many of the WELL's archives from this period were lost as the system migrated across a series of different servers. For overviews of the conferences and topics in this period, see Smith, "Voices from the WELL," 8–9; and Rheingold, *Virtual Community* (2000), 32–35.

8. Glossbrenner, *Handbook of Personal Computer Communications*, 156, 160–67.

9. Hafner, *The Well*, 11.

10. Coate, *Cyberspace Innkeeping*.

11. Quoted in Hafner, *The Well*, 13.

12. Cliff Figallo, "Small Town on the Internet Highway."

13. Barayón quoted in Hafner, "Epic Saga of the WELL"; Coate and Figallo, "Farm Stories," Coate quotations on 96, 99; Figallo quotation on 92.

14. Bates, *Post-Communal Experiments at the Farm*. See also Fike, *Voices from the Farm*. At its peak in the late 1970s, the Farm had about fifteen hundred members. Most lived on the Farm. Others lived in satellite communities in Washington, D.C., Manhattan's South Bronx, Wisconsin, Florida, California, and Missouri. In 1974 the Farm established its own version of the Peace Corps, which was called Plenty. Plenty created development and public health projects in Guatemala, Lesotho, Washington, D.C., and the South Bronx. Today Plenty

remains active in Central America and Mexico, at the Pine Ridge Indian Reservation, and at the Farm itself. In 2005, the Farm supported approximately two hundred residents.

15. On the WELL, for instance, members frequently sent each other "beams"—bursts of supportive energy made visible in the text of their postings. Figallo quoted in Hafner, "Epic Saga of the WELL."

16. Figallo, "Small Town on the Internet Highway."

17. Quoted in Hafner, "Epic Saga of the WELL," 111.

18. Figallo, "Small Town on the Internet Highway"; McClure quoted in Hafner, "Epic Saga of the WELL."

19. Lash and Urry, *End of Organized Capitalism*; Harvey, *Condition of Postmodernity*; Powell, "Neither Market nor Hierarchy"; Saxenian, *Regional Advantage*; Stark, "Ambiguous Assets for Uncertain Environments."

20. Powell, "Capitalist Firm in the Twenty-First Century," 55–62; Castells, *Rise of the Network Society*, 243–44.

21. *New York Times*, February 13, 1996, quoted in Powell, "Capitalist Firm in the Twenty-First Century," 40.

22. Castells, *Rise of the Network Society*, 381.

23. Many analysts, such as Manuel Castells (*Rise of the Network Society*, 151–200), have in fact suggested that computers played a strong role in decentralizing the firm. Yet AnnaLee Saxenian, in *Regional Advantage*, has shown that in the case of Silicon Valley, at least, the existence of firms with porous boundaries and strong interpersonal networks substantially predated the rise of computer networks. In her study of the deployment of computers in a number of manufacturing firms at this time (*In the Age of the Smart Machine*), Shoshanna Zuboff demonstrated that computers could often centralize rather than distribute power and control within a firm. Although computer networks have quite probably played a role in the disaggregation of the traditional firm, scholars do not yet agree on the nature of that role. For a comprehensive discussion of the role played by computer technologies in the development of networked organizational forms, see DeSanctis and Fulk, *Shaping Organization Form*.

24. Sturgeon, "How Silicon Valley Came to Be"; Leslie, "Biggest 'Angel' of Them All," 49; Leslie, *Cold War and American Science*, 51–75.

25. Wolfe, "Tinkerings of Robert Noyce." As Wolfe explained, "Everywhere the Fairchild émigrés went, they took the Noyce approach with them. It wasn't enough to start up a company; you had to start up a community, a community in which there were no social distinctions, and it was first come, first served in the parking lot, and everyone was supposed to internalize the common goals" (ibid.). This style was not simply a Fairchild phenomenon but a characteristic of engineering culture Valley-wide. Saxenian, *Regional Advantage*, 51.

26. Saxenian, *Regional Advantage*, 7, 2; Rogers and Larsen, *Silicon Valley Fever*, 28.

27. For figures on managers and engineers, see Saxenian, *Regional Advantage*, 35; for estimates of turnover among the Valley's manual laborers, see Rogers and Larsen, *Silicon Valley Fever*, 87. The engineer is quoted in Saxenian, *Regional Advantage*, 36. Workers have adopted multiple survival strategies under these conditions. See Neff, "Organizing Uncertainty"; and Ross, *No-Collar*.

28. Quoted in Hafner, "Epic Saga of the WELL."

29. Reva Basch, personal communication, September 21, 2004. Basch obtained this figure in a private conference made up of early WELL managers. The WELL's membership

records from this period were discarded several years ago, so precise numbers cannot be obtained. Even so, the figure is consistent with contemporary patterns of posts within archived topics. In 1993 WELL manager Gail Williams estimated that 18 percent of WELL members were female. "Experiences of Women On Line," posts 105 and 109. These numbers suggest that women on the WELL posted far more often than their male counterparts, since their posts account for approximately 40 percent of the comments in many archived public conferences. Apart from this one instance, however, WELL managers and journalists alike have consistently argued that women constituted between 40 percent and 50 percent of WELL users between 1990 and 1995. By 1997 journalist Wendy Grossman estimated that men and women were using the WELL in equal numbers. Grossman, *Net.wars*, 103.

30. The paper became Herring, "Gender Differences in Computer-Mediated Communication." The debate can still be found archived on the WELL within the Electronic Frontier Foundation Conference in topic 448, "The Experiences of Women On Line," and topic 476, "The Experiences of Women On Line (Continued)."

31. Weise, "A Thousand Aunts with Modems," xi–xii. The archives of the Women on the WELL conference are not available to readers who are not members of the conference, yet Weise's recollections are consistent with other accounts in a variety of other conferences and with the recollections of Reva Basch, who hosted the WOW conference from 1990 to 1995. Basch, interview, August 8, 2004.

32. Gardner, *Children of Prosperity*, 10. For a full accounting of *Whole Earth Catalog* finances 1968–1971, see Stewart Brand, "Money," in Brand, *Last Whole Earth Catalog*, 438.

33. Basch, "Living on the Net."

34. Rheingold, "Slice of My Life in My Virtual Community," 425; Howard Rheingold, "Da WELL Been Beddy, Beddy Goot to Me," post 6, December 7, 1989.

35. humdog, "Pandora's Vox," 438–39; Coate, "Cyberspace Innkeeping." Marc Smith notes that in 1992, 50 percent of the contributions to the WELL came from 70 people—approximately 1 percent of the overall membership. See Smith, "Voices from the WELL," 29.

36. Coate, "Cyberspace Innkeeping"; Basch, interview, August 8, 2004.

37. Howard Rheingold, interview, July 20, 2001; John Perry Barlow, interview, August 25, 2003; John Coate, interview, August 25, 2003.

38. Stark, "Ambiguous Assets for Uncertain Environments," 71. For an early and important application of Stark's theories of heterarchy to media production, see Boczkowski, *Digitizing the News*, 165.

39. Stark, "Ambiguous Assets for Uncertain Environments," 78.

40. Ibid., 90–91.

41. For an account of these processes in a journalistic setting, see Boczkowski, *Digitizing the News*, 164.

42. Rheingold has long been one of the most visible and articulate deployers of the gift-economy metaphor, and for that reason, I quote him here. Yet, the understanding of the exchange of information as the exchange of gifts permeated the WELL in its first decade. Perhaps the easiest way to explore the tension between the notion of information as gift and information as commodity is to examine the archives of the extensive debates around the "You Own Your Own Words" policy. The topics in which these debates occurred have been cataloged in the WELL's online archives. See "Word Ownership Discussions."

43. The giving of gifts without expectation of immediate return formed the basis of many countercultural activities in the San Francisco Bay area in the 1960s. By the middle of

the decade, for instance, a group called the Diggers could be found giving away free food daily in a Haight-Ashbury park as part of a larger effort to create a "Free City"—that is, a metropolis based substantially on giving rather than monetary exchange. The Diggers also established "Free Stores," where items could dropped off and taken away at no charge, and a free medical clinic as well. Many communes owed their existence to gifts of money, materials, and labor from their members—and their members' families. The "gift economy" paradigm ultimately outlived the commune movement. For a reading of the gift economy that was especially popular in Whole Earth circles in the 1980s, see Hyde, *The Gift*. Stewart Brand printed a selection from Hyde's book entitled "The Gift Must Always Move" in *CoEvolution Quarterly* 35 (Fall 1982). Richard Barbrook has argued that the gift-economy paradigm grew out of the New Left and has become a standard feature of the working world online. The history of the Whole Earth network suggests that in America, at least, it was the New Communalist movement rather than the New Left that drove the rise of the gift-economy paradigm. But Barbrook's work remains an early and influential account of the gift economy's role in the information economy. See Barbrook, "Hi-Tech Gift Economy."

44. Mauss and Halls, *The Gift*. For a critique and extension of Mauss's arguments, see Lévi-Strauss, "Selections from *Introduction to the Work of Marcel Mauss*." See also Bourdieu, "Selections from *The Logic of Practice*"; and Bourdieu, "Marginalia." For a broad-brush analysis of gift economies, see Cheal, *Gift Economy*. For a study of gift economies on the early public Internet, see Kollock, "Economies of Online Cooperation."

45. Mauss, *The Gift*, 73; Bourdieu, "Marginalia," 232, 214–19.

46. Rheingold, "Slice of My Life in My Virtual Community," 425.

47. For more on WOPs, see "The WELL History Project."

48. Both of these conferences, as well as others on similar topics, are still available in the WELL's online archives. See Boomers Conference, in the WELL, topic 86, "Communes"; and topic 15, "Communes—Spiritual and Otherwise"; topic 44, "Communes—Past, Present, and Pluperfect"; topic 210, "Memories on Morning Star in 1967," all in Archives Conference, in the WELL (these sources available to WELL subscribers).

49. For a clear view of the work that went into establishing the community metaphor, and for examples of alternatives in play, see "The WELL as Community." Coate, "Cyberspace Innkeeping."

50. Rheingold, "Virtual Communities"; Rheingold, "Slice of My Life in My Virtual Community"; Rheingold, *Virtual Community* (1993).

51. Rheingold, "Virtual Communities," 79.

52. Rheingold, *Virtual Community* (1993), 110.

53. It is hard to overestimate the impact of Rheingold's writing on new media scholarship. Before his articles and his 1993 book appeared, researchers generally did not take up the question of online communities as such. Rather, they focused on computer-mediated communication. Within this framework, they dealt principally with the ways in which computer technologies shaped interpersonal communication and, thereby, the performance of work groups, teams, and commercial organizations. For examples, see Rice, "Research on Computer-Mediated Communication Systems"; and Sproull and Kiesler, *Connections*. As Steve Jones has pointed out in "Understanding Community in the Information Age," 29, researchers in this period paid particular attention to the ways computers broke down barriers of time and distance. In the wake of Rheingold's book, researchers tended to adopt many of its core assumptions, including the notions that Americans needed new communities and that those communities could be established with technology (14). Many

studies focused on the ways in which computers helped create—or failed to create—interpersonal intimacy online and on the social and discursive norms shaping that process. See, e.g., Baym, "Emergence of Community in Computer-Mediated Communication"; Stoll, *Silicon Snake Oil*; and Barnes, *Online Connections*. Others attended to the ways in which "disembodied" forms of communication can lead to either feelings of increased intimacy or new and potentially disruptive forms of identity play. See Turkle, *Life on the Screen*; Stone, *War of Desire and Technology*; and Dibbell, *My Tiny Life*. More recently, scholars have focused on the ways in which online and off-line communications interact. See Wellman, "Electronic Group Is Virtually a Social Network"; Wellman and Gulia, "Virtual Communities as Communities"; Hampton and Wellman, "Examining Community in the Digital Neighborhood"; Wellman, "Physical Place and Cyber Place"; and Wellman et al., "Capitalizing on the Internet." See also Bakardjieva, "Virtual Togetherness." For comprehensive reviews of the literature on virtual communities, see Ellis, Oldridge, and Vasconcelos, "Community and Virtual Community"; Jankowski, "Creating Community with Media"; and Kendall, "Virtual Community."

54. For an astute critique of this logic, see Terranova, "Free Labor."

55. Hafner, "Epic Saga of the WELL"; Hagel and Armstrong, *Net Gain*; Werry, "Imagined Electronic Community."

56. Hafner, "Epic Saga of the WELL"; Rheingold, *Virtual Community* (2000), 323–91.

57. Sterling, *Hacker Crackdown*, 236; Hafner, "Epic Saga of the WELL"; Davis, *Techgnosis*, 107.

58. According to King, "Cultural Construction of Cyberspace," 152, Gibson first dreamed up the term *cyberspace* in 1981 as he searched for a way to describe electronic networks. He later recalled that the term emerged as a "neologic spasm: the primal act of pop poetics. Preceded any concept whatsoever. Slick and hollow—awaiting received meaning" (153). Although the technologies Gibson describes may belong to the future, the anger and anxiety that pervade the novel belong to the historical moment of its creation. The social and technological chaos of *Neuromancer* can be seen in many popular stories of the early and middle 1980s, including *Blade Runner* (1982), *The Terminator* (1984), and *First Blood* (the first Rambo film, 1982).

59. Stone, "Will the Real Body Please Stand Up?" 95–99.

60. Barlow, "Being in Nothingness," 38. See also Stone, "Will the Real Body Please Stand Up?" 98–99; King, "Cultural Construction of Cyberspace," 162; Rushkoff, *Cyberia*, 41–45.

61. King, *Cultural Construction of Cyberspace*, 165; Barlow, "Being in Nothingness," 41. The height of the Whole Earth group's involvement with virtual reality came on October 6 and 7, 1990, when a group of Whole Earth affiliates staged a twenty-four-hour virtual reality marathon called Cyberthon 1.0 at the Colossal Pictures sound stage in San Francisco. Among the attendees were Brand, William Gibson, Jaron Lanier, Colossal Pictures executive and founding member of the Global Business Network Lawrence Wilkinson, Wavy Gravy, members of the IBM Research Center, and Timothy Leary. In various press accounts, participants called the event "the acid test of the nineties" and "nerdstock."

62. Quoted in Sobchack, "Democratic Franchise and the Electronic Frontier," 14.

63. Boulware, "Mondo 1995."

64. Quoted ibid.

65. Sobchack, "New Age Mutant Ninja Hackers"; Barlow, "Being in Nothingness," 39, 37.

66. Barlow, interview, August 6, 2001.

67. Sterling, *Hacker Crackdown*, 234.

68. Barlow, interview, August 6, 2001.

69. Barlow, "@home.on.the.ranch."

70. Barlow, "Jack In, Young Pioneer!"

71. Sterling, *Hacker Crackdown*, 247.

72. For a full history of the case, see Hafner and Markoff, *Cyberpunk*.

73. Tough was introduced to the WELL by his father, a long-time subscriber to the *Whole Earth Review*.

74. Paul Tough, interview, February 8, 2002.

75. Hitt and Tough, "Forum," Barlow quoted on 47, Phreak quoted on 48.

76. Ibid., 52.

77. Tough, interview, February 8, 2002.

78. For a full account of Barlow's relations with Phreak and Optik, and of the founding of the Electronic Frontier Foundation, see Rheingold, *Virtual Community* (1993), 252–60; and Sterling, *Hacker Crackdown*, 247–305. Quotations in Barlow, "Crime and Puzzlement."

79. Quoted in Sterling, *Hacker Crackdown*, 41.

80. Sterling, *Hacker Crackdown*, 149.

81. Ibid., 234; Barlow, "Crime and Puzzlement."

82. Barlow, "Crime and Puzzlement."

83. Rheingold, *Virtual Community* (1993), 256; Sterling, *Hacker Crackdown*, 237.

84. Barlow, interview, August 6, 2001; quotation in Barlow, "Crime and Puzzlement."

85. Like the metaphor of virtual community, the image of cyberspace as an electronic frontier traveled far and wide. Often, the rhetoric of the electronic frontier was used explicitly, by scholars and others. See, e.g., Healy, "Cyberspace and Place." For a critical examination of gender issues entailed in the metaphor, see Miller, "Women and Children First." For a critical examination of the metaphor's links to neoliberalism, see Turner, "Cyberspace as the New Frontier?" Even when writers of the mid-1990s avoided Barlow's rhetoric, their vision of the Internet and cyberspace very much echoed his. This was true of local writers and international authors alike. See, e.g., Dyson, *Release 2.0*; and Lévy, *Collective Intelligence*.

86. Barlow, interview, August 6, 2001.

87. Barlow, "Crime and Puzzlement."

88. Ibid.

89. Ibid.

90. Ibid.

91. Barlow, "Jack In, Young Pioneer!"

Chapter 6

1. Reagan, quoted in Henwood, *After the New Economy*, 8.

2. Brand, *Inventing the Future*, xi.

3. Ibid., xiv.

4. Ibid., xiv, 33 (original emphasis).

5. Ibid., 207, 212, 255, quotations on 207 and 255.

6. Ibid., 6.

7. Ibid., 15.

8. Negroponte, quoted ibid., 252.

9. The book was translated into five languages (Spanish, German, Italian, Korean, and Japanese), was made a selection of the Quality Paperback Book Club, and was still in print ten years after publication. Elmer-DeWitt, "Dreaming the Impossible at M.I.T."

10. Kleiner, *Age of Heretics,* 142–55.

11. Schwartz, *Art of the Long View,* 95; Brand quoted in Kleiner, "Consequential Heresies," 17.

12. Kleiner, "Consequential Heresies," 18.

13. Ibid.

14. Schwartz, *Art of the Long View,* 92.

15. Kleiner, *Age of Heretics,* 199, quotation on 217; Harman and Rheingold, *Higher Creativity,* xvii.

16. For a fascinating study of countercultural entrepreneurialism in the food industry, see Belasco, *Appetite for Change.*

17. Schwartz, *Art of the Long View,* 7. For a comparison of the roles of operations research and systems analysis in World War II, see Edwards, *Closed World,* 113–21.

18. Edwards, *Closed World,* 115, 116; Ghamari-Tabrizi, *Worlds of Herman Kahn,* 48.

19. See Kahn, *On Thermonuclear War; Thinking about the Unthinkable;* and *On Escalation;* Kahn, Wiener, and Hudson Institute, *Year 2000.*

20. Kahn, quoted in Ghamari-Tabrizi, *Worlds of Herman Kahn,* 70, 75; Kahn, Brown, and Lovins, "New Class"; Kahn, "From Present to Future."

21. Kleiner, *Age of Heretics,* 163–70.

22. Ibid., 156; Gurdjieff, *Meetings with Remarkable Men,* quoted in Kleiner, *Age of Heretics,* 157.

23. Wack, "Uncharted Waters Ahead," 84.

24. Schwartz, *Art of the Long View,* 92.

25. Danica Remy, interview, July 27, 2001.

26. Schwartz, *Art of the Long View,* 96.

27. Paul Hawken, interview, July 24, 2001.

28. Schwartz, *Art of the Long View,* 96; Garreau, "Conspiracy of Heretics," 154. By contrast, McKinsey Consulting had approximately forty-five hundred consultants in eighty-one countries at this time. Lohr, "It's Long Boom or Bust for Leading Futurist."

29. Garreau, "Conspiracy of Heretics," 155. Ten years later the ratio of male to female and white to black had changed little. A 2005 review of staff and network members listed on GBN's Web site showed that 16 of 26 staff members on the site were women and 1 was a person of color. Of 126 network members listed, 123 were Caucasian and 20 were women.

30. Brand, interview, July 24, 2001.

31. Garreau, "Conspiracy of Heretics," 100. When asked what made a "remarkable person" remarkable, Brand replied, "One of the signs for me is each time you see these people they have news to report." Interview, July 24, 2001. His comment suggests that one measure of interest was in fact a person's extended network. After all, those who traveled more widely tended to bring more news. Schwartz, *Art of the Long View,* 97.

32. Warshall, "Informed Heart," 3; McIntire quoted ibid., 3; Wiener, *Human Use of Human Beings,* 96; Michael quoted in Warshall, "Informed Heart," 3.

33. Warshall, "Informed Heart," 6.

34. Ibid., 7.

35. Schwartz, and Brand, *1989 GBN Scenario Book,* 1; Einstein, "Think Tank Helps Prevent Future Shock."

36. Hoyt quoted in Stipp, "Stewart Brand," 172.

37. Stipp, "Stewart Brand," 172; Mauceli and Portante quoted ibid.

38. Kelly, interview, July 27, 2001.

39. "Cyberpunk Era"; Kadrey, "Cyberpunk 101 Reading List"; "Virtual Reality"; Dyson, "Groupware," 105–7; Brand, "Sticking Your Head In Cyberspace"; Barlow, "Crime and Puzzlement."

40. In the January 1985 issue of the *Whole Earth Review* (vol. 44), for instance, he and coeditor Art Kleiner published nine powerful critiques of the effect of computing. These included Langdon Winner's oft-cited "Mythinformation," Jerry Mander's "Six Grave Doubts about Computers," and Kleiner's own "Ambivalent Miseries of Personal Computing." On the front cover of the magazine, Kelly titled the issue "Computers as Poison." In the back of the issue, however, he printed an update of the *Whole Earth Software Catalog*. Stewart Brand explained the shift in his introduction to the update: "Having presented harsh words about computers in general, we here reveal our true colors with a whole section of largely kind words about computers in particular" (74).

41. Brand, "Introducing a Realm without Distance."

42. The ten categories of *Signal* were arranged in the following order: "Prime Information," "The Order of Languages," "Publishing Frontiers," "Network Societies," "Bodily Communication," "The Audible Signal," "Visual Knowledge," "Digital Thinking," "Information Civics," and "Mind Circuits."

43. Kelly, interview, July 27, 2001.

44. To get a feel for the role of biological metaphors at GBN, see Schwartz and Brand, *1989 GBN Scenario Book*, 6–9. Rothschild, *Bionomics*, xi, xv, quoted in Helmreich, "Artificial Life, Inc.," 502.

45. Helmreich, *Silicon Second Nature*; and "Artificial Life, Inc." For journalistic accounts of the Santa Fe Institute and artificial life, see Waldrop, *Complexity*; Levy, *Artificial Life*; and Lewin, *Complexity*.

46. Helmreich, *Silicon Second Nature*, 45.

47. As Helmreich suggests, this point of view represents the completion of a historical circle. In the postwar era, computers had helped give rise to an informational view of biological processes; now biology itself was being read back into computers in such a way that they could be seen as breeding grounds of "life." Ibid., 23.

48. Helmreich, "Artificial Life, Inc.," 491. Proceedings of both sessions were published as *The Economy as an Evolving Complex System: The Proceedings of the Evolutionary Paths of the Global Economy Workshop, Held September, 1987, in Santa Fe, New Mexico*.

49. See Langton, *Artificial Life*. Helmreich, *Silicon Second Nature*, 95–120; Kelly, "Nerd Theology," 388.

50. Kelly, "Nerd Theology," 390.

51. Kelly, *Out of Control*, 3.

52. Ibid., 1, 2, 3.

53. Ibid., 453, 5, 6.

54. Ibid., 7.

55. Ibid., 9.

56. Ibid., 21.

57. Ibid., 25.

58. Ibid., 25–26.

59. Ibid., 5, 189.

60. Ibid., 181.

61. Ibid., 385.

62. *Out of Control* was not widely reviewed at its release, but it was reviewed in several important publications and was extensively cited over the next several years. Early reviews included Poundstone, "Can You Trust Your Computer?"; Boisvert, "Weird Science"; Mitchell, "Mystifying the Net"; and Tetzeli, "Managing in a World Out of Control."

63. Taylor, "Control in an Age of Chaos," 65.

64. For critiques of Kelly's cyberrevolutionism, see Terranova, "Digital Darwin"; Best and Kellner, "Kelly's Complexity Theory"; Borsook, *Cyberselfish*.

65. As Walter Powell has pointed out, these forces included a flattening of corporate hierarchies, newly flexible employment structures for executives as well as laborers, globalization, and the integration of information technology into the firm. See Powell, "Capitalist Firm in the Twenty-First Century," esp. 40–61.

66. Ibid., 68.

67. The Long Now Foundation is still active at this writing. Founding members included computer designer Danny Hillis, Kevin Kelly, Esther Dyson, musician Brian Eno, Peter Schwartz, and others. In 1999 Brand published a book, *The Clock of the Long Now,* about the clock project.

Chapter 7

1. Rossetto, "Why Wired?"

2. John Plunkett, who, along with his wife, Barbara Kuhr, designed the magazine, explained, "If this magazine was supposed to be bringing news from the future, it had to look like it had just arrived from the future." Smith, "WiReD"; Rossetto, "Why Wired?"

3. Metcalfe, quoted in Gilbert, "Getting *Wired.*"

4. Barbrook and Cameron, "Californian Ideology." Louis Rossetto issued a famously fiery response to Barbrook and Cameron, which can be found at http://www.hrc.wmin.ac.uk/hrc/theory/californianideo/response/t.4.2.6.html. For critiques of *Wired* and of cyberlibertarianism more generally, see Borsook, *Cyberselfish;* Liu, *Laws of Cool;* Mosco, *Digital Sublime;* Terranova, *Network Culture.* As Thomas Streeter has pointed out, the Californian ideology emerged out of a wider tradition of Romantic individualism, within which Stewart Brand and the *Whole Earth Catalog* played an important role. See Streeter, "That Deep Romantic Chasm."

5. Gitlin, *Sixties,* 307.

6. Lehr and Rossetto, "New Right Credo," 24; Rossetto, interview, January 24, 2005.

7. Wolff, *Burn Rate,* 33–34.

8. "They were some of many people zooming by [and] not particularly memorable," Kelly recalled during an interview, July 27, 2001.

9. Keegan, "Reality Distortion Field."

10. Kelly, interview, July 27, 2001.

11. Gordon, "Does the 'New Economy' Measure Up?" 50. For more on developments in personal computing technology in this period, see Ceruzzi, *History of Modern Computing* (2003), 309–12.

12. Abbate, *Inventing the Internet*, 181, 196–99. Abbate has written the definitive history of the Internet; my account of the Internet and the rise of the World Wide Web in this period follows hers.

13. Ibid., 217.

14. Healtheon, for instance, saw its stock value rise 3,339 percent in this period; the price of eBay stock increased 3,269 percent. Perkins and Perkins, *Internet Bubble*, 13; Brenner, *Boom and the Bubble*, 2.

15. The relationship between information technology and productivity has been in dispute for some time. For a review and analysis of the literature on this issue in the late 1980s and early 1990s, see Brynjolfsson, "Productivity Paradox of Information Technology"; Gordon, "Does the 'New Economy' Measure Up?" 50, 57.

16. Shiller, *Irrational Exuberance*, 20–21, quoted in Thrift, "Romance Not the Finance Makes Business Worth Pursuing," 426; Alan Greenspan, "The American Economy in a World Context," at the 35th Annual Conference on Bank Structure and Competition, Federal Reserve Bank of Chicago, May 6, 1999, available at http://www.federalreserve.gov/board-docs/speeches/1999/19990506.htm, quoted in Gordon, "Does the 'New Economy' Measure Up?" 49.

17. Frank, *One Market Under God*, xiv, 356.

18. Rossetto quoted in Keegan, "Reality Distortion Field"; Battelle quoted in Smith, "WiReD."

19. Kelly, interview, July 27, 2001.

20. Smith, "WiReD."

21. Rossetto, interview, January 24, 2005; Rossetto, Metcalfe, et al., *Wired* business plan.

22. "Reader Report," internal document, *Wired*, January 1996, no pagination (in Louis Rossetto's personal collection).

23. Quittner, "Merry Pranksters Go to Washington," 79, 80, 81.

24. Ibid., 131.

25. Ibid., 80–81.

26. Ibid., 80, 81 (original emphasis).

27. Two years later, *Wired* ran a much shorter story on the Electronic Frontier Foundation, entitled "How Good People Helped Make a Bad Law" and written by Rogier van Bakel. The story detailed the EFF's role in passing a digital telephony bill that included a wiretapping provision, the foundation's financial and management troubles, and the return of its headquarters from Washington, D. C., to San Francisco. In this story, Barlow and other staffers appeared naive. As the story's extended headline put it, Washington had "reverse-engineered the EFF, driving it into dissension, debt, disgrace—and right out of town" (133). Yet, even as it detailed the personal failings of Barlow and others, the story left the larger metaphors of the earlier piece intact. Washington still needed reverse engineering—after all, it was entrenched bureaucrats who had driven the EFF away. The digital revolution was still under way—though the suits in Washington were trying to hold it back. And, like the countercultural revolution before it, the digital revolution would have to be headquartered in San Francisco.

28. Garreau, "Conspiracy of Heretics," 98; Best, quoted ibid., 154.

29. Michael McClure and Ramón Sender Barayón, respectively, quoted in Hafner, "Epic Saga of the WELL," 106, 109.

30. Hafner, "Epic Saga of the WELL," 112; Hapgood, "Media Lab at 10," 196.

31. Hapgood, "Media Lab at 10," 198.

32. Gilder and Dyson had known each other since the early 1980s, when Gilder had briefly covered semiconductors for Dyson's newsletter *Release 1.0*. For a thorough critical analysis of the "Magna Carta," see Moore, "Cyberspace Inc. and the Robber Baron Age."

33. Gilder, *Men and Marriage,* vii; Bronson, "George Gilder," 188.

34. For an account of these conferences, see Borsook, *Cyberselfish,* 59–61, 131–33.

35. Gilder, quoted in Kelly, "George Gilder," 39, 40.

36. Ibid., 40.

37. Wiener, *Human Use of Human Beings,* 96. Two years after running this piece, Kelly and *Wired* published a mild critique of Gilder's views by David Kline and Daniel Burstein, entitled "Is Government Obsolete?" Kline and Burstein took Gilder to task for supporting temporary monopolies in the telecommunications industries and for allowing the government virtually no role in shaping telecommunications markets. Yet even here, the authors celebrated the core tenets of the analogical agreement Kelly and Gilder had struck in their interview. Business, not government, was the "beating heart of all progress, the proving ground of all innovations in technology, and the creation of social wealth" (105). In Kline and Burstein's view, as in Gilder's, information systems were both a product of the "natural" system of free market capitalism and a sign of the progress that the system had made.

38. Bronson, "George Gilder," 188.

39. Borsook, "Release," 95, 97.

40. Ibid., 96.

41. Ibid., 124.

42. Brand, interview, July 24, 2001; Dyson, "Friend and Foe," 106.

43. Dyson et al., "Magna Carta," 295.

44. Ibid., 296, 297; U.S. Office of Scientific Research and Development, *Science, the Endless Frontier.*

45. Moore, "Cyberspace, Inc. and the Robber Baron Age," 317; Dyson et al., "Magna Carta," 303.

46. Dyson et al., "Magna Carta," 404.

47. Aufderheide, *Communications Policy and the Public Interest,* 4, 32, 37, 54, 78–81, 106–7.

48. Quarles quoted in Hipschman, "Who Speaks for Cyberspace?" For more coverage of the "Cyberspace and the American Dream II" conference, see Sayre, "Cyberspace and Newtonian Dreams"; and Kline, "'Friction-Free' Foolishness."

49. Brand's personal reaction to the libertarianism of the mid-1990s is hard to assess. When I spoke with him in 2001, he explained that he didn't "have a lot of patience for libertarianism these years." As he put it, "I don't like what Gingrich did to the country." Yet Brand had long shared Gingrich's rejection of interventionist government. "That whole victim mind-set—saying to government you're supposed to fix my problem—is total anathema to the Whole Earth," as Brand put it. Moreover, for many years Brand had celebrated business, technology, and the individual entrepreneur as key agents of social change, as had Gingrich. When asked about this connection and his rejection of Gingrich-style libertarianism in 2001, Brand replied, "I didn't make me a liberal. The Republicans made me a liberal." Interview, July 24, 2001.

50. Gingrich et al., *Contract with America;* Dyson, "Friend and Foe," 111.

51. Dyson, "Friend and Foe," 160.

52. Ibid., 107.

53. This is not to say Newt Gingrich saw himself in a countercultural light. On the contrary, in 1994 he told a gathering of Republicans, "There are profound things that went wrong starting with the Great Society and the counterculture and until we address them head-on we're going to have problems." *New York Times,* November 10, 1994, A1, quoted in Bromell, *Tomorrow Never Knows,* 7.

54. Schwartz and Leyden, "Long Boom," 118.

55. Ibid., 116.

56. Ibid., 168, 170.

57. Ibid., 171.

58. Kelly, *New Rules for the New Economy,* 6.

59. Ibid., 160. To get a feel for Internet-related work at the height of the dot-com bubble, see Bronson, *Nudist on the Late Shift;* and Ross, *No-Collar.* For a fascinating account of the social and psychological strategies dot-com workers used to manage the multiple risks of their employment, see Neff, "Organizing Uncertainty."

60. Byron, "Wired Ventures Is Worth Only $6 Million to $10 Million."

61. Throughout this expansion, *Wired* magazine remained the single most powerful source of income for the business. But according to some analysts, it too was losing money. In 1996, for instance, analysts estimated that *Wired* earned approximately $17 million in advertising revenues and approximately $10.4 million in circulation, for a gross income of $27.4 million. Gross total expenses, however, totaled $39.9 million. Its costs included $17.2 million in production and distribution, $15 million in sales and marketing, and $7.7 million for general and administration. All in all, *Wired* magazine alone lost something like $11.5 million in 1996 alone. Ibid.

62. For a detailed account of the offering process, see Wolf, *Wired,* 189–238; Byron, "Wired Ventures."

63. Wolff, *Burn Rate,* 47; Byron, "Wired Ventures."

Chapter 8

1. In this sense, these organizations resembled Max Weber's classic description of bureaucracies. See Weber, Gerth, and Mills, *From Max Weber,* 196–244. For an interpretation of the resemblances and their relationship to emerging forms of enterprise, see Paul DiMaggio, introduction to DiMaggio, *Twenty-First-Century Firm,* 10.

2. For accounts of this process at the macro-social level, see Harvey, *Condition of Postmodernity;* and Castells, *Rise of the Network Society.* For accounts of the ways that this process has affected employment and the structure of the firm, several edited collections are especially helpful, among them DiMaggio, *Twenty-First Century Firm;* and DeSanctis and Fulk, *Shaping Organization Form.* For an account of the rise of contracting and its effects on workers, see Barley and Kunda, *Gurus, Hired Guns, and Warm Bodies.*

3. Bell, *Coming of Post-Industrial Society;* Harvey, *Condition of Postmodernity;* Castells, *Rise of Network Society.* For related interpretations, see Piore and Sabel, *Second Industrial Divide;* and Lash and Urry, *End of Organized Capitalism.*

4. Castells, *Rise of Network Society,* 152–53. A number of scholars have disputed the notion that postindustrial society represents a break with the historical development of industrial capitalism. One of the earliest was James Beniger. In *Control Revolution,* Beniger traced to the late nineteenth century the increasing importance of information to economic life. James W. Cortada, in *Making of the Information Society,* has recently argued that information has been a key feature of Western and particularly American culture for

hundreds of years. For similar arguments on the knowledge worker, see Chandler and Cortada, *Nation Transformed by Information*. Scholars of a Marxist orientation have been particularly aggressive in challenging the notion that the postindustrial, postmodern, or network society models actually represent a new era in capitalism. For critiques in this vein, see Slack and Fejes, *Ideology of the Information Age;* Lyon, *Information Society;* and Garnham, "Information Society Theory as Ideology." For a thorough, critical introduction to the information society debates, see Webster, *Theories of the Information Society.*

5. Bell, *Coming of Post-Industrial Society,* 13.

6. Bell himself acknowledged this connection. "One might well say that 1945 to 1950 were the 'birth-years,' symbolically, of the post-industrial society," he wrote (ibid., 346). Yet, subsequent analysts have tended to downplay or ignore the role of cold war military research in shaping the network mode of production.

7. Ibid., 373. See, e.g., Lyon, *Information Society;* Zuboff, *In the Age of the Smart Machine;* Castells, *Rise of Network Society;* DeSanctis and Fulk, *Shaping Organization Form.* The impact of information technology on productivity per se remains an issue of substantial debate. See Gordon, "Does the 'New Economy' Measure Up?"

8. Bateson, *Mind and Nature,* 7.

9. Bell, *Coming of Post-Industrial Society,* 478, 480.

10. The classic statement of the power of loose connections to shape employment opportunities can be found in Granovetter, "The Strength of Weak Ties."

11. Inventors and designers have often played an entrepreneurial role in this regard. Bernard Carlson, for example, following Donald MacKenzie, has suggested that "inventors invent both artifacts and frames of meanings that guide how they manufacture and market their creations." Carlson, "Artifacts and Frames of Meaning," 176; see also MacKenzie, "Missile Accuracy." As Charles Bazerman has demonstrated in the case of the electric light, for instance, Thomas Edison was every bit as effective an inventor of new social and symbolic collaborations as he was of new wiring schemes. Bazerman, *Languages of Edison's Light.* Scholars focused on the social construction of technology have devoted similar attention to user communities. Wiebe Bijker, for example, in "Social Construction of Bakelite," has argued that the ensemble of beliefs and practices surrounding an emerging technology, an ensemble that he calls a "technological frame" (168) tends to emerge out of the interaction of user and inventor communities with each other and with the technology at hand. In a variation on this view, a number of digital media scholars have argued that new technologies, as they emerge, create new forms of embodied experience, which in turn lead users to turn both the machines and the new social experiences they afford into metaphors. See, e.g., Manovich, *Language of New Media;* and Wyatt, "Talking about the Future." Finally, many analysts have focused on the role of the press, both professional and popular, in shaping popular perceptions of new technologies. As Carolyn Marvin has shown in the case of electricity, for instance, the press can serve as both a powerful shaper of emerging technologies and a deep repository of the public's hopes and fears for the new devices. Marvin, *When Old Technologies Were New.*

12. Tesler, interview, July 26, 2001; Allison, interview, July 26, 2004.

13. For an overview of the traditional accounts and a critical study of the field, see Schudson, *Sociology of News.* Schudson, in *Discovering the News,* identifies journalistic norms as historical constructions.

14. Zelizer, *Covering the Body,* quotation on 8.

15. Gitlin, *Whole World Is Watching,* 78–129.

16. Turner, "How Digital Technology Found Utopian Ideology."

17. Fuller, *Ideas and Integrities*, 249.

18. Ullman, *Close to the Machine*, 126, 129.

19. Ibid., 100–101.

20. Ibid., 105.

21. For a compelling ethnography of contract workers in the United States, see Barley and Kunda, *Gurus, Hired Guns, and Warm Bodies*. Barley and Kunda demonstrate that although workers often leave full-time corporate employment in pursuit of self-fulfillment, they frequently find themselves transforming formerly personal time into time for training and the pursuit of new work. They also find that when contract workers are on the job, they often experience themselves as liminal members of work worlds in which they used to find feelings of community. For a compelling study of the effects of digital technologies on workers overseas, and particularly in India, see Aneesh, *Virtual Migration*.

22. Ullman, *Close to the Machine*, 127.

23. Barbrook and Cameron, "Californian Ideology."

24. The term *digerati* was almost certainly coined by John Brockman, a member of the downtown New York art scene of the early 1960s and an acquaintance of the USCO troupe; he went on to become a literary agent for many scientists and technologists. In 1996 he authored brief biographies of many of his friends and clients, including Brand, Dyson, Barlow, Kelly, Rheingold, and others, in a volume entitled *Digerati* and published by the fledgling book division of *Wired* magazine.

25. See Siegel and Markoff, *High Cost of High Tech*; and Hayes, *Behind the Silicon Curtain*.

26. Hayes, *Behind the Silicon Curtain*, 23, 54; Rogers and Larsen, *Silicon Valley Fever*, 144; Schoenberger, "Where Computers Go to Die."

27. Keniston, *Young Radicals*, 394.

Bibliography

Archival Sources

By far the richest collection of materials pertaining to the relationship between post–World War II technological research and the American counterculture resides in the Stanford University Library. I have made use of two kinds of resources there: collections of Whole Earth–related materials, including Stewart Brand's personal papers and diaries, and collections of papers and artifacts connected to the development of Silicon Valley.

Stanford hosts three collections of Whole Earth materials, two of which are open to the public. The first is the *Whole Earth Catalog* Records, 1969–1986 (Special Collections call number M1045). Although relatively thin on materials having to do with the *Catalog* between 1968 and 1972, these records offer extensive editorial files, correspondence, photographs, promotional materials, and issues of most editions of the *Catalog,* the *Supplement,* the *CoEvolution Quarterly,* and the *Whole Earth Review.* The Records of the Point Foundation, 1964–1975 (M1441), are also open to the public and give a comprehensive look at how the profits from the *Catalog* were disbursed in a series of small grants in the early 1970s. Finally, the library is custodian to the Papers of Stewart Brand, 1950–2000 (M1237). These papers include Brand's personal diaries, which I refer to as his "Notebooks" throughout the text. Brand's papers are not yet open to the public and most have not yet been cataloged. They include diaries and correspondence that span fifty years.

Stanford maintains a very large collection of materials related to computing in the region. For my purposes, I found several collections especially helpful. The Silicon Valley Ephemera collection (M0443) is a vast gathering of marketing materials, conference proceedings, technical manuals, and other materials pertaining to more than twenty firms from 1976 through the late 1990s. The Charles H. Irby Papers, 1962–1975 (M0671), also offer a varied assemblage of correspondence, memos, working notes, and technical reports. Irby was employed at SRI International and Xerox PARC, and his materials cover early work on ARPANET especially well. Lee Felsenstein's Papers, circa 1975–1995 (M1443), give a wide overview of Felsenstein's work in the heyday of personal computing and the decades that followed. Finally, programmer and computer educator Liza Loop's collection of computer club newsletters from the 1970s and the

1980s (Liza Loop Papers, 1972–1988, M1141), including complete collections of the Homebrew Computer Club newsletter and many editions of the *People's Computer Company*, offers a unique opportunity to read through debates among programmers, designers, hobbyists, and others in those years about what computers ought to become.

Printed and Electronic Sources

Abbate, Janet. *Inventing the Internet*. Cambridge, MA: MIT Press, 1999.

Alan and Heath [no surnames given]. "Centering." In Kahn et al., *Domebook One*, 46–47.

Albright, Thomas, and Charles Perry. "The Last Twelve Hours of the Whole Earth." In *The Seven Laws of Money*, edited by Michael Phillips, 121–27. Menlo Park, CA: Word Wheel; New York: Random House, 1974.

Anderson, Philip W., Kenneth Joseph Arrow, David Pines, and Santa Fe Institute. *The Economy as an Evolving Complex System: The Proceedings of the Evolutionary Paths of the Global Economy Workshop, Held September, 1987, in Santa Fe, New Mexico*. Redwood City, CA: Addison-Wesley, 1988.

Aneesh, A. *Virtual Migration: The Programming of Globalization*. Durham, NC: Duke University Press, 2006.

Ashby, Gordon, ed. *Whole Earth Catalog $1*. Menlo Park, CA: Portola Institute, July 1970.

Aufderheide, Patricia. *Communications Policy and the Public Interest: The Telecommunications Act of 1996*. New York: Guilford Press, 1999.

Bakardjieva, Maria. "Virtual Togetherness: An Everyday-Life Perspective." *Media, Culture, and Society* 25 (2003): 291–313.

Bakel, Rogier van. "How Good People Helped Make a Bad Law." *Wired*, February 1996.

Baldwin, J., and Stewart Brand. *Soft-Tech*. Sausalito, CA: Whole Earth Catalog, 1978.

Baltzell, E. Digby. *The Protestant Establishment: Aristocracy and Caste in America*. New York: Random House, 1964.

Barbrook, Richard. "The Hi-Tech Gift Economy." *First Monday* 3, no. 12 (December 1998). Available at http://www.firstmonday.org/issues/issue3_12/barbrook/index.html (accessed October 10, 2001).

Barbrook, Richard, and Andy Cameron. "The Californian Ideology (Extended Mix)." September 18, 1998. Available at http://www.hrc.wmin.ac.uk/hrc/theory/californianideo/main/t.4.2.html (accessed September 27, 2005).

Bardini, Thierry. *Bootstrapping: Douglas Engelbart, Coevolution, and the Origins of Personal Computing*. Stanford, CA: Stanford University Press, 2000.

Barley, Stephen R., and Gideon Kunda. *Gurus, Hired Guns, and Warm Bodies: Itinerant Experts in a Knowledge Economy*. Princeton, NJ: Princeton University Press, 2004.

Barlow, John Perry. "@home.on.the.ranch." 1998. Available at http://members.aye.net/~hippie/barlow/barlow01.htm (accessed November 15, 2004).

———. "Being in Nothingness: Virtual Reality and the Pioneers of Cyberspace." *Mondo 2000*, no. 2 (Summer 1990): 34–43.

———. "Crime and Puzzlement." Posted to the WELL June 8, 1990. Reprint in *Whole Earth Review*, no. 68 (Fall 1990): 44–57, available at http://www.eff.org/Misc/Publications/John_Perry_Barlow/HTML/crime_and_puzzlement_1.html (accessed September 27, 2005).

———. "A Declaration of the Independence of Cyberspace." 1996. Available at http://www.eff.org/~barlow/Declaration-Final.html (accessed November 15, 2004).

———. "Jack In, Young Pioneer! Keynote essay for the 1994 Computerworld College Edition." Available at http://www.eff.org/Misc/Publications/John_Perry_Barlow/ HTML/jack_in_young_pioneer.html (accessed September 27, 2005).

Barnes, Susan B. *Online Connections: Internet Interpersonal Relationships*. Creskill, NJ: Hampton Press, 2001.

Basch, Reva. "Living on the Net." *Artpaper*, December 1991. Available at http://www.well .com/user/reva/onthenet.mss (accessed September 27, 2005).

Bates, Albert. *Post-Communal Economic Experiments at the Farm in the Context of Developmental Communalism*. Available at http://www.thefarm.org/lifestyle/albertbates/akbp2.html (accessed October 14, 2005).

Bateson, Gregory. "Effects of Conscious Purpose on Human Adaptation." In Bateson, *Steps to an Ecology of Mind*, 446–53.

———. "Form, Substance, Difference." In Bateson, *Steps to an Ecology of Mind*, 454–71.

———. *Mind and Nature: A Necessary Unity*. New York: Dutton, 1979.

———. "The Roots of Ecological Crisis." In Bateson, *Steps to an Ecology of Mind*, 496–501.

———, ed. *Steps to an Ecology of Mind*. Chicago: University of Chicago Press, 1972.

Baym, Nancy. "The Emergence of Community in Computer-Mediated Communication." In Jones, *CyberSociety*, 138–63.

Bazerman, Charles. *The Languages of Edison's Light*. Cambridge, MA: MIT Press, 1999.

Belasco, Warren. *Appetite for Change: How the Counterculture Took on the Food Industry, 1966–1988*. New York: Pantheon, 1989.

Belgrad, Daniel. *The Culture of Spontaneity*. Chicago: University of Chicago Press, 1998.

Bell, Daniel. *The Coming of Post-Industrial Society: A Venture in Social Forecasting*. New York: Basic Books, 1973.

———. *The Cultural Contradictions of Capitalism*. New York: Basic Books, 1976.

Beniger, James R. *The Control Revolution: Technological and Economic Origins of the Information Society*. Cambridge, MA: Harvard University Press, 1986.

Berger, Bennett M. *The Survival of a Counterculture: Ideological Work and Everyday Life among Rural Communards*. Berkeley: University of California Press, 1981.

Berman, Morris. *The Reenchantment of the World*. Ithaca, NY: Cornell University Press, 1981.

Bertalanffy, Ludwig von. *General System Theory: Foundations, Development, Applications*. New York: G. Braziller, 1968.

Best, Steven, and Douglas Kellner. "Kevin Kelly's Complexity Theory: The Politics and Ideology of Self-Organizing Systems." *Organization and Environment* 12, no. 2 (1999): 141–62.

Bey, Hakim. *T.A.Z.: The Temporary Autonomous Zone, Ontological Anarchy, Poetic Terrorism*. Brooklyn, NY: Autonomedia, 1991.

Bijker, Wiebe E. "The Social Construction of Bakelite: Toward a Theory of Invention." In Bijker, Hughes, and Pinch, *Social Construction of Technological Systems*, 159–87.

Bijker, Wiebe E., Thomas Parke Hughes, and T. J. Pinch, eds. *The Social Construction of Technological Systems: New Directions in the Sociology and History of Technology*. Cambridge, MA: MIT Press, 1987.

Binkley, Sam. "The Seers of Menlo Park: The Discourse of Heroic Consumption in the Whole Earth Catalog." *Journal of Consumer Culture* 3, no. 3 (2003): 283–313.

Boczkowski, Pablo. *Digitizing the News: Innovation in Online Newspapers*. Cambridge, MA: MIT Press, 2004.

Boisvert, Bill. "Weird Science." *Voice Literary Supplement* 148 (September 1996): 14.

Borsook, Paulina. *Cyberselfish: A Critical Romp through the Terribly Libertarian Culture of High Tech*. New York: PublicAffairs, 2000.

———. "Release." *Wired,* November 1993.

Boulware, Jack. "Mondo 1995." *SF Weekly,* October 11, 1995. Available at http://www.suck .com/daily/95/11/07/mondo1995.html (accessed September 27, 2005).

Bourdieu, Pierre. "Marginalia—Some Additional Notes on the Gift." In Schrift, *Logic of the Gift,* 231–44.

———. "Selections from *The Logic of Practice*." In Schrift, *Logic of the Gift,* 190–230.

Bowker, Geoffrey C. "How to Be Universal: Some Cybernetic Strategies, 1943–1970." *Social Studies of Science* 23 (1993): 107–27.

———. *Science on the Run: Information Management and Industrial Geophysics at Schlumberger, 1920–1940*. Cambridge, MA: MIT Press, 1994.

Boyer, Paul S. *By the Bomb's Early Light: American Thought and Culture at the Dawn of the Atomic Age*. Chapel Hill: University of North Carolina Press, 1994.

Brand, Stewart. "Buckminster Fuller." In *Whole Earth Catalog,* edited by Stewart Brand, 3. Menlo Park, CA: Portola Institute, 1968.

———. "Civilization and Its Contents." In Rheingold, *Millennium Whole Earth Catalog,* 5.

———. *The Clock of the Long Now: Time and Responsibility*. New York: Basic Books, 1999.

———. *The Electronic Whole Earth Catalog*. San Rafael, CA: Broderbund Software, 1989.

———. *The Essential Whole Earth Catalog: Access to Tools and Ideas*. Garden City, NY: Double-day, 1986.

———. "History." In *Whole Earth Epilog,* edited by Stewart Brand, 752–53. San Francisco: Point Foundation, 1974.

———. *How Buildings Learn: What Happens after They're Built*. New York: Viking, 1994.

———. "How to Do a Whole Earth Catalog." In Brand, *Last Whole Earth Catalog,* 435–41.

———. *II Cybernetic Frontiers*. New York: Random House, 1974.

———. "Introducing a Realm without Distance." In Kelly, *Signal,* 3.

———. "'Keep Designing': How the Information Economy Is Being Created and Shaped by the Hacker Ethic." *Whole Earth Review* 46 (May 1985): 44–55.

———, ed. *The Last Whole Earth Catalog*. Menlo Park, CA: Portola Institute, 1971.

———. "Local Dependency." *CoEvolution Quarterly* 8 (Winter 1975): 5.

———. *The Media Lab: Inventing the Future at MIT*. New York: Viking, 1987.

———. "Money." In Brand, *Last Whole Earth Catalog,* 438.

———. *The Next Whole Earth Catalog: Access to Tools*. Sausalito, CA: Point Foundation, 1980.

———. "The Sky Starts at Your Feet." In Brand, *Space Colonies,* 5–7.

———, ed. *Space Colonies*. Sausalito, CA: Whole Earth Catalog, 1977.

———. "Space Colonies: Summary." *CoEvolution Quarterly* 9 (Spring 1976): 4.

———. "Spacewar: Fanatic Life and Symbolic Death among the Computer Bums." *Rolling Stone,* December 7, 1972.

———. "Sticking Your Head in Cyberspace." *Whole Earth Review* 63 (Summer 1989): 84–85.

———, ed. *The Updated Last Whole Earth Catalog: Access to Tools*. San Francisco: Point Foun-dation, 1974.

———. "We Owe It All to the Hippies." *Time* 145, special issue, Spring 1995.

———, ed. *Whole Earth Catalog*. Menlo Park, CA: Portola Institute, Spring 1969.

————, ed. *Whole Earth Catalog*. Menlo Park, CA: Portola Institute, Fall 1969.

————, ed. *Whole Earth Catalog One Dollar*. Menlo Park, CA: Portola Institute, January 1971.

————, ed. *Whole Earth Epilog: Access to Tools*. San Francisco: Point Foundation, 1974.

————. *Whole Earth Software Catalog*. Garden City, NY: Quantum Press/Doubleday, 1984.

————. *Whole Earth Software Catalog for 1986*. Garden City, NY: Quantum Press/Doubleday, 1985.

Brand, Stewart, Joe Bonner, Jan Ford, Diana Shugart, and Annie Helmuth, eds. *The Difficult but Possible Supplement to the Whole Earth Catalog*. Menlo Park, CA: Portola Institute, September 1969.

Brand, Stewart, Joe Bonner, and Ann Helmuth, eds. *The Difficult but Possible Supplement to the Whole Earth Catalog*. Menlo Park, CA: Portola Institute, January 1969.

————, eds. *The Difficult but Possible Supplement to the Whole Earth Catalog*. Menlo Park, CA: Portola Institute, July 1969.

Brand, Stewart, Ann Helmuth, Joe Bonner, Tom Duckworth, Lois Brand, and Hal Hershey, eds. *The Difficult but Possible Supplement to the Whole Earth Catalog*. Menlo Park, CA: Portola Institute, March 1969.

Brand, Stewart, Lloyd Kahn, and Sarah Kahn, eds. *Whole Earth Catalog*. Menlo Park, CA: Portola Institute, Spring 1970.

Brand, Stewart, Cappy McClure, Hal Hershey, Mary McCabe, and Fred Richardson, eds. *Whole Earth Catalog $1*. Menlo Park, CA: Portola Institute, January 1970.

Branwyn, Gareth. *Whole Earth Review*. A Web site available at http://www.streettech.com/bcp/BCPgraf/CyberCulture/wholeearthreview.html (accessed August 6, 2004).

Braunstein, Peter. "Forever Young: Insurgent Youth and the Sixties Culture of Rejuvenation." In *Imagine Nation*, edited by Peter Braunstein and Michael William Doyle, 243–73. New York: Routledge, 2002.

Breines, Wini. *Community and Organization in the New Left, 1962–1968: The Great Refusal*. New York: Praeger; South Hadley, MA: J. F. Bergin, 1982.

Brenner, Robert. *The Boom and the Bubble: The US in the World Economy*. London: Verso, 2002.

Brockman, John. *Digerati: Encounters with the Cyber Elite*. San Francisco: HardWired, 1996.

Bromell, Nicholas Knowles. *Tomorrow Never Knows: Rock and Psychedelics in the 1960s*. Chicago: University of Chicago Press, 2000.

Bronson, Po. "George Gilder." *Wired,* March 1996.

————. *The Nudist on the Late Shift*. New York: Random House, 1999.

Brooks, David. *Bobos in Paradise: The New Upper Class and How They Got There*. New York: Simon and Schuster, 2000.

Brown, John Seely, and Paul Duguid. *The Social Life of Information*. Boston: Harvard Business School Press, 2000.

Bryant, John, William Aspray, Andrew Goldstein, and Frederik Nebeker. *Rad Lab: Oral Histories Documenting World War II Activities at the MIT Radiation Laboratory*. Piscataway, NJ: IEEE Center for the History of Electrical Engineering, 1993.

Brynjolfsson, Erik. "The Productivity Paradox of Information Technology." *Communications of the ACM* 36, no. 12 (1993): 67–77.

Buderi, Robert. *The Invention That Changed the World: How a Small Group of Radar Pioneers Won the Second World War and Launched a Technological Revolution*. New York: Simon and Schuster, 1996.

Burner, David. *Making Peace with the 60s*. Princeton, NJ: Princeton University Press, 1996.

Burnham, Jack. "Art and Technology: The Panacea That Failed." In *The Myths of Information: Technology and Postindustrial Culture,* edited by Kathleen Woodward, 200–215. Madison, WI: Coda Press, 1980.

———. *Beyond Modern Sculpture: The Effects of Science and Technology on the Sculpture of This Century*. New York: G. Braziller, 1968.

———. "Systems Esthetics." *Artforum,* September 1968.

Burt, Ronald S. "The Network Entrepreneur." In *Entrepreneurship: The Social Science View,* edited by Richard Swedberg, 281–307. Oxford: Oxford University Press, 2000.

———. *Structural Holes: The Social Structure of Competition*. Cambridge, MA: Harvard University Press, 1992.

Bush, Vannevar. "As We May Think." *Atlantic Monthly,* July 1945. Reprint in *The New Media Reader,* edited by Noah Wardrip-Fruin and Nick Montfort, 35–48 (Cambridge, MA: MIT Press, 2003). (Page citations are to the 2003 reprint.)

Byerly, Victoria Morris. *Gerd Stern, "From Beat Scene Poet to Psychedelic Multimedia Artist in San Francisco and Beyond, 1948–1978": An Oral History Conducted in 1996*. Berkeley, CA: Regional Oral History Office, The Bancroft Library, University of California, Berkeley, 2001.

Byron, Christopher. "Wired Ventures Is Worth Only $6 Million to $10 Million." *Upside Today,* January 31, 1997. http://www.upside.com/texis/mvm/print- (accessed October 10, 2000; site now discontinued).

Cage, John. *A Year from Monday*. Middletown, CT: Wesleyan University Press, 1967.

Callon, Michel. "Some Elements of a Sociology of Translation: Domestication of the Scallops and the Fishermen of St. Brieuc Bay." In *Power, Action, and Belief: A New Sociology of Knowledge?* edited by John Law, 196–229. London: Routledge and Kegan Paul, 1986.

Carlson, W. Bernard. "Artifacts and Frames of Meaning: Thomas A. Edison, His Managers, and the Cultural Construction of Motion Pictures." In *Shaping Technology/Building Society: Studies in Sociotechnical Change,* edited by Wiebe E. Bijker and John Law, 175–98. Cambridge, MA: MIT Press, 1992.

Carroll, Peter N. *It Seemed Like Nothing Happened: The Tragedy and Promise of America in the 1970s*. New York: Holt, Rinehart, and Winston, 1982.

Case, John, and Rosemary C. R. Taylor. *Co-ops, Communes, and Collectives: Experiments in Social Change in the 1960s and 1970s*. New York: Pantheon, 1979.

Castells, Manuel. *The Rise of the Network Society*. Cambridge, MA: Blackwell, 1996.

Ceruzzi, Paul E. *A History of Modern Computing*. Cambridge, MA: MIT Press, 1998; 2nd ed., 2003.

Chandler, Alfred Dupont, and James W. Cortada. *A Nation Transformed by Information: How Information Has Shaped the United States from Colonial Times to the Present*. Oxford: Oxford University Press, 2000.

Chandler, John, and Lucy Lippard. "The Dematerialization of Art." *Art International,* February 20, 1968.

Cheal, David J. *The Gift Economy*. London: Routledge, 1988.

Coate, John. "Cyberspace Innkeeping: Building Online Community." January 1998 (rev. 1992, 1993, and 1998). http://www.sfgate.com/~tex/innkeeping (accessed February 15, 2001; site now discontinued).

Coate, John, and Cliff Figallo. "Farm Stories (From the True Confessions Conference on the WELL)." *Whole Earth Review* 60 (Fall 1988): 88–101.

Colstad, Ken. "Community Memory." *People's Computer Company* 4, no. 1 (1975): 16.

Conway, Flo, and Jim Siegelman. *Dark Hero of the Information Age: In Search of Norbert Wiener, the Father of Cybernetics.* New York: Basic Books, 2005.

Cortada, James W. *The Making of the Information Society: Experience, Consequences, and Possibilities.* Upper Saddle River, NJ: Prentice Hall, 2002.

———. *Rise of the Knowledge Worker.* Boston: Butterworth-Heinemann, 1998.

"Cyberpunk Era: Interviews with William Gibson." *Whole Earth Review* 63 (Summer 1989): 78–82.

Davidson, Sara. "Hippie Families on Open Land." *Harper's Magazine,* June 1970.

Davis, Erik. *Techgnosis: Myth, Magic, Mysticism in the Age of Information.* New York: Harmony Books, 1998.

"Da WELL Been Beddy, Beddy Goot to Me." Work Conference, in the WELL, topic 135, accessed September 15, 2004; no longer available.

Deloria, Philip Joseph. *Playing Indian.* New Haven, CT: Yale University Press, 1998.

Dery, Mark. *Flame Wars: The Discourse of Cyberculture.* Durham, NC: Duke University Press, 1994.

DeSanctis, Gerardine, and Janet Fulk, eds. *Shaping Organization Form: Communication, Connection, and Community.* Thousand Oaks, CA: Sage, 1999.

Diamond, Stephen. *What the Trees Said: Life on a New Age Farm.* New York: Delacorte Press, 1971.

Dibbell, Julian. *My Tiny Life: Crime and Passion in a Virtual World.* New York: Holt, 1998.

DiMaggio, Paul J., ed. *The Twenty-first Century Firm: Changing Economic Organization in International Perspective.* Princeton, NJ: Princeton University Press, 2001.

Draper, Hal. *Berkeley: The New Student Revolt.* New York: Grove Press, 1965.

Duberman, Martin B. *Black Mountain: An Exploration in Community.* New York: Dutton, 1972.

Dyson, Esther. "Friend and Foe." *Wired,* August 1995.

———. "Groupware." *Whole Earth Review* 64 (Fall 1989): 105–7.

———. *Release 2.0: A Design for Living in the Digital Age.* New York: Broadway Books, 1997.

Dyson, Esther, George Gilder, George Keyworth, and Alvin Toffler. "Cyberspace and the American Dream: A Magna Carta for the Knowledge Age (Release 1.2, August 22, 1994)." *Information Society* 12, no. 3 (1996): 295–308.

Echols, Alice. *Daring to Be Bad: Radical Feminism in America, 1967–1975.* Minneapolis: University of Minnesota Press, 1989.

Edwards, Paul N. *The Closed World: Computers and the Politics of Discourse in Cold War America.* Cambridge, MA: MIT Press, 1996.

Ehrlich, Paul R. "CoEvolution and the Biology of Communities." *CoEvolution Quarterly* 1 (Spring 1974): 40–44.

Ehrlich, Paul R., and Richard W. Holm. *The Process of Evolution.* New York: McGraw-Hill, 1963.

Einstein, David. "Think Tank Helps Prevent Future Shock." *San Francisco Chronicle,* June 10, 1995, D1.

Ellis, David, Rachel Oldridge, and Ana Vasconcelos. "Community and Virtual Community." In *Annual Review of Information Science and Technology,* edited by Blaise Cronin, 145–86. Medford, NJ: Information Today, 2004.

Elmer-DeWitt, Phillip. "Dreaming the Impossible at M.I.T." *Time,* August 31, 1987.

———. "Let Us Now Praise Famous Hackers." *Time,* December 3, 1984.

Engelbart's Unfinished Revolution. Stanford University Libraries and Institute for the Future, Palo Alto, 1998. Videorecording.

Estellachild, Vivian. "Hippie Communes." *Women: A Journal of Liberation* (Winter 1971): 40–43.

Evans, Sara M. *Personal Politics: The Roots of Women's Liberation in the Civil Rights Movement and the New Left.* New York: Knopf, 1979.

"Experiences of Women On Line." Electronic Frontier Foundation Conference, in the WELL, topic 448. This source available to WELL subscribers.

"Experiences of Women On Line (Continued)." Electronic Frontier Foundation Conference, in the WELL, topic 476. This source available to WELL subscribers.

Fairfield, Richard. *Communes U.S.A.* San Francisco: Alternatives Foundation, 1971.

Farber, David R., and Eric Foner. *The Age of Great Dreams: America in the 1960s.* New York: Hill and Wang, 1994.

Feigelson, Naomi. "We Are All One. Who R U." *Cheetah* 1 (1968): 30–35, 74–76.

Felsenstein, Lee. "Sol: The Inside Story." *ROM Magazine,* July 1977.

Figallo, Cliff. "Small Town on the Internet Highway System." Paper presented at the Public Access to the Internet Conference, John F. Kennedy School of Government, Harvard University, May 1993; updated for the Web September 1993. Available at http://www.eff .org/pub/Net_culture/Virtual_community/well_figallo.article (accessed June 13, 2000).

Fike, Rupert. *Voices from the Farm: Adventures in Community Living.* Summertown, TN: Book Publishing, 1998.

Fitzgerald, Frances. *Cities on a Hill: A Journey through Contemporary American Cultures.* New York: Simon and Schuster, 1986.

Florin, Fabrice, and New Dimension Films. *Hackers: Wizards of the Electronic Age.* New Dimension Films, Eugene, OR, 1985. 1 videocassette (VHS) (27 min.).

Frank, Thomas. *The Conquest of Cool: Business Culture, Counterculture, and the Rise of Hip Consumerism.* Chicago: University of Chicago Press, 1997.

———. *One Market Under God: Extreme Capitalism, Market Populism, and the End of Economic Democracy.* New York: Doubleday, 2000.

Freiberger, Paul, and Michael Swaine. *Fire in the Valley: The Making of the Personal Computer.* 2nd ed. New York: McGraw-Hill, 2000.

"FSM Newsletter." Available at http://lists.village.virginia.edu/sixties/HTML_docs/ Resources/Primary/Manifestos/FSM_fold_bend.html (accessed January 8, 2005).

Fuller, R. Buckminster. *Ideas and Integrities: A Spontaneous Autobiographical Disclosure.* Englewood Cliffs, NJ: Prentice-Hall, 1963.

Fuller, R. Buckminster, and Robert Snyder. *R. Buckminster Fuller: An Autobiographical Monologue Scenario Documented and Edited by Robert Snyder.* New York: St. Martin's Press, 1980.

Galbraith, John Kenneth. *The New Industrial State.* 4th ed. Boston: Houghton Mifflin, 1985.

Galison, Peter. "The Ontology of the Enemy: Norbert Wiener and the Cybernetic Vision." *Critical Inquiry* 21 (Autumn 1994): 228–66.

———. "Trading Zone: Coordinating Action and Belief." In *The Science Studies Reader,* edited by Mario Biagioli, 137–60. New York: Routledge, 1999.

Galison, Peter, Bruce Hevly, and Rebecca Lowen. "Controlling the Monster: Stanford and the Growth of Physics Research, 1935–1962." In *Big Science: The Growth of Large-Scale Research,* edited by Peter Galison and Bruce Hevly, 46–77. Stanford, CA: Stanford University Press, 1992.

Gardner, Hugh. *The Children of Prosperity: Thirteen Modern American Communes*. New York: St. Martin's Press, 1978.

Garnham, Nicholas. "Information Society Theory as Ideology: A Critique." *Loisir et Société (Society and Leisure)* 21, no. 1 (1998): 97–120.

Garreau, Joel. "Conspiracy of Heretics." *Wired,* November 1994.

Gaskin, Stephen. *Hey Beatnik! This Is the Farm Book, by Stephen and the Farm*. Summertown, TN: Book Publishing, 1974.

Gere, Charlie. *Digital Culture*. London: Reaktion, 2002.

Ghamari-Tabrizi, Sharon. *The Worlds of Herman Kahn: The Intuitive Science of Thermonuclear War*. Cambridge, MA: Harvard University Press, 2005.

Gibson, William. *Neuromancer*. New York: Ace Books, 1984.

Gilbert, Matthew. "Getting *Wired*." *Boston Sunday Globe,* September 18, 1994.

Gilder, George F. *Men and Marriage*. Gretna: Pelican, 1986.

———. *Telecosm: How Infinite Bandwidth Will Revolutionize Our World*. New York: Free Press, 2000.

———. *Wealth and Poverty*. New York: Basic Books, 1981.

Gingrich, Newt, Richard K. Armey, Ed Gillespie, and Bob Schellhas. *Contract with America: The Bold Plan by Rep. Newt Gingrich, Rep. Dick Armey, and the House Republicans to Change the Nation*. New York: Times Books, 1994.

Ginsberg, Allen. "The New Consciousness." In *Composed on the Tongue: Literary Conversations, 1966–1977*, edited by Donald Allen, 63–93. San Francisco: Grey Fox Press, 1980.

Gitlin, Todd. *The Sixties: Years of Hope, Days of Rage*. New York: Bantam Books, 1987.

———. *The Whole World Is Watching: Mass Media in the Making and Unmaking of the New Left*. Berkeley: University of California Press, 1980.

Glessing, Robert J. *The Underground Press in America*. Bloomington: Indiana University Press, 1970.

Glossbrenner, Alfred. *The Complete Handbook of Personal Computer Communications: Everything You Need to Go Online with the World*. 2nd ed. New York: St. Martin's Press, 1985.

Gordon, Robert J. "Does the 'New Economy' Measure up to the Great Inventions of the Past?" *Journal of Economic Perspectives* 14, no. 4 (2000): 49–74.

Gordon, W. Terrence. *Marshall McLuhan: Escape into Understanding: A Biography*. New York: Basic Books, 1997.

Gosse, Van. "A Movement of Movements: The Definition and Periodization of the New Left." In *A Companion to Post-1945 America,* edited by Jean-Christophe Agnew and Roy Rosenzweig, 277–302. Malden, MA: Blackwell, 2002.

Granovetter, Mark S. "The Strength of Weak Ties." *American Journal of Sociology* 78, no. 6 (1973): 1360–80.

Gravy, Wavy. *The Hog Farm and Friends*. New York: Links Books, 1974.

Grossberg, Lawrence. "On Postmodernism and Articulation: An Interview with Stuart Hall." In *Stuart Hall: Critical Dialogues in Cultural Studies,* edited by David Morley and Kuan-Hsing Chen, 131–50. London: Routledge, 1996.

Grossman, Wendy. *Net.Wars*. New York: New York University Press, 1997.

Guerlac, Henry. *Radar in World War II: The History of Modern Physics, 1800–1950*. Vol. 8. Los Angeles: Tomash; New York: American Institute of Physics, 1987.

Guilbaut, Serge. *How New York Stole the Idea of Modern Art: Abstract Expressionism, Freedom, and the Cold War*. Chicago: University of Chicago Press, 1983.

Gurdjieff, Georges Ivanovitch. *Meetings with Remarkable Men.* New York: Dutton, 1974.

Hafner, Katie. "The Epic Saga of the WELL." *Wired,* May 1997. Available at http://www
.wired.com/wired/archive/5.05/ff_well_pr.html (accessed September 22, 2003).

———. *The Well: A Story of Love, Death, and Real Life in the Seminal Online Community.*
New York: Carroll and Graf, 2001.

Hafner, Katie, and John Markoff. *Cyberpunk: Outlaws and Hackers on the Computer Frontier.*
New York: Simon and Schuster, 1991.

Hagel, John, and Arthur Armstrong. *Net Gain: Expanding Markets through Virtual Communities.* Boston: Harvard Business School Press, 1997.

Hampton, Keith N., and Barry Wellman. "Examining Community in the Digital Neighborhood: Early Results from Canada's Wired Suburb." In *Digital Cities: Technologies, Experiences, and Future Perspectives,* edited by Toru Ishida and Katherine Isbister, 194–208.
Berlin: Springer, 2000.

Hapgood, Fred. "The Media Lab at 10." *Wired,* November 1995.

Haraway, Donna J. "The High Cost of Information in Post–World War II Evolutionary
Biology: Ergonomics, Semiotics, and the Sociobiology of Communication Systems."
Philosophical Forum 13, nos. 2–3 (1981–82): 244–78.

Harman, Willis W., and Howard Rheingold. *Higher Creativity: Liberating the Unconscious for
Breakthrough Insights.* Los Angeles: J. P. Tarcher, 1984.

Harries-Jones, Peter. *A Recursive Vision: Ecological Understanding and Gregory Bateson.*
Toronto: University of Toronto Press, 1995.

Harvey, David. *The Condition of Postmodernity: An Enquiry into the Origins of Cultural Change.*
Oxford: Blackwell, 1989.

Hayes, Dennis. *Behind the Silicon Curtain: The Seductions of Work in a Lonely Era.* London:
Free Association Press, 1989.

Hayles, N. Katherine. *How We Became Posthuman: Virtual Bodies in Cybernetics, Literature, and
Informatics.* Chicago: University of Chicago Press, 1999.

Healy, Dave. "Cyberspace and Place: The Internet as Middle Landscape on the Electronic
Frontier." In *Internet Culture,* edited by David Porter, 55–68. New York: Routledge, 1997.

Hedgepeth, William. *The Alternative: Communal Life in New America.* New York: Macmillan,
1970.

Heelas, Paul. *The New Age Movement: The Celebration of the Self and the Sacralization of
Modernity.* Oxford: Blackwell, 1996.

Heims, Steve J. *Constructing a Social Science for Post-War America: The Cybernetics Group,
1946–1953.* Cambridge, MA: MIT Press, 1991.

———. "Gregory Bateson and the Mathematicians: From Interdisciplinary Interaction
to Societal Functions." *Journal of the History of the Behavioral Sciences* 13 (1977):
141–59.

———. *John Von Neumann and Norbert Wiener: From Mathematics to the Technologies of Life and
Death.* Cambridge, MA: MIT Press, 1980.

Helmreich, Stefan. "Artificial Life, Inc.: Darwin and Commodity Fetishism from Santa Fe to
Silicon Valley." *Science as Culture* 10, no. 4 (2001): 483–504.

———. *Silicon Second Nature: Culturing Artificial Life in a Digital World.* Berkeley: University
of California Press, 2000.

Henwood, Doug. *After the New Economy.* New York: New Press, 2003.

Herring, Susan. "Gender Differences in Computer-Mediated Communication: Bringing Familiar Baggage to the New Frontier." Paper presented at the American Library Association Annual Convention, Miami, FL, 1994.

Hiltz, Starr Roxanne, and Murray Turoff. *The Network Nation: Human Communication via Computer.* Reading, MA: Addison-Wesley, 1978.

Hiltzik, Michael A. *Dealers of Lightning: Xerox PARC and the Dawn of the Computer Age.* New York: HarperBusiness, 1999.

Hipschman, David. "Who Speaks for Cyberspace?" Posted September 14, 1995, to *Web Review* at http://www.gnn.org (site now discontinued); reposted December 5, 1995, to http://www.balikinos.de/dokfest/1995/reviewof.htm (accessed July 16, 2005).

Hitt, Jack, and Paul Tough. "Forum: Is Computer Hacking a Crime?" *Harper's Magazine,* March 1990.

Holloway, Mark. *Heavens on Earth: Utopian Communities in America, 1680–1880.* New York: Dover, 1966.

Horrocks, Christopher. *Marshall McLuhan and Virtuality.* Cambridge: Icon Books, 2000.

Houriet, Robert. *Getting Back Together.* New York: Coward McCann and Geoghegan, 1971.

Hughes, Thomas Park. *Rescuing Prometheus.* New York: Pantheon, 1998.

humdog. "Pandora's Vox: On Community in Cyberspace." In *High Noon on the Electronic Frontier: Conceptual Issues in Cyberspace,* edited by Peter Ludlow, 437–44. Cambridge, MA: MIT Press, 1996.

Hutchins, Edwin. *Cognition in the Wild.* Cambridge, MA: MIT Press, 1995.

Hyde, Lewis. *The Gift: Imagination and the Erotic Life of Property.* New York: Random House, 1983.

Innis, Harold Adams. *The Bias of Communication.* Toronto: University of Toronto Press, 1964.

———. *Empire and Communications.* Oxford: Clarendon Press, 1950.

Jamison, Andrew, and Ron Eyerman. *Seeds of the Sixties.* Berkeley: University of California Press, 1994.

Jankowski, Nicholas W. "Creating Community with Media: History, Theories, and Scientific Investigations." In *Handbook of New Media: Social Shaping and Consequences of ICTs,* edited by Leah A. Lievrouw and Sonia M. Livingstone, 34–49. London: Sage, 2002.

Jasanoff, Sheila. "Ordering Knowledge, Ordering Society." In *States of Knowledge: The Co-Production of Science and Social Order,* edited by Sheila Jasanoff, 13–45. New York: Routledge, 2004.

Jerome, Judson. *Families of Eden: Communes and the New Anarchism.* New York: Seabury Press, 1974.

Jones, Steve, ed. *CyberSociety: Computer-Mediated Communication and Community.* Thousand Oaks, CA: Sage, 1995.

———. *CyberSociety 2.0: Revisiting Computer-Mediated Communication and Community.* Thousand Oaks, CA: Sage, 1998.

———. "Understanding Community in the Information Age." In Jones, *CyberSociety,* 10–35.

Joselit, David. *American Art since 1945.* London: Thames and Hudson, 2003.

Kadrey, Richard. "Cyberpunk 101 Reading List." *Whole Earth Review* 63 (Summer 1989): 83.

Kahn, Herman. "From Present to Future: The Problems of Transition to a Postindustrial Society." *CoEvolution Quarterly* 11 (Fall 1976): 4–16.

———. *On Escalation: Metaphors and Scenarios.* New York: Praeger, 1965.

———. *On Thermonuclear War*. Princeton, NJ: Princeton University Press, 1960.

———. *Thinking about the Unthinkable*. New York: Horizon Press, 1962.

Kahn, Herman, Jerry Brown, and Amory Lovins. "The New Class." *CoEvolution Quarterly* 13 (Spring 1977): 8–39.

Kahn, Herman, Anthony J. Wiener, and Hudson Institute. *The Year 2000: A Framework for Speculation on the Next Thirty-Three Years*. New York: Macmillan, 1967.

Kahn, Lloyd, Jay Baldwin, Kathleen Whitacre, Cappy McClure, Jonathan Kanter, Sarah Kahn, and Robert Easton. *Domebook One*. Los Gatos, CA: Pacific Domes, 1970.

Kahn, Lloyd, and Pacific Domes. *Domebook Two*. 3rd ed. Bolinas, CA: Shelter, 1974.

Kanter, Rosabeth Moss. *Commitment and Community*. Cambridge, MA: Harvard University Press, 1972.

———, ed. *Communes: Creating and Managing the Collective Life*. New York: Harper and Row, 1973.

———. "Family Organization and Sex Roles in American Communes." In Kanter, *Communes*, 287–307.

———. "Leadership and Decision-Making." In Kanter, *Communes*, 143–49.

Kaprow, Allan. "Happenings Are Dead." In *Essays on the Blurring of Art and Life*, by Allan Kaprow; edited by Jeff Kelley, 59–65. Berkeley: University of California Press, 1993. Originally published in 1966.

———. "Happenings in the New York Scene." In *Essays on the Blurring of Art and Life*, by Allan Kaprow; edited by Jeff Kelley, 15–26. Berkeley: University of California Press, 1993. Originally published in 1961.

Kaprow, Allan, Gutai Bijutsu Kyokai, and Jean Jacques Lebel. *Assemblage, Environments, and Happenings*. New York: H. N. Abrams, 1966.

Kay, Alan. "Turning Points." Kyoto Prize Commemorative Lecture, Inamori Foundation, Kyoto, Japan. Delivered November 11, 2004.

Kay, Lily E. "How a Genetic Code Became an Information System." In *Systems, Experts, and Computers*, edited by Thomas P. Hughes and Agatha C. Hughes, 463–92. Cambridge, MA: MIT Press, 2000.

Keegan, Paul. "Reality Distortion Field." *UpsideToday*, January 31, 1997.

Kelly, Kevin. "The Birth of a Network Nation." *New Age Journal*, October 1984.

———. "The Computational Metaphor." *Whole Earth* 95 (Winter 1998): 5.

———. "George Gilder: When Bandwidth Is Free." *Wired*, September–October 1993.

———. "Nerd Theology." *Technology in Society* 21 (1999): 387–92.

———. *New Rules for the New Economy: 10 Radical Strategies for a Connected World*. New York: Viking, 1998.

———. *Out of Control: The Rise of Neo-Biological Civilization*. Reading, MA: Addison-Wesley, 1994.

———, ed. *Signal*. Sausalito, CA: Point Foundation, 1988.

Kendall, Lori. "Virtual Community." In *Encyclopedia of New Media*, edited by Steve Jones, 467–70. Thousand Oaks, CA: Sage, 2003.

Keniston, Kenneth. *Young Radicals: Notes on Committed Youth*. New York: Harcourt Brace and World, 1968.

Kennedy, John F. "Address Accepting the Democratic Party Nomination for the Presidency of the United States, July 15, 1960." John F. Kennedy Library and Museum. Available at http://www.jfklibrary.org/j071560.htm (accessed May 15, 2005).

Kenner, Hugh. *Bucky: A Guided Tour of Buckminster Fuller.* New York: Morrow, 1973.

Kerr, Clark. *The Uses of the University.* Cambridge, MA: Harvard University Press, 1963.

Kesey, Ken. "Ken Kesey Was a Successful Dope Fiend." In Brand, *Whole Earth Catalog One Dollar,* 3–4.

———. *One Flew Over the Cuckoo's Nest, a Novel.* New York: Viking Press, 1962.

King, James. "The Cultural Construction of Cyberspace." Ph.D. diss., King Alfred's College, University of Southampton, 2000.

Kirk, Andrew. "Appropriating Technology: The Whole Earth Catalog and Counterculture Environmental Politics." *Environmental History* 6, no. 3 (July 2001): 374–94.

———. "'Machines of Loving Grace': Alternative Technology, Environment, and the Counterculture." In *Imagine Nation: The American Counterculture of the 1960s and 70s,* edited by Peter Braunstein and Michael William Doyle, 353–78. New York: Routledge, 2002.

Kleiman, Jordan Benson. "The Appropriate Technology Movement in American Political Culture." Ph.D. diss., University of Rochester, 2000.

Kleiner, Art. *The Age of Heretics: Heroes, Outlaws, and the Forerunners of Corporate Change.* New York: Currency Doubleday, 1996.

———. "Appendix: A History of *CoEvolution Quarterly.*" In Kleiner and Brand, *News That Stayed News,* 331–37.

———. "Consequential Heresies: How 'Thinking the Unthinkable' Changed Royal Dutch/Shell." Global Business Network, Emeryville, CA, 1990.

Kleiner, Art, and Stewart Brand, eds. *News That Stayed News, 1974–1984: Ten Years of CoEvolution Quarterly.* San Francisco: North Point Press, 1986.

Kline, David. "'Friction-Free' Foolishness," *Hotwired,* September 11, 1995. http://webmonkey.wired/market/95/37/index1a.html (accessed July 16, 2005; site now discontinued).

Kline, David, and Daniel Burstein. "Is Government Obsolete?" *Wired,* January 1996.

Kollock, Peter. "The Economies of Online Cooperation: Gifts and Public Goods in Cyberspace." In Smith and Kollock, *Communities in Cyberspace,* 220–37.

Kostelanetz, Richard. "Scene and Not Herd—USCO." *Harper's Bazaar,* December 1967.

Krassner, Paul, and Ken Kesey, eds. *The Realist Presents: The Last Supplement to the Whole Earth Catalog (Realist,* no. 89). New York: Realist Association, March 1971.

Kuznick, Peter J., and James Burkhart Gilbert, eds. *Rethinking Cold War Culture.* Washington, DC: Smithsonian Institution Press, 2001.

Langton, Christopher G., *Artificial Life: The Proceedings of an Interdisciplinary Workshop on the Synthesis and Simulation of Living Systems, Held September, 1987, in Los Alamos, New Mexico.* Redwood City, CA: Addison-Wesley, 1989.

Langway, Lynn, and Pamela Abramson. "Whole Earth Revisited." *Newsweek,* November 17, 1980.

Lardas, John. *The Bop Apocalypse: The Religious Visions of Kerouac, Ginsberg, and Burroughs.* Urbana: University of Illinois Press, 2001.

Lash, Scott, and John Urry. *The End of Organized Capitalism.* Madison: University of Wisconsin Press, 1987.

Leamer, Laurence. *The Paper Revolutionaries: The Rise of the Underground Press.* New York: Simon and Schuster, 1972.

Lee, Martin A., and Bruce Shlain. *Acid Dreams: The CIA, LSD, and the Sixties Rebellion*. New York: Grove Press, 1985.

Lee, Pamela M. *Chronophobia: On Time in the Art of the 1960's*. Cambridge, MA: MIT Press, 2004.

Lehr, Stan, and Louis Rossetto Jr. "The New Right Credo—Libertarianism." *New York Times Sunday Magazine*, January 10, 1971.

Lenoir, Timothy, Henry Lowood, and Stanford Humanities Laboratory. *How They Got Game: The History of Video Games and Interactive Simulations*. Web site, http://htgg.stanford.edu/ (accessed September 9, 2004).

Leslie, Stuart W. "The Biggest 'Angel' of Them All: The Military and the Making of Silicon Valley." In *Understanding Silicon Valley: The Anatomy of an Entrepreneurial Region*, edited by Martin Kenney, 48–70. Stanford, CA: Stanford University Press, 2000.

———. *The Cold War and American Science: The Military-Industrial-Academic Complex at MIT and Stanford*. New York: Columbia University Press, 1993.

Lévi-Strauss, Claude. "Selections from *Introduction to the Work of Marcel Mauss*." In Schrift, *Logic of the Gift*, 45–69.

Levy, Frank. *Dollars and Dreams: The Changing American Income Distribution*. New York: Norton, 1988.

———. *The New Dollars and Dreams: American Incomes and Economic Change*. New York: Russell Sage Foundation, 1998.

Lévy, Pierre. *Collective Intelligence: Mankind's Emerging World in Cyberspace*. New York: Plenum Trade, 1997.

Levy, Steven. *Artificial Life: The Quest for a New Creation*. New York: Pantheon, 1992.

———. *Hackers: Heroes of the Computer Revolution*. Garden City, NY: Anchor Press/Doubleday, 1984.

Lewallen, Constance, and Steve Seid. *Ant Farm, 1968–1978*. Berkeley: University of California Press, Berkeley Art Museum, Pacific Film Archive, 2004.

Lewin, Roger. *Complexity: Life at the Edge of Chaos*. New York: Macmillan, 1992.

Lewis, Roger. *Outlaws of America: The Underground Press and Its Context*. Harmondsworth, Eng.: Penguin, 1972.

Licklider, J. C. R. "Man-Computer Symbiosis." *IRE Transactions on Human Factors in Electronics* 1, no. 4 (1960): 4–11. Reprint in *The New Media Reader*, edited by Noah Wardrip-Fruin and Nick Montfort, 74–82 (Cambridge, MA: MIT Press, 2003). (Page citations are to the 2003 reprint.)

Light, Jennifer S. *From Warfare to Welfare: Defense Intellectuals and Urban Problems in Cold War America*. Baltimore: Johns Hopkins University Press, 2003.

Lilienfeld, Robert. *The Rise of Systems Theory: An Ideological Analysis*. New York: Wiley, 1978.

Lipkin, Efrem. "A Public Information Network." *People's Computer Company* 4, no. 1 (1975): 17.

Liu, Alan. *The Laws of Cool: Knowledge Work and the Culture of Information*. Chicago: University of Chicago Press, 2004.

Lohr, Steve. "It's Long Boom or Bust for Leading Futurist." *New York Times*, June 1, 1998.

Lowood, Henry. "A Brief Biography of Computer Games." In *Playing Computer Games: Motives, Responses, and Consequences*, edited by Peter Vorderer and Jennings Bryant. Mahwah, NJ: Lawrence Erlbaum, 2006.

Lubar, Steven. "Do Not Fold, Spindle, or Mutilate: A Cultural History of the Punch Card." *Journal of American Culture* 15, no. 4 (Winter 1992): 43–55. Available at http://ccat.sas.upenn.edu/slubar/fsm.html (accessed September 21, 2004).

Lyon, David. *The Information Society: Issues and Illusions.* Cambridge: Polity Press; Oxford: Blackwell, 1988.

MacKenzie, Donald. "Missile Accuracy: A Case Study in the Social Processes of Technological Change." In Bijker, Hughes, and Pinch, *Social Construction of Technological Systems,* 195–222.

Manovich, Lev. *The Language of New Media.* Cambridge, MA: MIT Press, 2001.

Marable, Manning. *Race, Reform, and Rebellion: The Second Reconstruction in Black America, 1945–1982.* Jackson: University Press of Mississippi, 1984.

Marchand, Philip. *Marshall McLuhan: The Medium and the Messenger.* New York: Ticknor and Fields, 1989.

Markoff, John. *What the Dormouse Said . . . How the 60s Counterculture Shaped the Personal Computer Industry.* New York: Viking Penguin, 2005.

Markoff, John, Phillip Robinson, and Ezra Shapiro. "Up to Date." *Byte,* March 1985.

Marvin, Carolyn. *When Old Technologies Were New: Thinking about Electric Communication in the Late Nineteenth Century.* New York: Oxford University Press, 1988.

Mauss, Marcel, and W. D. Halls. *The Gift: The Form and Reason for Exchange in Archaic Societies.* New York: Norton, 1990.

May, Elaine Tyler. *Homeward Bound: American Families in the Cold War Era.* New York: Basic Books, 1988.

McClanahan, Ed, and Gurney Norman. "The *Whole Earth Catalog.*" *Esquire,* July 1970.

McLuhan, Marshall. *The Gutenberg Galaxy: The Making of Typographic Man.* Toronto: University of Toronto Press, 1962.

———. *Understanding Media: The Extensions of Man.* New York: McGraw-Hill, 1964.

Miller, Laura. "Women and Children First: Gender and the Settling of the Electronic Frontier." In *Resisting the Virtual Life: The Culture and Politics of Information,* edited by James Brook and Iain A. Boal, 49–58. San Francisco: City Lights Books, 1995.

Miller, Timothy. *American Communes, 1860–1960: A Bibliography.* New York: Garland, 1990.

———. *The 60s Communes: Hippies and Beyond.* Syracuse, NY: Syracuse University Press, 1999.

Mills, C. Wright. *The Power Elite.* New York: Oxford University Press, 1956.

———. *The Sociological Imagination.* New York: Oxford University Press, 1959.

Mindell, David A. "Automation's Finest Hour: Radar and System Integration in World War II." In *Systems, Experts, and Computers,* edited by Thomas P. Hughes and Agatha C. Hughes, 27–56. Cambridge, MA: MIT Press, 2000.

Mitchell, Melanie. "Mystifying the Net." *Technology Review* 98 (October 1995): 74–75.

Mitchell, William J. *City of Bits: Space, Place, and the Infobahn.* Cambridge, MA: MIT Press, 1995.

Moore, Richard K. "Cyberspace Inc. and the Robber Baron Age: An Analysis of PFF's 'Magna Carta.'" *Information Society* 12 (1996): 315–23.

Mosco, Vincent. *The Digital Sublime: Myth, Power, and Cyberspace.* Cambridge, MA: MIT Press, 2004.

Mumford, Lewis. *The Myth of the Machine: Technics and Human Development.* New York: Harcourt Brace and World, 1967.

Mungo, Raymond. *Total Loss Farm: A Year in the Life.* New York: Dutton, 1970.

Neff, Gina Sue. "Organizing Uncertainty: Individual, Organizational, and Institutional Risk in New York's Internet Industry, 1995–2003." Ph.D. diss., Columbia University, 2004.

Negroponte, Nicholas. *Being Digital*. New York: Knopf, 1995.

———. "Being Digital—A Book (P)review." *Wired*, February 1995.

Nelson, Theodor H. *Computer Lib; Dream Machines*. Rev. ed. Redmond, WA: Tempus Books, 1987.

———. *Computer Lib: You Can and Must Understand Computers Now*. Chicago: Nelson, 1974. Reprint in Nelson, *Computer Lib; Dream Machines*.

Norman, Gurney. "On Heroes." In Smith and Hershey, *Whole Earth Catalog One Dollar*, 13.

Norman, Gurney, and Diana Shugart, eds. *Whole Earth Catalog $1*. Menlo Park, CA: Portola Institute, March 1970.

———, eds. *Whole Earth Catalog One Dollar*. Menlo Park, CA: Portola Institute, September 1970.

O'Neill, Gerard K. *The High Frontier: Human Colonies in Space*. Garden City, NY: Anchor Books, 1982.

Orlikowski, Wanda J., and JoAnne Yates. "Genre Repertoire: Examining the Structuring of Communicative Practices in Organizations." *Administrative Science Quarterly* 39 (1994): 541–74.

Perkins, Anthony B., and Michael C. Perkins. *The Internet Bubble: Inside the Overvalued World of High-Tech Stocks—and What You Need to Know to Avoid the Coming Shakeout*. New York: HarperBusiness, 1999.

Perry, Charles. *The Haight-Ashbury: A History*. New York: Random House, 1984.

Perry, Paul, Ken Babbs, Michael Schwartz, and Neil Ortenberg. *On the Bus: The Complete Guide to the Legendary Trip of Ken Kesey and the Merry Pranksters and the Birth of the Counterculture*. New York: Thunder's Mouth Press, 1990.

Pfaffenberger, Bryan. "The Social Meaning of the Personal Computer: Or, Why the Personal Computer Revolution Was No Revolution." *Anthropological Quarterly* 61 (1988): 39–47.

Pickering, Andrew. "A Gallery of Monsters: Cybernetics and Self-Organisation, 1940–1970." Paper presented to the Dibner Institute for the History of Science and Technology, Massachusetts Institute of Technology, December 1, 1998.

———. *The Mangle of Practice: Time, Agency, and Science*. Chicago: University of Chicago Press, 1995.

Piore, Michael J., and Charles F. Sabel. *The Second Industrial Divide: Possibilities for Prosperity*. New York: Basic Books, 1984.

Poundstone, William. "Can You Trust Your Computer?" *New York Times Book Review*, July 24, 1994.

Powell, Walter W. "The Capitalist Firm in the Twenty-First Century: Emerging Patterns in Western Enterprise." In DiMaggio, *Twenty-first Century Firm*, 33–68.

———. "Neither Market nor Hierarchy: Network Forms of Organization." *Research in Organizational Behavior* 12 (1990): 295–336.

"Psychedelic Art." *Life*, September 9, 1966.

Quittner, Joshua. "The Merry Pranksters Go to Washington." *Wired*, June 1994.

Rabbit, Peter. *Drop City*. New York: Olympia Press, 1971.

Rau, Erik P. "The Adoption of Operations Research in the United States during World War II." In *Systems, Experts, and Computers*, edited by Thomas P. Hughes and Agatha C. Hughes, 57–92. Cambridge, MA: MIT Press, 2000.

Reich, Charles A. *The Greening of America*. New York: Random House, 1970.

Reich, Hanns, and Oto Bihalji-Merin. *The World from Above*. New York: Hill and Wang, 1968.

Rheingold, Howard, ed. *The Millennium Whole Earth Catalog: Access to Tools and Ideas for the Twenty-First Century*. San Francisco: HarperSanFrancisco, 1994.

———. "A Slice of My Life in My Virtual Community." In *High Noon on the Electronic Frontier: Conceptual Issues in Cyberspace,* edited by Peter Ludlow, 413–36. Cambridge, MA: MIT Press, 1996.

———. "Virtual Communities: The Computer Network as Electronic Watering Hole." *Whole Earth Review* 57 (Winter 1987): 78–80.

———. *The Virtual Community: Homesteading on the Electronic Frontier*. Reading, MA: Addison-Wesley, 1993.

———. *Virtual Reality*. New York: Summit Books, 1991.

Rice, Ronald E. "Issues and Concepts in Research on Computer-Mediated Communication Systems." In *Communication Yearbook 12,* edited by J. Andersen, 436–76. Beverly Hills, CA: Sage, 1988.

Rogers, Everett M., and Judith K. Larsen. *Silicon Valley Fever: Growth of High-Technology Culture*. New York: Basic Books, 1984.

Rosenblueth, Arturo, Norbert Wiener, and Julian Bigelow. "Behavior, Purpose, and Teleology." *Philosophy of Science* 10 (1943): 18–24.

Ross, Andrew. *No-Collar: The Humane Workplace and Its Hidden Costs*. New York: Basic Books, 2003.

Rossetto, Louis. *Response to the "Californian Ideology."* Available at http://www.hrc.wmin.ac .uk/theory-californianideology-responses1.html (accessed October 7, 1998).

———. "Why Wired?" *Wired,* March 1993.

Rossetto, Louis, Jane Metcalfe, et al. Executive summary, *Wired* Business Plan, Version 3.0, April 1992. Personal collection of Louis Rossetto and Jane Metcalfe.

Rossinow, Douglas C. "The New Left in the Counterculture: Hypotheses and Evidence." *Radical History Review* 67 (Winter 1997): 79–120.

———. *The Politics of Authenticity: Liberalism, Christianity, and the New Left in America*. New York: Columbia University Press, 1998.

Roszak, Theodore. *From Satori to Silicon Valley: San Francisco and the American Counterculture*. San Francisco: Don't Call It Frisco Press, 1986.

———. *The Making of a Counter Culture: Reflections on the Technocratic Society and Its Youthful Opposition*. Garden City, NY: Doubleday, 1969.

Rothschild, Michael L. *Bionomics: The Inevitability of Capitalism*. New York: H. Holt, 1990.

Royce, Joseph. *Surface Anatomy*. Philadelphia: F. A. Davis, 1965.

Rushkoff, Douglas. *Cyberia: Life in the Trenches of Hyperspace*. San Francisco: HarperSanFrancisco, 1994.

Rybczynski, Witold. *Paper Heroes: Appropriate Technology: Panacea or Pipe Dream?* New York: Penguin, 1991.

Savio, Mario. "California's Angriest Student." *Life,* February 26, 1965.

Saxenian, AnnaLee. *Regional Advantage: Culture and Competition in Silicon Valley and Route 128*. Cambridge, MA: Harvard University Press, 1994.

Sayre, Nora. "Cyberspace and Newtonian Dreams." *Nation,* September 25, 1995.

Schoenberger, Karl. "Where Computers Go to Die: Poor Cities in China Become Dumping Ground for E-Waste." *San Jose Mercury News,* November 23, 2002. Available at http://www.mercurynews.com/mld/mercurynews/4591233.htm (accessed March 21, 2005).

Schrage, Michael. "Hacking Away at the Future." *Washington Post,* November 18, 1984, F1.

Schrift, Alan D., ed. *The Logic of the Gift: Toward an Ethic of Generosity.* New York: Routledge, 1997.

Schudson, Michael. *Discovering the News: A Social History of American Newspapers.* New York: Basic Books, 1978.

———. *The Sociology of News.* New York: Norton, 2003.

Schwartz, Peter. *The Art of the Long View.* New York: Doubleday/Currency, 1991.

Schwartz, Peter, and Stewart Brand. *The 1989 GBN Scenario Book: Decades of Restructuring.* Emeryville, CA: Global Business Network, 1989.

Schwartz, Peter, and Blair Gibb. *When Good Companies Do Bad Things: Responsibility and Risk in an Age of Globalization.* New York: Wiley, 1999.

Schwartz, Peter, and Peter Leyden. "The Long Boom: A History of the Future, 1980–2020." *Wired,* July 1997.

Schwartz, Peter, Peter Leyden, and Joel Hyatt. *The Long Boom: A Vision for the Coming Age of Prosperity.* Reading, MA: Perseus Books, 1999.

Scribner, Sylvia, and Michael Cole. *The Psychology of Literacy.* Cambridge, MA: Harvard University Press, 1981.

Seidel, Robert. "The Origins of the Lawrence Berkeley Laboratory." In *Big Science: The Growth of Large-Scale Research,* edited by Peter Galison and Bruce Hevly, 21–45. Stanford, CA: Stanford University Press, 1992.

Shannon, Claude. "A Mathematical Theory of Communication." *Bell System Technical Journal* 27, no. 3 (July 1948): 379–423; no. 4 (October 1948): 623–56.

Shannon, Claude, and Warren Weaver. *The Mathematical Theory of Communication.* Urbana: University of Illinois Press, 1949.

Shiller, Robert J. *Irrational Exuberance.* New York: Broadway Books, 2001.

Siegel, Lenny, and John Markoff. *The High Cost of High Tech: The Dark Side of the Chip.* New York: Harper and Row, 1985.

Slack, Jennifer Daryl. "The Theory and Method of Articulation in Cultural Studies." In *Stuart Hall: Critical Dialogues in Cultural Studies,* edited by David Morley and Kuan-Hsing Chen, 112–30. London: Routledge, 1996.

Slack, Jennifer Daryl, and Fred Fejes, eds. *The Ideology of the Information Age.* Norwood, NJ: Ablex, 1987.

Smith, Douglas K., and Robert C. Alexander. *Fumbling the Future: How Xerox Invented, Then Ignored, the First Personal Computer.* New York: Morrow, 1988.

Smith, J. D., and Hal Hershey, eds. *The Whole Earth Catalog.* Menlo Park, CA: Portola Institute, Fall 1970.

Smith, Marc A. "Voices from the WELL: The Logic of the Virtual Commons." Master's thesis, University of California, Los Angeles, 1992.

Smith, Marc A., and Peter Kollock, eds. *Communities in Cyberspace.* London: Routledge, 1999.

Smith, Shannon James. "WiReD: Evolution of a New Media Company." Theseus Institute, Sophia Antipolis, France, April 4, 1996. Available at http://shannon.marketmatrix.com/wiredweb/ (accessed July 23, 2002).

Sobchack, Vivian. "Democratic Franchise and the Electronic Frontier." In *Cyberfutures: Culture and Politics on the Information Superhighway,* edited by Ziauddin Sardar and Jerome R. Ravetz. New York: New York University Press, 1996.

———. "New Age Mutant Ninja Hackers: Reading Mondo 2000." In *Flame Wars: The Discourse of Cyberculture,* edited by Mark Dery, 11–28. Durham, NC: Duke University Press, 1994.

Sproull, Lee, and Sara B. Kiesler. *Connections: New Ways of Working in the Networked Organization.* Cambridge, MA: MIT Press, 1991.

Stamps, Judith. *Unthinking Modernity: Innis, McLuhan, and the Frankfurt School.* Montreal: McGill–Queen's University Press, 1995.

Star, Susan Leigh. "Power, Technologies, and the Phenomenology of Conventions: On Being Allergic to Onions." In *A Sociology of Monsters: Essays on Power, Technology, and Domination,* edited by John Law, 26–56. London: Routledge, 1991.

Star, Susan Leigh, and James Griesemer. "Institutional Ecology, Translations, and Boundary Objects: Amateurs and Professionals in Berkeley's Museum of Vertebrate Zoology, 1907–1939." *Social Studies of Science* 19 (1989): 387–420. Reprint in *The Science Studies Reader,* edited by Mario Biagioli, 505–24 (New York: Routledge, 1999). (Page citations are to the 1999 reprint).

Stark, David. "Ambiguous Assets for Uncertain Environments: Heterarchy in Postsocialist Firms." In DiMaggio, *Twenty-first Century Firm,* 69–104.

Sterling, Bruce. *The Hacker Crackdown: Law and Disorder on the Electronic Frontier.* New York: Bantam Books, 1992.

Stipp, David. "Stewart Brand: The Electric Kool-Aid Management Consultant." *Fortune,* October 16, 1995.

St. John, Warren. "Agent Provocateur." *Wired,* September 1999.

Stockwell, Foster. *Encyclopedia of American Communes, 1663–1963.* Jefferson, NC: McFarland, 1998.

Stoll, Clifford. *Silicon Snake Oil: Second Thoughts on the Information Highway.* New York: Doubleday, 1995.

Stone, Allucquère Rosanne. *The War of Desire and Technology at the Close of the Mechanical Age.* Cambridge, MA: MIT Press, 1995.

———. "Will the Real Body Please Stand Up? Boundary Stories about Virtual Cultures." In *Cyberspace: First Steps,* edited by Michael Benedikt, 81–118. Cambridge, MA: MIT Press, 1991.

Streeter, Thomas. "The Romantic Self and the Politics of Internet Commercialization." *Cultural Studies* 17, no. 5 (2003): 648–68.

———. "'That Deep Romantic Chasm': Libertarianism, Neoliberalism, and the Computer Culture." In *Communication, Citizenship, and Social Policy: Rethinking the Limits of the Welfare State,* edited by Andrew Calabrese and Jean-Claude Burgelman, 49–64. Lanham, MD: Rowman and Littlefield, 1999.

Students for a Democratic Society (SDS). "Port Huron Statement." In *The New Left: A Documentary History,* edited by Massimo Teodori, 163–72. Indianapolis: Bobbs-Merrill, 1969.

Sturgeon, Timothy J. "How Silicon Valley Came to Be." In *Understanding Silicon Valley: The Anatomy of an Entrepreneurial Region,* edited by Martin Kenney, 15–47. Stanford, CA: Stanford University Press, 2000.

Taylor, William C. "Control in an Age of Chaos." *Harvard Business Review* 72, no. 6 (November–December 1994): 64–76.

Terranova, Tiziana. "Digital Darwin: Nature, Evolution, and Control in the Rhetoric of Electronic Communication." *New Formations* 29 (Autumn 1996): 69–83.

———. "Free Labor: Producing Culture for the Digital Economy." *Social Text* 18, no. 2 (2000): 33–58.

———. *Network Culture: Politics for the Information Age.* London: Pluto Press, 2004.

Tetzeli, Rick. "Managing in a World Out of Control." *Fortune,* September 5, 1994.

Theall, Donald F. *The Virtual Marshall McLuhan.* Montreal: McGill–Queen's University Press, 2001.

Thrift, Nigel. "'It's the Romance Not the Finance That Makes Business Worth Pursuing': Disclosing a New Market Culture." *Economy and Society* 30, no. 4 (2001): 412–32.

Toffler, Alvin. *Future Shock.* New York: Random House, 1970.

———. *The Third Wave.* New York: Morrow, 1980.

Tomkins, Calvin. *The Bride and the Bachelors: The Heretical Courtship in Modern Art.* New York: Viking Press, 1965.

———. "In the Outlaw Area." *New Yorker,* January 8, 1966.

Tung, Chung C. "The 'Personal Computer': A Fully Programmable Pocket Calculator." *Hewlett-Packard Journal,* May 1974. Reprint in Hewlett-Packard Company, *Inventions of Opportunity: Matching Technology with Market Needs: Selections from the Pages of the Hewlett-Packard Journal,* 273–78. Palo Alto, CA: Hewlett-Packard, 1983.

Turkle, Sherry. *Life on the Screen: Identity in the Age of the Internet.* New York: Simon and Schuster, 1995.

Turner, Fred. "Cyberspace as the New Frontier? Mapping the Shifting Boundaries of the Network Society." Red Rock Eater News Service, 1999. Available at http://legalminds .lp.findlaw.com/list/rre/msg00240.html (accessed October 4, 2005).

———. "How Digital Technology Found Utopian Ideology: Lessons from the First Hackers' Conference." In *Critical Cyberculture Studies: Current Terrain, Future Directions,* edited by David Silver and Adrienne Massanari. New York: New York University Press, 2006.

Ullman, Ellen. *Close to the Machine: Technophilia and Its Discontents.* San Francisco: City Lights Books, 1997.

U.S. Office of Scientific Research and Development. *Science, the Endless Frontier. A Report to the President by Vannevar Bush, Director of the Office of Scientific Research and Development, July 1945.* Washington, DC: Government Printing Office, 1945.

Vallee, Jacques. *The Network Revolution: Confessions of a Computer Scientist.* Berkeley, CA: And/Or Press, 1982.

Vesna, Victoria. "Networked Public Spaces: An Investigation into Virtual Embodiment." Ph.D. diss., University of Wales College, 2000. http://vv.arts.ucla.edu/publications/ thesis/official/thesis_frameset.htm.

"Virtual Reality: An Interview with Jaron Lanier." *Whole Earth Review* 64 (Fall 1989): 108–19.

Wack, Pierre. "Scenarios: Shooting the Rapids." *Harvard Business Review* 63, no. 6 (1985): 139–50.

———. "Scenarios: The Gentle Art of Reperceiving." Harvard Business School working paper. Harvard College, Cambridge, MA, 1984.

———. "Scenarios: Uncharted Waters Ahead." *Harvard Business Review* 63, no. 5 (September–October 1985): 73–89.

Waldrop, M. Mitchell. *Complexity: The Emerging Science at the Edge of Order and Chaos.* New York: Simon and Schuster, 1992.

———. *The Dream Machine: J. C. Licklider and the Revolution That Made Computing Personal.* New York: Viking, 2001.

Warshall, Peter. "Informed Heart: GBN Explores Rio Arriba." *Netview,* Fall 1993.

Warshaw, Steven. *The Trouble in Berkeley: The Complete History, in Text and Pictures, of the Great Student Rebellion against the "New University."* Berkeley: Diablo Press, 1965.

Weart, Spencer R. *Nuclear Fear: A History of Images.* Cambridge, MA: Harvard University Press, 1988.

Weber, Max, Hans Heinrich Gerth, and C. Wright Mills. *From Max Weber: Essays in Sociology.* New York: Oxford University Press, 1946.

Webster, Frank. *Theories of the Information Society.* London: Routledge, 1995.

Weise, Elizabeth Reba. "A Thousand Aunts with Modems." In Cherny and Weise, *Wired Women,* vii–xv.

"The WELL as Community." Archives Conference, in the WELL, topic 291. This source available to WELL subscribers.

"The WELL History Project: WOPs." Archives Conference, in the WELL, topic 10. This source available to WELL subscribers.

Wellman, Barry. "An Electronic Group Is Virtually a Social Network." In *Culture of the Internet,* edited by Sara Kiesler, 179–205. Mahwah, NJ: Lawrence Erlbaum, 1997.

———. "Physical Place and Cyber Place: The Rise of Personalized Networking." *International Journal of Urban and Regional Research* 25, no. 2 (2001): 227–52.

Wellman, Barry, and Milena Gulia. "Virtual Communities as Communities: Net Surfers Don't Ride Alone." In Smith and Kollock, *Communities in Cyberspace,* 163–90.

Wellman, Barry, Anabel Quan Hasse, James Witte, and Keith N. Hampton. "Capitalizing on the Internet: Network Capital, Participatory Capital, and Sense of Community." In Wellman and Haythornthwaite, *Internet in Everyday Life,* 291–324.

Wellman, Barry, and Caroline Haythornthwaite, eds. *The Internet in Everyday Life.* Malden, MA: Blackwell, 2002.

Werry, Chris. "Imagined Electronic Community: Representations of Virtual Community in Contemporary Business Discourse." *Firstmonday* 4, no. 9 (2001). Available at http://www.firstmonday.org/issues/issue4_9/werry/ (accessed October 14, 2005).

Whitfield, Stephen J. *The Culture of the Cold War.* 2nd ed. Baltimore: Johns Hopkins University Press, 1996.

Whyte, William Hollingsworth. *The Organization Man.* New York: Simon and Schuster, 1956.

Wiener, Norbert. *Cybernetics; or, Control and Communication in the Animal and the Machine.* New York: Wiley, 1948.

———. *The Human Use of Human Beings: Cybernetics and Society.* Boston: Houghton Mifflin, 1950.

———. *I Am a Mathematician: The Later Life of a Prodigy.* Garden City, NY: Doubleday, 1956.

———. "A Scientist Rebels." *Atlantic Monthly,* January 1947.

"Wild New Flashy Bedlam of the Discotheque." *Life,* May 27, 1966.

Willoughby, Kelvin W. *Technology Choice: A Critique of the Appropriate Technology Movement.* Boulder, CO: Westview; London: Intermediate Technology, 1990.

Winner, Langdon. *Autonomous Technology: Technics-Out-of-Control as a Theme in Political Thought.* Cambridge, MA: MIT Press, 1977.

———. "Building the Better Mousetrap." In *The Whale and the Reactor: A Search for Limits in an Age of High Technology,* edited by Langdon Winner. Chicago: University of Chicago Press, 1986.

Wolf, Gary. *Wired: A Romance.* New York: Random House, 2003.

Wolfe, Tom. *The Electric Kool-Aid Acid Test.* New York: Farrar, Straus, and Giroux, 1968.

———. "The Tinkerings of Robert Noyce." *Esquire,* December 1983.

Wolff, Michael. *Burn Rate: How I Survived the Gold Rush Years on the Internet.* New York: Simon and Schuster, 1998.

Woodward, Kathleen. "Art and Technics: John Cage, Electronics, and World Improvement." In *The Myths of Information: Technology and Postindustrial Culture,* edited by Kathleen Woodward, 171–91. Madison, WI: Coda Press, 1980.

"Word Ownership Discussions: A List [Yoyow/ You Own Your Own Words]." Archives Conference, in the WELL, topic 157. This source available to WELL subscribers.

Wyatt, Sally. "Talking about the Future: Metaphors of the Internet." In *Contested Futures: A Sociology of Prospective Techno-Science,* edited by Nik Brown, Brian Rappert, and Andrew Webster, 109–28. Aldershot, Eng.: Ashgate, 2000.

Yates, JoAnne. *Control through Communication: The Rise of System in American Management.* Baltimore: Johns Hopkins University Press, 1989.

———. *Structuring the Information Age: Life Insurance and Technology in the Twentieth Century.* Baltimore: Johns Hopkins University Press, 2005.

Zablocki, Benjamin David. *Alienation and Charisma: A Study of Contemporary American Communes.* New York: Free Press, 1980.

Zelizer, Barbie. *Covering the Body: The Kennedy Assassination, the Media, and the Shaping of Collective Memory.* Chicago: University of Chicago Press, 1992.

Zicklin, Gilbert. *Countercultural Communes: A Sociological Perspective.* Westport, CT: Greenwood Press, 1983.

Zuboff, Shoshana. *In the Age of the Smart Machine: The Future of Work and Power.* New York: Basic Books, 1988.

Index

abstract expressionism, 46, 47

"Access Mobile," 71

Acid Tests, 65, 66

Advanced Research Projects Agency (ARPA), 108, 213

Albrecht, Bob, 70, 101, 113, 114, 133

Alinsky, Saul, *Rules for Radicals,* 98

Allison, Dennis, 252

Alloy, 96–97, 273n54

Alpert, Richard (Baba Ram Dass), 61

Altair, 114, 274n1

alternative energy, 233

Alto, 111

American Indian Movement, 97

America Online, 161

analog computers, 20

Andreesen, Marc, 213

Ant Farm art and design collective, 86, 272n36

anti-aircraft predictor, 21, 25, 26, 95, 178

anti-automationists, 29

antiwar protests, 64, 74, 118, 209

AOL, 217

Apple Computer, 106, 116, 129, 139, 198, 247

Architecture Machine Group, 163, 177–78

Arcosanti, 81

ARPA community, 116

ARPANET, 28, 109, 117, 213

artificial intelligence, 177

Artificial Intelligence (AI) Laboratory, 116, 133, 134, 177

Artificial Life Conference, 198–99

artificial-life movement, 203

Ashby, Ross, 26, 178

"Aspen Summit: Cyberspace and the American Dream II," 230

Association for Computing Machinery / Institute of Electrical and Electronics Engineers (ACM/IEEE), 110

AT&T, 182, 193

Atari, 134, 163

Atkinson, Bill, 137

Atlas missile system, 19

atomic bomb, 18

atomic era, 17, 30–31, 243

atomic forecasting, 187

Aufderheide, Patricia, 230

Augmentation Research Center (ARC), 61, 106, 107–8, 109, 110

Autodesk, 163

automaton, 21

Baba, Meher, 75

back-to-the-land movement, 73, 76, 244, 245

Baer, Steve, 81, 95, 96, 97, 109; *Dome Cookbook,* 94

Baldwin, Jay, 94

Barayón, Ramón Sender, 65, 146

Barbrook, Richard, 208, 259, 279n43

Bardini, Thierry, 105, 274n1

Barlow, John Perry: and Aspen conference, 223; and computational metaphor, 16; conference on bionomics, 224; contributions to *Wired,* 217, 218; "Crime and Puzzlement," 171, 172–74, 195; "Declaration of

and Electronic Frontier Foundation, 172,
218; enthusiasm for computer-conferenc-
ing, 130; on faculty of School of Management and Strategic Studies, 129–30; fear of
living in a hyperrationalized world, 42–43;
fear of Soviet attack in 1950s, 41–42; first
experience with LSD, 61; forum on hacking on the WELL, 168–70; and Global
Business Network, 176, 184, 188, 189, 191,
192, 193; and Hackers' Conference, 139–
40, 254; helped computers to be seen as
"personal" technology, 105, 238; and Herman Kahn, 186; *How Buildings Learn,* 205;
idealized vision of Native Americans, 59;
idea that information-based products embodied an economic paradox, 136; imagined world as a series of overlapping information systems, 250; influence of Fuller
on, 57; influence of Kesey on, 60; integration of ideas and people of Whole Earth
into world of networked computing, 132;
interview with *Newsweek* in 1980, 128–29;
introduction to *Signal,* 196; issues facing
hackers to the themes of countercultural
work and the Whole Earth group, 139;
Kesey as role model, 65; and Learning
Conferences, 181–83; linking of information technologies to New Communalist
politics, 216; Long Now Foundation, 206,
285n67; as a manager, 79, 89–90; *The Media
Lab: Inventing the Future at MIT,* 178–81;
and the Merry Pranksters, 61–62; military
service, 46; mirror logic of cybernetics,
259; at MIT's Media Lab, 177; modeled the
synthesis of counterculture and research
culture, 253; multimedia pieces, 270n49;
networked cultural entrepreneurship, 251–
55; network forums, 239, 249–50; "New
Games Tournament," 120; in New York art
scene, 46; on outer space, 127; Point Foundation, 120; at Portola Institute, 70; por-
trayal of Nicholas Negroponte, 179–80;
principle of juxtaposition, 84; private online conference for software reviewers,
131; reaction to the libertarianism of the
mid-1990s, 287n49; reconfigured the cultural status of information and information
technologies, 8, 238–39, 249; repudiated
the *Catalog*'s New Communalist origins,
121; response to criticism of *Catalog*'s poli-

tics, 99–100; return to the *Whole Earth
Catalog,* 120; search for individual freedom,
45; search for new, flexible modes of living,
59; and *Software Catalog,* 130–31; "Spacewar: Fanatic Life and Symbolic Death
among the Computer Bums," 116–18;
"Sticking Your Head in Cyberspace," 195;
"Transcendental planning," 90–91; tran-
script of the Hacker Ethic forum, 138; trav-
els after discharge from the army, 48; and
Trips Festival, 65–68; turn back toward
the computer industry, 104; visit to Drop
City, 74; and the WELL, 141, 142–43, 145–
46; work with USCO, 49, 51; writing for
Wired, 217; and Xerox PARC, 246–47
Branwyn, Gareth, 81
Brautigan, Richard, "All Watched Over by
Machines of Loving Grace," 38–39
Breines, Wini, 267n80
Briarpatch Society, 70
Brilliant, Larry, 141, 142
Britton, Lois, 273n44
Brockman, John, 129, 130, 290n24
Broderbund Software Inc., 135
Bronson, Po, 225
Brown, Jerry, 186
Browning, Page, 61
Budge, Bill, 135
bulletin board system (BBS), 144, 247
Burnham, Jack, 268n13
Burroughs, William, 62
Burstein, Daniel, 287n37
Burt, Ronald, 5, 135
Bush, Vannevar, 17, 20, 24, 229; "As We May
Think," 106–7
Business 2.0 (magazine), 207
butterfly ecology, 43
Byte (magazine), 137

Cage, John, 43, 46–47, 67; Theatre Piece
No. 1, 47–48
"Californian Ideology," 208, 285n4
Callahan, Michael, 48, 51, 66
Callon, Michelle, 277n71
Calvert, Greg, 35
Calvin, William, 191
Cameron, Andy, 208, 259
Carlston, Doug, 135
Carpenter, Edmund, 53
Carroll, Jon, 143, 155